SELF-DETERMINATION IN THE INTERNATIONAL LEGAL SYSTEM

This open access book brings conceptual clarity to the study and practice of self-determination, showing that it is, without doubt, one of the most important concepts of the international legal order. It argues that the accepted categorisation of internal and external self-determination is not helpful, and suggests a new typology. This new framework has four categories: the polity-based, secessionary, colonial, and remedial forms. Each will be distinguished by the grounds, or the legitimacy-claim, on which it is based. This not only ensures consistency, it moves the question out of the purely conceptual realm and addresses the practical concerns of those invoking self-determination. By presenting international lawyers with a typology that is both theoretically consistent and more practically useful, the author makes a significant contribution to our understanding of this keystone of international law.

Self-Determination in the International Legal System

Whose Claim, to What Right?

Tom Sparks

•HART•

OXFORD • LONDON • NEW YORK • NEW DELHI • SYDNEY

HART PUBLISHING

Bloomsbury Publishing Plc

Kemp House, Chawley Park, Cumnor Hill, Oxford, OX2 9PH, UK

1385 Broadway, New York, NY 10018, USA

29 Earlsfort Terrace, Dublin 2, Ireland

First published in Great Britain 2023

A catalogue record for this book is available from the British Library.

A catalogue record for this book is available from the Library of Congress.

Library of Congress Control Number: 2022946553

ISBN: HB: 978-1-50994-506-1
ePDF: 978-1-50994-508-5
ePub: 978-1-50994-507-8

Typeset by Compuscript Ltd, Shannon

It will never rain roses: when we want
To have more roses, we must plant more roses.

—George Eliot, *The Spanish Gypsy*

ACKNOWLEDGEMENTS

This book began life as a part of my PhD thesis, written at the University of Durham. I have continued to develop the project subsequently, at the Max Planck Institute for Comparative Public Law and International Law in Heidelberg, and in total it has taken a little over eight years in the writing. In that time, I have been fortunate to have had wonderfully supportive colleagues, advisors and friends, who have enriched both my scholarship and all other aspects of my life.

I owe a profound debt of thanks to Robert Schütze, whose unfailing support and encouragement, generosity, and robust (but always constructive) criticism was invaluable in preparing the thesis which led to this book. To Gleider Hernández, too, I owe a huge debt, not only for his support and guidance in writing my PhD, but also that subsequently he has become one of my closest colleagues and friends. Gleider and Robert: thank you. I could not have hoped for a better supervisory team, nor a better start on my academic journey.

I was incredibly fortunate after completion of my PhD to gain a postdoctoral position at the Max Planck Institute, in the team of Anne Peters. As well as being an inspirational scholar, Anne has a true commitment to supporting junior scholars, something from which I have benefited immensely. Anne, your mentorship and encouragement has been invaluable, and I date my 'coming of age' as a scholar to reading *Beyond Human Rights*, which I did in a single, fascinated rush in the tranquil and beautiful setting of the reading room at the National Library of Scotland. It opened my eyes, and taught me what scholarship could be: rigorous, precise, and with an absolute commitment to the work of analysing the positive law, and yet imbued with heart, and a dedication to the emancipatory potential within international law.

I owe so much, too, to the friends and colleagues I have been fortunate to encounter in Durham, Heidelberg and elsewhere. To Verity Adams, Kanad Bagchi, Andrés Delgado Casteleiro, Julia Emtseva, Guillaume Futhazar, Angelo Golia, Eszter Harsanyi-Belteki, Laura Herring, Ruth Houghton, Henry Jones, Anette Kreutzfeld, Louis Kotzé, Raffaela Kunz, William Lucy, Roger Masterman, Carolyn Moser, Kyle Murray, Nataša Nedeski, Aoife O'Donoghue, Giacomo Rugge, Lucas Sánchez, Mark Somos, Silvia Steininger, Saskia Stucki, Ntina Tzouvala, Pedro A. Villarreal, Alex Wentker, and so many others: thank you. I have gained so much, too, from the members of Anne Peters's research group at the Max Planck Institute, past and present. It is a pleasure and a privilege to be able to engage with such a talented, supportive, and generous group of scholars.

I was extremely fortunate to spend some time as a Judicial Fellow in the team of HE Judge Peter Tomka at the International Court of Justice. I am hugely grateful to Judge Tomka for giving me that wonderful opportunity, for making me welcome, and for teaching me so much about the inner workings of international justice. I am grateful, too, for my wonderful fellow travellers on that journey: Iñaki Navarrete-Arechavaleta, Céline Braumann, Idriss Fofana, Mohit Khubchandani, Dean Rosenberg, Agathe Niveleau, Li Zhenni, Gertie Burgers and many others.

The text has also benefited from engagement with colleagues at a number of conferences and seminars: at the universities of Durham, Edinburgh, Tartu and as part of the conferences of the Socio-Legal Studies Association and the Intenationale Vereingung für Rechts- und Sozialphilosophie.

I have benefited from input on this text from a great many people, but above all from Anne Peters, Gleider Hernández, Mark Somos, Angelo Golia, and the anonymous reviewers. I am profoundly grateful for their input. Neither they, not anyone else, bears any responsibility for any of the text's many remaining flaws – they are mine alone.

The team at Hart publishing, and most particularly Sinéad Moloney and Sasha Jawed, have been wonderfully supportive – and supremely patient – during what has been a rather disrupted process of preparing the manuscript. Your assistance and encouragement have made this process possible.

My PhD research was funded by the European Research Council under the European Union's Seventh Framework Programme (FP/2007-2013) – ERC Grant Agreement No 312304. Subsequently, I have benefited from the institutional support of the Max Planck Gesellschaft and the Max Planck Institute for Comparative Public Law and International Law. I am very grateful to the support staff at the Max Planck Institute, and particularly to the library team.

My most profound thanks go to the people I love most in the world: Marion, Richard, Rosie and Jeanette. I owe you everything.

CONTENTS

Acknowledgements .... *vii*

1. A Struggle for Self-Determination: Whose Claim, to What Right? **1**
- I. Introduction 1
- II. The Self-Determination Problem 6
- III. Four Forms of Self-Determination 19
- IV. Vocabulary and Categorisation: The Forms of Self-Determination and their Interrelation 35
- V. Conclusion 38

2. Self-Determination's Origins: 1320–1920 .... **40**
- I. A Prehistory of Self-Determination? 40
- II. Self-Determination Takes Centre Stage: 1776 and 1789 63
- III. The Age of Revolution and the Long Nineteenth Century – 1789–1920 73
- IV. Conclusion 86

3. Self-Determination and Decolonisation: 1920–1970 .... **87**
- I. Imperialism and Decolonisation 88
- II. First World War Rhetoric: Lenin and Wilson on Self-Determination 90
- III. The Mandates System 98
- IV. The United Nations and the Trusteeship System 102
- V. Self-Determination in the Law of the United Nations 105
- VI. Conclusion 127

4. Judicial Treatments of Self-Determination 1945–2004 .... **129**
- I. Courts and Self-Determination 130
- II. Advisory Opinion on *Namibia (South West Africa)* 133
- III. The *Western Sahara* Advisory Opinion 137
- IV. Badinter Arbitration Commission 143
- V. *East Timor* 145
- VI. *Katangese Peoples' Congress v Zaire* 150
- VII. *Reference Re Secession of Quebec* 152
- VIII. The *Wall* Advisory Opinion 155
- IX. Conclusion 160

5. The *Kosovo* Advisory Opinion **162**
I. The Advisory Opinion 163
II. The Court's Decision 173
III. *Kosovo* Applied: Russian Rhetoric and the Invasions of Ukraine 185
IV. Conclusion 192

6. The *Chagos Archipelago* Advisory Opinion **194**
I. The Advisory Opinion 194
II. Self-Determination in the *Chagos* Advisory Opinion 212
III. Disambiguation: A Continuing Failure of Definition 220
IV. Conclusion 226

7. Interregnum **227**

Bibliography *234*
Index *249*

1

A Struggle for Self-Determination: Whose Claim, to What Right?

If the names are unknown knowledge of the things also perishes.[1]
Carl Linnaeus, *Philosophia Botanica*

I. Introduction

'This referendum is a normal, legal right of our people', asserted Masoud Barzani, President of the Kurdish Autonomous Region of Iraq (KAR), in an interview with *Foreign Policy*.[2] On 25 September 2017, the people of the KAR went to the polls.[3] As they did so, the world held its breath. The result was never in doubt – as expected, a resounding majority was returned in favour of independence[4] – but observers had other grounds for anticipation. In a region not lacking conflict, the idea of a united, independent Kurdistan continues to be seen as one of the most inflammable issues in contemporary politics.[5] Deeply desired by generations of Kurds, a united Kurdistan is implacably opposed by the four states whose territory is inhabited by the Kurdish minority, and previous attempts to create a Kurdish state have been 'brutally quashed'.[6] At first the fears seemed unnecessary: despite what followed, the referendum was peaceful and struck a tone both celebratory

[1] C Linnaeus, *Philosophia Botanica* (Matriti, 1791) 158: *Nomina si nescis, perit et cognition rerum.*

[2] Barzani was reporting a phone call with the Iraqi prime minister concerning 2017's independence referendum in the KAR: C MacDiarmid, 'Masoud Barzani: Why it's Time for Kurdish Independence' *Foreign Policy* (15 June 2017) www.foreignpolicy.com/2017/06/15/masoud-barzani-why-its-time-for-kurdish-independence/.

[3] 'Iraqi Kurdistan Votes in Independence Referendum' *BBC News* (25 September 2017) www.bbc.com/news/world-middle-east-41382494. The Kurds are a minority group concentrated in an area that is currently split between the four states, and have waged a long campaign for independent statehood.

[4] Ninety-two per cent of voters cast their ballots in favour of secession, with a turnout of 72 per cent: *BBC News* (27 September 2017) www.bbc.com/news/world-middle-east-41419633.

[5] The risk of a conflict between the KAR and the Iraqi central government led to ACLED Data listing Iraq as the country 'most at risk of returning to civil war' in 2019, for example: see ACLED Data, 'Ten Conflicts to Worry About in 2019', www.acleddata.com/2019/08/07/mid-year-update-ten-conflicts-to-worry-about-in-2019.

[6] 'Who Are the Kurds?' *BBC News* (15 October 2019) www.bbc.com/news/world-middle-east-29702440.

and conciliatory. Very consciously, the Kurdish regional government did not seek to declare immediate independence following the vote, instead calling for negotiations with the Iraqi government.[7] That call went unheeded, however, and the Iraqi government instead launched a military drive to regain control of the KAR, as well as the territory controlled by KAR forces since the defeat of the Islamic State in the region in 2014. Within a month, Iraq had retaken much of the disputed territory, and Barzani had been forced to resign.[8]

On 1 October, just a few days after the vote in the KAR, the Spanish region of Cataluña voted in its own unauthorised referendum. The vote had been called by the region's parliament and its president, Carles Puigdemont, but was vociferously opposed by the Spanish government which sought to disrupt preparations for the referendum by seizing ballot papers and closing polling stations.[9] Polling day itself descended into a chaos that sent shockwaves across Europe, with distressing footage of heavily armed and armoured police officers storming polling stations, seizing ballot boxes, and using batons and rubber bullets to disperse crowds.[10] Turnout was low, likely a result both of the police actions and a boycott of the poll by voters in favour of remaining part of Spain, and only 42 per cent of eligible voters cast a ballot.[11] Of those, however, just over 90 per cent backed independence.[12] The heavy-handed response has continued: direct rule over the region has been assumed by Madrid, and on the 14 October 2019, nine of the leaders of the separatist movement were sentenced by Spain's Supreme Court to between nine and thirteen years in prison for their roles in organising the referendum.[13]

Although it is far from true that every exercise of self-determination descends into violence and disorder, claims to self-determination – and in particular attempts to secede – have a worrying tendency to be flashpoints for conflict.[14] Still more concerning, international law seems to have a very limited facility to restrain

[7] 'Iraqi Kurds Decisively Back Independence in Referendum' (n 4).

[8] 'Iraq Kurds: Army Claims Full Control of Kirkuk Province' *BBC News* (20 October 2017) www.bbc.com/news/world-middle-east-41693143; 'Iraqi Kurdish Leader Massoud Barzani to Step Down' *BBC News* (29 October 2017) www.bbc.com/news/world-middle-east-41794083.

[9] S Burgen, 'Catalonia Riven with Tension as Referendum Day Arrives' *The Guardian* (30 September 2017) www.theguardian.com/world/2017/sep/30/catalonia-catalunya-independence-referendum-vote.

[10] 'Catalan Referendum: Clashes as Voters Defy Madrid' *BBC News* (1 October 2017) www.bbc.com/news/world-europe-41457238; S Jones and S Burgen, 'Catalan Referendum: Preliminary Results Show 90% in Favour of Independence' *The Guardian* (2 October 2017) www.theguardian.com/world/2017/oct/01/dozens-injured-as-riot-police-storm-catalan-ref-polling-stations.

[11] 'Final Results in Banned Catalan Independence Vote Put "Yes" on 90.18 Percent: Regional Government' *Reuters* (6 October 2017) www.reuters.com/article/us-spain-politics-catalonia-results/final-results-in-banned-catalan-independence-vote-put-yes-on-90-18-percent-regional-government-idUSKBN1CB272.

[12] 'Final Results in Banned Catalan Independence Vote Put "Yes" on 90.18 Percent: Regional Government' (n 11).

[13] 'Violent Clashes Erupt as Spanish Court Jails Catalonia Leaders' *BBC News* (14 October 2019) www.bbc.com/news/world-europe-49974289; S Jones and S Burgen, 'Violent Clashes over Catalan Separatist Leaders' Prison Terms' *The Guardian* (14 October 2019) www.theguardian.com/world/2019/oct/14/catalan-separatist-leaders-given-lengthy-prison-sentences.

[14] J Duursma, *Fragmentation and the International Relations of Micro-States: Self-Determination and Statehood* (Cambridge, Cambridge University Press, 1996) 1.

or resolve either these conflicts or the tensions underlying them. Indeed, international law itself seems to be highly conflicted on the question of self-determination. In spite of its long history, there are few other principles in international law the status, content and scope of which are so uncertain, and so contested.[15] It has a 'Jekyll and Hyde' character, reviled as a dangerous and anarchic force and simultaneously lauded as an 'essential' principle of the legal system[16] and one of the core purposes of the United Nations.[17] Attempts to self-determine often explicitly invoke the authority of international law and the 'right' to self-determination that international law instruments proclaim, even while the language of law is used to condemn and deny the rightfulness of those same actions.

A. Making Sense of Self-Determination

In this book I argue that the many contradictions and confusions surrounding the concept of self-determination evince a fundamental confusion concerning its nature, scope and content. A seemingly unbridgeable gulf yawns between the enthronement of self-determination as one of the keystones of modern international law, and the absolute condemnation from all sides that attempts to exercise the 'right' of peoples to self-determination receive.[18] Although international law has developed a vocabulary to apply to exercises of self-determination that seeks to reconcile these very different usages, of 'internal' versus 'external' claims, I argue that this binary tends to obscure rather than elucidate important distinctions within the concept, and does so at all levels – underlying legitimacy claim, legal status and practical implementation. Rather, in order coherently to understand self-determination and its place in the contemporary international legal order, I argue that it is necessary to divide self-determination into four independent and distinct forms: polity-based, colonial, remedial and secessionary self-determination.

To demonstrate the value of this four-part typology, this book offers a genealogy of self-determination. It traces the development of self-determination

[15] Mégret, for example, describes '[i]nternational law's attitude to self-determination [as having] oscillated in the last century between the temptation of encouraging group aspirations to forms of political and territorial power and a recoiling at the possible consequences for international order and stability'. F Mégret, 'The Right to Self-Determination: Earned, Not Inherent' in FR Tesón (ed), *The Theory of Self-Determination* (Cambridge, Cambridge University Press, 2016) 48.

[16] *East Timor (Portugal v Australia)*, Judgment, (1995) ICJ Reports 90, para 29: 'In the Court's view, Portugal's assertion that the right of peoples to self-determination, as it evolved from the Charter and from United Nations practice, has an *erga omnes* character, is irreproachable … it is one of the essential principles of contemporary international law.'

[17] Article 1(2) of the Charter of the United Nations and Statute of the International Court of Justice (San Francisco, 26 June 1945): 'The Purposes of the United Nations are: … To develop friendly relations among nations based on respect for the principle of equal rights and self-determination of peoples, and to take other appropriate measures to strengthen universal peace'.

[18] See below, nn 35–40, and accompanying text.

through its major events and usages, changes and ruptures, from the protogenous roots of the idea in fourteenth-century Scotland[19] to the 2019 advisory opinion of the International Court of Justice (ICJ) in the *Chagos Archipelago* matter.[20] In so doing, I am interested primarily in the development of self-determination as a legal concept, rather than with its wider intellectual history or its role as a moral-political idea (though there are, as will be seen, many overlaps). As such, I approach the history of self-determination not as a historian, but as a lawyer; self-determination claims are not viewed primarily as events in themselves, but as *precedents*.[21] There are many examples of the use and misuse of precedential reasoning in the history of self-determination, from the similarity of the 1776 American Declaration of Independence to the Plakkaat van Verlatinghe (Act of Abjuration) of 1581,[22] through the French revolution's influence on the independence declarations of the Age of Revolution,[23] and to the use of the ICJ's *Kosovo* Advisory Opinion by Russia in an attempt to justify its annexation of Crimea.[24] Through these successive invocations, as particular events are called upon as precedents in one case, and others in another, the four forms of self-determination that I identify become apparent. In the text, as in the history, these forms are allowed to emerge inductively. Although they appear first as claims primarily to a moral-political rightness rather than to a legal right (properly so-called), the major question I ask is: what legal status should each form of self-determination be understood to have today?

I answer that two forms of self-determination – the polity-based and the colonial forms – have achieved the character of norms of customary international law. They exist as legal rights, and hold a high position in the legal system. Certainly, the polity-based form should be understood to be a norm *ius cogens*, and it seems increasingly likely that the same status applies to colonial self-determination. By contrast, the secessionary form of self-determination certainly has not entered into customary law as a right of peoples. It remains a claim at a political level, though it seems increasingly clear that international law does not actively prohibit secession. Rather, it is grudgingly neutral – secession is tolerated but not welcomed; condemned but not forbidden – and international law will take account of the outcome of secession struggles without (to any great extent) regulating their conduct. Finally, remedial secession exists as a putative norm of international law.

[19] Declaration of Arbroath of 1320, discussed in ch 2, below.

[20] *Legal Consequences of the Separation of the Chagos Archipelago from Mauritius in 1965*, Advisory Opinion, (2019) ICJ Reports 95.

[21] A Orford, 'On International Legal Method' (2013) 1 *London Review of International Law* 166, *passim*, esp 177.

[22] Although note, as discussed in ch 2, that it remains a matter of speculation whether the similarity is coincidental or the result of an influence of the Dutch.

[23] The 'Age of Revolution' is used by Hobsbawm to signify the period from 1789 to 1848: EJ Hobsbawm, *The Age of Revolution: Europe 1789–1848* (London, Weidenfeld & Nicolson, 1962).

[24] For a discussion of this example, see ch 5, ss III.A–B.

Although it has long been on the verge of crystallising, I conclude that it has not yet done so. That it has not, I argue, is one of the clearest examples of the ongoing confusion surrounding self-determination and of the shortcomings of the internal/external vocabulary. The paucity of that framework means that the remedial form of self-determination is habitually – but inappropriately – categorised as a subset of 'external' self-determination, leading to what I name concerns of 'spillover' legitimacy. In other words, that the current framework offers no coherent way to distinguish between the remedial and secessionary forms means that both must be treated as unacceptable, lest the liberalisation of remedial self-determination echoes to the secessionary form. These answers are further developed through the historical and legal analysis in the remainder of the book, and are discussed in the book's conclusion.

The genealogical treatment of self-determination begins in chapter two. The current chapter, however, serves a different function. It offers an overview and a summary of the four-part typology of self-determination that emerges inductively through the remainder of the text. In relation to each form, I identify who the 'self' is that can claim to self-determine in that way, what the purported or expected consequences of its exercise will be, the rationale or underlying legitimacy narrative, and the legal character or status of the form. In so doing the chapter offers a brief overview of the material that will then be presented at greater length in the remainder of the text, and the conclusions that are reached. Section I.C takes up that task, before section I.D examines the nature of self-determination's forms at a deeper, ideational level. There I interrogate the relationship between the forms of self-determination and the wider self-determination category, and cast these in the relation of four species which sit within a single genus. Although they share the common attributes of the genus, each species is and should be understood as discrete and self-standing.

First, though, section II sets out the 'self-determination problem'. It identifies at both a conceptual and practical level that the current framework of self-determination reflects and perpetuates a deep-seated conceptual confusion. International law tends to treat self-determination as a unitary norm with two expressions: its 'internal' and 'external' manifestations. Neither that vocabulary nor the framework it reflects are fit for purpose. These terms lack appropriate descriptive content, and fail to discriminate between different claims to self-determination along rational lines. The result is a legal norm of self-determination of uncertain scope, application and consequences.[25] The events of 2017, which saw the holding of unauthorised independence referenda in both Cataluña and the KAR, provide an excellent example.

[25] FR Tesón, 'Introduction: The Conundrum of Self-Determination' in Tesón (ed), *The Theory of Self-Determination* (n 15) 1–2.

II. The Self-Determination Problem

Fernando Tesón declares that '[n]o other area of international law is more indeterminate, incoherent, and unprincipled than the law of self-determination'.[26] Although self-determination has been a common topic before international courts,[27] and although many hundreds of pages of academic literature have been written on the subject,[28] it remains unknowable, controversial and potentially inflammatory. This section will demonstrate that the current framework of self-determination is a significant contributor to – and perhaps a cause of – this confusion.

A. Self-Determination and Conflict

The dramatic events of 2017, introduced above, offer a snapshot of the fascinating and chaotic role played by self-determination in international law, as well as the Janus-faced and ineffectual role played by international law in self-determination. The international reactions to the referenda in the KAR and Cataluña were highly telling, particularly in the context of the violence employed by the Spanish police in an attempt to supress the Cataluñan referendum and the military campaign waged to bring the KAR back under the control of the Iraqi central government. They are all the more remarkable because in both cases it appears that the key players in the secessionist causes believed that they were acting in fulfilment of an international legal right. In the KAR, President Barzani (as noted above) referred to the 'legal right' of the region's people to hold a referendum,[29] although the source of that legal right was not spelled out. It seems likely that President Barzani referred to a right originating in international law: Iraq's 2005 Constitution does not provide for the right of its regions to hold secession referenda.[30] In Cataluña, meanwhile, the law establishing the referendum referred to the 'imprescriptible and inalienable right of Cataluña to self-determination',[31] and remarks by

[26] ibid 1; see further, M Sterio, *Secession in International Law: A New Framework* (Cheltenham, Edward Elgar, 2018).

[27] The ICJ, for example, has considered questions with a high degree of relevance to self-determination on no fewer than six occasions. Four of these judgments and opinions are discussed in ch 4, while chs 5 and 6 are dedicated to an analysis of its advisory opinions in *Kosovo* and *Chagos Archipelago*, respectively.

[28] See below, s II.C, for an extensive (although far from exhaustive) list of articles and books dedicated to self-determination, and an analysis of some common problems affecting that body of work.

[29] MacDiarmid, 'Masoud Barzani: Why it's Time for Kurdish Independence' (n 2).

[30] Constitution of the Islamic Republic of Iraq (UNAMI tr, 2005). Indeed, the constitution is described in Art 1 as the 'guarantor of the unity of Iraq', and Art 109 requires the 'federal authorities [to] preserve the unity, integrity, independence and sovereignty of Iraq'.

[31] Cataluña, Ley 19/2017, de 6 de septiembre, del referéndum de autodeterminación: 'El Parlamento de Cataluña ha expresado de forma continuada e inequívoca el derecho de Cataluña a la autodeterminación. Así se manifestó en la Resolución 98/III, sobre el derecho a la autodeterminación de la nación catalana, adoptada el 12 de diciembre de 1989, y ratificada en la Resolución 679/V, adoptada el 1 de

Cataluñan President Torra in January of 2019 confirm that it is an international right that was claimed. The referendum was 'based on every people's right to self-determination according to international law and treaties'.[32]

If, indeed, the Cataluñan referendum should be understood as a people exercising its international legal right to self-determination, the international reaction would be surprising indeed. No major power or international organisation offered support for the separatist cause – on the contrary, it was staunchly opposed – and even the responses to the violent means employed by the Spanish police were distinctly muted. Zeid Ra'ad Al Hussein, the United Nations High Commissioner for Human Rights, described being 'very disturbed by the violence' and called for 'thorough, independent and impartial investigations',[33] but his was amongst the strongest reactions. A statement issued by the European Commission on 2 October offered only a 'call' for 'all relevant players to now move very swiftly from confrontation to dialogue', and its statement that '[v]iolence can never be an instrument in politics' was seemingly addressed to both sides.[34] In parallel, it declared that 'yesterday's vote in Catalonia was not legal' under Spain's constitution, and concluded that any more significant international response would be inappropriate: 'this is an internal matter for Spain that has to be dealt with in line with the constitutional order'.[35] By contrast, the attempt on the part of the people of Cataluña to self-determine drew a much sterner reaction. In an interview with *el País* on 20 November 2017 Jean-Claude Juncker, then President of the European Commission, responded to the vote in Cataluña with '[n]ationalism is poison … and I don't accept regions going against nations'.[36] He went on to say that:

> [A]s president of the Commission, I support the position of the Spanish government. And do you know why? Because I am in favor of those who respect the law. The EU is based on the rule of law, and what my Catalan friends have done is the opposite: break

octubre de 1998, en la Resolución 631/VIII del Parlamento de Cataluña, sobre el derecho a la autodeterminación y sobre el reconocimiento de las consultas populares sobre la independencia, adoptada el 10 de marzo de 2010. Más recientemente, la Resolución 5/X del Parlamento de Cataluña, por la que se aprueba la Declaración de soberanía y del derecho a decidir del pueblo de Cataluña y la Resolución 306/XI, adoptada el 6 de octubre de 2016, sobre la orientación política general del Gobierno, han afirmado el derecho imprescriptible e inalienable de Cataluña a la autodeterminación y han constatado una mayoría parlamentaria favorable a la independencia.'

[32] Quim Torra i Pla, President de la Generalitat de Cataluña, 'Civil Rights and Self-Determination: A Catalan Perspective' (Stanford, 14 January 2019), www.govern.cat/govern/docs/2019/01/17/13/01/e700315f-46d0-415e-8575-f7f59660b411.pdf.

[33] OHCHR, 'Comment by the UN High Commissioner for Human Rights Zeid Ra'ad Al Hussein on the Situation in Catalonia, Spain' (2 October 2017) www.ohchr.org/en/press-releases/2017/10/comment-un-high-commissioner-human-rights-zeid-raad-al-hussein-situation.

[34] European Commission, 'Statement on the Events in Catalonia', 2 October 2017, STATEMENT/17/3626, www.europa.eu/rapid/press-release_STATEMENT-17-3626_en.htm.

[35] ibid; see further 'Catalonia Referendum Violence Prompts European Reaction' *Deutsche Welle* (2 October 2017) https://p.dw.com/p/2l4r0.

[36] C Pérez, 'Jean-Claude Juncker: "Nationalism Is Poison"' *El País* (20 November 2017) www.elpais.com/elpais/2017/11/20/inenglish/1511177283_048948.html.

> the law. I am with those who have respected the constitutional framework, I can't support those who violate it.[37]

The international response to the referendum in the KAR was, if anything, less sympathetic still. The Turkish Ministry of Foreign Affairs condemned the holding of the referendum as lacking legitimacy at the level both of constitutional and international law:

> The referendum, which is being held today (September 25th) in [Iraqi Kurdistan], is null and void in terms of its consequences. We do not recognize this initiative, which lacks legal basis and legitimacy with regard to the international law and the Iraqi constitution.[38]

Rex Tillerson, then US Secretary of State followed suit, declaring that the United States 'does not recognize the Kurdistan Regional Government's unilateral referendum', which he said, 'lack[s] legitimacy and we continue to support a united, federal, democratic and prosperous Iraq'.[39] Although less directly, both the United Nations Secretary-General and the Security Council similarly appeared to reject the referendum, affirming their 'respect for the sovereignty, territorial integrity, and unity of Iraq'.[40]

The unanimity and dour countenance of the responses to the referenda could lead the observer to question how it is that the organisers of the votes in Cataluña and the KAR came to the conclusion that international law offered them a right upon which to base their claims. Yet against this implacable wall of criticism, one can indeed set a plethora of references to the high status of self-determination in international law, and of the commitment all states have made to uphold that idea. A few examples will serve starkly to draw the contrast. A key reference is to be found in the UN Charter, where self-determination appears in Article 1. There it is declared that one of the purposes of the organisation is '[t]o develop friendly relations among nations based on respect for the principle of equal rights and self-determination of peoples'.[41] Self-determination is included, too, in the first article

[37] ibid; Ministry for Europe and Foreign Affairs of France, 'Spain – Catalonia – Statement by M Jean-Yves Le Drian, Minister for Europe and Foreign Affairs' (27 September 2017) www.diplomatie.gouv.fr/en/country-files/spain/events/article/spain-catalonia-statement-by-m-jean-yves-le-drian-minister-for-europe-and.

[38] Republic of Turkey Ministry for Foreign Affairs, 'Press Release Regarding the Referendum that Is Being Held in the KRG' (25 September 2017) www.mfa.gov.tr/no_-297_-ikby-referandumu-hk_en.en.mfa.

[39] US Department of State, 'Statement by Secretary Tillerson: Iraqi Kurdistan Regional Government's Referendum' (29 September 2017) www.translations.state.gov/2017/09/29/iraqi-kurdistan-regional-governments-referendum.

[40] UNSC, 'Security Council Press Statement on Iraq', 21 September 2017, UN Doc No SC/13036; UNSG, 'Secretary-General Expresses Concern about Potentially Destabilizing Effects of Referendum in Iraq's Kurdistan Region', 25 September 2017, UN Doc No SG/SM/18724; UNSC, 'Security Council Press Statement on Kirkuk', 18 October 2017, UN Doc No SC/13036.

[41] Art 1(2) of the UN Charter (n 17). More strikingly, in the French text this is rendered as the 'right' of peoples to self-determination: 'Développer entre les nations des relations amicales fondées sur le respect du principe de l'égalité de droits des peuples et de leur droit à disposer d'eux-mêmes, et prendre toutes autres mesures propres à consolider la paix du monde.'

common to both the United Nations human rights covenants, where it is stated that: 'All peoples have the right of self-determination. By virtue of that right they freely determine their political status and freely pursue their economic, social and cultural development.'[42] Moreover, self-determination holds a high and privileged position in the legal order as it is conceived by international courts. In its 1995 judgment in *East Timor* the ICJ declared that the 'assertion that the right of peoples to self-determination, as it has evolved from the Charter and from United Nations practice, has an *erga omnes* character, is irreproachable. … [I]t is one of the essential principles of contemporary international law.'[43] More recently Judge Robinson has developed that sentiment further in his separate opinion in the *Chagos Archipelago* Advisory Opinion, and argued that 'the Court's case law, State practice and *opinio juris*, and scholarly writing are sufficient to warrant characterising the right to self-determination as a norm of *jus cogens*'.[44]

In the face of the disparity between international reactions to these exercises of self-determination and the legal authorities that seem to apply to it, the immediate commentary by academic international lawyers on these events did not offer a clear way to reconcile those positions. Most authors agreed that efforts to secede fall into a legal grey zone – neither expressly enabled nor actually prohibited.[45] Although all seem to accept that some peoples in some circumstances have a right to independence that will be applied as a matter of international law, it remains unclear where to draw the line between cases to which a right to secede applies and those to which it does not. Indeed, the volume of academic work that continues to be dedicated to the subject of self-determination is itself testimony to the ways in which self-determination continues to defy attempts to bring it into order.[46]

[42] Art 1(1) of the International Covenant on Economic, Social, and Cultural Rights (New York, 16 December 1966); Art 1(1) of the International Covenant on Civil and Political Rights (New York, 16 December 1966). At the time of writing the ICESCR has 170 parties and the ICCPR 173.

[43] *East Timor* (n 16) para 29.

[44] *Legal Consequences of the Separation of the Chagos Archipelago from Mauritius in 1965*, Separate Opinion of Judge Robinson, (2019) ICJ Reports 294, para 50.

[45] M Sterio, 'Do Kurds Have the Right to Self-Determination and/or Secession?' *Opinio Juris* (28 September 2017) www.opiniojuris.org/2017/09/28/kurds-right-self-determination-andor-secession/; A Peters, 'Populist International Law? The Suspended Independence and the Normative Value of the Referendum on Catalonia' *EJIL:Talk!* (12 October 2017) www.ejiltalk.org/populist-international-law-the-suspended-independence-and-the-normative-value-of-the-referendum-on-catalonia; M Weller, 'Secession and Self-Determination in Western Europe: The Case of Catalonia' *EJIL:Talk!* (18 October 2017) www.ejiltalk.org/secession-and-self-determination-in-western-europe-the-case-of-catalonia; J Vidmar, 'Catalonia: The Way Forward Is Comparative Constitutional Rather than International Legal Argument' *EJIL:Talk!* (24 October 2017) www.ejiltalk.org/catalonia-the-way-forward-is-comparative-constitutional-rather-than-international-legal-argument; M Milanović, 'A Footnote on Secession' *EJIL:Talk!* (26 October 2017) www.ejiltalk.org/a-footnote-on-secession/; although note contra M Bak McKenna, 'The Referendum on Catalan Self-Determination: Long Shots and Legal Flair' *Völkerrechtsblog* (27 September 2017) www.voelkerrechtsblog.org/the-referendum-on-catalan-self-determination-long-shots-and-legal-flair/.

[46] Tesón puts it very well in his comment, already cited above, that '[n]o other area of international law is more indeterminate, incoherent, and unprincipled than the law of self-determination': Tesón, 'Introduction' (n 25) 1. See also below, s II.C, which notes many further examples of scholarship on this topic, albeit with no attempt to do so exhaustively.

And yet some form of resolution is badly needed.[47] These are matters laden with potentially deadly consequences, as the events in Cataluña and Kurdistan show all too clearly, and such conflicts have been distressingly common in the tragic and bloody history of this contested concept. Jorri Duursma's bleak assessment that 'practically all' conflicts in the modern world relate to self-determination has held worryingly true.[48] The multifaceted civil war in Syria over the proper governance and borders of the Syrian state has gradually dropped out of the news, but continues to decimate lives and livelihoods.[49] A similar and complex interaction between lack of confidence in governance and separatist ambitions has plunged Yemen into a prolonged and brutal civil war that has given rise to the 'worst humanitarian crisis in the world'.[50] Following decades of inter-ethnic violence and the partition of the country, Sudan remains one of the most dangerous places in the world in which to be displaced, according to Amnesty International.[51] Post 2017, the prospect of an independent Kurdistan continued to provoke significant disquiet in the region, and in 2019 prompted a swift and crushing intervention into majority Kurdish regions of Syria by Turkey.[52] In Europe, violence erupted again in

[47] See also Sterio, *Secession* (n 26) 1–6.

[48] Duursma, *Fragmentation* (n 14) 1. Although Duursma's comment, made in 1996, could not presage the so-called 'war on terror', even in a post-9/11 world in which the battle lines have been significantly redrawn it seems nevertheless to capture an important truth. Indeed, one could even ask whether the 'war on terror', with its roots in the Soviet and American interventions into Afghanistan, could itself be traced back to a self-determination conflict, although such a far-reaching conclusion is unnecessary for the general point to stand.

[49] 'Syria War: "World Shrugs" as 103 Civilians Killed in 10 Days' *BBC News* (26 July 2019) www.bbc.com/news/world-middle-east-49126523; 'Is the World Ignoring Syria's War?' *Al Jazeera* (27 July 2019) www.aljazeera.com/programmes/insidestory/2019/07/world-ignoring-syria-war-190727180524920.html; N Cummings-Bruce, 'UN Sounds Alarm Over Killings in Idlib as Syria Cease-fire Collapses' *New York Times* (9 August 2019) www.nytimes.com/2019/08/09/world/middleeast/syria-idlib-cease-fire.html.

[50] European Commission, 'EU Steps Up Support to Displaced and Crisis-Affected Communities in Yemen' *IP/18/6564* (27 November 2018) www.europa.eu/rapid/press-release_IP-18-6564_en.htm; K Schuster, 'Yemen's War Explained in 4 Key Points' *Deutsche Welle* (10 August 2018) https://p.dw.com/p/2i4cU; 'Yemen Crisis: Why Is There a War?' *BBC News* (21 March 2019) www.bbc.com/news/world-middle-east-29319423.

[51] Amnesty International, 'Sudan: Fresh Evidence of Government-Sponsored Crimes in Darfur Shows Drawdown of Peacekeepers Premature and Reckless' (11 June 2019) www.amnesty.org/en/latest/news/2019/06/sudan-fresh-evidence-of-government-sponsored-crimes-in-darfur-shows-drawdown-of-peacekeepers-premature-and-reckless/; Amnesty International, 'Sudan: Immediate Humanitarian Access for Victims of Conflict Essential as Ceasefire Deal Agreed' (22 October 2019) www.amnesty.org/en/latest/news/2019/10/sudan-immediate-humanitarian-access-for-victims-of-conflict-essential-as-ceasefire-deal-agreed/. Civilians and displaced persons are also at inordinately high risk of violence and abuse in South Sudan: Amnesty International, 'South Sudan: Sexual Violence "On a Massive Scale" Leaves Thousands in Mental Distress amid Raging Conflict' (24 July 2017) www.amnesty.org/en/latest/news/2017/07/south-sudan-sexual-violence-on-a-massive-scale-leaves-thousands-in-mental-distress-amid-raging-conflict/.

[52] For the events of 2019, see 'Turkish Military, Rebels to Cross Syrian Border "Shortly"' *Al Jazeera* (9 October 2019) https://aje.io/f6gsn; 'Turkey Launches Ground Offensive in Northern Syria' *BBC News* (9 October 2019) www.bbc.com/news/world-middle-east-49983357; 'Turkey Unleashes Airstrikes against Kurds in North-East Syria' *The Guardian* (9 October 2019) www.theguardian.com/world/2019/oct/09/turkey-launches-military-operation-in-northern-syria-erdogan.

Cataluña in 2019 in response to the imprisonment of a number of the organisers of the 2017 independence vote. Following the 2016 vote, the never-ending Brexit saga in the United Kingdom threatens the re-establishment of a border between the Republic of Ireland and British Northern Ireland, and with it a potential return to the intercommunity violence halted by the Good Friday Agreement.[53] Kosovo remains in an uneasy limbo between statehood and non-statehood following war, genocide and ethnic cleansing in the former Yugoslavia.[54]

Most recently, the final work to prepare this manuscript was undertaken in the shadow of the Russian invasion of Ukraine, launched on 24 February 2022.[55] This is a conflict about control, geopolitics, the decline of Russia post-Cold War and (very plausibly) the failing sanity of Russia's autocratic leader. But it is also a conflict of self-determination: as Ukraine has sought to move westward, seeking integration into Europe and guarantees of its independence through NATO membership, a Russia not prepared to countenance Ukraine's choice of its future political direction has sought to threaten, to coerce and now forcibly to suppress Ukrainian independence and nationhood. Ukraine, Vladimir Putin has declared, never had any 'real statehood'.[56]

International law is not a bystander in these conflicts; it is a contributor. It stands behinds both camps, saying both no and yes. When juxtaposed in this way, it seems absolutely apparent that the contrasting uses of self-determination exhibited in 2017 (and countless other similar scenarios) are the result of a conceptual confusion: when states hail a right to self-determination and separatists claim a right to self-determination they are, simply put, not talking about the same thing.[57] Recognising this duality, international lawyers have divided the self-determination idea into two components: 'internal' and 'external' self-determination.[58] The next section examines this vocabulary, and argues that it is not sufficient to resolve the conceptual uncertainty surrounding self-determination.

[53] Agreement on the withdrawal of the United Kingdom of Great Britain and Northern Ireland from the European Union and the European Atomic Energy Community (Brussels, 25 November 2018); The Belfast Agreement (Belfast, 10 April 1998).

[54] See further ch 5, s I.A.

[55] The invasion, and the extent to which it and the annexation of Crimea by Russia in 2014 were enabled by the *Kosovo* Advisory Opinion, are discussed in ch 5, ss III.A–B.

[56] B Perrigo, 'How Putin's Denial of Ukraine's Statehood Rewrites History' *Time* (22 February 2022) https://ti.me/3v9Dr21.

[57] This failure of vocabulary is also noted by Mégret, 'Earned, Not Inherent' (n 15) 50; Z Oklopcic, 'The Referendum on Catalan Self-Determination (Part I): Endemic Rhetoric, Interpretive Hypocrisy and Legal Imagination' *Völkerrechtsblog* (22 September 2017) www.voelkerrechtsblog.org/the-referendum-on-catalan-self-determination/; Z Oklopcic, 'The Referendum on Catalan Self-Determination (Part II): Endemic Rhetoric, Interpretive Hypocrisy and Legal Imagination' *Völkerrechtsblog* (25 September 2017) www.voelkerrechtsblog.org/the-referendum-on-catalan-self-determination-part-ii/.

[58] It is unclear who should be regarded as the originator of these terms, or when they first appeared. No mention of 'internal' or 'external' self-determination can be found in Cobban's classic 1944 study or its revised 1969 edition. It may be found, however, in Rigo Sureda's treatment of the topic in 1973 (eg p 117), and by 1978 Buchheit was able to refer to the vocabulary as having 'become popular' (p 14). The earliest use of the terms of which I am aware is Rupert Emerson's 1971 article, titled simply 'Self-Determination', and it seems reasonable to date its use to that time: A Cobban, *National*

B. The Meanings of Self-Determination

What is self-determination, and what do we mean when we use the term? As has been indicated in the foregoing, this question is at the heart of the enquiry in this book. At its most basic, the term itself is a portmanteau of two ideas that are simultaneously eloquent and undefined. It begins with the 'self'. Originally a reference to the individual – the internal, essential 'I' – political uses of the term extend the idea by analogy to groups that possess a collective identity. Such groups have sufficient echoes of the internal, mental life of the individual to be treated in similar ways. They consider themselves to be a unit, have a shared conception of the good and are able coherently to express themselves as a singularity. That is not to say that they are straightforward to identify, however; on the contrary, the criteria for and the practical task of the identification of 'selves' are highly controversial.[59] The second element – the 'determination' – indicates a moral conviction, drawing from the fact that it has its own conception of the good, that a 'self's' (whether individual or collective) decisions concerning the course of its life have moral significance.

The etymology of the term supports such a moral-theoretical definition. It may be that the English term 'self-determination' derives from the German term *Selbstbestimmung*, of which it is a literal translation. The German term is a similar composite of *Selbst-* (pertaining to the self) and *die Bestimmung*, which has a range of meanings from 'assignation' to 'identification'. In turn, *die Bestimmung* derives etymologically from *die Stimme*, meaning 'voice'.[60] The earliest use of the term of which I am aware appears in a 1571 German-language Bible commentary by Petrus Geduldius (Petrus the Patient),[61] and towards the end of the seventeenth century a number of English-language tracts appeared which used the term 'self-determination' in a theological context.[62] In these cases the term is

Self-Determination (Oxford, Oxford University Press, 1944); A Cobban, *The Nation State and National Self-Determination*, 2nd edn (London, Collins, 1969); R Emerson, 'Self-Determination' (1971) 65 *American Journal of International Law* 459, 465ff; A Rigo Sureda, *The Evolution of the Right of Self-Determination: A Study of United Nations Practice* (Leiden, AW Sijthoff, 1973) 117ff; L Buchheit, *Secession: The Legitimacy of Self-Determination* (New Haven, CT, Yale University Press, 1978) 14.

[59] I Jennings, *The Approach to Self-government* (Cambridge, Cambridge University Press, 1956) 56. See further, nn 123–24 and accompanying text.

[60] G Köbler, *Deutsches etymologisches Rechtswörterbuch* (Tübingen, Mohr, 1995) 53.

[61] Petrus Gedultius, *Concordantz und Zeiger über die gantze heilige biblische schrifft deß alten und Neuwen Testaments*, Erste Theil (Franckfurt am Mayn, Hieronymus Feyerabend/Georg Rab d. Ä., 1571) § 4.

[62] S Parker, *An Account of the Nature and Extent of the Divine Dominion and Goodnesse, Especially as They Refer to the Origenian Hypothesis Concerning the Pre-Existence of Souls, Together with a Special Account of the Vanity and Groundlessness of the Hypothesis Itself* (Oxford, R Davis, 1666) 31–32; *Richard Baxter's Catholick Theologie: Plain, Pure, Peaceable, for Pacification of the Dogmatical Word-Warriours* (London, Nevill Simmons, 1675) see eg 24, 33; V Alsop, *Melius Inquirendum, or a Sober Inquiry into the Reasonings of the Serious Inquiry: Wherein the Inquirers Cavils against the Principle, His Calumnies against the Preachings and Practices of the Non-Conformists Are Examined and Refelled* (1679) 339; J Corbet, *A Humble Endeavour of Some Plain and Brief Explication of the Decrees and Operations of God, about the Free Actions of Men: More Especially of the Operations of Divine Grace* (London, Tho Parkhurst, 1683) 16.

being used to refer to the ever-thorny theological problem of the free will of humanity on the one side, and its subjection to God on the other. Alsop says, for example, 'but as the self-determination of the will to one side prejudices not its liberty: so the determination of our *Christian liberty* (by our choice, guided by prudence and reason) is no extinguishment of its radical freedom'.[63]

It seems likely that the popularisation of the term was, at least in part, due to its use by Immanuel Kant. Kant's *Grundlegung zur Metaphysik der Sitten* (*Groundwork of the Metaphysics of Morals*), first published in 1785, uses *Selbstbestimmung* in a manner similar to its previous theological uses – to refer to an internal mental process of the individual – but in so doing transposed it from a theological to a moral philosophical plane. In the course of explaining his categorical imperative, he uses the term to refer to the externalisation of the individual's will:

> Nun ist das, was dem Willen zum objektiven Grunde seiner Selbstbestimmung dient, der *Zweck*, und dieser, wen er durch bloße Vernunft gegeben wird, muß für alle vernünftigen Wesen gleich gelten.[64]

This idea – of the self-determination of the individual as one of the basic pillars of moral philosophy – was further developed by Hegel,[65] and remains one of the staples of neo-Kantianism,[66] as well as of political philosophy more broadly.[67]

As a term of political application, self-determination is usually dated to the beginning of the twentieth century.[68] Even looking at these first usages, however, there is considerable disagreement in the literature concerning the initial claim intended by this term. Alfred Cobban and Andrés Rigo Sureda trace the concept to the popular sovereignty demands of the French revolution;[69] Hannum to

[63] Alsop, *Melius Inquirendum* (n 62) 339 (spelling and orthography modernised; emphasis in original).

[64] I Kant, *Grundlegung zur Metaphysik der Sitten*, ed C Horn, C Mieth and N Scarano (Frankfurt am Main, Suhrkamp, 2007) 60. 'Now it is, that that which serves the will as the objective basis of its self-determination is its *purpose*. And this, as it derives from the mere fact of reason, must be applied equally to all reasoning beings' (my translation, emphasis in original).

[65] GWF Hegel, *Grundlinien der Philosophie des Rechts, 2. Auflage*, ed G Lasson (Leipzig, Felix Meiner, 1921) §§105–14.

[66] CM Korsgaard, *The Sources of Normativity*, ed O O'Neill (Cambridge, Cambridge University Press, 1996) 136ff; see also CM Korsgaard, *The Constitution of Agency: Essays on Practical Reason and Moral Psychology* (Oxford, Oxford University Press, 2008); A Gewirth, 'The Basis and Content of Human Rights' (1978–79) 13 *Georgia Law Review* 1143; J Jowitt, 'Monkey See, Monkey Sue? Gewirth's Principle of Generic Consistency and Rights for Non-Human Agents' (2016) 19 *Trinity College Law Review* 71.

[67] R Dworkin, *Taking Rights Seriously* (London, Gerald Duckworth, 2005) 272–73; R Nozick, *Anarchy, State and Utopia* (Oxford, Basil Blackwell, 1974) ix; J Raz, 'The Rule of Law and its Virtue' in J Raz, *The Authority of Law: Essays on Law and Morality* (Oxford, Clarendon Press, 1979) 220.

[68] D Harper, '"Self-Determination" (n.)' *Online Etymology Dictionary* (2001–17) www.etymonline.com/word/self-determination; M Sterio, *The Right to Self-Determination under International Law: 'Selfistans,' Secession, and the Rule of the Great Powers* (London, Routledge, 2013) 1. The popularisation of the term is often attributed to Woodrow Wilson, although it should be noted that Vladimir Lenin's highly influential *The Right of Nations to Self-Determination* also appeared in the same time period (first publication 1914): VI Lenin, 'The Right of Nations to Self-Determination' in J Katzer (ed), B Isaacs and J Fineberg (trs), *VI Lenin: Collected Works*, vol 20 (Moscow, Progress Publishers, 1964).

[69] Cobban, *National Self-Determination* (n 58) 5; Rigo Sureda, *Evolution of Self-Determination* (n 58) 17.

the nationalism that provoked and followed the collapse of the Ottoman and Austro-Hungarian empires.[70] Milena Sterio's history begins in the decolonisation rhetoric of the First World War,[71] and Umozurike Oji Umozurike's with the political philosophy and demands of the international socialist movement of the late nineteenth and early twentieth centuries.[72] Although Robert McCorquodale describes a longer conceptual pedigree, he too dates the first use of the term in an international context to Woodrow Wilson.[73] None of these derivations are to be preferred over the others: there are elements of truth in each. As soon as the term was detached from the individualised, internal meaning it bore in moral philosophy, it acquired a composite character. Certainty of definition has consistently been defeated by the extent to which the 'self' and the 'determination' to which it refers have been in the eye of the beholder.

As a general definition of self-determination, then, it is difficult – if not impossible – to refine the concept beyond the general, all-purpose explanation given above: self-determination refers to the claim that the conception of the good that an individual or collectively holds for itself is morally (or politically) relevant. Such a definition, plainly, is not adequate to the needs of international law, and lawyers have therefore sought to overlay the internal/external binary as an additional level of specification.

C. The Internal/External Division of Self-Determination

Despite the divergent meanings identified as being the original usage of the idea, in international law self-determination is often understood to be a unitary concept.[74]

[70] H Hannum, *Autonomy, Sovereignty and Self-Determination: The Accommodation of Conflicting Rights* (Philadelphia, University of Pennsylvania Press, 1990) 27.

[71] Sterio, *Right to Self-Determination* (n 68) 1.

[72] UO Umozurike, *Self-Determination in International Law* (London, Archon Books, 1972) 3.

[73] R McCorquodale, 'Introduction' in R McCorquodale (ed), *Self-Determination in International Law* (Aldershot, Ashgate Dartmouth, 2000) xiii. Wilson, his philosophy and his influence on self-determination are discussed in ch 3, s II.

[74] Emerson, 'Self-Determination' (n 58); J Crawford, 'Outside the Colonial Context' in WJA Macartney (ed), *Self-Determination in the Commonwealth* (Aberdeen, Aberdeen University Press, 1988) 13; N Berman, 'Sovereignty in Abeyance: Self-Determination and International Law' (1988) 7 *Wisconsin International Law Journal* 51; A Whelan, 'Self-Determination and Decolonisation: Foundations for the Future' (1992) 3 *Irish Studies in International Affairs* 25; H Hannum, 'Rethinking Self-Determination' (1993) 34 *Virginia Journal of International Law* 1; P Thornberry, 'The Democratic or Internal Aspect of Self-Determination with Some Remarks on Federalism' in C Tomuschat (ed), *The Modern Law of Self-Determination* (Dordrecht, Martinus Nijhoff, 1993); A Cassese, *Self-Determination of Peoples: A Legal Reappraisal* (Cambridge, Cambridge University Press, 1995) 11–33; S Trifunovska, 'One Theme in Two Variations – Self-Determination for Minorities and Indigenous Groups' (1997) 5 *International Journal on Minority and Group Rights* 175; D Philpott, 'Self-Determination in Practice' in M Moore (ed), *National Self-Determination and Secession* (Oxford, Oxford University Press, 1998) 85–86; G Binder, 'The Case for Self-Determination' in R McCorquodale (ed), *Self-Determination in International Law* (Aldershot, Ashgate Dartmouth, 2000); E Chadwick, *Self-Determination in the Post-9/11 Era* (London, Routledge, 2011) 7–8; D French, 'Introduction' in D French (ed), *Statehood and Self-Determination: Reconciling Tradition and Modernity in International Law* (Cambridge, Cambridge

It is described as having two aspects or applications – the internal and the external.[75] Indeed, James Summers argues that this vocabulary is 'now almost standard practice in the academic literature',[76] even if – a fact which severely calls into question the value of the internal/external distinction – 'internal' and 'external' do not appear to bear the same meanings in the work of all authors. Compare, for example, Anthony Whelan, who uses the term 'external' to mean 'non-intervention',[77] with McCorquodale, who uses the term to refer to secession.[78] This section takes 'internal' to mean self-determination by the whole people of a state within its established borders, and 'external' to mean the secession of a sub-state unit, which appear to be the modal usages of these terms.

In sharp contrast to this general practice, I argue that this internal/external dichotomy amounts to a conflation of the forms of self-determination, and thus impedes their analysis and application. Such a view of self-determination produces (even to a greater extent than is warranted) histories which show its

University Press, 2013) 11; J Vidmar, 'Unilateral Declarations of Independence in International Law' in French (ibid) 71–73; K del Mar, 'The Myth of Remedial Secession' in French (ibid) *passim*; C Walter and A von Ungern-Sternberg, 'Introduction: Self-Determination and Secession in International Law – Perspectives and Trends with Particular Focus on the Commonwealth of Independent States' in C Walter, A von Ungern-Sternberg and K Abushov (eds), *Self-Determination and Secession in International Law* (Oxford, Oxford University Press, 2014) 2; JD Ohlin, 'The Right to Exist and the Right to Resist' in Tesón (ed), *The Theory of Self-Determination* (n 15) *passim*; P Macklem, 'Self-Determination in Three Movements' in Tesón (ed), *The Theory of Self-Determination* (n 15) 95; E Rodríguez-Santiago, 'The Evolution of Self-Determination of Peoples in International Law' in Tesón (ed), *The Theory of Self-Determination* (n 15); Mégret, 'Earned, Not Inherent' (n 15) 48–54.

[75] See inter alia Emerson, 'Self-Determination' (n 58) 465–466; Buchheit, *Secession* (n 58); DB Knight, 'Territory and People or People and Territory? Thoughts on Postcolonial Self-Determination' (1985) 6 *International Political Science Review* 248; S Senese, 'External and Internal Self-Determination' (1989) 16 *Social Justice* 19; Hannum, *Autonomy* (n 70); M Moore, 'Introduction: The Self-Determination Principle and the Ethics of Secession' in M Moore (ed), *National Self-Determination and Secession* (n 74); Whelan, 'Self-Determination and Decolonisation' (n 74); HR Berman, O Lyons and RA Falk, 'Indigenous Peoples and the Right to Self-Determination' (1993) 87 *Proceedings of the Annual Meeting of the American Society of International Law* 190; R McCorquodale, 'Self-Determination: A Human Rights Approach' (1994) 43 *ICLQ* 857; Cassese, *Self-Determination of Peoples* (n 74); H Quane, 'The United Nations and the Evolving Right to Self-Determination' (1998) 47 *ICLQ* 537; Duursma, *Fragmentation* (n 14); Trifunovska, 'One Theme in Two Variations' (n 74); D Raič, *Statehood and the Law of Self-Determination* (The Hague, Kluwer Law International, 2002) 226–307; J Klabbers, 'The Right to Be Taken Seriously: Self-Determination in International Law' (2006) 28 *Human Rights Quarterly* 186; Vidmar, 'Unilateral Declarations of Independence' (n 74) 71–73; del Mar, 'Myth of Remedial Secession' (n 74) 79ff; J Summers, 'The Internal and External Aspects of Self-Determination Reconsidered' in French (ed) (n 74) *passim*; K Strathopoulou, 'Self-Determination, Peacemaking and Peace-Building: Recent Trends in African Intrastate Peace Agreements' in French (n 74) 283–85; Rodríguez-Santiago, 'Evolution of Self-Determination' (n 74) 202ff; Sterio, *Secession* (n 26); A Cristescu, *The Right to Self-Determination: Historical and Current Development on the Basis of United Nations Instruments: Study Prepared by Aureliu Cristescu, Special Rapporteur of the Sub-Commission on Prevention of Discrimination and Protection of Minorities* (New York, United Nations, 1981). The internal/external classification was also discussed in some detail and employed by the Supreme Court of Canada in its decision in *Reference Re Secession of Quebec* (1998) 2 SCR 217, paras 126ff.

[76] Summers, 'Internal and External' (n 75) 230 (references omitted).

[77] Whelan, 'Self-Determination and Decolonisation' (n 74) 37.

[78] McCorquodale, 'A Human Rights Approach' (n 75) 863–64.

development to have been chaotic, and legal analyses which find its status to be at best indeterminate.[79]

i. 'Internal' Self-Determination

The internal/external vocabulary of self-determination is a distinction drawn on the basis of externalities. Under the heading of internal self-determination fall all those instances of self-determination that take place within the pre-drawn boundaries of a state.[80] It therefore refers primarily to what may be termed the political or the participatory aspects of self-determination; that no group within a state should be 'denied meaningful access to government to pursue their political, economic, social and cultural development'.[81] Secondarily, it refers to the principle of non-intervention:[82] if the legitimacy of political structures flows from an ongoing act of self-determination by the people within or creating those structures, external influence on those systems may sever the form of government from the act of self-determination that gives it authority. Finally, and depending on the strength ascribed to the principle *uti possidetis juris*, internal self-determination might also be conceived as encompassing self-determination by colonial possessions and other non-self-governing territories.[83]

Even if one accepts that these functions sit comfortably within the same category – a contention that will be challenged below – the vocabulary of 'internal' is insufficient as a descriptor. It is clear, first, that this principle is not a purely internal matter, but rather has both inward-facing and outward-facing aspects: 'internal' self-determination goes to the legitimacy of governments and political systems (inward-facing aspect),[84] and it guarantees the principles of sovereign equality and non-interference (outward-facing aspect).[85] In other words, the 'internal' form of self-determination posits two distinct principles: it asserts, first, that the *form* of government is legitimate only if it is in accordance with the wishes of the people to which the government applies;[86] and, secondly, that the form and functioning

[79] There are other, and more potentially serious, consequences of this false conflation, too, than its impediment of academic understanding of the idea. As Mégret notes, the endorsement by the international community of self-determination in the colonial context was seen by some as an affirmation of a broader right to secede, and by giving rise to unfulfilled expectations of international support, contributed to (often bloody) secession conflicts: Mégret, 'Earned, Not Inherent' (n 15) 50.

[80] Summers, 'Internal and External' (n 75) 253–42; Klabbers, 'Right to Be Taken Seriously' (n 75).

[81] *Quebec* (n 75) para 138.

[82] Whelan, 'Self-Determination and Decolonisation' (n 74) 37.

[83] For a discussion of the *uti possidetis juris* principle, see A Peters, 'The Principle of *Uti Possidetis Juris*: How Relevant Is it for Issues of Secession?' in Walter, von Ungern-Sternberg and Abushov (eds), *Self-Determination and Secession in International Law* (n 74).

[84] Patten calls this the 'democratic' idea of self-determination: A Patten, 'Self-Determination for National Minorities' in Tesón (ed), *The Theory of Self-Determination* (n 15). See *contra* J Waldron, 'Two Conceptions of Self-Determination' in S Besson and J Tasioulas (eds), *The Philosophy of International Law* (Oxford, Oxford University Press, 2010) 408, quoted at n 86 below.

[85] Patten calls this the 'statist' idea: Patten, 'National Minorities' (n 84).

[86] That is not to say, however, that the *government* must accord with the wishes of the population, nor that the government must be *democratic*. On the contrary, as Waldron has observed, '[i]t is important,

of their government is a matter for the people of the polity alone, that no power or people can impose its will upon the polity, and that interference by a foreign power or people is thus illegitimate.[87] For this reason Jeremy Waldron prefers to capture these ideas under the heading of *territorial* self-determination,[88] but while this vocabulary avoids the misnomer 'internal', it does not move beyond the effects or manifestations of the concepts and so does not advance understanding of the different legitimacy-claims involved.

ii. 'External' Self-Determination

'External' self-determination, by contrast, is usually taken to refer to claims to autonomy or to secession by territorially concentrated sub-state national groups.[89] It, too, encompasses a wide range of instances, from pure claims to secession based on a different identity, to secession *in ultimum remedium* as a result of severe abuses of rights of political participation or human rights;[90] and could provide an equally (un)comfortable home for the right of former colonies to self-determine as does the internal form.[91]

As with so-called 'internal' self-determination, the 'external' label is too broad a church to be useful as an analytical or legal tool. Here it is the effect – the displacement of sovereignty – which is treated as the hallmark of the category,[92] but this focus on effects causes a conflation of different kinds of claims: the claim by a minority group of a right to independence purely as a function of its identity qua minority (that part of self-determination that Waldron calls 'identity-based',[93]

however, not to identify self-determination and democracy. The right of self-determination is prior to democracy, for it includes the right to decide whether to have a democracy around here, and if so, what sort of democracy to have. Self-determination is violated when we forcibly impose democracy on a country from the outside': Waldron, 'Two Conceptions' (n 84) 408.

[87] B van der Vossen, 'Self-Determination and Moral Variation' in Tesón (ed), *The Theory of Self-Determination* (n 15) 13–14. It is under this second heading that self-determination by a colonial entity would sit, if included in the 'internal' category.

[88] Waldron, 'Two Conceptions' (n 84) 397–398.

[89] Trifunovska, 'One Theme in Two Variations' (n 74); McCorquodale, 'A Human Rights Approach' (n 75) 863–864;.

[90] *Katangese Peoples' Congress v Zaire*, African Commission on Human and Peoples' Rights, Communication no. 75/92 (1995); Written Statement of the Kingdom of the Netherlands, *Kosovo* Advisory Opinion, para 3.6.

[91] *Quebec* (n 75) para 138; Cassese, *Self-Determination of Peoples* (n 74) 71–99.

[92] Cassese, *Self-Determination of Peoples* (n 74) 19. As Mégret correctly observes, the displacement of sovereignty and the creation of a new State is the most extreme of a series of possible outcomes of self-determination claims of the kinds discussed here, and it may be that it is therefore artificial and misleading to categorise them according to their effects. Claims of the kinds discussed here could seek, rather than secession and statehood, increased minority protections, a degree of autonomy, federalism, or other outcomes entirely: Mégret, 'Earned, Not Inherent' (n 15) 45–46. Nevertheless, the focus on independence and the displacement of sovereignty is appropriate, it is submitted, not only because it is those manifestations of the claim which are archetypal of the categories, but also because those are the claims which are of the greatest interest to international law.

[93] Waldron, 'Two Conceptions' (n 84) 398.

and Christopher Morris 'national' self-determination)[94] is a vastly different *kind* of appeal to legitimacy than that of a victimised minority which seeks secession as a remedy of last resort,[95] and different again from the claim of a people under colonial rule to independence and self-government.[96] That these different legitimacy-claims are subsumed under a single heading constrains the ability of international law and international lawyers to draw principled distinctions between claims deemed worthy and those considered unworthy of international support. It raises the spectre of 'spillover' effects, where a decision to tolerate or to facilitate secession in certain cases appears to confer legitimacy on secession by sub-state groups more broadly. Indeed, such indiscriminate echoes can hardly be avoided, given the lack of an appropriately discriminatory vocabulary.[97]

That paucity of the standard vocabulary thus produces two tendencies in the legal treatment of so-called 'external' self-determination, both of which will readily be observed in the analysis of the forms and their development in later chapters. First, it tends towards a conservatism that constrains the very real potential of self-determination to further human rights and international equality. It is very credible to argue that the form defined below as *colonial self-determination* has suffered to some extent from this conservative tendency, that its application and scope was delayed and reduced for fear that its affirmation would unleash a broader and unintended secessionary pressure, and it will be argued that *remedial self-determination* shows signs of a similar affliction at present. Secondly, it produces a confused legal picture in which groups seeking independence can receive no clear guidance from international law, and consequently the potential of law to guide events is compromised. This, too, can be seen in practice: as the analysis in later chapters will show,[98] the forms bundled under the heading of 'external' self-determination have indeed received different legal treatment, although the deficiency of vocabulary makes it difficult to draw lines between them. Law's inability to govern has effects beyond the lecture theatre: when law offers no guide to events pure power rules unmitigated, and force is the only court it knows.[99] The example of Crimea, in which the *Kosovo* Advisory

[94] CW Morris, 'The Case for National Self-Determination' in Tesón (ed), *The Theory of Self-Determination* (n 15); see also Moore, 'Introduction' (n 75); M Koskenniemi, 'National Self Determination Today: Problems of Legal Theory and Practice' (1994) 43 *ICLQ* 241.

[95] Ohlin characterises this as a combination of the right to exist and the right to resist: Ohlin, 'Right to Exist' (n 74).

[96] Cassese, *Self-Determination of Peoples* (n 74) 71–99. As Binder points out, the decision to treat cases of colonial secession separately from secessions from unitary or postcolonial states is a political decision based on a perceived difference between these cases, which she argues is unjustifiable: Binder, 'The Case for Self-Determination' (n 74) 226ff.

[97] Mégret, 'Earned, Not Inherent' (n 15) 50.

[98] See in particular ch 3, and further chs 4–6.

[99] This point is derived from Smith: FE Smith, *International Law*, 4th edn (London, JM Dent & Sons, 1911) 37. The observation holds true, however, in contemporary international law. For a more recent observation along similar lines, see A Peters, 'Has the Advisory Opinion's Finding that Kosovo's Declaration of Independence Was Not Contrary to International Law Set an Unfortunate Precedent?' in M Milanović and M Wood (eds), *The Law and Politics of the Kosovo Advisory Opinion* (Oxford, Oxford University Press, 2015) 299ff.

Opinion's reasoning was (mis)applied as a precedent to support the incorporation of the region into Russia starkly shows the ways in which legal indeterminacy is inimical to legal authority.[100]

III. Four Forms of Self-Determination

In contrast to the standard conception of an internal and an external application of the same unitary idea,[101] in this book I will argue that at least four forms of self-determination can be identified which together may be considered as four species within a common genus. These are:

- First, a claim on the part of a people of a political society (a polity) that they form a single political unit, and should be treated as such for the purposes of the governance of their shared social and political life. Within that are the twin corollary claims that all individuals within a given society should have the opportunity to participate in its governance on the basis of equality, and that only those individuals within a given society should do so: external interference in its sociopolitical life is illegitimate. I call this a claim to *polity-based self-determination.*
- Secondly, an identity-based claim to secession and independence that treats the separate character of a group as sufficient justification for its independent nationhood, which I term *secessionary self-determination.* The same principle can also ground a claim on the part of a group with a single identity but which is split between several entities to unify itself within a single state, either through parallel secessions and unification, or irredentism.
- Thirdly, a claim by a group which has suffered a severe abuse of its rights vis-a-vis other groups within a state, and which seeks autonomy, secession or irredentism as a remedy of last resort. That principle will be called *remedial self-determination.*[102]
- Finally, a claim by a colonial possession or other non-self-governing territory to independence and self-government; this will be termed *colonial self-determination.*

[100] See ch 5, s III.A and further s III.B.

[101] Senese, for example, describes them as 'two inseparable aspects of the same principle': Senese, 'External and Internal' (n 75) 19; see also Duursma, *Fragmentation* (n 14) 78–80; Trifunovska, 'One Theme in Two Variations' (n 74). Tesón perhaps goes further still, treating the nationalistic and the remedial arguments as two competing justifications which apply to the same self-determination idea: Tesón, 'Introduction' (n 25) 8–11.

[102] The first use of the term 'remedy' in relation to self-determination of which I am aware is Buchheit's: Buchheit, *Secession* (n 58) 59. The label 'remedial' is, though, often attributed to Buchanan, in whose work it acquired a wider popularity: A Buchanan, 'Secession, Self-Determination, and the Rule of International Law' in J McMahan and R McKim (eds), *The Morality of Nationalism* (Oxford, Oxford University Press, 1997); A Buchanan, 'Theories of Secession' (1997) 26 *Philosophy & Public Affairs* 31; A Buchanan, 'Democracy and Secession' in M Moore (ed), *National Self-Determination and Secession* (n 75).

Each will be examined in turn, in order to demonstrate that these delineations reflect relevant historical or ideational differences, and that such a typology offers a more coherent framework for the treatment of claims to self-determination by international law. I will argue that this categorisation captures differences in legal treatment which have already begun to emerge in the practice of international law, but which lack an adequate vocabulary for their expression.

A. Polity-based Self-Determination

Polity-based self-determination is the longest-established of the four forms of self-determination discussed here, and has the unusual distinction that two of its earliest invocations are among its most iconic – indeed, are among the most influential documents in the development of the Western world. In 1776 and in 1789 the American and French revolutions sent shockwaves through the West's political foundations,[103] and set in train the 'age of revolution',[104] a period of extraordinary political and social change which was typified by independence claims consciously modelled on the American[105] or (to an even greater extent) the French declarations.[106] Both declarations are best understood as claims to polity-based self-determination, and particularly to its internal aspect: they assert that the form of government in a state should be determined by the collective will of the people who are subject to it. The French declaration proclaimed that: 'The principle of any Sovereignty lies primarily in the Nation. No corporate body, no individual may exercise any authority that does not expressly emanate from it.'[107] Here the claim is to the aggregated political rights of individuals assembled into a body politic. It avers that *authority* is distinct from *power*;[108] that rule is not self-justificatory, and

[103] D Armitage, *The Declaration of Independence: A Global History* (Cambridge, MA, Harvard University Press, 2007) 67.

[104] Hobsbawm, *Age of Revolution* (n 23) 1–4.

[105] Armitage, *Declaration of Independence* (n 103) 108.

[106] Hobsbawm, *Age of Revolution* (n 23) 75.

[107] Declaration of Human and Civic Rights of 26 August 1789, www.conseil-constitutionnel.fr/en/declaration-of-human-and-civic-rights-of-26-august-1789, article 3.

[108] Here a distinction is drawn between mere power and true or legitimate authority along the lines described by Weber, who distinguishes between *Herrschaft* and *Macht*:

> „Herrschaft" soll, definitionsgemäß … , die Chance heißen, für spezifische (oder: für alle) Befehle bei einer angebbaren Gruppe von Menschen Gehorsam zu finden. Nicht also jeder Art von Chance, „Macht" und „Einfluß" auf andere Menschen anzuüben. Herrschaft („Autorität") in diesem Sinn kann im Einzelfall auf den verschiedensten Motiven der Fügsamkeit: von dumpfer Gewöhnung angefangen bis zu rein zweckrationalen Erwägungen, beruhen. Ein bestimmtes Minimum an Gehorchen*wollen*, also: *Interesse* (äußerem oder innerem) am Gehorchen, gehört zu jedem echten Herrschaftsverhältnis.

M Weber, 'Wirtschaft und Gesellschaft' in K Borchardt, E Hanke and W Schluchter (eds), *Max Weber: Wirtschaft und Gesellschaft*, vol 23 (Tübingen, Paul Siebeck, 2013) 449 (emphasis in original), see also 210. While *Herrschaft* for Weber connotes a legitimate relationship of authority, *Macht* (power; force) could be analogised to Austin's concept of obedience through sanction; that 'you will visit me with an evil in case I comply not with your wish': J Austin, *The Province of Jurisprudence Determined*

that it cannot be justified by historical or external factors (such as by reference to a divine right). Rather, in order to be legitimately exercised, power must have a legitimate source.[109]

Inherent in this statement, too, is a parallel claim which may be described as the outward-facing aspect of polity-based self-determination: the principle of non-intervention. If, as the French declaration proclaimed, the exercise of power and authority is legitimate only where it flows from the population, it is necessarily true that the exercise of power over the internal affairs of a nation from sources external to it is similarly illegitimate. Although this aspect of polity-based self-determination was not the major focus of the 1789 declaration and received less attention in the years that followed, it has come to be its dominant aspect. It is a foundational principle of modern-day international law. It is primarily this aspect of the self-determination idea that is referred to in the Charter of the United Nations, and (alongside references to colonial self-determination, discussed below) which has been developed in the practice of the United Nations and the ICJ.

The most important reference to self-determination in the UN Charter appears in Article 1, which declares that the development of 'friendly relations among nations based on the principle of equal rights and self-determination of peoples' to be a purpose of the organisation.[110] Although of huge rhetorical significance, it is likely that Article 1(2), in and of itself, did not create a legal right of any kind.[111] These were obligations directed to the organisation, rather than to its Member States. It found a counterpart, however, in Article 2, and particularly in Article 2(1) – the guarantee of the equality of Member States – and Article 2(4):

> All Members shall refrain in their international relations from the threat or use of force against the territorial integrity or political independence of any state, *or in any other manner inconsistent with the Purposes of the United Nations*.[112]

(Cambridge, Cambridge University Press, 1995) 21. Raz further complicates the categorisation, distinguishing between *legitimate authority*, *de facto authority* and *naked power*: legitimate authorities rule by right, de facto authorities claim such a right to rule (but lack it), and naked power makes no claim of right: J Raz, 'Introduction' in J Raz (ed), *Authority* (New York, New York University Press, 1990) 3.

[109] Note, however, as discussed above, that the principle expressed in this claim is not necessarily an affirmation of democracy (although in practice it is difficult to conceive of a real-world situation in which it would be necessary to draw this distinction). Rather, the polity-based form of self-determination corresponds to an analytically prior idea that the *form* of government must flow from the people. In other words, a dictatorship could conform with this principle if that were the form of government selected by the people of a political society, and to the extent that this form of government (as opposed to the specific actions *of the* government) continues to be willed by them. See Waldron, 'Two Conceptions' (n 84) 408, quoted above at n 86.

[110] Art 1(2) UN Charter (n 17).

[111] Certainly, that was the conclusion of Kelsen's analysis: H Kelsen, *The Law of the United Nations: A Critical Analysis of its Fundamental Problems* (London, Stevens & Sons, 1951) 15; although for an indication that the Art 1 purposes were intended directly to bind members, see Rapporteur, 'Report of the Rapporteur to Subcommittee I/1/A to Committee I/1' in United States of America Department of State, *The United Nations Conference on International Organization; San Francisco, California, April 25 to June 26, 1945: Selected Documents* (Washington, DC, US Government Printing Office, 1946) 478ff.

[112] Art 2(4) UN Charter (n 17) (emphasis added).

Reading Articles 2(1) and 2(4) as the mirror image of Article 1(2) indicates the latter's content: Article 1(2) concerns the polity-based form of self-determination in its outward-facing aspect. That principle, as it was interpreted by the judgment of the ICJ in its decision in *Nicaragua*, extends to 'the choice of a political, economic, social and cultural system, and the formulation of foreign policy'.[113] It is probable that through Article 2(1) and (especially) Article 2(4), the outward-facing aspect of polity-based self-determination did acquire the status of a legal obligation on States Parties to the Charter. Its status has subsequently been confirmed in the Declaration on Friendly Relations;[114] in common Article 1 of the International Covenants on Human Rights;[115] and in the case law of the ICJ, most notably its judgment in *East Timor*[116] and its opinion in the *Wall* advisory proceedings.[117] Indeed those sources, taken together and read in accordance with the four-part typology of self-determination proposed here, strongly imply that polity-based self-determination has not only acquired the status of a norm of international law, but also that of a norm *ius cogens*.[118]

In international law, then, the norm of polity-based self-determination is a right of peremptory status which attaches to the people of a recognised political entity – that is to say, of a state – and which guarantees the right of that polity to make core decisions concerning its governance without external interference. It is the underlying rationale beneath the prohibition on intervention and coercive interference; that is to say, of the rights of a state which amount to, and derive from, its *sovereignty*. Alf Ross equates 'sovereign' and 'self-governing' (or, as I would prefer it, self-determining, in the polity-based sense), saying that 'sovereignty in its two branches is *merely another term for self-government*'.[119] He goes on to argue that the consequence of a community being 'sovereign' (ie self-governing/self-determining) is 'that of the "sovereign" community being invested with the duties (and rights) called international'. 'What these duties and rights are cannot be deduced from this definition',[120] Ross says, but certainly we can derive a *claim*: inherent in each self-determining political community's identification of itself as such is a claim *to remain that way*.

[113] *Military and Paramilitary Activities in and Against Nicaragua (Nicaragua v United States of America)*, Merits, Judgment, (1986) ICJ Reports 14, para 205.

[114] Declaration on Principles of International Law concerning Friendly Relations and Co-operation among States in accordance with the Charter of the United Nations, annexed to UN General Assembly Resolution 2625 (XXV), 24 October 1970.

[115] Art 1(1)–(3) of the ICESCR/ICCPR (n 42).

[116] *East Timor* (n 16) para 29.

[117] *Legal Consequences of the Construction of a Wall in the Occupied Palestinian Territory*, Advisory Opinion, (2004) ICJ Reports 136, paras 121–22, 159.

[118] For further discussion of the status of polity-based self-determination, see chs 3 and 4.

[119] A Ross, *A Textbook of International Law: General Part* (London, Longmans, Green and Co, 1947) 36.

[120] ibid 37.

In the post-Charter legal order, sovereignty in these descriptive (per Ross) and normative senses are united under the legal order of the Charter, which is premised on this foundation. In other words, polity-based self-determination is of fundamental importance to the contemporary legal order.

B. Secessionary Self-Determination

If polity-based self-determination can be treated as international law's primary understanding of the term, the secessionary form is its antithesis. Although it is ever-present as a feature of the discourse, it has been invoked only on a handful of occasions, and successfully in still fewer. While polity-based self-determination – and particularly its external, non-intervention aspect – is frequently cited as a necessary component of the post-Charter world order, secessionary self-determination is largely reviled as a dangerous and anarchic force that threatens instability, discord and conflict.

The different ideational foundations and legal treatment of remedial and colonial self-determination (discussed further below) require that the secessionary form be construed as a narrow category, defined only as those claims to independence which are premised purely on the separate character or identity of a group within a state. Historical examples of its use are few and far between, with separatist movements generally preferring claims to remedial self-determination – a better and longer established form and one that carries a stronger perception of legitimacy – but its presence can occasionally be felt. It was a claim of this kind that was (successfully) made in the 1814 and 1905 secessions of Norway,[121] and was the background to the Canadian Supreme Court's judgment in the *Quebec* case.[122] In recent years it may have been increasing in frequency, although it is as yet too early to detect any definite trend. It appears to have been the justification invoked by the pro-independence movement in the 2014 referendum on Scotland's status, and was invoked in 2017 in Cataluña and (perhaps) Kurdistan. In another guise, the same logic – here relating to similarity rather than difference – was a factor in the unifications of Italy and of Germany in the nineteenth century.

Secessionary self-determination is premised on a conviction that 'peoples', howsoever defined, have a right to determine how they are governed. This differs from the principle that underpins the polity-based form – that the members of a society (as it presently exists) should determine their own governmental arrangements – because of the strength of the identity element. The secessionary

[121] K Gjerset, *History of the Norwegian People*, vol 2 (New York, AMS Press, 1969) 417; K Larsen, *A History of Norway* (Princeton, NJ, Princeton University Press, 1948) 376–87. Norway's claim to independence cited no historical wrongs, nor did it claim a subsisting sovereignty, but rather expressed a claim of a right to independence as a result of Norway's separate character and nationhood. The Norwegian secessions are analysed in ch II, ss III.A–B.

[122] *Quebec* (n 75).

form does not apply to existing polities, but seeks instead to redesign them to accord with the identities that their inhabitants feel themselves to belong to. It attaches instead to 'peoples', although there is a distinct lack of clarity about what this term means (Ivor Jennings's acerbic remark that 'the people cannot decide until somebody decides who are the people' captures that uncertainty well).[123] Most definitions include both subjective and objective elements, however. David Raič, for example, defines a 'people' as having a common history, ethnic identity, language, culture or religion, coupled with a 'belief of being a distinct people distinguishable from any other people'.[124] For this reason, secessionary self-determination is sometimes criticised as being a profoundly illiberal principle, one that highlights national, ethnic or other identities over a common humanity, and which perpetuates and deepens divisions between people that are essentially arbitrary.[125] Together with the fear that its application could prompt a destabilising disintegration and balkanisation of international society,[126] it is seen as embodying a radical nationalism which contrasts starkly with the tolerant conservatism of the polity-based form. This renders the secessionary form suspect in many eyes, and equally so from liberal, progressive and conservative points of view.[127] The polity-based form is rooted in an historical reality: it accepts as a given the existence of societies and transforms that contingent *is* into an *ought*. The secessionary form engages in a process of social engineering, seeking to remake society in its own image, and transform its conception of *ought* into an *is*.

In contrast to polity-based self-determination, too, it has long been assumed that secessionary self-determination is contrary to international law. The so-called 'safeguard clause' found in many of the international proclamations of self-determination has contributed to this view, and has been taken as affirming the relative primacy of the principle of territorial integrity:

> Any attempt aimed at the partial or total disruption of the national unity and the territorial integrity of a country is incompatible with the purposes and principles of the Charter of the United Nations.[128]

[123] Jennings, *Self-Government* (n 59) 56.

[124] Raič, *Law of Self-Determination* (n 75) 262.

[125] For an argument along these lines, see D Held, *Cosmopolitanism: Ideals and Realities* (Cambridge, Polity Press, 2010) 93–94; Tesón, 'Introduction' (n 25) 8ff; Buchheit, *Secession* (n 58) 28–31; A Etzioni, 'The Evils of Self-Determination' (1992–93) 89 *Foreign Policy* 21, *passim*.

[126] See inter alia R Higgins, *The Development of International Law through the Political Organs of the United Nations* (Oxford, Oxford University Press, 1963) 104; Cassese, *Self-Determination of Peoples* (n 74) 328; Buchheit, *Secession* (n 58) 28–29.

[127] No endorsement of this suspicion of the secessionary form is intended. Although there are, in my opinion, strong arguments in favour of restricting secession on identitarian grounds, there are also numerous arguments which would speak in favour of its liberalisation, and my sympathies fall rather on the latter side of the scale. The assessment of these arguments is not the task of this book, however, which is concerned with identification of the forms rather than their evaluation from a policy point of view. For academic contributions in favour (at least to some extent) of a liberalised secessionary self-determination regime, see, among others, D Ronen, *The Quest for Self-Determination* (New Haven, CT, Yale University Press, 1979); Duursma, *Fragmentation* (n 14); Binder, 'The Case for Self-Determination' (n 74); Sterio, *Secession* (n 26).

[128] UN General Assembly Resolution 1514 (XV), 14 December 1960, para 6.

However, that position was called into question by the opinion of the ICJ in the *Kosovo* advisory proceedings. There the Court characterised territorial integrity as a negative obligation on states (as an obligation *not to infringe*) rather than as a positive right accruing to them, with the implication that states receive no protection from international law against threats to their territorial integrity that arise from within their own borders. It declared that 'State practice during [the eighteenth, nineteenth and twentieth centuries] points clearly to the conclusion that international law contained no prohibition of declarations of independence.'[129] The Court treated secession as a legally neutral act: one of which international law would take account, but which is neither prohibited nor facilitated. Although the Court's reasoning on this point has been sharply criticised,[130] it has cast doubt on the status of secessionary self-determination.[131]

The *Kosovo* opinion indicates that the (legal) treatment of secessionary self-determination may be moving from the hostile to the equivocal, although significant ambiguities remain. One aspect is clear, however: there is at present no international law *right* to secede on purely secessionary grounds. Two possible exceptions to this rule exist but, as will be discussed below, it is more appropriate to class these as separate forms with different justification narratives and legal histories: colonial and remedial self-determination.

C. Remedial Self-Determination

In many ways remedial self-determination is its most intriguing form. Like the polity-based form it has deep historical roots, and indeed it shares many instances and philosophical ties to that idea. It might be appropriate even to describe it as an offshoot or subdivision of that branch, but here it will be treated as separate but akin; although it is premised on the polity-based form, it merits a separate

[129] *Accordance with International Law of the Unilateral Declaration of Independence in Respect of Kosovo*, Advisory Opinion, (2010) ICJ Reports 403, para 79.

[130] *Accordance with International Law of the Unilateral Declaration of Independence in Respect of Kosovo*, Declaration of Judge Simma, (2010) ICJ Reports 478, para 8. For criticism along the same lines see *Accordance with International Law of the Unilateral Declaration of Independence in Respect of Kosovo*, Dissenting Opinion of Judge Koroma, (2010) ICJ Reports 467, paras 21–23; GI Hernández, *The International Court of Justice and the Judicial Function* (Oxford, Oxford University Press, 2014) 263–76, esp 264–66; P Hilpold, 'The International Court of Justice's Advisory Opinion on Kosovo: Perspectives of a Delicate Question' (2009) 14 *Australian Review of International and European Law* 259, 287; A Orakhelashvili, 'The International Court's Advisory Opinion on the UDI in Respect of Kosovo: Washing Away the "Foam on the Tide of Time"' (2011) 15 *Max Planck Yearbook of United Nations Law* 65, 73; N Beal, 'Defending State Sovereignty: The ICJ Advisory Opinion on Kosovo and International Law' (2012) 21 *Transnational Law & Contemporary Problems* 549; M Jovanović, 'After the ICJ's Advisory Opinion on Kosovo: The Future of Self-Determination Conflicts' (2012) 3 *Annals of the Faculty of Law in Belgrade – International Edition* 292, 300–02; M Weller, 'The Sounds of Silence: Making Sense of the Supposed Gaps in the Kosovo Opinion' in M Milanović and M Wood (eds), *The Law and Politics of the Kosovo Advisory Opinion* (Oxford, Oxford University Press, 2015) 188.

[131] Peters, 'Unfortunate Precedent' (n 99).

treatment because of its different legal status and different history. Yet despite its close links to the polity-based form, in its outward appearances it is sometimes seen as having more in common with secessionary self-determination, and so is often (mis)categorised as a subtype of 'external' self-determination. I argue that this habitual conflation is inappropriate in light of the philosophical foundations of the remedial form and the justification-claim it represents, and that this misrepresentation has contributed to an inconsistent legal treatment.

Remedial self-determination has been invoked on many occasions in international law, including in a substantial number of successful claims to independence. Prior to the decolonisation era, it was the major justification-claim employed by entities seeking independence, and played a very significant role in reshaping the international order of states during the period Eric Hobsbawm calls 'the age of revolution'.[132] Like many of the ideas that defined the age, the foundations of remedial self-determination can be found in the American and French declarations of 1776 and 1789.

The 1776 American Declaration of Independence was, as discussed above, one of the earliest expressions of the principles underpinning polity-based self-determination: that the form of government to which a society is subject should be determined by the members of that society, and that the imposition of any other political will upon them, either by a group within the society or by external actors, is illegitimate. The declaration stood for more than this, however: it was a claim to secession, and was intended to demonstrate to the world that the American action in throwing off British rule was just. Importantly, these two functions were linked: the declaration did not make a claim to independence in pursuance of a positive right to secede, but rather cast its claim negatively, as a final resort to long privations and abuses that amounted to a vacation of the link between government and the governed.

> That to secure the[ir unalienable] rights, Governments are instituted among Men, deriving their just powers from the consent of the governed, – That whenever any Form of Government becomes destructive of these ends, it is the Right of the People to alter or to abolish it, and to institute new Government.[133]

In other words, the basis of the claimed right to remove the American territory from the control of the British state was the denial to the people of America of their right to polity-based self-determination. *In extremis* this denial generated a secession claim as a remedy of last resort.

A similar link between a government detached from the interests of wishes of the population and a right to secede was a (less central) feature of French revolutionary thought,[134] and reliance on a negative, remedial legitimacy-claim can be

[132] Hobsbawm, *Age of Revolution* (n 23).

[133] The Declaration of Independence: A Transcription, US National Archives & Records Administration, www.archives.gov/exhibits/charters/declaration_transcript.html.

[134] Rigo Sureda, *Evolution of Self-Determination* (n 58) 17–18; Cassese, *Self-Determination of Peoples* (n 74) 11–12, 174; Hobsbawm, *Age of Revolution* (n 23) 75ff. See further, discussion in ch 2, s II.B.

seen in a great many of the declarations of independence of the years that were to follow.[135] This feature is particularly clear in, for example, the declarations of independence of Flanders, Venezuela, Liberia and Hungary,[136] and can be seen in most declarations of the period.[137]

In the modern day the use of remedial self-determination has somewhat diminished, replaced in its dominance by the colonial form. But modern expositions of the idea, too, show its link to polity-based self-determination. In the course of the *Kosovo* advisory proceedings, for example, the Netherlands and Germany explicitly linked the denial of polity-based self-determination and the right to secede. The written statement of the Netherlands argued that:

> [T]he right to political [ie polity-based] self-determination may evolve into a right to external self-determination in exceptional circumstances, ie in unique cases or cases *sui generis*. This is an exception to the rule and should therefore be narrowly construed. The resort to external self-determination is an *ultimum remedium*.[138]

Similarly, Germany argued that the denial of a right to secede would

> render the internal right of self-determination meaningless in practice. There would be no remedy for a group which is not granted the self-determination that may be due to it under international law. The majority in the state could easily and with impunity oppress the minority, without any recourse being open to that minority.[139]

Similar principles were discussed in the *Katanga* and *re Secession of Quebec* cases and both hinted at the existence of a norm (properly so-called) of remedial self-determination, although it was applied in neither case.[140]

[135] Armitage, *Declaration of Independence* (n 103) 108–13ff; Hobsbawm, *Age of Revolution* (n 23) 73–75ff.

[136] Manifesto for the Province of Flanders, in Armitage, *Declaration of Independence* (n 103) 187–91; Venezuelan Declaration of Independence, in Armitage, *Declaration of Independence* (n 103) 199–207; Declaration of Independence of Liberia, in CH Huberich, *The Political and Legislative History of Liberia*, vol 1 (New York, Central Book, 1947) 828ff; Hungarian Declaration of Independence, in H de Puy, *Kossuth and His Generals* (Buffalo, NY, Phinney, 1852) 202–25; see also Armitage, *Declaration of Independence* (n 103) 124. For discussion of these declarations in their historical context, see ch 2, s III.

[137] For an excellent table listing many of the post-1776 declarations of independence, see Armitage, *Declaration of Independence* (n 103) 146–55.

[138] Written Statement of the Netherlands, *Kosovo* Advisory Opinion, 17 April 2009, para 3.6.

[139] Written Statement of Germany, *Kosovo* Advisory Opinion, 15 April 2009, 33–34.

[140] *Katangese Peoples' Congress v Zaire* (n 90) para 6: '[I]n the absence of evidence that the people of Katanga have been denied the right to participate in Government as guaranteed by Article 13(1) of the African Charter, the Commission holds the view that Katanga is obliged to exercise a variety of self-determination that is compatible with the sovereignty and territorial integrity of Zaire'; *Quebec* (n 75) para 138: 'In summary, the international law right to self-determination only generates, at best, a right to external self-determination … where a people is oppressed, as for example under foreign military occupation; or where a definable group is denied meaningful access to government to pursue their political, economic, social and cultural development. In [these] situations, the people in question are entitled to a right to external self-determination *because they have been denied the ability to exert internally their right to self-determination*' (emphasis added).

Perhaps the most intriguing statement of the principle in the modern day, however, is to be found in the Declaration on Friendly Relations, proclaimed by the General Assembly on 24 October 1970. The 'safeguard clause' of the Declaration asserts that:

> Nothing in the foregoing paragraphs shall be construed as authorizing or encouraging any action which would dismember or impair, totally or in part, the territorial integrity or political unity of sovereign and independent States *conducting themselves in compliance with the principle of equal rights and self-determination of peoples as described above* and thus possessed of a government representing the whole people belonging to the territory without distinction as to race, creed or colour.[141]

Although the reference is oblique, the clause appears to accept the link between the protection of a state's territorial integrity and its compliance with polity-based self-determination. Indeed, the clause has been interpreted as declaring the existence of an international law right to secede *in ultimum remedium* where polity-based self-determination is denied.[142] It is, however, not necessary to accept so far-reaching a conclusion in order to agree that the paragraph does speak of a link between the forms. It would be equally possible to read the clause as expressive of a legal *lacuna* to the effect that there exists a general prohibition on secession, but that an exception applies where polity-based self-determination is denied. Secession for these groups may not be enabled or facilitated, but would at least *not be prohibited.*

A choice between the interpretations of the Declaration's safeguard clause cannot be made on the basis of current international practice. The author tends towards agreement with the states, commentators and judges cited above that the better reading of the clause is that it does recognise an international law right to secede in extremis where polity-based self-determination is denied. However, practice remains mixed, and responses to claims to remedial secession are generally ad hoc, incompletely theorised and have a tendency to stress the sui generis character of the event,[143] all of which present obstacles to the search for

[141] Declaration on Friendly Relations, annexed to UN General Assembly Resolution 2625 (XXV), 24 October 1970 (emphasis added).

[142] The proposition is supported by the written submissions of a number of states to the Court in the course of the proceedings in the *Kosovo* Advisory Opinion, as well as academic commentators and ICJ Judges. See, for example, Written Statement of the Netherlands, *Kosovo* Advisory Opinion, paras 3.6–3.7; Written Statement of Estonia, *Kosovo* Advisory Opinion, para 2.1; Written Statement of Finland, *Kosovo* Advisory Opinion, para 8; Written Statement of Poland, *Kosovo* Advisory Opinion, paras 6.8–6.9; Written Comment of Switzerland, *Kosovo* Advisory Opinion, para 60; Written Statement of Germany, *Kosovo* Advisory Opinion, 32–37; Cassese, *Self-Determination of Peoples* (n 74) 108–119; Duursma, *Fragmentation* (n 14) 25; Sterio, *Right to Self-Determination* (n 68) 12–13; Rodríguez-Santiago, 'Evolution of Self-Determination' (n 74) 235; *Accordance with International Law of the Unilateral Declaration of Independence in Respect of Kosovo*, Separate Opinion of Judge Cançado Trindade, (2010) ICJ Reports 523, paras 175–81; *Accordance with International Law of the Unilateral Declaration of Independence in Respect of Kosovo*, Separate Opinion of Judge Yusuf, (2010) ICJ Reports 618, paras 11–12.

[143] That the secession of Kosovo was a case sui generis was, for example, a feature of the statements to the Court of Denmark, Estonia, France, Ireland, Japan, Latvia and the Maldives.

a consistent interpretation. In the case law of the ICJ, too, the status of remedial self-determination is officially uncertain, with the Court having noted only that 'radically differing views' exist among states on its legality.[144]

I argue that the conflation of forms plays a part in the status confusion that afflicts the remedial form (and other forms) of self-determination. While it might be expected from the discussion here that remedial self-determination, viewed as a near-relative of the polity-based form, would be similarly received, it has more often been categorised as an 'external' manifestation on the basis of its displacement of sovereignty. Remedial self-determination has suffered from being viewed as the thin end of the secessionary wedge. Such an interpretation is suggested, for example, by the tendency of states to discuss remedial secession as an exception to a general rejection of 'external' self-determination, without apparent recognition of the different legitimacy-claims involved.[145] That is not to say, of course, that no other considerations exist which could justify remedial self-determination's status as illegal or non-legal, but rather that those have not yet adequately been assessed. The inappropriate categorisation of the form as a subset of 'external' self-determination impedes a principled appraisal of its current and future role in the international legal system.

D. Colonial Self-Determination

Colonial self-determination does not have the deep historical roots of the remedial or polity-based forms. On the contrary, it is a relatively recent development, having come about as a result of the decolonisation process under the auspices of the United Nations and (to a lesser extent) its predecessor, the League of Nations. Despite its relative youth it has swiftly been firmly entrenched, however: in the last century it has been by magnitudes the most commonly applied form of the self-determination, and has had at least as vast an impact on the shape and structure of the international order of states in recent history as the remedial form had in the age of revolution.

The decolonisation process began almost accidentally. Although a desire for decolonisation was growing ever stronger in the colonial possessions of the European powers, in the years leading up to the First World War power imbalances between colonies and colonisers were sufficient to perpetuate the status quo. During that war, however, the words and actions of the great powers themselves set in train a process that was intended perhaps only by Lenin's Russia

[144] *Kosovo* (n 129) para 82. This finding was criticised by Judges Cançado Trindade and Yusuf in their separate opinions. See further, discussion in ch 5, s II.B.

[145] See, for example, the written statements of Egypt, Estonia, Ireland, Norway, Russian Federation, Serbia and Switzerland to the ICJ in the *Kosovo* advisory proceedings.

and, though to a less ambitious extent, Wilson's America. During this globalised European war colonies became frontlines, both as direct theatres of engagement and battlegrounds of ideas.[146] The colonies of the European powers were vital to their prosecution of the conflict – they were sources of supplies, of raw materials, and of vital manpower – and both sides sought to gain an advantage by disrupting the ability of their rivals to access the resources of the colonies. In an effort to maintain the loyalty of their own colonies and to win allies in their enemies', both sides made extravagant promises of greater independence or self-government,[147] a process that intensified following the rise to power of the Bolsheviks in Russia.[148]

Coupled with the growing strength of the independence causes in the colonies, these events probably made some form of decolonisation process inevitable. But it was the intervention of Wilson that provided the spark. Wilson's commitment to self-determination is questionable – unlike that of Lenin which, for all the later failings of the Soviet Union on this point, appears to have been strongly held – and was likely born from convenience rather than conviction. But Wilson's intervention did have the effect of instituting self-determination as a principle to be – cautiously – taken into account in the disposal of colonies, alongside a number of other considerations (including the interests of the colonial powers).[149] His primary concern appears to have been to prevent the absorption of the colonies of the defeated powers into the empires of the victors,[150] but his declaration that '[n]ational aspirations must be respected; peoples may now be dominated and governed only by their own consent' took on a life of its own.[151] It was the impetus needed to start the process which ultimately resulted in the mandates system of the League of Nations, and the trusteeship system of the United Nations.

Later, in the years following the Second World War, a political consensus gradually emerged that colonial rule is illegitimate.[152] The trusteeship system of the UN built on the foundations of the mandates system, but while the latter had applied

[146] TD Musgrave, *Self-Determination and National Minorities* (Oxford, Clarendon Press, 1997) 15.

[147] Musgrave, *National Minorities* (n 146) 15–17.

[148] The right of nations to self-determination was a mainstay of Lenin's political thought, and was the official policy of the Bolshevik movement. See Lenin, 'Right of Nations' (n 68) 413, 453–54.

[149] W Wilson, 'Fourteen Points' (8 January 1918); Cassese, *Self-Determination of Peoples* (n 74) 21.

[150] W Wilson, 'Reply to the Pope of 27th August 1917' (27 August 1917).

[151] W Wilson, 'President Wilson's Address to Congress, Analyzing German and Austrian Peace Utterances' (11 February 1918).

[152] Note, however, that 'colony' in this context has generally been interpreted in line with the so-called 'saltwater' test – that is to say, it applies only to those territories geographically separated from the colonising state. See further J Trinidad, *Self-Determination in Disputed Colonial Territories* (Cambridge, Cambridge University Press, 2018) 17. The existence of the saltwater criterion was likely applied as (yet another) attempt to draw a line between 'acceptable' and 'unacceptable' exercises of 'external' self-determination, lacking a more coherent means to differentiate between different 'external' cases. There is no principled reason why a contiguous territory should not be understood as a colony, if it follows the all-too familiar patterns of colonial domination elsewhere (an example might be South Africa's mandate over Namibia, for example – see ch 4). Freed from the unhelpful internal/external vocabulary, then, it may be that the 'saltwater' test is no longer needed. However, given that the 'saltwater' test remains, at present, a part of the positive law, I refer to it here as an element of the norm in a descriptive sense and without endorsement.

only to those territories which were stripped from the defeated powers in the First World War, Article 77 of the Charter made provision for states to place their colonial possessions into the system voluntarily.[153] This change made the important declaration of principle that there existed no difference *in kind* between the territories stripped from colonial powers as a result of the two world wars, and those held by the European states in their own right. Moreover, it was accompanied by a number of statements on the proper governance of all non-self-governing territories:

> Members of the United Nations which have or assume responsibilities for the administration of territories whose people have not yet attained a full measure of self-government recognise the principle that the interest of the inhabitants of these territories are paramount.[154]

That line of thought was carried further in resolution 1514 (XV) of the General Assembly, the '[d]eclaration on the granting of independence to colonial countries and peoples'.[155] The resolution demonstrates that a tipping-point had been reached. Its paragraph 1 declares that: 'The subjection of peoples to alien subjugation, domination and exploitation constitutes a denial of fundamental human rights, is contrary to the Charter of the United Nations and is an impediment to the promotion of world peace and co-operation.'[156] That strong anticolonial statement was accompanied by an equally strong assertion of the means to bring about its end: paragraph 2 declares the existence of a right to self-determination of colonies, 'by virtue of [which] they freely determine their political status and freely pursue their economic, social and cultural development'.[157]

That a right to self-determination by colonial peoples emerged during this period was confirmed by the ICJ in its decisions and opinions in *Namibia*,[158] *Western Sahara*[159] and *East Timor*.[160] Most recently, the Court has returned to the subject of colonial self-determination in its 2019 advisory opinion in *Chagos Archipelago*.[161] There it specified more concretely that colonial self-determination had emerged as a legal norm by 1965 when the separation of the Chagos archipelago from Mauritius took place, and it laid particular importance on the effect of resolution 1514 in crystallising the norm.[162] It also implied that colonial self-determination has a high status, although it was criticised by certain of its

[153] Ch XII, Art 77(c) UN Charter (n 17).
[154] Ch XI, Art 73 UN Charter (n 17).
[155] UNGA Res 1514.
[156] UNGA Res 1514, para 1.
[157] UNGA Res 1514, para 2.
[158] *Legal Consequences for States of the Continued Presence of South Africa in Namibia (South West Africa) notwithstanding Security Council Resolution 276 (1970)*, Advisory Opinion, (1971) ICJ Reports 16, para 53.
[159] *Western Sahara*, Advisory Opinion, (1975) ICJ Reports 12, para 162.
[160] *East Timor* (n 16) para 29.
[161] The *Chagos* opinion is the subject of ch 6.
[162] *Chagos* (n 20) paras 150–61.

members for its failure (as they saw it) to declare the norm unequivocally to be *ius cogens*.[163] Although chapter six will conclude that these Judges were correct in according colonial self-determination peremptory status, I argue that their reasoning conflates elements of the colonial and polity-based forms, and thus leaves something to be desired. I argue, too, that the Court may have declined to make such a finding for fear of spillover legitimacy.[164]

Colonial self-determination is something of an outlier; a form of self-determination that is marked out as different by the existence of a political consensus rather than by a philosophical argument. That political consensus declares that there is a difference in kind between the rule by a state of a territory in the character of a colony and its rule as an integral part of the state. Interestingly, however, that difference does not appear primarily to be remedial: although the historical experience of colonial rule (which, in general, well deserved its characterisation in resolution 1514 as subjugation, domination and exploitation) is likely to have informed the approach, it is *colonial rule itself*, and not *abusive* colonial rule, which is treated as wrong and requiring remediation. It could nevertheless be considered a subset of the remedial form of self-determination: after all, a people governed by a presence external to its society is a clear violation of the principle of polity-based self-determination as described above, and thus could generate a remedial right. It is better conceived as separate, however: despite the overlapping themes, the unambiguous political acceptance of colonial self-determination marks it out as different. The right of colonial peoples to self-determination has been proclaimed by states, and by national and international courts, even while the status of the remedial form has been hedged, doubted or avoided altogether.[165] For the sake of legal, if not philosophical, coherence, then, it must be treated as a separate species.

E. The Four Forms of Self-Determination in Overview

In this section, I have introduced the four-part typology of self-determination which this book argues offers a clearer and more coherent framework for self-determination in international law. The four forms which have been identified I term the *polity-based*, *secessionary*, *remedial* and *colonial* forms of self-determination. Each has a different rationale, makes a different legitimacy

[163] *Legal Consequences of the Separation of the Chagos Archipelago from Mauritius in 1965*, Separate Opinion of Judge Cançado Trindade, (2019) ICJ Reports 156, paras 118, 120–50; Separate Opinion of Judge Robinson, *Chagos* (n 44) paras 48–82; *Legal Consequences of the Separation of the Chagos Archipelago from Mauritius in 1965*, Separate Opinion of Judge Sebutinde, (2019) ICJ Reports 270, *passim*, esp paras 30–43.

[164] See further, ch 6, s III.

[165] Compare, for example, the statements highlighted in nn 158–63 with the Canadian Supreme Court in *Quebec* (n 75) paras 135, 138; or the ICJ in *Kosovo* (n 129) para 82.

claim and applies to a different 'people'.[166] Polity-based self-determination applies to the populations of existing political communities as recognised by international law (in other words: to states) and guarantees their independence, as well as the right of their populations to participate in their governance. Secessionary self-determination, by contrast, seeks to redraw the boundaries of those communities so that they accord with the experienced identities of the people who comprise them. It stands for the principle that population groups – like individuals – should be able to choose to which state they belong, and stands ready to create new polities if such is their choice. The remedial and colonial forms have certain outward similarities to secessionary self-determination – they, too, countenance the creation of new states – and so have often been conflated with it. But here the similarities end. The colonial form is restricted to the colonial context, and stands for a political conviction that peoples ruled from afar (usually by European powers) have a right to achieve independence. The remedial form, meanwhile, does indeed offer a right to a new state (as one of a range of options that can also include regional autonomy or irredentism in appropriate circumstances), but does so only as a last resort. It applies to excluded and victimised minorities, and is triggered when the group's polity-based self-determination is denied; that is to say, where a group is wholly excluded from the polity, remedial self-determination offers the group an opportunity also to remove themselves from that polity's zone of control.

I have characterised these as four separate and independent ideas, and not as manifestations of a single self-determination concept. I emphasise that point, as it is one of the crucial outcomes of the analysis. That they are separate and independent forms means that they can have – and it has been argued above that they do have – different statuses under international law. Two forms, polity-based and colonial self-determination, have acquired the character of customary law rights. Moreover, as will be seen in the course of chapters three, four and six, the polity-based form of self-determination has acquired the status of a norm *ius cogens*, and I argue that colonial self-determination should also be understood to be a peremptory norm. By contrast, it is clear that international law does not recognise a right of peoples to secessionary self-determination, although it also seems likely following *Kosovo* (discussed in chapter five) that there is also no active prohibition as a matter of international law. Finally, the status of remedial self-determination remains uncertain. Although it was possible to argue pre-*Kosovo* that an international consensus was slowly forming that it is an international law norm, it was again cast into doubt by the Court's remarks on that occasion. I argue that it is

[166] Jennings's remark that the 'people cannot decide until somebody decides who are the people' was quoted above: Jennings, *Self-Government* (n 59) 56, and further above, nn 123–24 and accompanying text. Although there remain controversies to resolve concerning the identification of the relevant 'people' for each form, the uncertainty identified by Jennings is also partly a result of the conceptual uncertainty around self-determination: the 'people' relevant to each form of self-determination are different. Indeed, it is possible to envisage a situation in which a person is (almost) simultaneously a member of four 'peoples', each corresponding to a different form of self-determination.

the most conspicuous casualty of what I have termed 'spillover' legitimacy, or the concern that liberalising the regime applicable to remedial cases of self-determination opens the door also to the secessionary form. The concern is unwarranted, but understandable: the unitary and binary conceptions of self-determination conflate these forms and erase the boundaries between them.

The four-fold division that I propose here is founded in a few, key, definitional questions: what is the 'self' that claims the right to self-determine, and in what circumstances can it do so? What range of possibilities are within the scope of its determination, and what are the legal consequences of any given choice? The answers to these questions are summarised in Figure 1.1.

Figure 1.1 Distinguishing features of the four forms of self-determination

Genus/ Category	SELF-DETERMINATION			
Species/ Forms	Polity-Based	Secessionary	Colonial	Remedial
To whom?	Populations of States	Self-defined groups	"Salt-water" colonial territories	Groups denied polity-based form
When?	Ongoing process	At the discretion of the group	All colonies post c.1965	As a last resort when other remedies fail
Outcomes?	Popular sovereignty; non-interference	Autonomy; irredentism; independence	Independent statehood within existing borders	Autonomy; irredentism; independence
Legal status?	Norm of CIL; ius cogens status	No existing right under CIL; no prohibition	Norm of CIL; likely of ius cogens status	Legal status currently unclear

These divisions will be further substantiated in the remainder of the text. Before embarking on that examination, however, it is salient to consider further what the nature of the forms are and the relationship between them, to show that concerns of spillover legitimacy are indeed unjustified. To do so it is necessary to consider what is meant by the term 'forms' of self-determination, and how these relate to the overarching self-determination 'category'. It is to these questions that the next section turns.

IV. Vocabulary and Categorisation: The Forms of Self-Determination and their Interrelation

I have argued that the conceptual confusion that attends self-determination can be resolved by understanding self-determination as a category that comprises four sub-types: polity-based, secessionary, remedial and colonial self-determinations. I have described these as the four 'forms' of self-determination, and situated them within a broader self-determination 'category'. The relationship between these levels has to this point been implied – the metaphor of species and genus has been used to illustrate it – but much remains to be explained about their interrelation as I conceive it here. This section takes up that task to demonstrate that the forms of self-determination are interrelated to the extent that they are all members of the same category, and therefore share a set of common attributes, but are nevertheless independent things-in-themselves and should not be understood as facets or aspects of a unitary idea.[167]

That enquiry offers an opportunity, too, to clarify and explain the terminology used in this chapter, and in the book as a whole. It is appropriate that an argument that criticises the existing use of vocabulary should itself take care over the terms it employs. For that reason, I avoid the term 'norm', which has the potential to be misinterpreted in a legal discussion, and use it only in the context of 'norm of customary international law'. Instead, the term 'form' of self-determination is adopted, and is so rather for its lack of semantic content than for any particular explanatory virtue.

A. Taxonomy of Self-Determination

'Categorization', George Lakoff observes, 'is not a matter to be taken lightly. There is nothing more basic to our thought, perception, action and speech.'[168] Although the concept of categorisation is now more commonly discussed in epistemology or biology, it has no less relevance for the lawyer than it did for the early taxonomists. Illegal and legal, law and non-law, judgment and dissent, subject and object, innocence and guilt, whether the circumstance precluding wrongfulness applies, which court has jurisdiction, what system of law governs the dispute, and many others besides are basic divisions which structure the legal universe and are necessary for the pursuit of the lawyer's craft. But the need to categorise in law

[167] Gleider Hernández and I have elsewhere discussed the importance of semantics in understanding concepts such as self-determination in international law, with reference to the theory of language. See G Hernández and T Sparks, 'Categorising Self-Determination: Four Forms' (2020) 63 *German Yearbook of International Law* 223, 226–30.

[168] G Lakoff, *Women, Fire, and Dangerous Things: What Categories Reveal about the Mind* (Chicago, University of Chicago Press, 1987) 5.

runs deeper than these practical distinctions: law is a conceptual science, both in its academic study and in its 'real' application.[169] At a basic level the making and the application of law are exercises in categorisation, a fact which can be seen in the structure of norms and rules. Laws do not in general take the form of specific orders addressed to named individuals, but instead refer to categories of actions or events: a norm governs all those situations which fall within its ambit (spatial, temporal, factual), and leaves unaffected all those which do not. That definitional proposition is simply and elegantly captured in the principle demand of the rule of law, that like cases should be treated alike and different cases differently.[170] A similar observation is made by Lon Fuller, who lists the failure to categorise as 'the first and most obvious' of his 'eight routes to disaster' in the law-making enterprise;[171] in which a lawmaker which finds itself 'incapable of making … generalizations',[172] as a result cannot 'achieve rules at all'.[173]

In other words: categorisation is an inherent element of law. Laws that do not appropriately distinguish between categories are not law at all,[174] but discretion.[175] It has been argued here that the usual categorisation applied to self-determination claims – the language of 'internal' and 'external' – is inappropriate, and that this miscategorisation has a distorting effect with consequences both academic and practical.[176] It seeks to compare things that are not alike, and it lacks a conception of the ideal to which each category corresponds. The 'indeterminate, incoherent'[177] character of the law on self-determination is, at least in part, a result of that failure of categorisation. What is more, the lens of categorisation also suggests a better way to understand the relationships between different usages of the term 'self-determination'. To borrow a metaphor from the natural sciences, it is I think helpful to conceive of the forms of self-determination in terms of taxonomy: self-determination and its forms stand in a relation much like that of species and genus.

[169] Bianchi says that 'categories are fundamental to legal thinking': A Bianchi, 'Textual Interpretation and (International) Law Reading: The Myth of (in) Determinacy and the Genealogy of Meaning' in P Bekker, R Dolzer and M Waibel (eds), *Making Transitional Law Work in the Global Economy – Essays in Honour of Detlev Vagts* (Cambridge, Cambridge University Press, 2010) 43 ff.

[170] N MacCormick, *Legal Reasoning and Legal Theory* (Oxford, Clarendon Press, 1978) 53.

[171] L Fuller, *The Morality of Law* (New Haven, CT, Yale University Press, 1969) 39.

[172] ibid 34.

[173] ibid 39. Many other scholars have also noted the importance of categories in law, and have highlighted many different aspects of law's categorical structure. See, for example, J Derrida, 'Force of Law: The "Mystical Foundation of Authority"' in G Anidjar (ed), J Derrida, *Acts of Religion* (Longdon, Routledge, 2013) 252–53; K Larenz, *Methodenlehre der Rechtswissenschaften*, 3rd edn, ed C-W Canaris (Berlin, Springer-Verlag, 1995) 17–18, 71, 294ff.

[174] Fuller, *The Morality of Law* (n 171) 34–39.

[175] Derrida, 'Mystical Foundation' (n 173) 252–54.

[176] See eg Mégret, 'Earned, Not Inherent' (n 15) 50; and further s II.A above. In more general terms, d'Aspremont and Singh argue that '[m]odes of thought that seek to reduce the complexities … of our social world to inadequate categories are not merely unwarranted but potentially dangerous': J d'Aspremont and S Singh, 'Introduction: The Life of International Law and Its Concepts' in J d'Aspremont and S Singh (eds), *Concepts for International Law: Contributions to Disciplinary Thought* (Cheltenham, Edward Elgar, 2019) 1.

[177] Tesón, 'Introduction' (n 25) 1; see further, Sterio, *Secession* (n 26).

The unitary term 'self-determination' as it has been employed for many years by international law is, this book argues, better understood as a genus. It is a category; it designates a subset of objects that share certain common attributes, but is not a *thing* in itself.[178] 'Self-determination' cannot be an international law norm, because there is nothing behind the word 'self-determination' to tell us specifically *what it means*. Long usage has obscured the extent to which the lack content may be obvious to the observer, but it is (I think) strongly indicated by the examples given above of self-determination being invoked as simultaneously law and not law, supporting this outcome or that, attaching to specific regions or whole countries.

To push the taxonomic metaphor further, the four different kinds of self-determination that have been identified above can be described as *species*. Although these species all share certain characteristics, they are sufficiently different to be regarded as wholly separate ideas. Gleider Hernández and I illustrate this interrelation with the example that 'a lion, a tiger, and a leopard are distinct species with unique features. However, they share a number of attributes – in particular, a common cranial structure that enables them to roar – and which marks them out from other [cats].'[179] Together with the jaguar and the snow leopard, these species make up the genus *Panthera*, and certainly these five animals have significant commonalities. However, while only one of them is likely to be found hunting Cape buffalo on the African savanna, so too only one of them can survive in the thin air and harsh weather above 3,000 meters in the Himalaya: their differences are just as important as their shared bone structure.

Much the same applies to the forms of self-determination: polity-based, colonial, remedial and secessionary self-determination. Each corresponds to different contexts and claims – different habitats, to push the metaphor further – although all share the common attributes of the self-determination category. Each of the forms contains a range of possible applications, justifications, and modalities, and they remain distinguishable as discrete types by the specific differentiating features identified above. That holds true in particular for their status at law: although it will be argued that two of the forms – polity-based and colonial self-determination – have acquired the character of legal norms, simultaneously it will be argued that an assertion of their existence as norms (properly so-called) has no implications for the legal status of either the remedial or secessionary self-determination forms.

That is not to say that they will never overlap: different self-determination claims can be advanced in relation to the same factual scenario by different actors – such as when two schools of thought within an independence movement stress variously the secessionary and remedial aspects of their claim. Different claims can also be advanced simultaneously – such as where an independence declaration cites not only a colonial context but a history of active abuses to substantiate a territory's right to independence. Claims can be consciously connected, as where

[178] 'Genus, n.' Oxford English Dictionary (2019).
[179] Hernández and Sparks, 'Categorising Self-Determination' (n 167) 229.

independence movements conceive of remedial self-determination as being consequent upon a denial of the polity-based form. And conflations can occur as a direct result of the confusion I identify here, as I will argue has been the case in relation to the reasoning of courts on some occasions.[180] Numerous such examples will be identified in the analysis that follows. Nevertheless, I argue that over the course of their development the forms here identified have acquired the status of separate ideas, separate precedents and (in some cases) of separate norms. Greater conceptual clarity will, what is more, reduce the frequency of such overlaps by offering a clear and defined vocabulary that enables a coherent delineation of self-determination's forms.

It is not argued that the four species identified here need necessarily exhaust the category 'self-determination' entirely. None of the forms encompasses, for example, concepts of self-determination that apply to individuals rather than to collectivities,[181] and it is distinctly possible – even likely – that further developments in international society's treatment of different kinds of self-determination claims will alter the boundaries of these categories, may collapse them, and may give rise to new forms. But neither the elimination of any penumbral uncertainty nor timeless validity is necessary for the claim made in this book to be accepted. Rather, this book argues that a division of the self-determination genus into the four species identified here is better able to explain the distinctions and discontinuities observable in the operation of 'self-determination' in international law at present and as it has developed, and provides a more useable framework for future claims. If it does that much, it has achieved its aims.

V. Conclusion

International law has a self-determination problem. Not only do the vagaries of the idea present challenges for scholars and scholarship, but the conceptual confusion that veils self-determination has real, and potentially serious, practical consequences. The panoply of references to the 'essential' principle of self-determination,[182] the 'right' of 'all peoples … freely [to] determine their political status',[183] are wont to be interpreted by population groups seeking to change their relationship with their state as indicating that international law stands behind their claim, whether it be to regional autonomy, to irredentism, or to secession. Such groups, Frédéric Mégret notes, have often learned 'painfully' that no such endorsement of their aspirations is intended by these references.[184] And

[180] See, in particular, the discussion of the *East Timor* decision, ch 4, s V; and the *Chagos* Advisory Opinion, ch 6.

[181] See above, nn 64–67 and accompanying text.

[182] *East Timor* (n 16) para 29.

[183] Art 1 ICESCR/ICCPR (n 42).

[184] Mégret, 'Earned, Not Inherent' (n 15) 50.

yet such interpretations of the authorities – treaties, General Assembly resolutions and international court judgments – are hardly unreasonable.

Indeed, the conceptual confusion surrounding self-determination runs deeper than this. It cannot be waved away as the product of the overenthusiastic and inexpert interpretations of a handful of obsessive nationalists; on the contrary, self-determination has seemed to defeat even sober and measured analysis. Such a conclusion is indicated, for example, by the fact that even the explanatory framework overlaid on the idea by international lawyers – the internal/external binary – is not used to mean the same thing by all authors.[185] Even were it so, I have argued here that this framework is inherently incapable of capturing the complexities of self-determination. By drawing distinctions between different claims to self-determination on the basis of their intended effects, the internal/external binary groups together claims to self-determination that have very little in common. Whether viewed at the level of the underlying source of legitimacy each claim invokes or the legal treatment each claim receives, the binary is inadequate: it requires that unlike cases are treated alike, and it erases relevant differences between different manifestations of the concept. Rather, I have argued that the kinds of self-determination should be divided on the basis of the justification-claims that each form makes, an exercise which results in a four-part typology of self-determination: the polity-based, secessionary, remedial, and colonial forms.

This chapter has briefly introduced those four forms of self-determination, which will be used as analytical foci for the analysis to come, and has interrogated their nature. In contrast to the prevailing view in international law, which categorises self-determination as a unitary norm with two facets or applications, I have argued that 'self-determination' must be understood instead as a category or a genus. Although it designates a set of connected ideas that share certain common attributes, it remains noumenal and not phenomenal. It is not a claim in itself, but only a structure of thought that collects together the individual forms of self-determination and designates them as being examples of a kind. Absent the specificity that is provided by the forms, 'self-determination' means little: it is too vague and undefined to serve as a legal concept, still less a legal norm. Rather that character, of an actual or potential legal norm, can be borne only by the forms.[186]

Over the course of the following five chapters, this book will trace the development of these four self-determination ideas from their early expressions in the major European and American declarations, through the age of revolutions, the practice of the League of Nations and the United Nations, the decolonisation era, and to its most recent treatment by the ICJ in *Chagos Archipelago*. It will argue that four distinct traditions, legitimacy claims and legal treatments can be discerned, and in consequence that it is necessary to understand the interactions between states, nations and peoples in terms of these four self-determinations.

[185] See above, nn 77–78 and accompanying text.

[186] For a summary overview of these forms and their legal status, see Figure 1.1.

2

Self-Determination's Origins: 1320–1920

This chapter will trace the development of the self-determination idea through its major milestones, from its prehistory in Scotland in 1320 and the Low Countries in 1571, to the (totemic) expressions in the American and French declarations of 1776 and 1789 where most histories begin, and to the Åland Islands dispute in 1920, the first occasion on which self-determination was subject to institutionalised adjudication. It will argue that the four-part typology of self-determination set out in chapter one is better suited to an analysis of self-determination's early history than either a unitary or binary (internal/external) conception of the norm. By contrast, dividing the self-determination category into four forms – the political, colonial, remedial and secessionary ideas – has the effect of clarifying much about the development of the self-determination norms as legal and political claims. It demonstrates that self-determination claims can usually be characterised as referring to one or other of these forms, and that the different forms have been accepted by international law to differing degrees. Chapter three will then continue this history, turning in particular to the decolonisation practice of the League of Nations and the United Nations.

I. A Prehistory of Self-Determination?

The idea of self-determination has evolved and changed significantly during the course of its development. Most scholars find its first expression in the American Declaration of Independence of 1776, or in the closely contemporaneous French Declaration of 1789.[1] It is, however, difficult to pinpoint the genesis of concepts with any degree of certainty, and nearly always an arbitrary decision to label any idea or expression wholly original. Although they may be hidden beneath the surface, most concepts have roots stretching far back into the past. In her account of self-determination, Elizabeth Rodríguez-Santiago reaches back past the American Declaration to the fifteenth century, finding precursor ideas in European debates

[1] See eg A Cassese, *Self-Determination of Peoples: A Legal Reappraisal* (Cambridge, Cambridge University Press, 1995) 11; D Raič, *Statehood and the Law of Self-Determination* (The Hague, Kluwer Law International, 2002) 172–73.

concerning the colonisation of the Americas, for example.[2] Indeed, it is possible to look yet further back: A US Senate resolution of 1997 designated 6 April annually to be 'National Tartan Day' in the United States, in recognition of the inspiration provided to the 1776 drafters of the American Declaration of Independence by a much earlier Scottish document, the Declaration of Arbroath of 6 April 1320.[3]

A. The Declaration of Arbroath

The story of the Declaration of Arbroath begins in 1286. Alexander III was King of Scotland, and had suffered great tragedy: he was a widower and in 1273 his only surviving child, his daughter, had died in childbirth. With the royal succession in disarray, Alexander remarried in November 1275. On 19 March 1286, riding through the night to be with his new queen on her birthday, Alexander fell from his horse, tumbled down a steep, rocky embankment and died.[4]

i. The Scottish War of Independence

When in 1286 Alexander III died, the crown passed to his last surviving descendent, Margaret, Maid of Norway – Alexander's granddaughter and daughter of the King of Norway – who was then just three years old. What was an unorthodox succession became a succession crisis when, en route to Scotland to take up her throne in 1290, the then seven-year-old Margaret also died, leaving no direct heir to the Scottish crown. There were four main contenders for the Scottish crown, but as many as thirteen hopefuls declared themselves as claimants. The most notable were John Balliol, John Hastings, Floris V, Count of Holland, and Robert Bruce – grandfather of another Robert Bruce who was to be known to history as Rob 'the' Bruce. With Scotland on the verge of civil war, the Guardians of Scotland – a committee of regents appointed by Parliament to assist Margaret until she came of age – petitioned the English King Edward I to arbitrate the succession. Edward agreed and established a commission of Auditors, which declared John Balliol to be the rightful King of Scotland in accordance with primogeniture. But in the process Edward sought to establish himself as Lord Paramount of Scotland[5] – that England be Scotland's suzerain – a claim based on the somewhat dubious authority of the 1174 Treaty of Falaise which established English suzerainty over Scotland for a period of fifteen years, until the Treaty was annulled by the Quitclaim of

[2] E Rodríguez-Santiago, 'The Evolution of Self-Determination of Peoples in International Law' in FR Tesón (ed), *The Theory of Self-Determination* (Cambridge, Cambridge University Press, 2016) 202–204.

[3] As I discuss below, there are good reasons for doubting that the 1320 Declaration of Arbroath was, in fact, an influence on the 1776 drafters: See below, s I.C.

[4] R Chambers (ed), 'Alexander III', *A Biographical Dictionary of Eminent Scotsmen*, vol I, 2nd edn (Glasgow, Blackie and Son, 1857) paras 47–49.

[5] AAM Duncan, *The Kinship of the Scots, 842–1292: Succession and Independence* (Edinburgh, Edinburgh University Press, 2016) 220ff, 340–44.

Canterbury in 1189.[6] With Edward having won important concessions – to the point of reducing Scotland to a vassal of the English crown – John Balliol was allowed to ascend the throne of Scotland on 30 November 1292.[7]

Edward was not content to treat his newly won suzerainty over Scotland as formal; rather, he seemed to relish the title. He demanded that King John pay homage to him, he levied charges against Scotland to pay for his wars against France and required that Scotland send troops to support the English army, and claimed legal authority in any dispute between English and Scottish subjects. Infuriated by these humiliations and the inability of their new king to stand up for Scotland, the Scottish barons met at Stirling in 1295, and appointed a new Council of Twelve to take over the administration of Scotland, effectively deposing John Balliol, who resigned his kingship in favour of Edward,[8] fled the country, and ended his days in exile.[9] One of the new Council's first acts was to negotiate a mutual defence treaty with France,[10] decisively breaking with the suzerainty claim of an England that was then at war with France. Edward responded with force, ordering the English army to muster at Newcastle upon Tyne in the north of England, in March 1296.[11]

Scotland struck first – burning Carlisle, Tindale, Corbridge and two monasteries in the border region of Northumberland[12] – but England struck harder. The English army poured north through Scotland, sacking towns, and slaughtering townspeople. It is estimated that between 7,000 and 17,000 were killed in the town of Berwick,[13] and some sources even put the number at as many

[6] D Carpenter, *The Struggle for Mastery: Britain 1066–1284* (London, Penguin Books, 2004) 226–29; R de Hoveden, *The Annals of Roger de Hoveden: Comprising the History of England and of Other Countries of Europe from AD 732 to AD 1201*, vol I, tr HT Riley (London, HG Bohn, 1853) 382, 398–400; R de Hoveden, *The Annals of Roger de Hoveden: Comprising the History of England and of Other Countries of Europe from AD 732 to AD 1201*, vol II, tr HT Riley (London, HG Bohn, 1853) 130–32.

[7] AH Dunbar, *Scottish Kings: A Revised Chronology of Scottish History, 1005–1625*, 2nd edn (Edinburgh, David Douglas, 1906) 115–16.

[8] ibid 116.

[9] Balliol abdicated following the Scots defeat at Dunbar in April 1296. He was first imprisoned in the Tower of London, before being allowed to go to France in 1299. As he tried to cross the Channel, it was found that he had with him the Crown of Scotland and the Royal Seal in his baggage, which were seized by the English king. He was released into the custody of the pope and lived in the papal residence until 1301, when he was released. He moved to his family estates in Picardy, where he lived for the rest of his life. His son, Edward Balliol, 'the pretender', with the assistance of Edward III of England and a number of disillusioned members of the Scottish nobility, invaded Scotland in an attempt to take Scottish crown following the death of Robert I (Rob the Bruce) in 1329. Edward Balliol was crowned king in September 1332, but was forced to flee just three months later. Further (unsuccessful) attempts to take Scotland followed in 1333, 1334, 1335, 1336 and 1346, in what was to become known as the second war of independence. See RC Reid, 'Edward de Balliol' (1956) 35 *Transactions of the Dumfriesshire and Galloway Natural History & Antiquarian Society* 38, 38–48.

[10] R Tanner, 'Franco-Scottish Alliance' in R Crowcroft and J Cannon (eds), *The Oxford Companion to British History*, 2nd edn (Oxford, Oxford University Press, 2015).

[11] M Prestwich, *Edward I* (New Haven, CT, Yale University Press, 1997) 373.

[12] P de Langtoft, *The Chronicle of Pierre de Langtoft: In French Verse, from the Earliest Period to the Death of King Edward I*, vol 2, tr T Wright (London, Longmans, Green, Reader and Dyer, 1866) 233–41.

[13] JP Lawson, *Historical Tales of the Wars of Scotland, and of the Border Raids, Forays, and Conflicts*, vol I (Edinburgh, A Fullarton & Co, 1839) 115–16.

as 60,000, although this has been regarded by later sources as an unreliable estimate.[14] Whatever the true number, accounts agree that the events at Berwick in March 1296 were nothing short of a massacre: men, women and children were slaughtered in the streets, and the English forces even (a horrendous crime by the standards of the time) desecrated the sanctity of the cloister, entering churches to kill those sheltering within and to pillage the altar ornaments. Certainly, the victims would (in modern terms) be understood as civilians: the sack of Berwick was conducted before the castle was invested and its surrender obtained.[15] Having taken Berwick, the English army continued northwards, routing the Scottish army at Dunbar,[16] and taking the castles at Edinburgh and Stirling, and the Palace of Linlithgow. By the end of July, Edward's advance had reached as far north as Banff and Cullen, on the Moray Firth, before turning west and south to return to Berwick by way of Perth and Dunfermline. Edward I had all but conquered Scotland. The Scottish army had been scattered; its castles were taken; its nobility either taken captive or had sworn themselves to his service. Not satisfied now with suzerainty, Edward set about eliminating markers of Scottish independent identity: the Scottish crown and the other trappings of the Scottish monarchy – the Black Rood of St Margaret (said to be a fragment of the True Cross) and the Stone of Destiny (the Stone of Scone) – were removed to Westminster Abbey.[17]

Scotland, however, if conquered was not entirely defeated: rebellions began in 1297 in both the north and south of the country, led in the north by Andrew Moray and in the south by William Wallace. Wallace won a storied battle against the English forces left to hold Scotland at Stirling Bridge,[18] followed by a string of other victories, prompting Edward to invade Scotland once again in 1298. Edward's forces entered Scotland in July, and on the 22nd met Wallace's forces at Falkirk. The Scottish army was slaughtered by the English longbowmen, which allowed the English army to engage the Scottish lines while remaining out of range of the Scottish spearmen and cavalry.[19] Wallace, humiliated by the defeat, resigned his guardianship of Scotland,[20] and lived the rest of his life as a hunted man, until he was captured and executed in 1305.

Wallace's retreat from leadership left space for a new set of Scottish Guardians, and he was replaced in 1299 by John Comyn (the Red Comyn) and Robert the Bruce, alongside John de Soulis and William Lamberton, Bishop of St Andrews.[21]

[14] ibid 116. Certainly, it seems far-fetched, given that 60,000 people may have amounted to around 15 per cent of the Scottish population in the period, which Cooper estimates at around 400,000 people: TM Cooper, 'The Numbers and the Distribution of the Population of Medieval Scotland' (1947) 26 *Scottish Historical Review* 2, 9.

[15] Lawson, *Wars of Scotland* (n 13) 115–17.

[16] DJ Breeze, *The Stone of Destiny: A Symbol of Nationhood* (Edinburgh, Historic Scotland, 1997) 22.

[17] ibid 21–23.

[18] Lawson, *Wars of Scotland* (n 13) 173–78.

[19] P Armstrong, *Stirling Bridge and Falkirk 1297–98: William Wallace's Rebellion* (Hailsham, Osprey Publishing, 2003) 77–78.

[20] ibid 80.

[21] J Mackintosh, *Historic Earls and Earldoms of Scotland* (Aberdeen, W Jolly, 1898) 86.

The relationship between Bruce and the Red Comyn was to be a key factor leading to the Declaration of Arbroath.[22] Both Bruce and Comyn had a potential genealogical claim to the Scottish crown, and both at different points switched loyalties – whether as a matter of convenience or semblance – allying themselves at times with the English throne. By 1306, however, matters came to a head: Comyn was at this time sworn to the English thrown but Bruce, although outwardly maintaining his loyalty to Edward, was planning a new attempt at restoring the Crown of Scotland. Edward somehow came to hear of Bruce's plans – with suspicion falling ultimately upon Comyn – but Bruce managed to extricate himself from the English court, returning to Scotland before he could be captured.[23] On the 10 February 1306, Bruce and Comyn met at the Friary of Dumfries where, in an interview before the high altar in the chapel, Bruce sought to win Comyn's support for the independence cause. Bruce offered to support Comyn's claim to kingship in return for the Comyn family lands, or offered Comyn the Bruce family estates in return for his support for Bruce's claim. Comyn refused, professing his loyalty to Edward, whereupon Bruce accused him of revealing Bruce's plans to the English court.[24] With their argument becoming furious, Bruce drew his dagger and stabbed Comyn, wounding him. Bruce turned and rushed from the chapel, apparently distressed, shouting to his followers that he had killed Comyn. On their entry into the chapel, and finding Comyn still alive, Bruce's followers immediately killed him outright.[25]

Bruce had reasons to be distressed: the die had been cast and war with England was now again inevitable. Just as concerning, he had committed an act of sacrilege by stabbing Comyn on consecrated ground and, although he received absolution from Robert Wishart, Bishop of Glasgow,[26] Bruce was excommunicated by the Archbishop of York on the authorisation of Pope Clement V.[27] Despite his excommunication, just six weeks after Comyn lay dying before the altar at Greyfriars, in March 1306, Bruce was rushed to Scone to be crowned King of Scotland.[28]

[22] Their term as Guardians began poorly: Mackintosh reports that at (what must have been an early) meeting of the Guardians in 1299, 'Comyn leaped upon [the Bruce] and took him by the throat … until the Steward and others went between them and stopped the scuffle': Mackintosh, *Earls and Earldoms* (n 21) 87.

[23] This account (or a variation on it) is, as Barrow says, dominant, although note that Barrow himself doubts that it can be true in at least some respects, and writes that there is 'no evidence that Bruce was with the king' in this period: GWS Barrow, *Robert Bruce and the Community of the Realm of Scotland* (Berkeley, University of California Press, 1965) 197–98.

[24] ibid 198–99.

[25] See Mackintosh, *Earls and Earldoms* (n 21) 93; although note the inconsistencies which Barrow describes in the accounts of Comyn's death: see Barrow, *Robert Bruce* (n 23) 197–99, 206–08.

[26] Barrow, *Robert Bruce* (n 23) 210–11; RM Scott, *Robert the Bruce: King of the Scots* (Barnes & Nobel, 1982) 74.

[27] D Dalrymple, *Annals of Scotland from the Accession of Robert I. Surnamed Bruce, to the Accession of the House of Stewart* (Edinburgh, Balfour & Smellie, 1779) 3–4. Bruce was actually crowned king twice in quick succession, on 25 and 27 March, the second ceremony taking place to allow the Countess Isabel Duncan to perform the role traditionally afforded to her family, the Clan Macduff (of Macbeth fame), to crown the Scottish kings: Barrow, *Robert Bruce* (n 23) 212–213.

[28] Barrow, *Robert Bruce* (n 23) 208.

Only a few of Scotland's noble families rallied to his banner, however. It is not surprising that support for Bruce was initially so minimal; perhaps more surprising was that he was crowned at all. Bruce had a claim to the throne, certainly,[29] but he was not the only man in Scotland who harboured royal ambitions, nor the only one with a bloodline to back them up. He had recently been – outwardly – an ally of the English king, whatever true opinions he might have held. He was a murderer and an excommunicate. The act of crowning a king of any family would provoke the English into another war, and seating Bruce upon the thrown would pit the new king's forces also against the Comyns – still Scotland's most powerful family[30] – and their followers; many noble families who remained loyal to Edward; and those who themselves had designs on the throne.[31] Last but not least: Scotland still had a deposed king yet living – John Balliol in exile – and there were those in Scotland who believed the divine right to rule was vested in him. Nevertheless, however inauspiciously, however controversially, Robert the Bruce was crowned.

The following years were a time of abject suffering for the new king. He enjoyed a string of swift victories,[32] but once the English were mobilised soon encountered his first real defeat – a crushing loss at Methven in June 1306. Many of his followers were killed or captured, and Bruce himself barely escaped.[33] His forces broken, and with a strong English force in control of Scotland once again, Bruce was forced to go into hiding. The momentum started to shift in 1307, however, with the death of Edward I and the ascension of Edward II, at the age of twenty-three. Edward I had been a shrewd and experienced military strategist; his son proved to be less artful, and English strategy started to go awry.[34] Bruce returned to mainland Scotland – probably from a hideout in the Hebrides or Ireland[35] – and began to chip away at English positions. As Edward I lay dying in his encampment at Burgh by Sands,[36] just south of the Scottish border, Bruce won battles against the English army at Glen Trool and Loudoun Hill, before capturing the castles at Inverlochy and Urquhart, and burning the castle at Inverness.

By the end of 1308, Bruce had torn through the Comyn lands in the north of Scotland, destroying their castles and garrisons, breaking the power of what had once been the most significant family of Scotland, before destroying the English garrison at Aberdeen. As the victories continued, support grew for the man who

[29] ibid 204.

[30] ibid 205.

[31] Mackintosh, *Earls and Earldoms* (n 21) 94; Barrow, *Robert Bruce* (n 23) 206.

[32] Barrow, *Robert Bruce* (n 23) 214–215.

[33] J Barbour, *The Bruce: Edited and with an Introduction by AAM Duncan*, ed AAM Duncan (Edinburgh, Canongate Books, 2010) 96.

[34] In 1310, Edward II was to face a petition in parliament, charging that '[s]quandering the inheritance of his father … [he] had lost Scotland and dismembered his lands in England and Ireland': RM Haines, *King Edward II: Edward of Caernarfon, His Life, His Reign, and Its Aftermath, 12841330* (Montreal, McGill-Queen's University Press, 2003) 75.

[35] Barrow, *Robert Bruce* (n 23) 231–33, 237.

[36] Prestwich, *Edward I* (n 11) 556–57. As Barrow noted, Edward I was clearly in failing health as early as 1304: Barrow, *Robert Bruce* (n 23) 204.

called himself King of Scotland, and in 1310 the Scottish clergy officially recognised Bruce as Scotland's king at its general council, a significant development given Bruce's status as an excommunicate. English strongholds continued to fall throughout the next years – Linlithgow in 1310, Dunbarton in 1311, and Perth in 1312 – before Bruce, in what was to be a decisive development, laid siege to Stirling castle in 1314. Edward II, determined to put a definitive end to the Bruce's campaign, marched to Stirling's rescue with a huge army[37] – it is estimated that England fielded 15,000–20,000 men against the Bruce's forces of around 6,000. The Scots surprised the English forces just shy of Stirling, at Bannockburn, where the heavily armed and armoured cavalry and foot soldiers of the English forces were bogged down in the marshy ground either side of the Bannock Burn itself. In what has been described as a 'calamity of stunning proportions',[38] the English army was destroyed and routed by a force of Scots less than a third the size, and Edward II barely escaped with his life.

With English power in Scotland de facto broken, the Scottish focus shifted from control to sovereignty. Although Scotland now had the upper hand in military terms – indeed, Scottish forces were conducting ever more, and ever more vicious, raids into England – the diplomatic contest still seemed to be going in favour of Edward II. In 1319, a Scottish force cut a swathe through the towns of the north of England, burning barns and harvests, characterised by Haines as 'one of the most heartless and senseless of a lengthening series of raids against a defenceless population',[39] and though the Scots won the military engagement, they handed to Edward something of a propaganda victory. In February 1320, and following entreaties by Edward, the Pope dispatched a series of six Bulls aimed at the Scots: the Bulls sentenced all those involved in the invasion of England to excommunication, and reiterated Bruce's excommunication for the murder of Comyn.[40] The meeting at the Abbey of Arbroath in April 1320 was the Scots' diplomatic response.[41] The barons of Scotland wrote an appeal to the Pope, seeking to put their own case. In addition to their hope that the interdict on Scotland and Bruce's excommunication would be lifted,[42] they were no doubt aware that papal recognition would strengthen the claim of right on behalf of the kingship of Robert the Bruce, as well as offering some degree of protection to the newly independent kingdom that its larger neighbour would not be able to attack it again without questioning papal authority.

[37] Haines, *King Edward II* (n 34) 94.

[38] ibid 259–60.

[39] ibid 267.

[40] ibid 268.

[41] Or riposte – see Hill's characterisation of the affair: RMT Hill, 'Belief and Practice as Illustrated by John XXII's Excommunication of Robert Bruce' (1972) 8 *Studies in Church History* 135, 137–38.

[42] But see, *contra*, Hill, who comments that Bruce 'clearly believed that he had never been excommunicated' and 'disregarded the whole affair': ibid 137.

ii. *The Text of the Declaration of Arbroath*

It was likely a cold and wet spring when,[43] on 6 April 1320, a group of men gathered at the abbey of the Tironesian Benedictine community at Arbroath on the east coast of Scotland to write a letter. The men were the earls and barons of Scotland who met, together with Bernard of Kilwinning, Abbot of Arbroath, to address an appeal to the Pope. Bernard was probably the author of the Declaration of Arbroath as well as its draftsman,[44] and the men who met with him on 6 April were the earls and barons of Scotland. It is not known whether there was any discussion or dissent, or whether all present on that day endorsed the text, but it is thought that as many as fifty seals may have originally been attached to the Declaration[45] – each one authenticating the document and signalling the assent of the noble house to which it pertained.

The Declaration begins with paragraphs proclaiming the separate nationhood of the Scots,[46] and their status as a Christian people.[47] It then complains of the deeds of Edward I, committed against the Scottish population, declaring that:

> The deeds of cruelty, massacre, violence, pillage, arson, imprisoning prelates, burning down monasteries, robbing and killing monks and nuns and yet other outrages without number which he committed against our people, sparing neither age nor sex, religion nor rank, no-one could describe nor fully imagine unless he had seen them with his own eyes.
>
> But from these countless evils we have been set free, by the help of Him who though He afflicts yet heals and restores, by our most tireless prince, King and lord, the lord Robert.

It then proclaims Robert Bruce's kingship according to 'divine providence, the succession to his right according to our laws and customs which we shall maintain to the death, and the due consent and assent of us all' – a statement that some have argued amounts to a proteogenic expression of (what would later be called) popular sovereignty.[48]

[43] K Pribyl, 'The Study of the Climate of Medieval England: A Review of Historical Climatology's Past Achievements and Future Potential' (2014) 69 *Weather* 116, 119; M Rydval et al, 'Reconstructing 800 Years of Summer Temperatures in Scotland from Tree Rings' (2017) 49 *Climate Dynamics* 2951, 2957.

[44] References to the Declaration of Arbroath correspond to the revised version compiled by Alan Borthwick (2005) based on Sir James Fergusson *The Declaration of Arbroath, 1320* (1970) 5–11, with reference to AAM Duncan, *The Nation of Scots and the Declaration of Arbroath* (Historical Association pamphlet, 1970) 3437 and DER Watt (ed), *Scotichronicon*, vol 7 (Aberdeen, Aberdeen University Press, 1996) 49.

[45] Although only nineteen of the seals have survived until the present day.

[46] '[W]e know and from the chronicles and books of the ancients we find that among other famous nations our own, the Scots, has been graced with widespread renown.'

[47] 'Nor did He wish them to be confirmed in that faith by merely anyone but by the first of His Apostles – by calling, though second or third in rank – the most gentle Saint Andrew, the Blessed Peter's brother, and desired him to keep them under his protection as their patron for ever.'

[48] Cowan describes it as 'the first national or governmental expression … of the principle of the contractual theory of monarchy which lies at the root of modern constitutionalism': EJ Cowan, *The Declaration of Arbroath, 1320: 'For Freedom Alone'* (Edinburgh, Birlinn, 2020) ch 4. McLean

Certainly, as Kellas has argued, '[t]he signatories of the 1320 Declaration of Arbroath could have [had] no concept of participant popular sovereignty',[49] if understood either as a reference to that term, or to the articulated version of that theory, which most authors date to the Renaissance and the works of John Locke and Jean-Jacques Rousseau.[50] Even if, as some have argued, those ideas can be traced back further – to the School of Salamanca and the sixteenth century[51] – nevertheless they long post-date the events at Arbroath.[52] Nor, in the context of the structure of the social order in thirteenth- and fourteenth-century Scotland, would it be credible to interpret the barons as expressing a *popular* sovereignty theory: at most, this would have been a statement of an oligarchic *pouvoir constitué*. Even that, however, seems to be an overreading of, or reading backwards into, the text: Robert the Bruce's divine right to the kingship of Scotland is given foremost precedence in the Declaration, followed in the same sentence by the 'consent and assent' of the Scottish nobles, and his right to succession according to the laws of Scotland.

The Declaration may not have contained a refutation of the divine right of kings in and of itself, but it does seem to declare a right of revolution. Having established Robert I as the rightful king of Scotland, the declaration forewarns that:

> Yet if he should give up what he has begun, seeking to make us or our kingdom subject to the King of England or the English, we should exert ourselves at once to drive him out as our enemy and a subverter of his own right and ours, and make some other man who was well able to defend us our King; for, as long as a hundred of us remain alive, never will we on any conditions be subjected to the lordship of the English. It is in truth not for glory, nor riches, nor honours that we are fighting, but for freedom alone, which no honest man gives up but with life itself.

and McMillan repeat the claim, although noting that they doubt that it is accurate: I McLean and A McMillan, *State of the Union: Unionism and the Alternatives in the United Kingdom since 1707* (Oxford, Oxford University Press, 2005) 247.

[49] JG Kellas, *The Politics of Nationalism and Ethnicity*, 2nd edn (Basingstoke, Macmillan, 1998) 35.

[50] J Locke, *Two Treatises of Government* (London, Awnsham Churchill, 1690); J-J Rousseau, *Du contrat social; ou principles du droit politique* (Amsterdam, Marc Michel Rey, 1762).

[51] Alves and Moreira find consonant ideas in the work of Francisco Suárez, for example: AA Alves and JM Moreira, *The Salamanca School* (New York, Bloomsbury USA, 2009) 50; AS Campos, 'Francisco Suárez's Conception of the Social Contract' (2019) 75 *Revista Portuguesa de Filosofia* 1195; and further AS Campos, 'The Idea of the Social Contract in the History of "Agreementism"' (2019) 24 *The European Legacy* 579. Notably, there is a direct line between Suárez's expression of ideas akin to popular sovereignty and those of John Locke: Suárez's theory of state formation was criticised by Robert Filmer in his *Patriarcha*, on the grounds that he unduly diminished God's role in establishing the state. In turn, the first of John Locke's *Two Treatises* is dedicated to a ferocious rebuttal of Filmer's *Patriarcha*, before Locke lays out his theory of the social contract in the second treatise: R Filmer, *Patriarcha: Or the Natural Power of Kings* (London, Richard Chiswell, 1680); Locke, *Two Treatises* (n 50).

[52] Note, *contra*, that Gough has traced the idea of popular sovereignty back to ancient Greece, and the philosophy of the Sophists, as reported by Plato in the *Republic*: JW Gough, *The Social Contract: A Critical Study of its Development*, 2nd edn (Oxford, Clarendon Press, 1957) 10–12. Campos instead suggests roots in fourteenth- and fifteenth-century works by Manegold of Lautenbach, Engelbert of Volesdorf, John of Paris, Nicholas of Cusa and Marius Salamonius: Campos, 'Suárez's Social Contract' (n 51) 1197.

Here the right of revolution vests in the nation, and more specifically, in its *nationhood*. The drafters do not allege that they would have a right to replace Robert as king if he levies unfair taxes, failed in the administration of justice, or even if he committed acts of war against his own people.[53] But by betraying the nationhood of Scotland, the king would lose his right to rule[54] – would have 'unkinged himself', as Mayhew later coined the phrase.[55]

Having thus tied together Robert's divine right to rule the Scots, the contingency of his right on the preservation of nationhood and the dedicated wish of the Scots to remain a people of their own and distinct from the English, the Declaration begs the Pope to

> look with the eyes of a father on the troubles and privations brought by the English upon us and upon the Church of God. May it please you to admonish and exhort the King of the English, who ought to be satisfied with what belongs to him since England used once to be enough for seven kings or more, to leave us Scots in peace, who live in this poor little Scotland, beyond which there is no dwelling-place at all, and covet nothing but our own.

In the final analysis, the Declaration of Arbroath must be viewed as a piece of political propaganda. The Scots were not – at this point in time – the meek, beleaguered people that the Declaration seeks to portray, a people seeking only to live in peace but prevented by relentless aggression on the part of their overbearing neighbour. Rather, in the years immediately preceding the Declaration, the Scots had more often been the aggressor. Nevertheless, the Scottish people had suffered hugely through the military campaigns of Edward I, and there remained little prospect that Scotland would be able to defend itself against a well-organised and determined offensive by an equivalently able tactician – the power balance between Scotland and England was simply too great. As with the best pieces of propaganda, there was enough truth in the Declaration to give force to its claims.

As with other great acts of communication, too, there is something in the Declaration that deeply touches the reader. Certainly, it served its purpose – the Pope did consent to intercede with the English on the Scots' behalf and,[56] when a peace treaty – which recognised Scottish independent nationhood – was signed

[53] All these (and many more) were charges laid by the drafters of the 1776 American Declaration of Independence against King George III. See below, s II.

[54] This statement doubtless served the dual purpose of buttressing Bruce's claim to kingship over John Balliol and his children, as well as expressing the core contention of the Scots cause, that Scotland had a right to maintain its independent nationhood.

[55] J Mayhew, *A Discourse, Concerning Unlimited Submission and Non-Resistance to the Higher Powers: With Some Reflections on the Resistance Made to King Charles I, & on the Anniversary of His Death: In Which the Mysterious Doctrine of That Prince's Saintship & Martyrdom Is Unriddled: The Substance of Which Was Delivered in a Sermon Preached in the West Meeting-House in Boston the Lord's Day after the 30th of Jan, 1749–50* (Boston, D Fowle, 1750) 47. Mayhew's remarks were made in the context of the execution of King Charles I in 1649.

[56] B Webster, 'Robert I (Robert the Bruce) (1274–1329)' in R Crowcroft and J Cannon (eds), *The Oxford Companion to British History*, 2nd edn (Oxford, Oxford University Press, 2015).

between the two states in 1328,[57] the Pope lifted the interdict against Scotland and Robert's excommunication.[58] Beyond its immediate historical context, the Declaration has continued to have a gravitational pull that is almost palpable. Barrow comments that historians 'hold that Scottish nationalism was the product rather than the cause of the war of independence',[59] and certainly the Declaration has played its part in building and sustaining the Scots national identity in the close to seven-hundred years since it was written. Its statement that '[i]t is in truth not for glory, nor riches, nor honours that we are fighting, but for freedom alone, which no honest man gives up but with life itself' continues to hold a resonance, and not (I think) for its belligerence or patriotism. This was an expression of an idea – still in a nebulous form, not yet couched in familiar vocabulary – which has continued to have a world-shaping effect, and which had probably already been at work in the world for many thousands of years. The claim made by the Declaration – that the Scottish nation had a right to govern itself without the interference of another people or their king – did not appeal to law or to a legal right; rather it appealed to something deeper within the reader, some sense of moral right or legitimacy.

As the following sections track the development of self-determination through time, a similar structure will often be observed. The claim was sometimes the same, and sometimes different in important ways. In some cases, claims have invoked the precedential authority of prior self-determination claims, and increasingly so after 1776. But always the claim has been primarily one of rightness – of moral and political legitimacy – and only secondarily (if at all, until much more recently) an appeal to law. Just as the Pope faced the thorny question of how to deal with the Scottish claim to be free of English suzerainty in 1320, the question of whether – and how – to incorporate, tame or give effect to claims of self-determination has been one of the key concerns for international law and politics since its earliest days.

B. The Plakkaat van Verlatinghe (Act of Abjuration)

An interesting comparison may be drawn with another declaration which, falling almost two hundred years before the American revolution, has also been suggested as a model for the 1776 Declaration.[60] In 1581, the States General of the United Provinces of the Low Countries adopted a declaration that was every bit as remarkable as the Declaration made at Arbroath two centuries earlier, and

[57] J Cannon, 'Edinburgh, Treaty of, 1328' in R Crowcroft and J Cannon (eds), *The Oxford Companion to British History*, 2nd edn (Oxford, Oxford University Press, 2015).

[58] Scott, *Robert the Bruce* (n 26) 225.

[59] Barrow, *Robert Bruce* (n 23) 119.

[60] See S Lucas, 'The Rhetorical Ancestry of the Declaration of Independence' (1998) 1 *Rhetoric & Public Affairs* 143, 159–69; but *contra* D Armitage, 'The Contagion of Sovereignty: Declarations of Independence since 1776' (2005) 52 *South African History Journal* 1, 5–6.

that which was to be given at Philadelphia two centuries on. The Plakkaat van Verlatinghe, usually translated as 'Act of Abjuration', announced the independence of the Low Countries from Philip II of Spain, purporting instead to transfer the 'government and sovereignty' of those lands to 'the illustrious Prince and Duke of Anjou, upon certain conditions stipulated with his highness', 'by common consent of their members'.[61]

There are some intriguing parallels between the Plakkaat and the Declaration of Arbroath, and one passage in particular stands out. The Plakkaat declares the rights of people to throw off the rule of a tyrannical monarch with the phrase:

> This is the only method left for subjects whose humble petitions and remonstrances could never soften their prince or dissuade him from his tyrannical proceedings; and this is what the law of nature dictates for the defense of liberty, which we ought to transmit to posterity, even at the hazard of our lives.

The statement that the law of nature demands the defence of liberty, even at great personal risk, certainly resonates with the feeling that inspired the Scottish barons to declare their cause the defence of 'freedom alone, which no honest man gives up but with life itself'.[62] Here, however, the similarities end. While the Declaration was drafted in the aftermath of conflict, with the Scots seeking a moral buttress to their de facto independence, the drafters of the Plakkaat were in the midst of what was, in effect, a civil war. While the Declaration proclaims Robert I's divine right to rule Scotland, albeit with limits, the Plakkaat rejects the divine right to rule, seeking to vitiate Philip II's sovereignty over the Low Countries and to set a chosen ruler in his place. The Plakkaat is also a much more extensive and more fully argued text: in the original Dutch it runs to almost five thousand words, compared to the Latin text of the Declaration, which is just over one thousand.

i. Background to the Plakkaat van Verlatinghe

In the late sixteenth century, religious conflict was sweeping Europe. King Philip II of Spain ruled the Low Countries. Also called the Habsburg Netherlands or the Seventeen Provinces, the Low Countries were each under the feudal authority of Philip II, but were not regarded as a single political unit.[63] It was seven of those provinces which sought to remove Philip's sovereignty in 1581, pushed to take that (virtually unprecedented) step by concerns over high taxes, attempts to change the governmental structure of the provinces and, not least, the arrival in

[61] References to the English translation of the Act of Abjuration relate to: OJ Thatcher (ed), 'Act of Abjuration, 1581', *The Library of Original Sources*, vol V (Milwaukee, WI, University Research Extension Co, 1907).

[62] For an analysis of whether these similarities are the result of a direct influence of Arbroath on the drafters of the Plakkaat see below, nn 98–107 and accompanying text.

[63] R Lesaffer, 'A Short Legal History of the Netherlands' in S Taekema (ed), *Understanding Dutch Law* (Den Haag, Boom Juridische Uitgevers, 2004) 38.

the Netherlands of the Inquisition.[64] Between 1556 and 1568, amid increasing political and interreligious tensions, petitions and contestation by the nobility in the Low Countries were answered with repression, which in turn sparked armed resistance. An important inflection point was reached in 1565. Coinciding with the start of the Little Ice Age in Europe,[65] the winter of 1564–65 was exceptionally harsh in the Low Countries, and the harvest of 1565 failed.[66] As food prices rocketed, bread riots began to break out. As dissatisfaction grew, it also spread to other issues: religious freedom became an increasing point of contention, especially as French Calvinists sought refuge in the Low Countries following the 1562 massacre of Calvinists at Vassy,[67] and the religious conflict which followed.[68] Fearing a spiral of violence, two of the leading statesmen of the Low Countries – Lamoral, Count of Egmont (himself a devout catholic) and William of Nassau, Prince of Orange (also known as William the Silent) – argued strongly that greater tolerance of Protestantism was necessary.[69] In 1564, Egmont travelled to Spain to petition the King, and started his return to the Low Countries convinced that the King has been persuaded to relax the heresy laws.[70]

He was mistaken: Philip II had no intention of loosening his heresy laws, and the leaders of the Low Countries were forced to consider their next moves. In 1565, the nobles took a more muscular step, presenting to Margaret of Parma – Philip's half-sister and regent in the Low Countries – a petition demanding an end to the religious inquisition, supported by a sworn statement of their mutual (including military) support.[71] Although still understated and short of outright rebellion, the threat was clear, and Margaret seemed ready to seek a compromise. Events took over, however: in 1566 Calvinists, dissatisfied with their exclusion from churches,

[64] It was often inaccurately stated (including contemporaneously) that this was an importation into the Low Countries of the Spanish Inquisition. In fact, the Low Countries suffered under an inquisition all their own, although certainly one that enjoyed the support and encouragement of the King of Spain. This fact is probably where the confusion originates, as Gielis and Soen observe, although it seems likely that the distinction was also deliberately blurred by Lutheran propagandists: G Gielis and V Soen, 'The Inquisitorial Office in the Sixteenth-Century Habsburg Low Countries: A Dynamic Perspective' (2015) 66 *Journal of Ecclesiastical History* 47, 49; and further A Duke, 'A Legend in the Making: News of the "Spanish Inquisition" in the Low Countries in German Evangelical Pamphlets, 1546–1550' (1997) 77 *Nederlands Archief voor Kerkgeschiedenis/Dutch Review of Church History* 125.

[65] M Mann, 'Little Ice Age' in T Munn, MC MacCracken and JS Perry (eds), *Encyclopedia of Global Environmental Change*, vol 1 (Chichester, Wiley, 2002).

[66] P Limm, *The Dutch Revolt 1559–1648* (London, Routledge, 2014) 20.

[67] S Carroll, *Martyrs and Murderers: The Guise Family and the Making of Europe* (Oxford, Oxford University Press, 2011) 16–18; S Carroll, 'The Rights of Violence' (2012) 214 *Past & Present* 127, 133–35.

[68] Carroll, 'Rights of Violence' (n 67) 138–58; MP Holt, *The French Wars of Religion, 1562–1629* (Cambridge, Cambridge University Press, 1995) 49–52.

[69] As van Nierop observes, in this they were in agreement with much of the political class, notwithstanding that most of its members were – like Egmont – themselves committed Catholics: H van Nierop, '*Alva's Throne* – Making Sense of the Revolt in the Netherlands' in G Darby (ed), *The Origins and Development of the Dutch Revolt* (London, Routledge, 2001) 36.

[70] Limm, *Dutch Revolt* (n 66) 20.

[71] HH Rowen, 'The Dutch Revolt: What Kind of Revolution?' (1990) 43 *Renaissance Quarterly* 570, 572–73.

launched the *Beeldenstorm* (the Iconoclasm), storming through churches and destroying statuary, paintings, stained-glass, and other ornamentation.[72] Beginning in the south-west of the Low Countries, within a month it had spread over much of the territory.[73] Philip's patience broke: he was not prepared to leave it to Margaret or the local nobility to deal with the religious and political unrest any longer. Instead, he would stamp his authority onto the Low Countries.[74]

The wielder of that boot was to be the Duke of Alba. Fernando Álvarez de Toledo, or the Iron Duke as he came to be known in the Low Countries, was a trusted advisor and close councillor to the King, and a brilliant military leader – remembered as one of the greatest military minds of history.[75] He was also an absolutist: both in his loyalty to his King and his zeal for the Catholic faith. He resolved to bring the Low Countries to heel swiftly, even if that meant doing it brutally.[76] He brought with him an army of well-trained troops and set about meting out punishment for questioning the King and his faith. Thousands were hanged or drowned by Alba's Council of Troubles – or 'Council of Blood', as it was known.[77] Any disloyalty, small or large, was punishable by death: Egmont's temerity in petitioning the King to show tolerance was sufficient to see him executed, and William of Orange was forced to flee the country.[78] Watching from abroad, William was horrified by the brutality being inflicted on the Low Countries, and his dissatisfaction hardened to rebellion. Twice in 1568 William rallied troops in Germany and marched on the Low Countries, hoping to provoke a general uprising and overthrow Alba's governorship, but the country was gripped by a terror of Alba, and William was twice forced to retreat.[79]

William in this period started issuing letters of marque in his capacity as the Prince of Orange, creating a force of privateers operating in the waters to the north of the Low Countries. That proved decisive: with Alba's forces concentrated in the south to repel William's invasions, the *Watergeuzen* (Sea Beggars) in 1572 attacked Brielle and succeeded in seizing control of the town.[80] Encouraged by their victory, and with some scattered support in the local populations,[81] they succeeded in taking further towns along the northern coast, with the unforeseen effect that, when a further attempted invasion by William went awry later that year, William fled north only to find that a small territory was now held by friendly forces.[82]

[72] Rowen, 'Dutch Revolt' (n 71) 573.
[73] P Arnade, *Beggars, Iconoclasts, and Civic Patriots: The Political Culture of the Dutch Revolt* (Ithaca, NY, Cornell University Press, 2008) 90–91.
[74] Rowen, 'Dutch Revolt' (n 71) 574.
[75] J Belda Plans, *Grandes Personajes del Siglo de Oro Español* (Madrid, Ediciones Palabra, 2013) 20ff.
[76] Lesaffer, 'Legal History of the Netherlands' (n 63) 40–41.
[77] Rowen, 'Dutch Revolt' (n 71) 575.
[78] Rowen, 'Dutch Revolt' (n 71) 575.
[79] JC Kennedy, *A Concise History of the Netherlands* (Cambridge, Cambridge University Press, 2017) 124; Rowen, 'Dutch Revolt' (n 71) 575–76.
[80] Rowen, 'Dutch Revolt' (n 71) 576.
[81] HG Koenigsberger, *Monarchies, States Generals and Parliaments: The Netherlands in the Fifteenth and Sixteenth Centuries* (Cambridge, Cambridge University Press, 2001) 241.
[82] Kennedy, *History of the Netherlands* (n 79) 126; Rowen, 'Dutch Revolt' (n 71) 576.

William's presence in the north provided a rallying point: the scattered support for the rebellion of the *Watergeuzen* coalesced around his leadership, and William was named *Stadtholder* (effectively a regent) of Holland and Zeeland. Now with a territorial and economic base, and supported by the funds of these wealthy trading provinces,[83] William succeeded in halting Alba's march to retake the territory. In 1573, embarrassed by his failure, Alba returned to Spain.

Alba was replaced as leader of the Spanish forces and head of the civil government by Luis de Requesens y Zúñiga. Another talented military leader, Requesens was sent with permission to attempt a more conciliatory approach.[84] He pursued a dual strategy, pressing a military strategy but halting Alba's campaign of executions and making diplomatic overtures to the local Catholic nobility. It might have succeeded: By 1576 Requesens's troops were making substantial inroads into Zeeland, but a shortage of funds halted the military advance.[85] Having gone many months without pay, Requesens's army mutinied, and the setback was compounded when Requesens died suddenly in Brussels aged forty-seven. Lacking both military force and civil leadership, Spanish power in the Low Countries was left devoid of authority, a void that was filled – to some extent – by William of Orange.[86] In November 1576, the provinces of the Low Countries agreed to the Pacification of Ghent, an agreement between the rebellious provinces of the north and the loyalist south jointly to combat the mutineer Spanish army, which was then plundering its way through the territory. The fiction was maintained that the conflict with Spain was the fault of the Spanish provincial authorities in the Low Countries and not the King himself, and the Pacification declared that the authority of Philip II would be restored, once the marauding Spaniards had been driven out.[87]

The Pacification was never fully implemented: in response to an attempt by Spain to roll back the political authority of the provinces, and fearful of a further attempt by Catholic Spain to suppress Protestantism in the Calvinist north, Holland and Zeeland refused to surrender the fortresses they had occupied to Spanish authority.[88] The disintegration of the Pacification created a decisive split, one which laid the foundations for the separate states of Belgium and the Netherlands that were to follow. Suspicious of the Calvinist north and fearful of the consequences of another revolt, the French-speaking, Catholic southern provinces formed the Union of Arras, an alliance under the Spanish crown.[89] In response, in 1579 the northern provinces agreed their own defensive alliance: the Union of Utrecht.[90] By the end of 1580, most of the northern provinces had joined the Utrecht Union, as well as a number of cities and smaller counties in the central

[83] Rowen, 'Dutch Revolt' (n 71) 577.
[84] ibid 577; Koenigsberger, *Monarchies & States Generals* (n 81) 237.
[85] Rowen, 'Dutch Revolt' (n 71) 577–78.
[86] ibid 579.
[87] Koenigsberger, *Monarchies & States Generals* (n 81) 272.
[88] Rowen, 'Dutch Revolt' (n 71) 580–581.
[89] van Nierop, '*Alva's Throne*' (n 69) 39; Rowen, 'Dutch Revolt' (n 71) 581.
[90] Koenigsberger, *Monarchies & States Generals* (n 81) 292–93.

belt of the Low Countries. The Utrecht Union, too, initially conceived of itself as an aligned block within the Spanish Netherlands, and not as a declaration of independence.[91] The formation of this new powerbase in the predominantly Calvinist north of the Low Countries, however – notwithstanding that the Union explicitly recognised the rights of both Catholics and Protestants to practice freely within its boundaries – was seen in Spain as a challenge to the King's authority, and relations continued to deteriorate. 1581 brought a decisive break: the provinces adopted the Plakkaat van Verlatinghe, declaring their intention of throwing off the sovereignty of Spain entirely.

ii. The Text of the Plakkaat van Verlatinghe

The Plakkaat is a substantial and closely argued text, but two passages deserve particular attention.

The Plakkaat begins with a powerful declaration of the responsibilities of the prince to his people – the text's major premise, as Lucas has it.[92] Significantly, the text denies the idea that kings rule over their populations, accountable only to God for their conduct. Although it does not challenge the idea that kingship is created by God, it nevertheless drove an important wedge into the divine right of kings as it was then understood, stating that:

> As it is apparent to all that a prince is constituted by God to be a ruler of a people, to defend them from oppression and violence as a shepherd his sheep; … God did not create the people slaves to their prince, … but rather the prince for the sake of his subjects (without which he could be no prince).

It follows, in view of the drafters, that:

> [W]hen he does not behave thus, but, on the contrary, oppresses them, seeking opportunities to infringe their ancient customs and privileges, exacting from them slavish compliance, then he is no longer a prince, but a tyrant, and the subjects are to consider him in no other view. And particularly when this is done deliberately, unauthorized by the states, they may not only disallow his authority, but legally proceed to the choice of another prince for their defense. This is the only method left for subjects whose humble petitions and remonstrances could never soften their prince or dissuade him from his tyrannical proceedings; and this is what the law of nature dictates for the defense of liberty, which we ought to transmit to posterity, even at the hazard of our lives.

Stated another way: the prince is not unconstrained in his rule over the people, but rather has limits on his power. When he commits abuses against the population at a certain threshold, he crosses from legitimate rule into tyranny. Tyranny, if it continues and cannot be remedied by less drastic means, may be resisted and,

[91] Rowen, 'Dutch Revolt' (n 71) 582.
[92] Lucas, 'Rhetorical Ancestry' (n 60) 163.

in extremis, gives the population the legitimate right to throw off the authority of the prince entirely.

Although certainly no such vocabulary would – or could – have been employed at the time,[93] it is no great stretch to characterise the Plakkaat as expressing the same logic as *remedial self-determination*, as it was described above.[94] In terms that are a closer (though still not exact) chronological match, it expresses a *right of rebellion*: it expresses the notion of limited government, and the conviction that government becomes illegitimate when it breaches those limits. Once those limits have been crossed, the people are entitled to *decide* to remove it, and to *decide* on a new ruler. Importantly, the prince does not cease to be the prince on account of his tyranny by some automatic operation of the universe; rather, the tyrant ceases to be the prince when the people choose to remove him.

Importantly, too, the Plakkaat is emphatically not an espousal of what would later come to be known as popular sovereignty. Although the provinces which signed the Plakkaat were ultimately to constitute themselves as a republic – the Republic of the Seven United Netherlands – in 1588, there was certainly no republicanism evident in the Plakkaat itself. On the contrary, the Plakkaat declared the right of a people to 'cho[ose] another prince for their defense' and, indeed, it declares that 'the United Provinces have, by common consent of their members, submitted to the government and sovereignty of the illustrious Prince and Duke of Anjou'.[95] In other words, although it stands firmly for the proposition that the prince's power is limited in important ways, it can also be interpreted as standing for – or at least not challenging – the proposition that the people must be governed by a blood member of one of Europe's great monarchic dynasties.

Having established its major premise – in syllogistic terms – the Plakkaat turns its attention to the minor premise: that Philip II of Spain had, indeed, acted towards the Low Countries as a tyrant and not a prince. By far the largest part of the Plakkaat is dedicated to this task, and what follows is a damning inditement of Philip's conduct. He had 'tyrannize[d] at pleasure' and 'sought by all means possible to reduce this country (stripping them [the provinces] of their ancient privileges) to slavery'. He 'would have introduced the Spanish inquisition' and sought 'not only … to tyrannize over their persons and states, but also over their consciences, for which they believed themselves accountable to God only'. He 'put to death … ambassadors, and confiscated their estates, contrary to the law of nations', and 'sent the Duke of Alva with a powerful army to oppress this land, who for his inhuman

[93] See below, s II.

[94] See ch 1, s III.C.

[95] Anjou's rule in the seven provinces was to be both disastrous and abortive. He ruled only until 1583 – and then only in name. Attempts to convince Elizabeth I of England to assume sovereignty over the Netherlands failed, and William of Orange himself was then approached to become Count of Holland and assume the lordship, but fell victim to the dagger of a Spanish assassin in 1584, before he assumed the role. A short period under a governor-general appointed by the English queen was equally unsuccessful, and in 1588 the provinces became a republic.

cruelties is looked upon as one of its greatest enemies'. The Plakkaat contains much more along the same lines, and concludes:

> So, having no hope of reconciliation, and finding no other remedy, we have, agreeable to the law of nature in our own defense, and for maintaining the rights, privileges, and liberties of our countrymen, wives, and children, and latest posterity from being enslaved by the Spaniards, been constrained to renounce allegiance to the King of Spain, and pursue such methods as appear to us most likely to secure our ancient liberties and privileges. Know all men by these presents that being reduced to the last extremity, as above mentioned, we have unanimously and deliberately declared, and do by these presents declare, that the King of Spain has forfeited, ipso jure, all hereditary right to the sovereignty of those countries, and are determined from henceforward not to acknowledge his sovereignty or jurisdiction, nor any act of his relating to the domains of the Low Countries, nor make use of his name as prince, nor suffer others to do it.

Rarely, before or since, has the syllogistic form been so effectively wielded.[96] The Plakkaat's third section then declares the transfer of sovereignty to the Duke of Anjou, and the remainder of the text deals with practical details: forbidding the use of the Spanish royal seal, ordering that no coinage be minted bearing the arms of the King of Spain, and discharging the holders of public offices in the provinces of their oaths to the Spanish crown.

The Plakkaat did not produce a clean break from Spain. Certainly, the Spanish crown has not ruled in the Seven Provinces since the proclamation of Dutch independence in this period, but the Dutch revolution sparked one of the longest conflicts in European history, often called the eighty years' war. That conflict – and the thirty years' war with which it shared much – were to come to an end with the Peace of Westphalia in 1648, the event often credited with creating both the modern concept of the sovereign state, and with the birth of the law of nations.[97]

C. From Prehistory to History

Certainly, the Declaration of Arbroath and Plakkaat van Verlatinghe were, and remain, significant documents in their historical contexts. They are stirring, powerful, epoch-making declarations that continue to hold treasured places in the national identity of, respectively, Scotland and the Netherlands. It may even be possible to argue that they were globally significant documents, though that is

[96] Although equalled, perhaps, in the 1776 Declaration, and here some have drawn a parallel and suggested that 1776 may have been influenced by 1581.

[97] For all that it was very significant, there are good reasons for doubting both of these orthodoxies concerning Westphalia: P Piirimäe, 'The Westphalian Myth and the Idea of External Sovereignty' in H Kalmo and Q Skinner (eds), *Sovereignty in Fragments: The Past, Present and Future of a Contested Concept* (Cambridge, Cambridge University Press, 2010); and further S Beaulac, 'The Westphalian Legal Orthodoxy – Myth or Reality' (2000) 2 *Journal of the History of International Law/Revue d'histoire du droit international* 148.

perhaps an argument easier to make in the case of the Plakkaat – which led to the Republic of the Seven Provinces and, in due course, the Verenigde Oostindische Compagnie (Dutch East India Company) and the Dutch colonial empire – than the Declaration of Arbroath. It is less clear, however, whether they should be considered of any direct consequence – rather than purely historical interest – for the development of self-determination. Can a link be drawn between these two documents, or even from this prehistory to 1776 and 1789, the more familiar starting points of the self-determination story?

It has long been assumed that the Declaration of Arbroath vanished from view after its conclusion in 1320, until it was transcribed and published (for what was long assumed to be the first time) in 1680.[98] According to this history, the Declaration could have had no influence on the Plakkaat van Verlatinghe, the conclusion of which in 1581 would have pre-dated the Declaration's publication by a century. It is still overwhelmingly likely that the Declaration was not known to the drafters of the Plakkaat, but more recent archival work has recalled that there indeed were copies (or part copies) of the Declaration in circulation in medieval Scotland: the Community of the Realm of Scotland research project has identified twenty-six manuscript copies of the Declaration which were in circulation around the turn of the sixteenth century.[99] Two of these certainly made it to mainland Europe in this period: the Herzog August Bibliothek in Wolfenbüttel holds a copy of the *Copiale prioratus Sancti Andreae*, produced in St Andrews between 1425 and 1445, which includes a transcription of the Declaration. The *Copiale* was acquired in 1553 by Marcus Wagner, who travelled in Scotland as a research assistant to Matthias Flacius Illyricus.[100] In turn, the library of Illyricus was acquired by Duke Heinrich Julius von Braunschweig-Lüneburg for the Bibliotheca Julia in Wolfenbüttel in 1587.[101]

Perhaps more significantly, the KBR (formerly: Koninklijke Bibliotheek) in Brussels, holds a copy of the *Scotichronicon*, a history of the Scottish people in legend-form compiled in the fifteenth century by Walter Bower, building on the earlier *Chronica Gentis Scotorum* by John of Fordun. The *Scotichronicon* recounts the Declaration as well as the period which produced it, and remains perhaps the most important medieval account of Scottish history. The KBR dates its version

[98] RA Mason, 'The Declaration of Arbroath in Print, 1680–1705' (2021) 72 *Innes Review* 158, 158–59. Archival work by Murray Tod (discussed below) has, too, demonstrated that the Declaration was read in the late-medieval period: MAL Tod, 'The Narrative of the Scottish Nation and its Late-Medieval Readers: Non-textual Reader Scribal Activity in the MSS of Fordun, Bower and Their Derivatives' (PhD thesis, University of Glasgow, 2005) 205–09, www.theses.gla.ac.uk/1396/1/2005todphd.pdf.

[99] Mason, 'Arbroath in Print' (n 98) 158–59; JR Davies and D Broun, 'The Manuscripts of the Declaration' in D Broun et al (eds), *The Dynamic Edition of the Declaration of Arbroath*, www.cotr.ac.uk/guidelines/dynamic-declaration-arbroath.

[100] M Hartmann, *Humanismus und Kirchenkritik: Matthias Flacius Illyricus als Erforscher des Mittelalters* (Stuttgart, Thorbecke, 2001) 64, 110; Davies and Broun, 'Manuscripts' (n 99).

[101] 'Beschreibung von Cod Guelf 411 Helmst' (*Herzog August Bibliothek Wolfenbüttel – Manuscript Database*) www.diglib.hab.de/?db=mss&list=ms&id=411-helmst&catalog=Lesser&lang=en.

of the text to *c*.1510 and gives its provenance as having been acquired by David Dowthiltz in *c*.1565.[102] Coincidentally or otherwise, it is in this manuscript that the Declaration seems to have received the most attention: in archival work examining the reception of Fordun/Bower and their derivatives in the late-medieval period, Murray Tod identifies twenty-five manuscript copies containing late-medieval marginalia, in which thirty-four readers could be individuated.[103] Of those, Tod finds annotations of the Declaration in three manuscripts, by six individual readers. Three of those readers left marginalia on the copy now held by the KBR.[104] Tod does not (seek to) identify these readers, however, and it is not clear where the manuscript was located when these readers engaged with the text.[105] Neither from Tod's archival work nor the provenance note of the KBR is it clear when the manuscript arrived in Belgium, or whether it was available for consultation during the drafting of the Plakkaat van Verlatinghe. Still less can we assume that any of the readers whom Tod identifies as engaging with the section containing the Declaration post-dated the manuscript's departure from the British Isles. Thus, although it seems plausible that a version of the Declaration was present in the Low Countries in the decade before the Plakkaat was drafted, nevertheless any suggestion that it was known to the drafters would be conjecture.

While it is likely that the Declaration of Arbroath was not known to the drafters of the Plakkaat van Verlatinghe, there are certain similarities in the structure of the appeal both documents make, and also to some of the phraseology each employs. In particular, the Plakkaat's statement that 'the law of nature dictates … the defense of liberty, which we ought to transmit to posterity, even at the hazard of our lives' strongly recalls the Declaration's best-known phrase, that Scotland seeks 'freedom alone, which no honest man gives up but with life itself'. The similarity seems to invite comparison, but given that no direct link between the Declaration and the Plakkaat's drafters has been established, it is more likely that the two documents drew – at least in part – from the same sources: it is clear that classical (particularly Roman) literature was an influence on both sets of drafters. While the suggestion that the Scottish barons drew on Tacitus seems unlikely,[106]

[102] '[Scotichronicon (f. 2r–231v)] = [Chronica gentis Scotorum, cum continuatione]: [ms 7396 (Van den Gheyn 4628)] [Iohannes de Fordun]' (*KBR*) www.opac.kbr.be/LIBRARY/doc/SYRACUSE/17038463.

[103] Tod, 'Non-textual Reader Scribal Activity' (n 98) 13–50.

[104] ibid 39–41, 209–11.

[105] Although note that Tod characterises these marginal notes as the 'activity of late-medieval readers, both Scottish and English'. It is not clear on what basis Tod identifies Scottish and English readers: ibid 213.

[106] This suggestion has been made, for example, by Riach, and Cowan notes similarities between Tacitus and the Bannockburn-inspired Scottish anthem, 'Scots Wha Hae'. However, as Tacitus's manuscripts were not rediscovered until the Renaissance (the *Annales* in 1508, and the minor works in 1425), there could have been no direct influence: GB Conte, *Latin Literature: A History*, ed DP Fowler and GW Most, tr JB Solodow (Baltimore, MD, Johns Hopkins University Press, 1994) 543; and compare Cowan, '*For Freedom Alone*' (n 48) 38–39; A Riach, 'Scotland Emergent IV: From Tales of Merlin and Arthur to the Agricola of Tacitus' (*Glasgow University ePrints*, 1 May 2018) www.eprints.gla.ac.uk/161614/.

Sallust may well have been read and invoked in Arbroath.[107] Philip has argued influentially that the famous passage in the Declaration draws on Sallust's *Bellum Catiline*,[108] a text which was 'commonly found in mediaeval monastic libraries'[109] and the popularity of which is unlikely to have waned by the end of the sixteenth century.[110] Whether or not Sallust's *Catiline* was a direct influence on the drafters of the Plakkaat, it seems clear that just seven years later Sallust was an influence on the Republic of the Seven United Netherlands that was its direct descendent. Norris et al have identified that the motto of the Republic, *Concordia res parvae crescent* (later rendered as: *Eendracht maakt macht*/Unity makes strength) is a direct quotation of Sallust's *Bellum Jugurthinum*.[111] The suggestion that both texts drew inspiration from *Catiline* is, thus, likely a better explanation for any similarities than a direct link between the two.

Also of interest is the question of whether either document inspired the next generation of declarations, in particular the American Declaration of Independence of 1776, where most authors begin their histories of self-determination. Certainly, some have claimed a link between the Declaration of Arbroath and the 1776 Declaration.[112] Supporting a resolution submitted by Senator Trent Lott of Mississippi in 1997 which asked the Senate to designate 6 April each year 'National Tartan Day', the US Senate declared that 'April 6 has a special significance for all Americans … because the Declaration of Arbroath, the Scottish Declaration of Independence, was signed on April 6, 1320 and the American Declaration of Independence was modeled on that inspirational document'.[113] In his remarks, Trent Lott further claimed that the drafters of the 1776 Declaration 'used the Arbroath Declaration as the template for their own thoughts'. This was, he said,

[107] See, most influentially, JR Philip, 'Sallust and the Declaration of Arbroath' (1947) 26 *Scottish Historical Review* 75, *passim*. Philip's statement that '[i]t has been observed more than once that these words ['It is in truth not for glory …'] from the [Declaration of Arbroath] are too good not to be a quotation' perhaps neglects the extent to which exemplum and analogy were an essential aspect of appeals to authority in pre-Renaissance argumentation: F Iurlaro, 'From Exemplary Individuals to Private Persons with Rights – International Law 1500–1647: Vitoria, Gentili, and Grotius' in T Sparks and A Peters (eds), *The Individual in International Law – History and Theory* (forthcoming).

[108] Philip provides a side-by-side comparison of the Latin texts, and the similarity is certainly striking: Philip, 'Sallust' (n 107) 75.

[109] ibid 76–77.

[110] Patricia Osmond identifies a debate in the Low Countries and Germany at the end of the sixteenth century, concerning whether Sallust or Tacitus should be regarded as the more important classical historian (in both cases, the other being placed second): PJ Osmond, '"*Princeps Historiae Romanae*": Sallust in Renaissance Political Thought' (1995) 40 *Memoirs of the American Academy in Rome* 101, 101–02. Although, as Ophelia Norris et al note, questions of Sallust's influence on the Low Countries have thus far received less attention than vis-a-vis other countries, 'there are indications of it to have been of a similar magnitude': O Norris et al, '"Bellum Catilinae" by Sallust' (Utrecht University Library: Special Collections, July 2020) www.uu.nl/en/special-collections/collections/manuscripts/other-medieval/bellum-catilinae-by-sallust.

[111] Norris et al, '"Bellum Catilinae" by Sallust' (n 110).

[112] Armitage, 'Contagion of Sovereignty' (n 60) 5.

[113] US Congressional Record, vol 143, no 158 (Senate – 10 November 1997) S12478–S12479, S12478.

'natural' because 'almost half' of the men who signed the Declaration 'were of Scottish ancestry', and he claimed that one of the ancestors of Thomas Jefferson – the primary drafter of the 1776 text – 'had signed the Arbroath Declaration, all those centuries before'.[114]

As far as I have been able to ascertain, Lott's comments were mistaken in almost every detail. The claim about Jefferson's ancestry appears to be based on the coincidence that Jefferson's mother was born Jane Randolph, while Thomas Randolph, Earl of Moray, was one of the signatories at Arbroath. Although a Scottish ancestry for Jefferson seems to be established through his maternal grandmother,[115] it seems more credible to trace Jane Randolph's paternal ancestry to the Randolphs of Sussex, England, and before that to the Fitzrandolph family, the hereditary lords of Spennithorne in North Yorkshire. Thomas Jefferson himself appears to have been largely ignorant of his ancestry, although family tradition seems to have placed more emphasis on a Welsh heritage than a Scottish one.[116] Summing up, David Armitage is scathing of claims such as Lott's that 1776 was based on Arbroath, saying that 'the lazy assumption that one depended on the other … cannot be too often debunked'.[117]

Nevertheless, Armitage notes that Arbroath may – among many other sources and influences – have had some presence in 1776. He refers to 'the only [book] we can prove to have been in the hands of the drafters of the Declaration', Emer de Vattel's *Droit de gens*.[118] Benjamin Franklin reported seeking out the 1773 edition of *Droit de gens*, printed in Amsterdam and edited by Dumas – that edition had been, Franklin said, 'continually in the hands of the members of our congress, now sitting'.[119] Dumas had (after Vattel's death) inserted a footnote into that edition which included a long quotation from the 1320 Declaration, including the famous phrase, 'for freedom alone, which no honest man gives up but with life itself'.[120] Nevertheless, just as, '[a]bsence of evidence … is not evidence of absence', Armitage

[114] ibid S12478.

[115] Although the line appears to have departed Scotland for England long before Arbroath: the line can be traced to Saier de Quincy, born in Scotland but one of the leaders of the English Baronial rebellion of 1215 which led to the Magna Carta, of which de Quincy was one of the sureties: LS Kaplan, *Thomas Jefferson: Westward the Course of Empire* (Plymouth, Rowman & Littlefield Publishers, 1998) 12.

[116] Kaplan, *Thomas Jefferson* (n 115) 11–12.

[117] D Armitage, '1320, 1776, and All That: A Tale of Two "Declarations"' (Forthcoming) 101 *Scottish Historical Review* 2 (footnotes omitted).

[118] ibid 14. Although Vattel may have been the only authority whose presence in the negotiations can be proven, there is ample evidence that the drafters – and others around them – discussed and consulted a very wide range of sources in the process of what was a rich and well-theorised debate in the decade preceding the Second Continental Congress in 1776: see M Somos, *American States of Nature: The Origin of Independence, 1761–1775* (New York, Oxford University Press, 2019) *passim*, eg 52–75.

[119] Armitage, 'Tale of Two "Declarations"' (n 117) 15; referencing Benjamin Franklin to CGF Dumas (9 December 1775), in *The Papers of Benjamin Franklin*, gen eds Leonard W. Labaree et al (New Haven, 1959) xxii. 287.

[120] Armitage, 'Tale of Two "Declarations"' (n 117) 23–24; referencing Emer de Vattel, *Le Droit des gens*, ed CGF Dumas (Amsterdam, 1775) i.31.

says, so 'the presence of evidence is not evidence of the presence of Arbroath in the Declaration'.[121] Neal Ascherson concludes that 'there is not a scrap of evidence that any of the Americans gathered on that "steamy" Pennsylvania day gave even a moment's thought to the Declaration of Arbroath'.[122]

Although the same caveats apply – as Armitage argues, '[t]here could be no single model for such a complex text' as the 1776 Declaration[123] – the evidence is better for a Dutch heritage. Stephen Lucas has argued influentially that:

> The persuasive design of the [1776] Declaration was neither accidental nor original. Indeed, there was a remarkably precise template for it, a template of which Jefferson and other members of the Committee of Five were surely aware. That template can be found in the Plakkaat van Verlatinge.[124]

Lucas refers in particular to the syllogistic form of both documents, as well as to an 'inescapable affinity' between them: 'Both affirm the existence of a compact in which a ruler can lawfully demand obedience only as long as he protects the rights and privileges of his subjects.'[125] Lucas catalogues a number of other similarities and overlaps between the two documents, and concludes that the resemblance is 'so striking that we must give serious consideration to the possibility that [it was considered] as a paradigm for the argumentative structure' of the 1776 Declaration.[126] Nevertheless, he concedes that drawing any such parallel will remain speculation: 'the documentary record regarding the drafting of the Declaration is too scanty' to settle the question.[127] Armitage notes that the evidence here, too, is 'at best only circumstantial',[128] but recounts that in eighteenth-century Netherlands a link was drawn, albeit that the comparison was not seen as flattering: William V of Orange, the descendent of that William of Orange who had been the moving force in the events of 1581, called the Declaration a 'parody of the proclamation issued by our forefathers against king Philip II'.[129]

[121] Armitage, 'Tale of Two "Declarations"' (n 117) 25.

[122] N Ascherson, *Stone Voices: The Search for Scotland* (London, Granta Books, 2014) 265; and further E Hague, 'National Tartan Day: Rewriting History in the United States' (2014) 38 *Scottish Affairs* 94.

[123] Armitage, 'Tale of Two "Declarations"' (n 117) 21. Recent archival work by Mark Somos has revealed just how wide the range of sources accessed by the drafters was. He has demonstrated that a 'sophisticated state of nature argument against British encroachments existed in the colonies before Blackstone's 1765 *Commentaries*, and blended Grotius, Hobbes, Locke, Montesquieu, Vattel, Rousseau, and other authorities': Somos, *American State of Nature* (n 118) 75. More significantly, the discourse did not stop at the boundaries of this multitude of authorities, but developed and went beyond them. As Somos identifies, a specifically American state of nature theory emerged during this period: 'It combined already existing semantic ranges, excluded others in clear and specific contestation over the term's use, and it gained specifically American connotations while it was used to justify independence.' See Somos, *American State of Nature* (n 118) 10 and *passim*; and further M Somos, 'Boston in the State of Nature, 1761–1765' (2018) 3 *Jus Gentium* 63.

[124] Lucas, 'Rhetorical Ancestry' (n 60) 161.

[125] ibid 162.

[126] ibid 165.

[127] ibid 165.

[128] Armitage, 'Contagion of Sovereignty' (n 60) 5.

[129] ibid 5, citing William V, Prince of Orange, to H Fagel, 20 August 1776, in FJL Krämer (ed), *Archives ou correspondance inédite de la maison d'Orange-Nassau*, 5th series, 3 vols (Leiden, 1910–15) vol I,

Ultimately, and whether or not the declarations of 1320, 1581 and the eighteenth century can be directly linked in a genealogical sense, it may be that establishing a twelfth- or sixteenth-century heredity for self-determination is less important than simply noting how deeply rooted the idea – and its close counterparts – are in human history. Even if understood purely as separate and entirely novel geneses, that some variant on a self-determination idea shaped events in 1320 just as it continues to do in the present day is in itself extraordinary. In fact, perhaps we should see it as yet more significant if these three declarations did *not* in fact provide any inspiration for each other – how many other concepts can be said to have been generated independently on so many different occasions?[130] And yet, as I will argue, precedential reasoning was to become a core feature of self-determination. While a link between 1776 and the declarations which preceded it is ambiguous – if it exists at all – there is a clear influence from the American Declaration in 1776 and the French Declaration in 1789 to those that followed them.

II. Self-Determination Takes Centre Stage: 1776 and 1789

As noted above, most histories of self-determination begin with either 1776 or 1789.[131] To do so is both correct and incorrect. It is, to begin with, equally valid – or invalid – to describe the declarations of 1776 and 1789 as acts of self-determination. Certainly, neither used that term, which would not have borne its modern significance in the mind of their drafters. As noted above,[132] in the eighteenth century the term had not yet acquired its political meaning, and was largely confined to theology. In the same period, it was making the transition to moral philosophy – the first use of the term *Selbstbestimmung* in moral philosophy of which I am aware was in 1785, by Immanuel Kant in his *Grundlegung*

449, cited by JM Schulte Nordholt, *The Dutch Republic and American Independence*, tr HH Rowen (Chapel Hill, NC, 1982) 221.

[130] There are probably other instances. See, for example, Rodríguez-Santiago, who argues convincingly that a similar logic can be discerned in fourteenth-century debates concerning the colonisation of the Americas: Rodríguez-Santiago, 'Evolution of Self-Determination' (n 2) 202–04ff; and further Hannum, who begins with the collapse of the Ottoman and Austro-Hungarian empires: H Hannum, *Autonomy, Sovereignty and Self-Determination: The Accommodation of Conflicting Rights* (Philadelphia, University of Pennsylvania Press, 1990) 27.

[131] A Cobban, *National Self-Determination* (Oxford, Oxford University Press, 1944) 5; A Rigo Sureda, *The Evolution of the Right of Self-Determination: A Study of United Nations Practice* (Leiden, AW Sijthoff, 1973) 17; Cassese, *Self-Determination of Peoples* (n 1) 11; Raič, *Law of Self-Determination* (n 1) 172–73; but *contra* Rodríguez-Santiago, 'Evolution of Self-Determination' (n 2) 202–04; Hannum, *Autonomy* (n 130) 27.

[132] See ch 1, s II.B.

zur Metaphysik der Sitten.[133] It was not until much later, however – probably the start of the twentieth century – that the term was applied to political processes.[134] In that sense, any application of the term 'self-determination' to the declarations of 1776 and 1789 – or those that preceded or followed them until the start of the twentieth century – is inevitably anachronistic.

And yet, it is also true to say that 1776 and 1789 are vitally important for self-determination's story. If a genealogic line between 1776 and the declarations which preceded is elusive, the importance of 1776 and 1789 for the declarations which followed is a bright thread that can be followed with ease. The 1789 Declaration in 'France made [the nineteenth century's] revolutions and gave them their ideas', Hobsbawm declares.[135] And further: 1776 and 1789 gave the declarations that followed *authority*. They became totemic documents, precedents invoked directly or indirectly by almost every declaration of independence which has followed them as a source of legitimacy. Although perhaps not *the* beginning, 1776 and 1789 were certainly *a* beginning for self-determination's story.

A. The American Declaration of Independence 1776

The American Declaration of Independence was drafted by Thomas Jefferson, and was adopted in Congress by the (then) thirteen states of America on 4 July 1776.[136] In the Declaration, Jefferson derives the right of the people of America to throw off the sovereignty of the King of England from his statement, said to be 'one of the best-known sentences in the English language',[137] that:

> We hold these truths to be self-evident, that all men are created equal, that they are endowed by their Creator with certain unalienable Rights, that among these are Life, Liberty and the pursuit of Happiness.

As Lucas notes, the scope, and thus the true significance, of this statement is contested:

> It has been studied and restudied by historians, critics, philosophers, and political theorists – usually in an effort to determine what Jefferson and the Congress intended by

[133] I Kant, *Grundlegung zur Metaphysik der Sitten*, ed C Horn, C Mieth and N Scarano (Frankfurt am Main, Suhrkamp, 2007) 60.

[134] D Harper, '"Self-Determination" (n.)' (*Online Etymology Dictionary*, 2001–17) www.etymonline.com/word/self-determination; M Sterio, *The Right to Self-Determination under International Law: 'Selfistans,' Secession, and the Rule of the Great Powers* (London, Routledge, 2013) 1.

[135] EJ Hobsbawm, *The Age of Revolution: Europe 1789–1848* (London, Weidenfeld & Nicolson, 1962) 73.

[136] References to the text of the Declaration of Independence relate to: The Declaration of Independence: A Transcription, US National Archives & Records Administration, www.archives.gov/exhibits/charters/declaration_transcript.html.

[137] S Lucas, 'Justifying America: The Declaration of Independence as a Rhetorical Document' in T Benson (ed), *American Rhetoric: Context and Criticism* (Carbondale, IL, Southern Illinois University Press, 1989) 85.

> such phrases as 'created equal' and 'the pursuit of Happiness.' But there are no definitive answers – partly because Jefferson never explained what he meant, partly because the words of the Declaration did not mean the same thing to all members of Congress (or to all readers).[138]

The definitional uncertainty noted by Lucas also applies to much of the remainder of the text. While the declaration as a whole clearly represents a claim by the American People of a right to separate from Britain, the basis and ambit of the right are not self-evident. If, as some have suggested, the Declaration represents the first recognisable expression of a self-determination claim, it is not sufficient to identify it simply by *genus*; in order to understand the origin of the principle and the precedent set by the Declaration, it is necessary to understand the *source* of the claimed right, and thus to understand the legitimacy-claim made by its authors. In other words, it is necessary to examine the declaration and its language in more detail, to identify the *species* of self-determination it invokes.

The Declaration holds that, in order to protect the 'unalienable Rights' of man, 'Governments are instituted among Men, deriving their just powers from the consent of the governed.' Further:

> That whenever any Form of Government becomes destructive of these ends, it is the Right of the People to alter or to abolish it, and to institute new Government, laying its foundations on such principles and organizing its powers in such a form, as to them shall seem most likely to effect their Safety and Happiness.

Certain principles can be derived from these statements. To begin with, and whatever its influence may (or may not) have been, a parallel can be drawn with the Plakkaat. As the Plakkaat declared that a king lost his right to rule when he became a tyrant, Jefferson declares that government 'destructive' of the 'unalienable Rights' of man may be abolished. Here the parallel ends, however: in one respect the 1776 Declaration breaks decisively with the ideas expressed in 1581. While the Plakkaat argues that a king who acts as a tyrant has failed to act as a king (has 'unkinged himself' as Mayhew put it in 1648, albeit in another context[139]) and may therefore be removed without contravening the heavenly mandate of kingship generally, the 1776 Declaration derives the right to remove a government 'destructive of [its proper] ends' from the fact that governments 'deriv[e] their just powers from the consent of the governed'. Put another way: the Plakkaat bends, but does not break, the divine right of kings; the 1776 Declaration denies it entirely.[140]

In that sense, unlike Arbroath and the Plakkaat, the 1776 Declaration recognises what may loosely be described as popular sovereignty.[141] It is unclear why the 1776 drafters were able to make this leap while the drafters of the Plakkaat

[138] ibid 85.
[139] Mayhew, *Discourse Concerning Unlimited Submission* (n 55) 47.
[140] Armitage, contrasting 1776 with what came before, highlights this point by naming the Plakkaat – and Arbroath – declarations of *dependence*: Armitage, 'Contagion of Sovereignty' (n 60) 11, 19.
[141] Although note that this vocabulary, too, is an anachronism.

did not – and perhaps could not – but Mark Somos can help us to understand the building blocks which allowed the 1776 drafters to do so. Somos highlights the importance of the state of nature as a philosophical idea as an underpinning for the theories of government and sovereignty developed in the United States in the decade leading up to the Declaration, and which gave it shape. Although a distinct, American state of nature discourse emerged in the period, it drew heavily from thinkers such as Grotius, Hobbes, Locke, Montesquieu, Vattel and Rousseau.[142] State of nature theories certainly predated Grotius – medieval state of nature theories were expounded by Thomas Aquinas and William of Ockham, and in ancient Greek and Roman literature the device can be found in Plato, Cicero and others[143] – but it was in the early modern period and the Renaissance that the idea came to dominate political theory. For the drafters of the 1776 Declaration, these thinkers provided an important philosophical vocabulary and set of ideas which, recrafted through their distinct discourse, seemed to them to describe perfectly the situation in which they found themselves;[144] in a new land, creating a new society, in which proper governmental authority had been substituted for discretion.

Given that the 1776 Declaration lays emphasis on the 'consent of the governed' as the source from which the 'just powers' of the government derive, it might be expected that the withdrawal of consent would, in and of itself, be held up as sufficient to delegitimise the current governmental order and allow a new one to take its place. It seems a better interpretation of the text, however, not to cast self-determination as one of the 'unalienable' rights of man, but rather as a contingent, secondary right, which exists only as a result of governmental abuses – a government 'destructive' of its proper ends. Three factors suggest that conclusion.

First, it is indicated by the reliance on the state of nature. As Somos has shown, in the understanding of the drafters of the Declaration, the state of nature was more than a thought experiment that enabled them to puzzle out the rights and wrongs of political communities: it was a lived reality. The British government had, in their view, actually placed the colonies into a state of nature through its hostile actions, most particularly with the passage of the Stamp Act of 1765. The effect of the Stamp Act was that the courts in the colonies were unable to conduct business for extended periods, leading James Otis Jr – a lawyer identified by Somos as one of the most important thinkers of the period – to declare that 'when the King "shuts his Courts, he unkings himself in the most essential point"',[145] echoing, consciously or unconsciously, Mayhew's comments on Charles I fourteen years

[142] Grotius – the earliest of these – was born in Delft, the seat of the Prince of Orange and de facto capital of the (then) newly independent Seven Provinces in 1583, just seventeen months after the Plakkaat was adopted, and grew up in the country – and continent – which that document helped to create.

[143] Somos and Peters identify Hesiod, Plato, Aristotle, Cicero and Lucretius: M Somos and A Peters, 'Introduction' in M Somos and A Peters (eds), *The State of Nature: Histories of an Idea* (Leiden, Brill, 2022) 3.

[144] Somos, *American State of Nature* (n 118) 5–6.

[145] Somos, 'Boston in the State of Nature' (n 123) 107, citing James Otis Jr, *The Rights of the British Colonies Asserted and Proved* (1764).

previously.[146] John Adams would later argue explicitly that British actions had placed the colonies into a state of nature during this period.[147] In other words, the exceptional action of removing themselves from the British State was effected in a state of nature, in which British political authority was first vitiated by its own actions before a new polity could arise in its place.

A second indication is the syllogistic form of the Declaration itself. Simply put, that a syllogistic form was chosen would indicate that the major premise and the conclusion were understood as being logically connected. On that view, that the drafters chose to frame their right to secede as deriving from the fact that their 'Form of Government [has] become[] destructive of [its proper] ends', because they understood those two ideas as standing in a logical relation to one another. Lucas has, however, cast doubt on that conclusion. We should not, he argues, understand the Declaration as an exercise in pure logic; rather, by the standards of logical argument in the period, the Declaration would not have been understood as meeting the criteria of a logical syllogism:

> Its 'self-evident' truths are not self-evident in the rigorous technical sense …; it does not provide the definition to terms that [logicians] regard[] as a crucial first step in syllogistic demonstration; and it does not follow [the] injunction that both the major premise and the minor premise must be self-evident if a conclusion is to be conclusively demonstrated in a single act of reasoning.[148]

Rather, Lucas says, we must look beyond an appeal to formal logic: he concludes that the Declaration consciously mirrors the rhetorical form of the Plakkaat.[149] Lucas may be correct that the drafters were influenced by the Plakkaat, but (as discussed above) unless new archival evidence comes to light it is impossible to know for sure.[150] He is also clearly correct to conclude that the Declaration does not meet the standards of formal logic as it was then practised. Nevertheless, and *pace* Lucas, it may be that the two documents adopt the same form because it is, in both cases, useful for the same reasons. That the Declaration does not meet the standards of formal logic does not demonstrate that the drafters adopted the syllogistic form *in spite of* their subject matter; rather, it nevertheless implies that they *did* understand that the right to secede was *consequent upon* the abuses and failures of the existing political order. Given that belief, the legitimacy of an actual secession could be demonstrated only by proving that the political order had, in fact, failed.

A third indication is that while the intended *effect* of the document was secession, the text of the document speaks of the legitimacy of *governments*, and not of

[146] Mayhew, *Discourse Concerning Unlimited Submission* (n 55) 47.

[147] For a full discussion of these developments with references to the primary sources, see Somos, 'Boston in the State of Nature' (n 123) 110–12 and *passim*; Somos, *American State of Nature* (n 118) esp 107–58.

[148] Lucas, 'Rhetorical Ancestry' (n 60) 161.

[149] ibid 161–65.

[150] See above, s I.C.

states. It begins from the premise that 'Governments are instituted among Men, deriving their just powers from the consent of the governed', or what has here loosely been described as popular sovereignty, and that 'whenever any Form of Government becomes destructive of these ends, it is the Right of the People to alter or to abolish it'. The Declaration makes no claim that the people of the thirteen colonies had a right to remove themselves from Britain because they constituted a separate 'People'. On the contrary, the Declaration seems to recognise that 'The people' to whom the right would apply in this instance would be all the people subject to the government in question: or subjects of the British Crown, both overseas and in Britain. But in representations to the British people, the American people found no common cause:

> We have appealed to their native justice and magnanimity, and we have conjured them by the ties of our common kindred to disavow these usurpations, which, would inevitably interrupt our connections and correspondence. They too have been deaf to the voice of justice and of consanguinity.

It is as a direct consequence of the lack of an internal remedy that the people of the thirteen colonies must seek a remedy externally, the Declaration makes clear. The paragraph continues: 'We must, therefore, acquiesce in the necessity, which denounces our Separation.'

In other words, the Declaration makes no claim to secession as of right. Rather, secession is justified on the basis of a final resort: having exhausted the possibility of a change in the form of government of the state as a whole, the American people could secure their 'unalienable' rights only by ridding themselves of the control of the British State. This is an example of what has subsequently been termed the right to secede in extremis, or *remedial self-determination*.[151]

There are two different incarnations of self-determination engaged in the Declaration. The first is expressed in the major premise of the Declaration: governments derive their legitimacy from 'the consent of the governed'. That is not to say that governments must shape themselves to the wishes of their people in everything they do; nor does it make any statement about what form a government must take. As Waldron would later identify, the principle here neither requires, nor is analogous to, democracy; rather it is a prior and more basic concern:

> It is important, however, not to identify self-determination and democracy. The right of self-determination is prior to democracy, for it includes the right to decide whether to have a democracy around here, and if so, what sort of democracy to have.[152]

[151] This, too, it shares with the Plakkaat, as discussed above.

[152] J Waldron, 'Two Conceptions of Self-Determination' in S Besson and J Tasioulas (eds), *The Philosophy of International Law* (Oxford, Oxford University Press, 2010) 408. Note that Waldron was not commenting directly on the Declaration, here, but rather on the principle which – I argue – can be discerned from it.

The principle expressed in the Declaration requires that the people subject to a government be the authors of the *form* of that government, that they determine its ends, and that its most fundamental purpose it 'to secure' 'certain unalienable rights' of its people. Importantly, that principle could be violated equally by an internal threat (that an individual or group within the polity establish a power structure that is inimical to the wishes and needs of (certain of) its other subjects[153]) as by an external threat (the erasure of the political independence of the polity through the intervention of another polity[154]). That principle was above given the label of *polity-based self-determination*.[155]

The second form of self-determination is closely connected to the polity-based form, to the extent that it can be considered almost a derivative form. Where a section of a population is denied the right to determine along with others in the state the form of its government (in other words, the denial of political self-determination), there results an exceptional right to secede. That secession does not come about because of a general principle allowing separation, but rather as a remedy of last resort for the lack of polity-based self-determination.[156] It is thus named *remedial self-determination*.

In referring to the 1776 Declaration as claiming a right to self-determination – either polity-based or remedial – on behalf of the people of the thirteen colonies it is important to note, however, that the American Declaration appealed not to remedial self-determination as an idea conferring *legality*, but as an idea conferring *legitimacy*.[157] This was a moral and political claim made by the authors that, as a people subject to abuses amounting to a denial of their internal self-determination, the secession of the thirteen colonies from the British Empire was permissible and legitimate. They did not invoke a *legal* right to self-determination – at least as a matter of international law – and there is no indication that they considered in writing the Declaration that they were acting in accordance with, with the support of, or, indeed, in violation of international law norms.

[153] Examples might include military dictatorships, wealth oligarchies or polities which deny rights of political participation to minority communities, although note that autocracy and oligarchy are not – from the point of view of self-determination – invalid forms of government in and of themselves (though they may be illegitimate per se on other grounds): As Waldron reminds us, it would be theoretically possible for a people to *choose* a monarchy (for example) through a valid process of self-determination, however unlikely we may regard such an even in practice: Waldron, 'Two Conceptions' (n 152) 408.

[154] Colonialism is, perhaps, the best example.

[155] See ch 1, s III.A.

[156] Rodríguez-Santiago also identifies this as an act of remedial secession: Rodríguez-Santiago, 'Evolution of Self-Determination' (n 2) 206–07.

[157] Although note that any such conclusion must have due regard to the context of the times, and particularly to the fact that the distinctions between morality and legality were not conceived as being sharply defined. It may be that (some of) those involved in the drafting considered that they were acting in a manner authorised by natural law, although note that (as Somos has shown) the role of natural law, and whether natural law continued to apply outside of a state of nature, was a matter of active debate in the years leading up to the Declaration: Somos, 'Boston in the State of Nature' (n 123) 81–83; and compare JP Reid, *Constitutional History of the American Revolution: The Authority of Rights* (Madison, WI, University of Wisconsin Press, 1986) esp 7–10, 65–66.

As a political document, the American Declaration of Independence is and will doubtless remain highly significant, including for its discussion of self-determination. The reader is presented with an apparent paradox: the intended effect of the document is secession, but the rhetoric relates to polity-based self-determination. A further examination, however, reveals an implied connection between polity-based self-determination and secession and shows that denial of the former is conceived as the basis for the latter. This was a consequential right of secession and not a pure appeal to nationhood or distinctiveness. It seems that it should, therefore, be categorised as an appeal to remedial self-determination, a form which finds its roots in the political rather than the secessionary idea. The Declaration was, however, merely the starting point, and the ideas inherent in the Declaration have been reconceptualised and restated in many different forms in the interim. Among the most significant of these subsequent statements was the product of the 1789 French Revolution.

B. The French Revolution of 1789

The Déclaration des droits de l'homme et du citoyen was adopted on 26 August 1789, marking the height of the 1789 Revolution. It represented a powerful recognition of polity-based self-determination, both in its denial of the divine right of kings, and its declaration of the right of peoples to self-government.[158]

Like the American Revolution, the French Revolution of 1789 espoused a philosophical conviction that '[m]en are born and remain free and equal in rights'.[159] Those rights, variously referred to as 'unalienable' and 'imprescriptible', are declared to be 'Liberty, Property, Safety and Resistance to Oppression'. Like the American Revolution, the French Revolution too recognised the principle of popular sovereignty: 'The principle of any Sovereignty lies primarily in the Nation. No corporate body, no individual may exercise any authority that does not expressly emanate from it.'

Unlike in earlier cases, there is no ambiguity about the influence of the 1776 Declaration on that of 1789: some of the French revolutionaries themselves noted the intellectual debt that their document owed to its American predecessor.[160] Nevertheless, the 1789 revolution did not simply apply the principles of the 1776 Declaration. Although they may be recognisable as expressions of the same idea, they have notably developed. Where the 1776 Declaration holds that 'all men are created equal [and] are endowed … with certain unalienable rights', the 1789

[158] Raič, *Law of Self-Determination* (n 1) 174–175; Cassese, *Self-Determination of Peoples* (n 1) 11–13.

[159] References to the Déclaration in English translation relate to: 'Declaration of Human and Civic Rights of 26 August 1789', www.conseil-constitutionnel.fr/en/declaration-of-human-and-civic-rights-of-26-august-1789.

[160] D Armitage, *The Declaration of Independence: A Global History* (Cambridge, MA, Harvard University Press, 2007) 67.

Déclaration has it that '[m]en are born *and remain* free and equal in rights'. Similarly, there is a significant step made in the Déclaration's statement that 'the principle of any Sovereignty lies primarily in the Nation', compared to the 1776 Declaration's formulation that government is 'instituted' among men, with its powers derived 'from the consent of the governed'. While the 1776 formulation implies a static relationship – an exercise of *pouvoir constituent*, albeit one that can be overturned when a 'Form of Government becomes destructive of these ends' – the French Déclaration employs the concept of sovereignty to create a dynamic relationship of continuous reconstitution of government. The Déclaration also makes an additional – and significant – specification which goes beyond the 1776 Declaration when it declares that: 'The Law is the expression of the general will. All citizens have the right to take part, personally or through their representatives, in its making.' What is more, 1789 deserves far more than any preceding document the label of a 'declaration'. The text does not take the form of an appeal (as does Arbroath) or a logical justification (as do the Plakkaat and the 1776 Declaration); rather, the 1789 Déclaration baldly states principles that its drafters believe to be true, and does so in absolute terms.[161]

Antonio Cassese comments that taken together, the events of 1776 and 1789 'marked the demise of the notion that individuals and peoples, as subjects of the King, were objects to be transferred, alienated, ceded, or protected in accordance with the interests of the monarch'.[162] He is correct to highlight the significant role played by each event, as well as the still greater significance of the two taken together. A doctrine of polity-based self-determination can be derived in outline from the 1776 Declaration, and in 1789 it is developed, and laid out in full detail: the constitutional order of a polity is created – both originally and dynamically – by the will of its people. Those people are equal in their rights, and must all have an equal opportunity to take part in the political life of the state, to make the law and be 'equally eligible for all high offices, public positions, and employments'.

In other words, the legitimacy of the form of government derives from the will of the people, and that the people, as a corporate entity comprising all members of the polity, has the right to alter that form of government.[163] The statement of principle made in 1789 has continued to be virtually definitive of polity-based self-determination ever since.

However, the French Revolution also contemplated an infant right to secessionary self-determination, in the form of irredentism. Self-determination was proposed as the governing principle in transfers of territory as early as 1790, and the principle was codified in the Draft Constitution presented to the National

[161] Examples include: 'Men *are* born and remain free'; 'The principle of any Sovereignty *lies* primarily in the Nation'; 'The Law *is* the expression of the general will'; 'every man *is* presumed innocent until he has been declared guilty'.

[162] Cassese, *Self-Determination of Peoples* (n 1) 11.

[163] Raič, *Law of Self-Determination* (n 1) 174.

Convention in 1793.[164] As David Raič notes, 'the plebiscite as a means of determining the political fate of a territory was an invention of the French Revolution'.[165] Although the proffered choice was between existing states (independence was not envisaged), the plebiscite as the primary tool of territorial delimitation appears to be based on a conviction that peoples are entitled to determine their own political fate, even to the extent of choosing which state to belong to. Thus, Andrés Rigo Sureda argues that the most noteworthy aspect of the philosophy of the French Revolution was that it severed the link between state 'ownership' and territory: 'the territorial element in a political unit lost its feudal predominance in favour of the personal element: people were not to be any more a mere appurtenance of the land'.[166]

If the recognition of self-determination as a right of peoples in determining their political status was significant, however, the principle as applied did not live up to these noble ideals. Although the revolution yielded a number of statements which repudiated wars of conquest and territorial acquisitions,[167] this ideal was ultimately subsumed by a conception of the freedom of mankind that went beyond the polity.[168] The Revolution's conviction was that individuals should no longer be in thrall to a social elite, and it therefore followed quite logically that populations should be enabled to join the new, free, France. Revolutionary thought therefore recognised a doctrine of secessionary self-determination premised on the freedom of the individual and the right of peoples 'not content with the government of the country to which they belong … to secede and organise themselves as they wish'.[169] In practice, however, the freedom of the individual was mythologised to the extent that actions which detracted from an individual's ability to freely self-determine were justified in its pursuit.[170] Self-determination was deployed to rationalise the transfer of territories to France if the populace voted in favour of incorporation,[171] and sometimes even if it did not:

> At first, the French revolutionaries consistently with their ideals renounced all wars of conquest and agreed to annexations of territory to France only after a plebiscite. However, when they considered that their democratic ideals were threatened, they tried to impose them by force upon other peoples: how could men choose not to be free?[172]

Whatever the deficiencies in the application of the principle, the French revolutionary conception of self-determination should be seen as highly significant.

[164] Cassese, *Self-Determination of Peoples* (n 1) 11.
[165] Raič, *Law of Self-Determination* (n 1) 174 (footnotes omitted).
[166] Rigo Sureda, *Evolution of Self-Determination* (n 131) 17.
[167] Rodríguez-Santiago, 'Evolution of Self-Determination' (n 2) 206.
[168] As Hobsbawm notes, 'the French [Revolution] was ecumenical. Its armies set out to revolutionize the world; its ideas actually did so.' Hobsbawm, *Age of Revolution* (n 135) 75.
[169] Rigo Sureda, *Evolution of Self-Determination* (n 131) 17.
[170] Internally, these included the 'terror', see D Edelstein, 'What Was the Terror?' in D Andress (ed), *The Oxford Handbook of the French Revolution* (Oxford, Oxford University Press, 2015).
[171] Cassese, *Self-Determination of Peoples* (n 1) 12.
[172] Rigo Sureda, *Evolution of Self-Determination* (n 131) 18 (footnotes omitted).

Although the application of self-determination principles was not consistent with the ideals which underpinned them, there can be no doubt that the principles enunciated in 1789 and the years that followed further advanced the sense that self-determination conferred legitimacy, and were a significant contribution to the development of the concept.

III. The Age of Revolution and the Long Nineteenth Century - 1789–1920

The 'Age of Revolution' is a term used by Hobsbawm to refer to the years 1789–1848 – a period of extraordinary political and social change in Europe.[173] During this period, which saw the beginning of the Industrial Revolution,[174] democratic uprisings threatened many of Europe's monarchies, in some cases successfully,[175] and the period had a significance that went far beyond Europe. Armitage identifies this as the first of four independence 'moments' – points in time that saw the creation of many new states and the diminution of empires.[176]

The influence of the American and French declarations on the would-be revolutionaries or secessionists of this period is difficult to quantify but almost impossible to overstate. It is clear that the American declaration was an influence on the French revolutionaries, and that the potential of both documents to inspire or incite others was amply appreciated. As Armitage observes:

> The claim of some French revolutionaries that their movement owed its inspiration to the United States rendered key documents like the [1776] Declaration suspect and dangerous in the eyes of those who feared the wholesale destruction of the political and diplomatic order of the Atlantic world.[177]

The fear was justified: the American influence on many of the declarations of independence in the period was clear to see,[178] and the influence of the French Revolution was arguably greater still. As Hobsbawm notes, 'France made [the nineteenth century's] revolutions and gave them their ideas, to the point where a tricolour of some kind became the emblem of virtually every emerging nation.'[179]

[173] Hobsbawm, *Age of Revolution* (n 135) 1–4.
[174] ibid 27ff.
[175] ibid 109–12.
[176] Armitage, *Declaration of Independence* (n 160) 107.
[177] ibid 67.
[178] ibid 108.
[179] Hobsbawm, *Age of Revolution* (n 135) 73. Hobsbawm goes on to say that the French Revolution created a set of political ideas the contestation for and against which defined the politics of the era (73), and created the 'concept and vocabulary of nationalism' (73–74). More significantly still, he argues that it was decidedly more radical than its American close contemporary. In a characteristically beautiful

While the American revolution is a 'crucial event in American history, … [t]he French Revolution is a landmark in all countries'.[180]

Hobsbawm is undoubtedly correct to highlight the importance of the French Revolution. It is here that the inward-facing aspect of the idea of political self-determination – that the form of government should be determined by the people – finds its most influential roots. Nevertheless, the influence of the American declaration should not be underestimated: it remains true that there was, as identified by Armitage, an (US) 'American component' to many of the revolutions of the long nineteenth century,[181] composed of a combination of substance and form. Substantively, the American Declaration sought to establish an independent state with full external sovereignty.[182] To that extent, it signalled an intention on the part of the Declaration's authors to 'play within the rules' of the international system. By conforming to the established models of statehood and sovereignty, they chose to 'affirm the maxims of European statecraft, not affront them'.[183] Truistic though it may appear, it is significant that the great majority of subsequent declarations of independence, too, sought independent statehood. That revolutionary approaches to political authority conformed so closely to the established norm served further to entrench that norm, and the state was thus (re)established as the single viable form of non-dependent sociopolitical community within this international legal paradigm. To this extent, the American independence struggle and those that followed it were 'decidedly *un*-revolutionary' revolutions.[184]

More significantly still, the form of the 1776 Declaration proclaimed the principle of remedial self-determination, and this is (at least in this area) arguably its most profound and lasting legacy. Like the American Declaration, the majority of independence movements which followed made claims to remedial self-determination. Their focus is on the rights (individual or collective) of the people, and they begin with an exposition of the iniquities suffered by the would-be state on the understanding that to cast their claim as a remedy to long suffering confers legitimacy. This feature is particularly clear in, for example, the declarations of independence of Flanders,[185]

passage he notes that: 'The results of the American revolutions were, broadly speaking, countries carrying on much as before, only minus the political control of the British, Spaniards and Portuguese. The result of the French Revolution was that the age of Balzac replaced the age of Mme Dubarry' (74–75).

[180] ibid 75.

[181] Armitage, *Declaration of Independence* (n 160) 108.

[182] ibid 112–13.

[183] ibid 65.

[184] ibid 65; see also Hobsbawm, *Age of Revolution* (n 135) 74–75.

[185] Manifesto for the Province of Flanders, in Armitage, *Declaration of Independence* (n 160) 187–91:

> [I]t is incontestable that the Emperor has broken all of his agreements with us. By violating the social and inaugural pact, he freed the Nation to sever its bond of obedience. Moreover, he has remained deaf to the humble and renewed appeals of a Nation that sought redress for its grievances until the final hour. In waging was upon us, the Emperor obliged us to meet force and to claim all those rights granted by the Law of Nations to victorious parties.

Venezuela,[186] Liberia[187] and Hungary,[188] and can be seen in most declarations of the period.[189] These appeals to remedial self-determination, although unlikely to have created a legal right, are very likely to have further instituted the growing *sense of right* that was a hallmark of both the American and French declarations:[190] an exercise of remedial self-determination following the denial of the political form was seen by secession movements as a legitimate justification for rebellion, and each declaration which appealed to those principles further entrenched the status of remedial self-determination as conferring legitimacy on those who invoked it.

[186] Venezuelan Declaration of Independence, in Armitage, *Declaration of Independence* (n 160) 199–207:

> We, the Representatives of the united Provinces of Caracas, Cumana, Varinas Margarita, Barcelona, Merida, and Truxillo, forming the American Federation of Venezuela, in the South Continent, in Congress assembled, considering the full and absolute possession of our Rights, which we recovered justly and legally from the 19th of April, 1810, in consequence of the occurrences in Byona, and the occupation of the Spanish Throne by conquest, and the succession of a new Dynasty, constituted without our consent: are desirous, before we make use of those Rights, of which we have been deprived by force for more than three ages, but now restored to us by the political order of human events, to make known to the world the reasons which have emanated from these same occurrences, and which authorise us in the free use we are now about to make of our own Sovereignty.

[187] The declaration of Independence of Liberia, in CH Huberich, *The Political and Legislative History of Liberia*, vol 1 (New York, Central Book Co, 1947) 828ff:

> We, the people of the Republic of Liberia, were originally the inhabitants of the United States of North America.
>
> In some parts of that country we were debarred by law for all rights and privileges of man – in other parts, public sentiment, more powerful than law, frowned us down.
>
> We were excluded from all participation in the government.
>
> We were taxed without our consent.
>
> We were compelled to contribute to the resources of a country with gave us no protection.
>
> We were made a separate and distinct class, and against us every avenue of improvement was effectively closed. Strangers from other lands, of a color different from ours, were preferred before us.

[188] Hungarian Declaration of Independence, in H de Puy, *Kossuth and His Generals* (Buffalo, NY, Phinney & Co, 1852) 202–25; see also Armitage, *Declaration of Independence* (n 160) 124:

> WE, the legally constituted representatives of the Hungarian nation, assembled in Diet, do by these presents solemnly proclaim, in maintenance of the inalienable natural rights of Hungary, with all its dependencies, to occupy the position of an independent European State – that the house of Hapsburg-Lorraine, as perjured in the sight of God and man, has forfeited its right to the Hungarian throne. At the same time we feel ourselves bound in duty to make known the motives and reasons which have impelled us to this decision, that the civilised world may learn we have taken this step not out of overweening confidence in our wisdom, or out of revolutionary excitement, but that it is an act of the last necessity, adopted to preserve from utter destruction a nation persecutes to the limit of its most enduring patience.
>
> Three hundred years have passed since the Hungarian nation, by free election, placed the house of Austria upon its throne, in accordance with stipulations made on both sides, and ratified by treaty. These three hundred years have been for the country, a period of uninterrupted suffering.

[189] For an excellent table listing many of the post-1776 declarations of independence, see Armitage, *Declaration of Independence* (n 160) 146–55.

[190] See above, ss II.A–B.

Few secession movements during this period appealed to justifications other than remedial self-determination, but there are notable exceptions. One such example is Norway. In both 1814 (ultimately unsuccessfully) and 1905 (successfully), the Norwegian people sought their independence from the Scandinavian powers. Norway's 1814 declaration of independence, in particular, is noteworthy, because of its claim to secessionary self-determination.

A. The Secessions of Norway – 1814

At the beginning of 1814 Norway was, and had been since 1380, a territorial possession of the Danish monarchy.[191] While the union began as a consensual union of two states under a common ruler, Norway's independent character was gradually eroded.[192] The decisive moment in this decline was the declaration, in the 1536 Charter, 'that the country should cease to be a separate kingdom, and be incorporated in Denmark'.[193] Thereafter Norway was ruled from Denmark and had no international representation, becoming little more than a region in a Danish state. The Permanent Court of International Justice (PCIJ) has subsequently concluded that during this period the Norwegian state ceased to exist.[194]

Norway remained a Danish possession until 1814, when it gained a short-lived independence.[195] The Napoleonic wars wrought significant changes in the power structures of Scandinavia. Although initially neutral, Denmark, Sweden and Russia were drawn into the wars. Denmark allied itself to France; Russia to Great Britain. Sweden initially joined Napoleon, but following the 1809 Finnish War and the loss of Finland to Russia, Sweden made overtures to the Anglo-Russian coalition.[196] Its crown prince, Karl Johan, sought to gain the friendship of Russia by renouncing its claim to Finland, hoping instead to acquire Norway.[197] By October 1813 the Danish cause had been defeated at the Battle of Leipzig and, on 14 January 1814, Denmark and Sweden concluded the Treaty of Kiel, by which Norway would be transferred 'with all rights, entitlements and incomes, in full ownership and full sovereignty to His Majesty the King of Sweden'.[198] The implementation of the Treaty was frustrated by Norway's claim to independence, however. This situation was remarkable because Norway claimed a right to

[191] K Larsen, *A History of Norway* (Princeton, NJ, Princeton University Press, 1948) 373–95, esp 390.
[192] ibid 208–276, esp 232, 243.
[193] ibid 232.
[194] *Legal Status of Eastern Greenland*, (1933) PCIJ Series A/B, no 53, 22, 27–30.
[195] I Libæk, Ø Sternersen and S Asle, *The History of Norway after 1814*, tr J Irons (Oslo, Font Forlag, 2012) 10.
[196] Larsen, *History of Norway* (n 191) 367–68; K Gjerset, *History of the Norwegian People*, vol 2 (New York, AMS Press, 1969) 407–10.
[197] Larsen, *History of Norway* (n 191) 368; Gjerset, *History of the Norwegian People* (n 196) 407; *Legal Status of Eastern Greenland* (n 58) 30.
[198] Art IV Der Kieler Frieden (Kiel, 1814) (my translation).

independence based solely on its separate national character and the will of its people:[199] it did not claim a subsisting sovereignty, or that it had gained a right to independence as a result of historical wrongs. In other words, Norway's claim was one of secessionary self-determination. Although it did not yield Norway's independence – the kings of Sweden would rule Norway from 1814 to 1905 – the situation was remarkable, too, in that Norway's claim appears to have been accepted by Sweden. Indeed, Norway was de facto independent for some months, and when united with Sweden – compelled by the threat of vastly superior Swedish military force, lack of sympathy among the great powers and a British naval blockade – it was as a distinct state under a joint monarchy, and not as the territorial possession envisaged by the Treaty.

Following the conclusion of the Treaty of Kiel there was widespread resentment against Denmark and Sweden in Norway; the one for bargaining away the country without consultation, the other for seeking to gain control of Norway against the wishes of its population.[200] An assembly of elected delegates was called and, on 17 May 1814, a new constitution was signed at Eidsvoll.[201] It included a statement that 'Norway … shall be a free, independent, and indivisible kingdom.'[202] At a similar time, Karl Johan ordered that a force be sent to occupy Norwegian fortresses, stating that 'Norway is to be taken possession of, not as a province, but only to be united with Sweden in such a way as to form with it a single kingdom.'[203] The intention of Sweden was very clear: Norway would not be independent, but would be incorporated as a part of the Swedish state.

As the war in Europe came to an end, and Karl Johan was able to refocus on the acquisition of Norway, so too did Norway's short-lived independence.[204] As Swedish forces returned to Sweden, it became increasingly obvious that resistance against the far-superior Swedish military was doomed to fail and, indeed, hostilities lasted only from 29 July to 14 August, when the Convention of Moss was signed.[205] During the brief conflict the Norwegian forces had been significantly overmatched,[206] and there can be little doubt that, had the war been prosecuted to its conclusion, heavy defeat for Norway would have resulted.[207] Nevertheless, a number of significant concessions were made to Norway. Notably, the Convention of Moss made no reference to the Treaty of Kiel, and did not seek to effect the union of the two states. On 20 October 1814 the Norwegian Storthing,

[199] Gjerset notes that the people of Norway 'felt that they had been bartered away in a manner disgraceful to a free people.' Gjerset, *History of the Norwegian People* (n 196) 417.

[200] Larsen, *History of Norway* (n 191) 376.

[201] ibid 385.

[202] ibid 384.

[203] Gjerset, *History of the Norwegian People* (n 196) 416.

[204] Larsen, *History of Norway* (n 191) 381.

[205] ibid 390–91.

[206] Gjerset notes that not only was the Swedish army and navy significantly larger than those of Norway, but that England, Russia and Prussia were ready to commit troops and naval vessels to assist the Swedish cause: Gjerset, *History of the Norwegian People* (n 196) 440.

[207] Libæk, Sternersen and Asle, *The History of Norway after 1814* (n 195) 12.

the parliament established under the Eidsvoll constitution, voted in favour of the union of Norway and Sweden as independent states under a common monarchy, and Karl Johan proclaimed the 'freedom of each nation'.[208]

It may seem strange to speak of a successful claim to self-determination on the part of Norway when, as the result of a short war and the threat of force, Norway ultimately entered into an unpopular union with Sweden. The change in the Swedish position over the course of 1814 is, however, striking. At the beginning of the year Sweden claimed absolute sovereignty and title over Norway as a result of the Treaty of Kiel, and there can be little doubt that at the beginning of 1814 Norway was not a state, having lost its independence in 1536. However, when the union was carried into effect in October 1814, Norway entered the joint monarchy consensually, as the result of an international treaty – the Convention of Moss – concluded between Sweden and Norway, and with an established constitution that (contrary to the wishes of Sweden) was amended in the course of the incorporation negotiations to strengthen Norway's independence. During this process, Sweden treated Norway not as a rebellious province to which it already had title, or as a conquered territory, but as a sovereign state with international capacity.[209] Nor, it appears, was Norway's independent personality lost as a result of the union, as the events of 1905 were to demonstrate.

B. The Secessions of Norway – 1905

In 1905 the ninety-one-year union between Sweden and Norway came to an end. While some within Sweden considered Norway an inferior partner in the union, Norway regarded itself as an equal, sovereign state.[210] Both in matters of internal governance and external relations Norway sought to exercise its independence, creating a running conflict with the king of Sweden. The events leading to the dissolution of Norway/Sweden in 1905 suggest that Norway not only achieved independence in 1814, but that it did not lose that independence when it united with Sweden.[211] When it sought to leave the Swedish union, it was as a state asserting its sovereign right.

[208] Larsen, *History of Norway* (n 191) 391–95; Gjerset, *History of the Norwegian People* (n 196) 441.

[209] 'The Act of Union, like the constitution of Norway, recognized the Union as resting, not on the Treaty of Kiel, but on the free consent of the Norwegian people, and the complete equality of the two realms.' Gjerset, *History of the Norwegian People* (n 196) 445.

[210] Larsen, *History of Norway* (n 191) 484.

[211] Although perhaps a strange claim to the ear of a modern international lawyer, it was at that time and in the preceding century common for entities seeking independence to do so on the basis that their incorporation with another state had not extinguished their separate personality, which could be revived. This was a particular feature of claims to independence by regions which retained a measure of self-government (as, for example, in the case of several of those US states which seceded to form the Confederacy in 1860–61), and in states which had the structure of a dual- or common monarchy (as, for example, in the case of Hungary in 1848–49, see above n 188), but was not confined to those contexts (see, for example, the Declaration of Independence of Venezuela in 1811, above, n 186). Norway's claim to independence appears to have fallen into this category: given that it consensually

The political structure of Norway/Sweden was complex and contested, with both sides of the union claiming a greater degree of power and control (on Sweden's part) or autonomy (on Norway's) than the other would accept.[212] Thus, while the Storthing and the Norwegian government had a day-to-day competence for the internal governance of Norway, the government was an appointment of the king, and he had (and made use of) the power to veto legislation. Two incidents in particular are especially demonstrative of the conflict over Norway's political status. The first came to a head in 1884, and concerned the power of the Norwegian Storthing to amend the constitution without the king's approval. Three successive Storthings had passed a constitutional amendment intended to seat the Norwegian ministers in the Storthing, but on all three occasions the king vetoed the measure.[213] While it was clear that the king had the power to veto ordinary legislation, many within the Storthing refused to accept that the king had the power of veto over constitutional amendments. No such power was granted to the king by the constitution of March 1814, nor the subsequent amendments. Indeed, the signing of the Eidsvoll constitution was completed without the involvement of the then regent, Christian Frederick, and he neither signed nor affirmed it either before or after his election as Norway's king.[214] This, it was suggested, was authority for the suggestion that the Storthing alone had the authority to amend the constitution.[215] Accordingly, on 9 June 1880, the Storthing overwhelmingly passed a resolution declaring that the constitution had been successfully amended and instructing the government both to promulgate and comply with it. This the government, anxious to avoid a conflict with Sweden, refused to do.[216] No further action was taken until 1882. The final card left to the Storthing was its power to impeach the ministers for their failure to comply with the constitution, and there was an understandable reluctance to pursue such a radical course. Following the 1882 election, however, which gave the majority within the Storthing a clear mandate from the electorate to pursue the amendment, impeachment proceedings were begun against the ministers.[217] On 27 February 1884, the ministers were found guilty of failing to comply with the constitution following a prolonged process before a special court. Eight ministers were sentenced to loss of office, and a further three were fined for their part in the affair.[218] Perhaps surprisingly,

entered into a dual monarchy with Sweden by means of an international agreement, the argument runs, it retained its status as an international person and could, by denouncing the treaty that effected it, unilaterally bring the union to an end.

[212] Gjerset, *History of the Norwegian People* (n 196) 477.

[213] Larsen, *History of Norway* (n 191) 456.

[214] Indeed, Gjerset notes that at the Eidsvoll assembly it was against, rather than according to, the wishes of the Christian Frederick that the constitution was adopted, and that he was proclaimed only as regent *ad interim* until his election could be confirmed by the whole of the Norwegian people, rather than (as he hoped) full monarch. Gjerset, *History of the Norwegian People* (n 196) 418–420.

[215] Larsen, *History of Norway* (n 191) 457.

[216] ibid 457.

[217] Gjerset, *History of the Norwegian People* (n 196) 541.

[218] Larsen, *History of Norway* (n 191) 458.

the king chose to ratify the decision, and dismissed the government. Having first failed to form a new government of the unionist right, the king asked majority leader Johan Sverdrup to form a government and, on 2 July 1884 Sverdrup and his new ministers took their seats in the Storthing.[219] In defying the king's veto of the constitutional amendment Norway was asserting its independence. The Storthing had declared that the monarch's legitimate power stemmed from the constitution, rather than constitutional legitimacy flowing from the monarch. In doing so, it asserted the control of Norway over the legal basis of the union.

A second source of conflict was the external competences of the two states, and it was to precipitate the end of the union. In 1885 Sweden proposed a new council of foreign affairs, consisting of 'the minister of foreign affairs … two *other* members of the Swedish and three of the Norwegian ministry'.[220] The proposal created outrage – never before had it been specified that the minister of foreign affairs of Norway/Sweden had to be a *Swedish* minister[221] – and it was seen as proof of Norway's inferior position in the union.[222] Norway by this time had the third-largest merchant marine in the world, and there was widespread feeling among its shipowners and seamen that its unique interests were not being catered to by the Swedish diplomatic service.[223] Old desires for distinct Norwegian international representation were reawakened and, in 1891, the Storthing passed a bill establishing a Norwegian consular service. Despite Norway's opinion that such an action was within its area of concern as stipulated in the Act of Union, Sweden held that the establishment of a consular service was a matter for the union and, accordingly, the king vetoed the bill.[224] A period of low-level conflict followed for several years evidenced by a succession of short-lived Norwegian governments until, on 11 March 1905, a government was formed under the charismatic Christian Michelson.[225]

Michelson's actions swiftly brought the crisis to a head. On 27 May 1905, the Norwegian ministers in Stockholm presented the king with a new bill establishing a Norwegian consular service. Once again the king vetoed the measure.[226] On this occasion, however, refusing to accept the veto, the ministers offered the king their resignation, and immediately returned to Norway.[227] On 7 June, the Michelson government resigned en masse, and presented to the Storthing two resolutions, which were adopted without debate.

> The first stated that whereas a primary duty of a constitutional monarch was to supply the country with a responsible government and the king was unable to do this, the royal

[219] ibid 458; Gjerset, *History of the Norwegian People* (n 196) 544.
[220] Larsen, *History of Norway* (n 191) 485 (emphasis added).
[221] ibid 485–86; Gjerset, *History of the Norwegian People* (n 196) 560.
[222] OJ Falnes, *Norway and the Nobel Peace Prize* (New York, AMS Press, 1938) 125–31.
[223] Larsen, *History of Norway* (n 191) 486–87.
[224] ibid 487.
[225] ibid 488–89.
[226] Gjerset, *History of the Norwegian People* (n 196) 577.
[227] ibid 577.

> power had ceased to function. Oscar II had therefore ceased to be king of Norway, and thereby the union, which had existed by virtue of a common monarch, had come to an end.[228]

In the second, the Storthing communicated the end of the union to King Oscar II, and asked his leave to elect a prince of the Bernadotte line to the throne of Norway. The Storthing's actions were subsequently endorsed by the electorate by a huge margin in a referendum.[229]

The Storthing's declaration almost provoked a war. Surprisingly, Sweden appeared to be willing to allow Norway to leave the union, but Sweden demanded that a series of concessions be made, not least that a neutral zone be implemented along the border, and that several frontier forts be demolished. In Norway, these demands were seen as quite unacceptable, and for a time it appeared that no compromise could be reached. Troops were mobilised, and it appeared that the two countries might slide once more into conflict.[230] Eventually, however, the countries negotiated the demilitarisation of certain Norwegian frontier forts rather than their demolition and on 23 September 1905, the Karlstadt agreement was signed, repealing the Act of union. On 27 October, Oscar II abdicated the throne of Norway, and the union was at an end.[231]

Although a constituency within Sweden advocated the forcible suppression of the Norwegian independence movement, ultimately Norway's competence to bring the union to an end appears to have been accepted.[232] In 1814, despite being bartered away in the grand pan-European power games of the Napoleonic era, Norway declared itself independent, and it was as an independent state that it had entered into the union with Sweden later that year. In the constitutional conflicts that characterised the latter years of the union, Norway's independence was often vindicated and, in 1905, when Norway declared the union to be at an end, Sweden acceded. Throughout the period of union, the nature of the bond between the nations was viewed differently on either side of the border. Norway entered into the union on the understanding that it did so as a sovereign state, and that its independent character was preserved. To Norwegians, the union with Sweden was a joint monarchy, a loose and consensual affiliation of equals. In Sweden, however, the union was seen as the permanent acquisition of the territory of Norway. Despite these different perspectives, however, there appears to have been recognition by Sweden of Norway's independence at several points.

[228] Larsen, *History of Norway* (n 191) 490.

[229] 'Over 84 per cent of the voters turned out, and the events of June 7 were approved by a vote of 368,208 against 184.' ibid 491. Significantly, Gjerset notes that it was *Sweden* which demanded that the independence desire be confirmed by plebiscite, and that the king agreed to concede the separation of Norway on that basis: Gjerset, *History of the Norwegian People* (n 196) 582. This appears to be a recognition of the competence of the Norwegian people to determine their political future.

[230] Larsen, *History of Norway* (n 191) 492.

[231] ibid 492.

[232] Gjerset notes that Sweden ultimately agreed to concede the separation of Norway provided that it be shown in a general plebiscite that the Norwegian people favoured the dissolution. Gjerset, *History of the Norwegian People* (n 196) 582.

In 1814, although Norway was compelled to enter into the union under the threat of force, Sweden officially abandoned the idea that title to Norway had been transferred to Sweden under the Treaty of Kiel. During the negotiations on the formation of the union, the Norwegian Storthing amended the constitution to emphasise Norway's independence, and refused to make certain modifications required by the Swedish king. The king's accession was not considered necessary to bring the amended constitution into force either in 1814 or in 1880, when the Storthing sought to create a parliamentary democracy in Norway.

Despite the opposition of the Swedish king, the 1880 constitutional crisis and the 1885/91 consular conflicts served only to emphasise the degree of independence the Norwegian state still possessed. Most notably, when the union was dissolved in 1905, the Norwegian Storthing did not declare its desire for independence, but the *fact* of it: the Storthing declared that the joint monarchy had come to an end, and thus the link between Norway and Sweden had been severed. Prior to 1814, Norway had ceased to be a state in any meaningful sense – a conclusion eloquently proven by the Treaty of Kiel. In a popular movement, however, Norway demanded its independence, drafted and adopted a liberal constitution, and elected a king of its choosing. In 1814 Norway's claim was to secessionary self-determination: the sense in a people of nascent nationhood, and the claim of a *right* to be independent of the control of others stemming simply from a *desire* to be independent of their control. The factor that makes the Norwegian example fascinating, however, and shows it to be worthy of consideration alongside the most significant of historical secession struggles, is that the events of 1905 suggest that Norway's 1814 claim to secessionary self-determination was successful.

The Norwegian secessions are examples of a trend that typified the Age of Revolution, and which has arguably continued until the present day: the growing acceptance that self-determination confers legitimacy. Like the Declaration of Independence of 1776 and the French Declaration of 1789, Norway's invocation of self-determination principles was a claim of legitimacy. It is a rare and intriguing example, however, in that the claim of the Norwegian people was to secessionary self-determination, and did not cite the abuses of the sovereign as justification. On the contrary, Norway claimed its independence on the basis of its will. Equally unusual was Sweden's apparent acceptance of the legitimacy of Norway's claim: few claims to secessionary self-determination have been made, fewer have been successful, and fewer still received the blessing of the previous sovereign. The pattern holds true in the modern day, where secessionary self-determination continues to be repudiated by the majority of states (although it is in the modern day, too, that one may find echoes of the Norwegian example).[233] Notwithstanding its singular

[233] In the 2014 Scottish independence campaign, the UK government accepted that Scotland's future was a matter to be decided by the people of Scotland, which may suggest a similar legitimacy-belief. See Agreement Between the United Kingdom Government and the Scottish Government on a Referendum on Independence for Scotland (15 October 2012), www.gov.scot/About/Government/concordats/Referendum-on-independence. Similar acceptance that a group has a (politico-moral) right

character, the Norwegian secessions suggest that the concept of self-determination was, by this time, seen as conferring a substantial legitimacy on those invoking it.

Although the Norwegian example is in many respects unique, it should be noted that, like the declarations of 1776 and 1789, Norway's was a political and a moral claim, and not an appeal to international law. It is clear, therefore, that the example can reveal little about the legality of self-determination. It was in the years that followed, however, that the first internationalised dispute concerning self-determination – the Åland Islands dispute of 1920 – was decided, and the question of self-determination's legality, rather than legitimacy, came to the fore.

C. The Åland Islands

The Åland Islands 'case' remains a renowned example of a self-determination claim, and one of the first to be subject to international adjudication.[234] The Åland Islands are a Swedish-speaking archipelago off the coast of Finland, and in 1920 Sweden asked the Council of the League of Nations to decide whether the islanders had a right to secede and join Sweden. Following agreement by Finland, the Council of the League appointed a Committee of Jurists to pronounce on the jurisdiction of the Council.[235] Following their determination that the Council had jurisdiction, the Council appointed a Commission of Rapporteurs to make substantive recommendations.[236] Both reports considered the claims of the Åland islanders to self-determination, and reveal a great deal about the ambit and nature of self-determination as it was then understood. The process was all the more remarkable, too, because the Jurists and the Rapporteurs reached very different conclusions.

The Jurists began their analysis with an examination of the relationship between self-determination and state sovereignty. Their conclusion was that state sovereignty, in the absence of an express limitation, remains dominant:

> [T]he right of disposing of national territory is essentially an attribute of the sovereignty of every State. Positive International Law does not recognise the right of national groups, as such, to separate themselves from the State of which they form part by the simple expression of a wish, any more than it recognises the right of other States to claim such a separation.[237]

to secessionary self-determination can be seen in the 1983 Constitution of St Kitts and Nevis (The Saint Christopher and Nevis Constitutional Order, 1983, s 113(1–80)), and the 1994 Ethiopian Constitution (Constitution of Ethiopia, 1994, ss 39(1), 39(5)). A right of the individual regions to secession also appeared in the 1974 Constitution of Yugoslavia (Constitution of the Socialist Federal Republic of Yugoslavia, 1974, s I). As discussed further in relation to Kosovo, however, it was the attempt of Croatia and Slovenia to secede that, in 1991, triggered the Balkan war. See ch 5.

[234] TD Musgrave, *Self-Determination and National Minorities* (Oxford, Clarendon Press, 1997) 32.

[235] Report of the International Committee of Jurists entrusted by the Council of the League of Nations with the task of giving an advisory opinion upon the legal aspects of the Aaland Islands question, Official Journal of the League of Nations, Special Supplement No 3, October 1920, 5.

[236] Report Presented to the Council of the League of Nations by the Commission of Rapporteurs, B7 21/68/106 (1921).

[237] Report of the International Committee of Jurists (n 235).

Nevertheless, the Jurists accepted that self-determination has a role to play in the formation of states. Where a State is, as yet, unformed and its sovereignty is imperfect, 'aspirations of certain sections of a nation … may come to the surface and produce effects which must be taken into account in the interests of the internal and external peace of nations'.[238] Indeed, the Jurists cast national self-determination as 'the most important of the principles governing the formation of States',[239] but one that is nevertheless confined to the pre-state context.[240] Any other finding, they argued, would be 'contrary to the very idea embodied in the term "State"'.[241] While it is clear that the Jurists understood self-determination to be a right attaching to 'nations', they construed it as a weak right and one that is subordinate to the right of the state to territorial integrity. Nevertheless, that weak right was applied in this case: the Committee concluded that the League of Nations had the competence to address the question because 'Finland had not yet acquired the character of a definitively constituted State'.[242] Thus, it was because Finland had not yet achieved statehood and its rights over the territory were less than sovereign that the claim to self-determination should be considered, and not because self-determination was a right capable of defeating the claim of the sovereign state over its territory.

Far from recognising an effective right to secede, therefore, the report of the Committee of Jurists declared that sovereignty prevails over self-determination. Nor, as has been wrongly suggested,[243] did the Jurists assert that remedial principles may operate to 'internationalise' an ostensibly domestic dispute:

> The Commission, in affirming these principles, does not give an opinion concerning the question as to whether a manifest and continued abuse of sovereign power, to the detriment of a section of the population of a State, would, if such circumstances arose, give to an international dispute, arising therefrom, such a character that its object should be considered as one which is not confined to the domestic jurisdiction of the State concerned, but comes within the sphere of action of the League of Nations.[244]

It is important to note, first, that the Committee declined to give an opinion on the question. Regardless, however, interpretation of their statement as an endorsement of remedial self-determination would be questionable, given that the passage considers only who should have jurisdiction over the dispute, and not on what principles it should be decided. Indeed, the passage even suggests that the abuse of sovereign power by a state would not be sufficient, in itself, to confer jurisdiction on the League of Nations, but that the dispute would first have to be 'internationalised' by other means.[245]

[238] ibid para 3.
[239] ibid para 3.
[240] This, perhaps, recalls the state of nature argument advanced by some US revolutionaries in the decade leading up to 1776. See above, s A, and further Somos, 'Boston in the State of Nature' (n 123) 110–12; Somos, *American State of Nature* (n 118) *passim*, esp 107–58.
[241] Report of the International Committee of Jurists (n 235), para 2.
[242] ibid Conclusion 2.
[243] Cassese, *Self-Determination of Peoples* (n 1) 31.
[244] Report of the International Committee of Jurists (n 235) para 2.
[245] ibid para 2.

While the Jurists decided that the right to self-determination had relevance for the question because Finland had not yet attained full sovereignty, the Rapporteurs were emphatic that no right to secessionary self-determination then existed in international law:

> This principle is not, properly speaking a rule of international law and the League of Nations has not entered it into its Covenant. ... It is a principle of justice and liberty, expressed by a vague and general formula which has given rise to the most varied interpretations and differences of opinion. ... To concede to minorities, either of language or religion, or to any fractions of a population the right of withdrawing from the community to which they belong ... would be to uphold a theory incompatible with the very idea of the State as a territorial and political unity.[246]

Unlike the Committee of Jurists, though, the Rapporteurs did explicitly recognise a right to remedial secession 'as a last resort when the State lacks either the will or the power to enact and apply just and effective guarantees' of minority rights.[247] They stressed, however, that such a secession 'can only be considered as an altogether exceptional solution'.[248] Applying the criteria for such a right to the case of the Åland islanders, they found that no such exceptional situation existed, and that Finland was prepared to offer the islanders protection of their rights as a minority.[249] They therefore concluded that the islanders did not have a right to separate from Finland.[250]

Although the reports disagree on a great many points, it is clear that self-determination was considered by both to be subordinate to territorial sovereignty. While the Jurists believed that secessionary self-determination existed as a right, albeit a weak right which would only have application where the state's sovereignty was imperfect, the Rapporteurs denied its legal character altogether.[251] Concurrently, in a conclusion which lends further support to the ideational separation between the secessionary and the remedial forms, the Rapporteurs recognised that a right to remedial secession may exist in international law (although they were emphatic that it would not apply to the circumstances of the Åland Islands), a point on which the Jurists made no determination.[252] Overall, the Åland Islands question did not greatly clarify either the legal status of the various forms of self-determination, or their ambits. Even if a right either to secessionary or to remedial self-determination existed at this time, any such right must be regarded as weak and imperfect, and to be at least as much a question of politics as a question of law. It was only through the decolonisation process that this was to change, and that a form of self-determination with an unambiguously legal status was to emerge.

[246] Report of the Commission of Rapporteurs (n 236) 3–4.
[247] ibid 4.
[248] ibid 4.
[249] ibid 5.
[250] ibid 5; see also Musgrave, *National Minorities* (n 234) 36.
[251] Report of the Commission of Rapporteurs (n 236) 3.
[252] ibid 4; Report of the International Committee of Jurists (n 235).

IV. Conclusion

Whether the self-determination story starts in 1776 or earlier, certain things hold true. Tracing the early history of self-determination shows clearly that different kinds of idea are engaged. The claim to independence on grounds of a separate national character that motivated the Declaration of Arbroath and the independence claims of Norway has little in common with the rejection of the divine right of kings by the French revolutionaries, and is different again from the claim made in 1581 and 1776 that a train of abuses gives rise to a right against the government. There are three different kinds of appeal embedded in these claims; three narratives, each of which seeks to locate the legitimacy of its intended outcome in a different source – separate nationhood, popular will or the imperative of remedy. In other words, as early as 1789 three different self-determination logics can be individuated.

It also became clear through this survey of self-determination's early history how important precedent is in this area. From at least the start of the long nineteenth century – and, if we follow Lucas,[253] before that – self-determination declarations make a double appeal to legitimacy: to the legitimacy inherent in their respective logic (to nationhood, popular sovereignty, or arising from past abuses), and to the past. That appeal can be seen, for example, in the manifold independence declarations of the long nineteenth century which make a remedial claim, formulated in recognisably US American terms,[254] and giving rise to new states which then promptly adopted a tricolour.[255] That reliance on precedential authority has continued to be a feature of self-determination up to – and in – the present day.[256]

By the end of the period surveyed in this chapter, three forms of self-determination are manifest. A fourth form was, however, to emerge following the end of the long nineteenth century, which more than any other had a world-making effect in the twentieth century: colonial self-determination. The next chapter turns to the experience of colonialism, and the emergence of the specific decolonial form of self-determination.

[253] See above, nn 123–29 and accompanying text.

[254] Armitage, *Declaration of Independence* (n 160) 108.

[255] Hobsbawm, *Age of Revolution* (n 135) 73; and see further above, nn 185–89 and accompanying text.

[256] See, for example, the discussion of the Russian attempt to cast its invasion of Ukraine in 2014 as following the precedent set by Kosovo in ch 5, s III.A.

3

Self-Determination and Decolonisation: 1920–1970

Although since 1776 it had been invoked by many states and peoples, at the beginning of the twentieth century self-determination remained an inherently controversial concept among states. In the aftermath of the First World War, however, self-determination began to gain currency and acceptance as a tool in the decolonisation process. Over time, a separate form of *colonial self-determination* was to emerge, and this chapter will trace its emergence and growth in the period from the end of the First World War to the height of the decolonisation era in the 1960s and 1970s. Although the colonial self-determination idea has a number of links or similarities to other forms of self-determination – it shares a similarity of outcomes with the secessionary form, while its ideational foundations bear close similarities to the political form – it merits its own category because of its political status.

Here, as in the long nineteenth century, the precedential nature of the development of self-determination is on full view. In small and incremental steps, each building on the one before, a legal norm of self-determination grew without the intention of – and often despite – the major international powers. While in the age of revolution, it was primarily an appeal to the legitimacy of the remedial logic that dominated, in the twentieth century it was overtaken by a distinctive, anticolonial appeal. Although there are overlaps – colonialism was, more than almost any other example, a source of abuses in need of remedy – it was not against abuses *under* colonialism on which the legitimacy narrative focused, but rather against colonialism itself.

In the same period, polity-based self-determination re-emerged as a key principle in international affairs. Although the American and French declarations of 1776 and 1789 had a hugely significant impact on the development of political thought, they had little immediate impact on international law. Following the First and – even more so – Second World Wars, however, polity-based self-determination was given a key position in the attempts to construct a new international order. Its injunction against foreign domination, interference and aggression was incorporated into the UN Charter as one of its most central principles: the guarantee of the political independence of states and the prohibition on the use of force. From small beginnings, polity-based self-determination was transformed almost overnight into one of the key principles of international organisation, a fundamental norm of the post-1945 legal order, and almost certainly a norm of *ius cogens* status.[1]

This chapter proceeds as follows. Section I briefly introduces the discussion of decolonisation, and section II discusses the origins of the decolonisation process in the First World War. Section II.A reconsiders the legacy of Woodrow Wilson and his role in establishing the post-First World War legal order in the light of the contemporary reassessment of his presidency following the Black Lives Matter movement, and section II.B argues that in self-determination, too, his legacy is often overstated. Although Marxist scholars have often highlighted the (in my view equally or more significant) role of Lenin in beginning the process of decolonisation,[2] it bears repeating that (what was to become) the norm of colonial self-determination owes much of its initial impetus – if not its actual implementation – to the Bolsheviks. Sections III and IV then trace the development of colonial self-determination through its institutionalisation first in the mandates system of the League of Nations, and then the trusts system of the United Nations. In this period, the form developed from a vague principle to be applied as one of many considerations in handling colonial territories, to a firmly embedded principle of the system. Section V continues that analysis by considering in detail the practice and documents of the United Nations, most notably the Charter itself (section V.A), the international human rights covenants (section V.B), resolution 1514 (XV) of the General Assembly (section V.C) and the Declaration on Friendly Relations (section V.D). It will become clear that multiple forms of self-determination are often engaged in these documents, and this section will thus also track the institutionalisation of polity-based self-determination (in particular in the Charter and the covenants), and will make some remarks on remedial self-determination (in the Declaration on Friendly Relations). Section VI concludes.

I. Imperialism and Decolonisation

European imperialism saw the conquest and domination of most of the world's peoples by foreign powers in a series of waves, beginning with the Portuguese and Spanish empires of the fifteenth and sixteenth centuries, Dutch mercantile capitalism between the sixteenth and eighteenth, and the French and British struggle for dominance thereafter.[3] Although colonialism and its legacies continue

[1] The status to be accorded to the polity-based and colonial forms of self-determination are discussed further in ch 4.

[2] R Knox and N Tzouvala, 'Looking Eastwards: The Bolshevik Theory of Imperialism and International Law' in K Greenman et al (eds), *Revolutions in International Law* (Cambridge, Cambridge University Press, 2021) *passim*, esp 31–42.

[3] A Anghie, *Imperialism, Sovereignty and the Making of International Law* (Cambridge, Cambridge University Press, 2004) 13–114.

in pernicious forms to this day, the most recent wave of saltwater empires were largely dismantled in the period leading up to and following the Second World War, with the decolonisation movement reaching its height in the 1960s.[4]

During the decolonisation period, and in particular in the years 1945–1960, there was a remarkably rapid shift of international legality. Prior to the Second World War, the centuries-old practice of European colonisation continued to be regarded as legally permissible by European-dominated international law. Indeed, as Anthony Anghie (most influentially) and others have demonstrated, over the course of international law's development, its doctrines were shaped in order to – at the least – permit and often actively to facilitate the acquisition and retention of colonial possessions by the European states.[5]

And yet, in many ways the story of the twentieth century is the story of decolonisation. In 1920 – at the 'territorial zenith of modern colonialism'[6] – the two largest European colonial powers (Britain and France) between them controlled almost 35 per cent of the Earth's land surface, and the international community had only around fifty acknowledged members. By the turn of the century, the European powers had (largely) been reduced to their municipal territories, and the United Nations counted 189 Member States.[7] Although in many cases old patterns of domination have continued, albeit in less overt forms, the change wrought in the international community during the twentieth century is, on any reckoning, remarkable.

Decolonisation is typically characterised as a process that began with the end of the Second World War.[8] While describing decolonisation both as a 'moment and a process', Jan Jansen and Jürgen Osterhammel note that decolonisation is typically taken to refer to 'the simultaneous disintegration of several intercontinental empires within the short timeframe of three decades (1945–1975)'.[9] Certainly, the most striking developments – both legally and in terms of real-world effects – took place in this post-war period, but there were significant developments too which both preceded and followed the three decades identified by Jansen and Osterhammel.[10] B.S. Chimni notes the founding of the League Against Imperialism in 1927,[11]

[4] ibid 115–194 and *passim*; A Anghie, 'Bandung and the Origins of Third World Sovereignty' in L Eslava, M Fakhiri and V Nesiah (eds), *Bandung, Global History, and International Law: Critical Pasts and Pending Futures* (Cambridge, Cambridge University Press, 2018); J Trinidad, *Self-Determination in Disputed Colonial Territories* (Cambridge, Cambridge University Press, 2018) *passim*, esp 6–16, 21–24.

[5] Anghie, *Imperialism* (n 3) 13–114 and *passim*; BS Chimni, 'The Past, Present and Future of International Law: A Critical Third World Approach' (2007) 8 *Melbourne Journal of International Law* 499; N Tzouvala, *Capitalism as Civilisation: A History of International Law* (Cambridge, Cambridge University Press, 2020).

[6] RF Holland, *European Decolonization, 1918–1981: An Introductory Survey* (New York, St Martin's Press, 1985) 1.

[7] By 2011: 193. See UN Membership, www.un.org/en/about-us/growth-in-un-membership.

[8] JC Jansen and J Osterhammel, *Dekolonisation: Das Ende der Imperien* (München, Verlag CH Beck, 2013) 7.

[9] ibid 7 (my translation).

[10] M Mazower, *Governing the World: The History of an Idea* (London, Penguin Books, 2013) 250.

[11] BS Chimni, 'The Grotian Tradition, Grotian Moment, and Decolonization: A TWAIL Perspective' (2021) 42 *Grotiana* 252, 268.

for example, while Jansen and Osterhammel themselves pose the question of whether the (subsequent) dissolution of the Soviet Union should be considered as a part of the process of decolonisation, or as a process of a separate character.[12] Similar mention could be made of other independence moments in pre-war history: the independence declarations of the Irish Republic in 1916 and 1919; non-violent civil resistance in Egypt leading to its (partial) independence in 1922; the (unsuccessful) Berber independence war in Morocco in 1921–1926; and status-change of certain British colonies – notably Australia, Canada, New Zealand and South Africa – from dominions to Commonwealth members as a result of the 1931 Statute of Westminster.[13] Particularly notable, too, was the growing independence movement in India which, although ongoing since at least 1885, gathered force and worldwide acclaim under the leadership of Mohandas Gandhi from 1921. India – albeit split into India and Pakistan – was to gain independence in 1947.

Despite these precursors, there is a sense in which the decolonisation process began almost accidentally. Although a desire for decolonisation was growing ever stronger in the colonial possessions of the European powers, in the years leading up to the First World War power imbalances between colonies and colonisers were sufficient to perpetuate the status quo. During that war, however, the words and actions of the great powers themselves set in train a process the end result of which was not intended; or perhaps was intended only by Lenin's Russia. During the conflict, the colonies of the European powers became frontlines in an information and propaganda war:[14] by fomenting dissolution and rebellion, as well as through cutting supply lines, the combatants sought to disrupt their opponents' access to the supplies, raw materials and manpower of their overseas empires. In an effort to maintain the loyalty of their own colonies and to win allies in the colonies of their enemies, both sides made extravagant promises of greater independence or self-government.[15] These wartime actions provided the last spark needed to set the beacon of decolonisation ablaze.

II. First World War Rhetoric: Lenin and Wilson on Self-Determination

The First World War was a globalised European war. The main participants were European powers, but the involvement of the colonies held by those powers resulted in a war with a truly global impact and global implications. The colonies not only provided vital supplies to their respective municipal powers during the conflict but also provided manpower to bolster the European armies,[16] and it was

[12] Jansen and Osterhammel, *Dekolonisation* (n 8) 17–18.
[13] UK: Statute of Westminster 1931, ch 4.
[14] TD Musgrave, *Self-Determination and National Minorities* (Oxford, Clarendon Press, 1997) 15.
[15] ibid 15–17.
[16] H Grimal, *Decolonization: The British, French, Dutch and Belgian Empires 1919–1963*, tr S de Vos (Boulder, CO, Westview Press, 1978) 9.

thus clear to both sides that by ridding the other of its colonial supply-chain they could gain a considerable advantage. In due course, therefore, the colonies became frontlines, both as direct theatres of engagement and battlegrounds of ideas.[17] Wishing to destabilise enemy colonies and guarantee the loyalty of their own, both sides promised greater independence or full self-governance in an effort to win and keep allies.[18]

That process only gathered momentum with the rise to power of the Bolsheviks in Russia. The right of nations to self-determination was a mainstay of Lenin's political thought, and was the official policy of the Bolshevik movement.[19] As Thomas Musgrave notes: 'Following the overthrow of the Tzarist regime in Russia the provisional government promised autonomy to many regions, while the Bolsheviks promised full independence.'[20] Indeed, the promise of self-determination was a significant aspect of the Bolsheviks' political appeal in many of Russia's outlying regions, where Russian rule was considered an alien imposition. But self-determination held a position in the movement beyond political convenience: according to Lenin's political theory, the actualised right of all nations that wished it to secessionary self-determination was a first and necessary step towards the great socialist awakening.[21] Importantly – and interestingly – Lenin's self-determination was a non- and even anti-nationalist concept: it was, Lenin argued, the duty of all to reject nationalism in all its forms, including by encouraging the self-determination of people subject not only to saltwater colonialism, but also the land-imperialism of European history:

> In this situation, the proletariat of Russia is faced with a twofold or, rather, a two-sided task: to combat nationalism of every kind, above all, Great-Russian nationalism; to recognise, not only fully equal rights for all nations in general, but also equality of rights as regards polity, ie, the right of nations to self-determination, to secession.[22]

In other words: accepting a strong right of peoples to self-determination is a necessary corollary of accepting that all peoples are equal in rights.[23] Lenin's

[17] Musgrave, *National Minorities* (n 14) 15.

[18] ibid 15–17.

[19] See VI Lenin, 'The Right of Nations to Self-Determination' in J Katzer (ed), B Isaacs and J Fineberg (trs), *VI Lenin: Collected Works*, vol 20 (Moscow, Progress Publishers, 1964) 413, 453–54; and further Musgrave, *National Minorities* (n 14) 17–18; Knox and Tzouvala, 'Looking Eastwards' (n 2).

[20] Musgrave, *National Minorities* (n 14) 17–18.

[21] Lenin, 'Right of Nations' (n 19) 413; although see, *contra*, L Mälksoo, 'The Soviet Approach to the Right of Peoples to Self-Determination: Russia's Farewell to the *Jus Publicum Europaeum*' (2017) 19 *Journal of the History of International Law/Revue d'histoire du droit international* 200, 202–04 and *passim*.

[22] Lenin, 'Right of Nations' (n 19) 453–54.

[23] Here it is important to distinguish between self-determination in Lenin's political theory as expressed in the years during and immediately following the First World War, and self-determination as it was subsequently practised by the Soviet Union. As discussed above – compare, for example, ch 2, s II.B – the Bolsheviks would hardly be the first revolutionaries to fail to live up to the high principles they declared in their campaign to replace the former order. For (contrasting) accounts of subsequent Soviet attitudes to self-determination and imperialism, see Mälksoo, 'Soviet Approach' (n 21) 207–16; Knox and Tzouvala, 'Looking Eastwards' (n 2) 31–45.

thought on self-determination was to prove to be highly influential, both in itself and through the competition for influence between Lenin's Russia and Woodrow Wilson's United States.

1919 saw the end of the war, and the defeat of Germany, Austria-Hungary and Turkey. By that time most of the colonies of the central powers had fallen into Allied hands, and it became increasingly important to determine their future.[24] It was the leaders of the Russian revolution who first advocated that the colonies be permitted to self-determine, but their calls were swiftly echoed by others.[25] In particular, Lenin's call for self-determination influenced Henry Balfour, who was the first to moot the idea of international control of the territories. In turn, Balfour's ideas were taken up by Woodrow Wilson who, during the course of the war and the subsequent peace process, became a strong advocate of self-determination. It seems clear that his was a narrower conception than the principled, absolutist form advocated by Lenin,[26] however: Lenin's commitment to self-determination was clear, but the intention behind Wilson's call for self-determination has often been debated. It may be that Wilson was, if in a less radical form, equally as committed as Lenin to the principle that repressed and subject peoples should be released from colonialism and achieve self-rule.[27] Equally, it may be that he simply saw some form of internationalisation as a preferable option to further growing the European empires, in realpolitik terms.[28] In order fully to understand his commitment to self-determination, and what that principle meant within his worldview, a brief excursus to examine his political thought is worthwhile.

A. Self-Determination and Woodrow Wilson's Political Philosophy

Woodrow Wilson is among the most complex and fascinating personalities of US political history. Undoubtedly one of the most influential US presidents, and

[24] The League of Nations, *The Mandates System: Origin – Principles – Application* (Geneva, Series of League of Nations Publications, 1945) 13 www.un.org/unispal/document/auto-insert-176218.

[25] ibid 14.

[26] Although see, *contra*, Mälksoo, 'Soviet Approach' (n 21) 204–05. Mälksoo argues that 'for Lenin and his Bolsheviks – unlike for Wilson – the right of peoples to self-determination was not a political end in itself'. Here the view is preferred, with Knox and Tzouvala, that 'the accusation of insincerity ignores the Bolshevik analysis of imperialism': Knox and Tzouvala, 'Looking Eastwards' (n 2) 28ff. Mälksoo's analysis also seems, as discussed in s II.A, to give too much credit to Wilson's good intentions in his formulation of self-determination.

[27] Saladin Ambar argues that Wilson 'was the first statesman of world stature to speak out not only against European imperialism but against the newer form of economic domination sometimes described as "informal imperialism." For repressed ethnic and national groups around the world, his call for "national self-determination" was the herald's trumpet for a new era.' See: S Ambar, 'Woodrow Wilson: Impact and Legacy' (Miller Center of Public Affairs, University of Virginia, 2016) millercenter.org/president/wilson/impact-and-legacy.

[28] The League of Nations, *Mandates System* (n 24) 14–15.

long regarded as one of the most progressive,[29] Wilson is a figure of surprising complexity. It has often been noticed by observers of Wilson that his presidency was marked by a distinct conservatism,[30] but his legacy has received an additional level of scrutiny in the years following the death of George Floyd at the hands of Minnesota police officers in May 2020.[31] The reassessment of US society post-2020 has called attention to Wilson's overt and ingrained racism, an aspect of his character and presidency that had hitherto escaped proper attention.[32] It was not a merely incidental aspect of his social policy, however, which could be explained as an unexamined precept of the time: rather, it was a motivating force. More than perhaps any other US president post the Civil War, Wilson was a political philosopher – he was the author of several works of political theory and remains the only US president to have held a PhD – and his presidency was shaped by his theoretical convictions. Prominent among them was his view of the nature of the state and the source of its authority.

Wilson was a revolutionary thinker in US constitutional terms. He rejected flatly many of the doctrines and assertions that underpinned the US constitution, as set down in that document and in the Declaration of Independence.[33] In particular, Wilson criticised the Declaration of Independence as being founded on a Hobbesian fiction;[34] a naturalism that he regarded not only as being theoretically unsound but historically disproved.[35] The Declaration's famous proposition as 'self-evident' that 'all men are created equal' was, Wilson argued, 'a mere "assertion"':[36] government is 'accountable to Darwin, not to Newton'.[37]

Unable to appeal to naturalism, Wilson was left with a need to find another basis for the authority of states, and he found it in community will. But like many historically minded social contractarian thinkers both before and since, he was not satisfied with the Hobbesian solution of positing a contract 'moment' at which the state was formally constituted: the state is not founded upon 'conscious mutual consent of individuals', either to its authority in particular or 'to abstract principles

[29] Rightly, although not without contradiction. See Ambar, 'Wilson' (n 27).

[30] CR Kesler, 'Woodrow Wilson and the Statesmanship of Progress' in BCS Watson (ed), *Progressive Challenges to the American Constitution* (Cambridge, Cambridge University Press, 2017) 228–29.

[31] J Goyette, 'Hundreds Demand Justice in Minneapolis after Police Killing of George Floyd' *The Guardian* (27 May 2020) www.theguardian.com/us-news/2020/may/26/george-floyd-killing-minneapolis-protest-police.

[32] JJ Jablonski Jr, 'The Dark Side of President Woodrow Wilson's Progressive Political Thought: Its Race-Historicism and Other Anti-Democratic Aspects' (unpublished thesis, Claremont Graduate University, 2018) 2–3. The renewed attention has led to the removal of Wilson's name from numerous memorials and honorific positions. See eg Office of Communications, Princeton University, 'Press Release: Board of Trustees' Decision on Removing Woodrow Wilson's Name from Public Policy School and Residential College' (*princeton.edu*, 27 June 2020).

[33] RW Van Alstyne, 'Woodrow Wilson and the Idea of the Nation State' (1961) 37 *International Affairs* 293, 295; Kesler, 'Statesmanship of Progress' (n 30) 228–32 and *passim*.

[34] Kesler, 'Statesmanship of Progress' (n 30) 232.

[35] Van Alstyne, 'Wilson and the Nation State' (n 33) 295.

[36] Kesler, 'Statesmanship of Progress' (n 30) 240, citing Woodrow Wilson, *Constitutional Government in the United States* (1908).

[37] Woodrow Wilson, cited in Kesler, 'Statesmanship of Progress' (n 30) 234.

like universal equality'.[38] Rather, Wilson found the basis of its authority in a shared sense of community and in the values of that community. Notably, however, for Wilson that shared sense of statehood was not social, but national: his was a racially defined community, and his state a nation State. It was the 'unconscious in-bred habits and customs of a racially superior unified homogenous community' which Wilson posited as the basic unit of a state.[39]

Wilson's commitment to ethnonationalism has not been extensively studied in relation to his self-determination doctrine, but would certainly make for a fascinating and revealing subject-matter. Preliminarily, it certainly appears to have relevance for his post-war commitment to self-determination as a principle of the new international order, and to do so in two ways. To begin with, his belief in the need for a racially homogeneous community as the basis for statehood certainly seems to lead him to a commitment to a (mediated) form of decolonisation. Put into modern vocabulary, we could perhaps see this as a form of political self-determination principle, albeit a deeply illiberal one: through recognition of its shared identity, customs and culture, the nation is able to constitute itself as the nation state. Minority-governed states, among them colonial possessions, could never be true states according to Wilson's theory. But Wilson was not purely a racial isolationist; he also had a firm belief in the superiority of the Caucasian race, and in particular of those of Anglo-Saxon descent.[40] Whether as a corollary of that superiority belief or as an accessory to it, Wilson also saw the post-war realignment as the moment at which the United States would assume its proper position at the pinnacle of the international order. The United States was the true inheritor of white European racial superiority:

> Europe, he assumed, would henceforth subordinate herself to the United States; and the world at large, including Russia, would fall under American influence. It was a new dream of universal empire, allegedly confined to the exercise of moral influence but backed up by the new position of dominance attained by the United States.[41]

Wilson's influence on the post-war international order was profound, but not unrivalled. Although Wilson is now often given sole credit as the (Western) architect of decolonisation,[42] to do so unfairly neglects not only the agency of the colonised peoples, but also the vital influence of a second Global North leader. As Richard Van Alstyne observes, there were two 'prophets' of this new system, each of whom 'in his own way, but in fulfilment of the peculiar mission of his respective

[38] Jablonski, 'Wilson's Race-Historicism' (n 32) 4.

[39] ibid 4 (references omitted). Notably, community identity (without the ethnonationalism of Wilson's theory) remains an element of many modern theories of statehood. See, for example, Anna Stilz, who puts the idea to much more progressive use than does Wilson: A Stilz, *Territorial Sovereignty: A Philosophical Exploration* (Oxford, Oxford University Press, 2019).

[40] Jablonski, 'Wilson's Race-Historicism' (n 32) 6; Kesler, 'Statesmanship of Progress' (n 30) 241.

[41] Van Alstyne, 'Wilson and the Nation State' (n 33) 307–08.

[42] This argument is made passionately, for example, by Mälksoo, who argues that it is 'a misunderstanding to mention in one breath Lenin's (the Bolsheviks') and Wilson's concepts of self-determination': Mälksoo, 'Soviet Approach' (n 21) 203ff; and further Knox and Tzouvala, 'Looking Eastwards' (n 2).

nation, struck a mortal blow' at the European-dominated imperial order.[43] The second 'prophet' of the new international order was Vladimir Lenin, and it was Lenin and the Bolsheviks' – in many ways, much more coherent[44] – commitment to self-determination that set in train many of the post-war developments. As Van Alstyne notes, Wilson's famous 'Fourteen Points was his response to [Lenin's] challenge'.[45] In considering Wilson's role in setting the decolonisation process in train it is important to recall both that geopolitical context, as well as the centrality of what would today be called self-determination in Wilson's own – in some respects, contradictory – political theory. Here to, in assessing the legacy of this most multifaceted of presidents, complexity rules.

B. Internationalisation: Decolonisation and Wilson's Illiberal Liberalism

In January 1917, Wilson addressed a joint session of Congress. His address was entitled 'Peace Without Victory', and in the course of the speech he laid out a vision for peace in Europe which, he hoped, would encourage the central powers to submit to a negotiated ceasefire. Central to that vision of a stable Europe was the principle of political self-determination:

> No peace can last, or ought to last, which does not recognize and accept the principle that governments derive all their just powers from the consent of the governed, and that no right anywhere exists to hand peoples about from sovereignty to sovereignty as if they were property.[46]

This liberal clarion call is somewhat at odds with Wilson's political philosophy, although it may fit more comfortably if 'peoples' is interpreted to refer to 'nations' and to exclude a similar status applying to national minorities. It is not clear from this passage whether Wilson was advocating a strong right of national (nation-) statehood, a principle of popular consent to government, or whether his goal was to ensure that the war would not result in the acquisition of territories by Bolshevik Russia or the European powers.[47] There are indications, however, that it was realpolitik that was foremost in his mind; certainly, it was the impermissibility of territorial acquisitions which was the focus of Wilson's letter to Pope Benedict XV on 27 August 1917.[48]

Although it seems clear that Wilson was not seeking to institute a right to secessionary self-determination – and certainly not one which would give rights

[43] Van Alstyne, 'Wilson and the Nation State' (n 33) 307.
[44] Lenin, 'Right of Nations' (n 19) 413, 451–54; Knox and Tzouvala, 'Looking Eastwards' (n 2) 31–42.
[45] Van Alstyne, 'Wilson and the Nation State' (n 33) 306–07.
[46] W Wilson, 'Peace Without Victory' (22 January 1917).
[47] Tzouvala, *Capitalism as Civilisation* (n 5) 91–92.
[48] W Wilson, 'Reply to the Pope of 27th August 1917' (27 August 1917).

to national minorities – or to establish definitive principles for the determination of territorial claims, he insists on the superiority of the rights of 'peoples' over the rights of 'Governments'. Here his rejection of what he saw as Hobbesian/Newtonianism in favour of a 'people' defined in ethnonational terms seems clearly to play into his post-war espousal of self-determination:[49] '"If any one ask me what a free government is," Wilson quotes Burke as saying, "I reply, it is what the people think so."'[50] Peoples, he argues, have a right to freedom and self-government. These statements established Wilson as an advocate of political self-determination in the peace process in Europe, and of the United States' position that the process should take self-determination principles into consideration. At the same time, in the East, Lenin's Russia was yet more definite in its espousal of self-determination, a principle that was central to Lenin's interpretation of Marxist thought.[51] As Van Alstyne notes, Russia and Lenin 'forced the pace' on many of the developments in the period:[52] Wilson's desire to position the United States as the leading nation of the post-war world – to be 'the Messiah of the New Order'[53] – pushed him to keep pace with Lenin. His 'response to this challenge', as Van Alstyne notes, was his famous 'Fourteen Points' speech in January of 1918,[54] which refined, formalised and extended his thoughts on the peace process. Wilson's fourth point stated that there must be:

> A free, open-minded, and absolutely impartial adjustment of all colonial claims, based upon a strict observance of the principle that in determining all such questions of sovereignty the interests of the populations concerned must have equal weight with the equitable claims of the government whose title is to be determined.[55]

While the address was not a ringing endorsement of self-determination, Wilson established that the will of the population was a factor to be considered in the determination of colonial claims, and did so authoritatively: 'Liberals and Christians accepted [the Fourteen Points] as gospel, so that any disagreement or disposition to disregard them was instantly looked upon as unworthy and as a breach of faith.'[56] Cassese is, of course, correct to strike the cautionary note when he comments that, for Wilson, 'self-determination should not be the sole or even the paramount yardstick in this area, but must be reconciled with the interests of colonial powers'.[57] Nevertheless, it is difficult to overstate the importance of the

[49] Kesler, 'Statesmanship of Progress' (n 30) 232–34, 240; Jablonski, 'Wilson's Race-Historicism' (n 32) 10ff.

[50] Kesler, 'Statesmanship of Progress' (n 30) 240, citing Wilson. It is likely that the remark Kesler quotes derives from an address given by Wilson in Madison, Wisconsin on 5 January 1910, in *The Papers of Woodrow Wilson*, vol 19, ed AS Link (Princeton, NJ, Princeton University Press, 1975) 726.

[51] Lenin, 'Right of Nations' (n 19) 453 and *passim*; Musgrave, *National Minorities* (n 14) 17–18.

[52] Van Alstyne, 'Wilson and the Nation State' (n 33) 306.

[53] ibid 306.

[54] ibid 306–07.

[55] W Wilson, 'Fourteen Points' (8 January 1918).

[56] Van Alstyne, 'Wilson and the Nation State' (n 33) 307.

[57] A Cassese, *Self-Determination of Peoples: A Legal Reappraisal* (Cambridge, Cambridge University Press, 1995) 21.

idea that colonial peoples should be given some measure of influence over their future circumstances.

> Peoples are not to be handed about from one sovereignty to another by an international conference or an understanding between rivals and antagonists. National aspirations must be respected; peoples may now be dominated and governed only by their own consent. 'Self-determination' is not a mere phrase. It is an imperative principle of actions which statesmen will henceforth ignore at their peril.[58]

It is surprising – or, given subsequent history, perhaps not surprising at all – that the role of the second 'prophet'[59] of the post-war order in the institution of self-determination as the guiding principle of the decolonisation era has been comparatively neglected. Lenin's commitment to self-determination was likely decisive in this history,[60] both in its direct influence and in the 'challenge' it presented to Wilson. There were notable differences between the ideas of self-determination held by the two men, and ultimately neither was adopted unaltered: while Wilson's was a nationalist principle of internal political freedom, which placed the (ethnonationalistically defined) people above the structures of government; Lenin's was an antinationalist idealism, which believed that peoples would be enabled to achieve the communist liberation more readily by dismantling structures of foreign domination. As will be seen in what follows, elements of both ideas are present in the norm of colonial self-determination that was to emerge in the decades which followed. In their individual actions – and perhaps especially, in their competition – the twin 'prophets of the new international order'[61] had set in motion a process which would eventually yield a political conviction that colonialism is inherently reprehensible, and that colonial peoples should be granted self-government.[62] In determining the form that self-government should take in any particular case, self-determination became the accepted tool of the international community.

[58] W Wilson, 'President Wilson's Address to Congress, Analyzing German and Austrian Peace Utterances' (11 February 1918).

[59] Van Alstyne, 'Wilson and the Nation State' (n 33) 307.

[60] Tzouvala, *Capitalism as Civilisation* (n 5) 93.

[61] Van Alstyne, 'Wilson and the Nation State' (n 33) 307.

[62] I refer, here, to colonialism as a whole. Although individual cases of colonial rule had previously been seen as illegitimate, and although colonialism was often (if not always) seen as illegitimate by those under colonial rule (a prime example is Haiti under French rule pre-1804), the international community continued to recognise colonial rule as acceptable, or even laudable – for many years colonialism was arrogated as part of a 'civilising mission' – and the great powers were understood to have a perfect right to continued possession of the colonial holdings. 1918 marks a watershed moment: before this, claims by colonies to independence were generally justified on the basis of mistreatment or other failure by the colonial power (and thus fall more readily under the heading of remedial self-determination). The Haitian declaration of independence falls into this category (1804, see D Armitage, *The Declaration of Independence: A Global History* (Cambridge, MA, Harvard University Press, 2007) 193–98), as does the 1776 American declaration (see ch 2). In the years that were to follow, however, it was increasingly widely believed that colonies have a right to independence because of their status as such, and not only as a result of abuse by the colonial power.

III. The Mandates System

The end of the First World War left the international community with a dilemma over the colonial possessions of the defeated central powers. While it was considered unacceptable for the colonies to revert to their pre-war masters, many states – including Wilson's America – were reluctant to see the empires of France and the United Kingdom grow yet larger. And yet most states, too, were not yet willing to embrace Lenin's proposal of self-determination for the colonies.[63] Their answer was to place the colonies into international stewardship, under a system devised by General Smuts.[64] Smuts considered that the task of administering the territories could not practicably be carried out at the international level, and so proposed a system of *mandates*.[65] Article 22 of the League of Nations Covenant established the mandates system:

> To those colonies and territories which as a consequence of the late war have ceased to be under the sovereignty of the States which formerly governed them and which are inhabited by peoples not yet able to stand by themselves under the strenuous conditions of the modern world, there should be applied the principle that the well-being and development of such peoples form a sacred trust of civilisation and that securities for the performance of this trust should be embodied in this Covenant.[66]

Elizabeth Rodríguez-Santiago describes this as an embryonic form of the right to colonial self-determination that would later evolve under the auspices of the United Nations: individual states would be given responsibility for mandated territories under the supervision of the League, and the principle was established that the purpose of the arrangement was the care and development of the territories, and not the ownership of or profit from them.[67] Three categories were established: the 'A', 'B' and 'C' mandates.[68] The A mandates were those territories seen

[63] Nevertheless, and alongside realpolitik considerations, Leninian and Wilsonian self-determination probably contributed to the unwillingness of states to see the colonies incorporated into the European empires.

[64] The League of Nations, *Mandates System* (n 24) 16–17; Tzouvala, *Capitalism as Civilisation* (n 5) 92–93. For a detailed account of the negotiation history of the mandates system, see PB Potter, 'Origin of the System of Mandates under the League of Nations' (1922) 16 *American Political Science Review* 563.

[65] The League of Nations, *Mandates System* (n 24) 16–17.

[66] Art 22 of the Covenant of the League of Nations (Paris, 28 June 1919).

[67] E Rodríguez-Santiago, 'The Evolution of Self-Determination of Peoples in International Law' in FR Tesón (ed), *The Theory of Self-Determination* (Cambridge, Cambridge University Press, 2016) 213. Although note that such a right to self-determination was not envisioned. As Pedersen puts it, 'the League, against its own desires and intentions, helped to bring the European empires down': S Pedersen, *The Guardians: The League of Nations and the Crisis of Empire* (Oxford, Oxford University Press, 2015) 406.

[68] The League of Nations, *Mandates System* (n 24). For an outline of the different classifications of mandates and their differences, see Tzouvala, *Capitalism as Civilisation* (n 5) 99–102; and further N Matz, 'Civilization and the Mandate System under the League of Nations as Origin of Trusteeship' (2005) 9 *Max Planck Yearbook of United Nations Law* 47, 72–73. For an account of the negotiation history of the different mandate categories, see Pedersen, *The Guardians* (n 67) 52–56.

as closest to independence, the 'existence [of which] as independent nations can be provisionally recognized'.[69] At the other end of the spectrum, the C mandates 'came closest to colonial rule'.[70] As Ntina Tzouvala observes, '[b]oth international lawyers and League administrators at the time struggled to establish a distinction between the C mandates relationship and outright annexation',[71] a matter that was ultimately to require adjudication by the ICJ.[72]

The mandates system has been described by Quincey Wright as a form of tutelage. The colonies of the defeated powers were placed under the control of one or more of the allied powers to hold in trust on behalf of the international community.[73] While the colonial possessions of the European powers that remained outside the mandates system were conceived as the property of those states, the mandate territories were treated quite differently. Michael Callahan observes, for example, that the mandate territories were often subject to better treatment than the mandatory's own colonial possessions.[74] A similar distinction can be seen in that, while the mandatories tended to regard their own colonies as permanent possessions over which their rights were absolute, it was accepted that the ultimate goal of the mandates was the independence of the territories:

> [T]he phrase 'peoples not *yet* able to stand by themselves' is used [in Article 22 of the League Covenant]. It follows from this and from the very conception of tutelage that this mission is not, in principle, intended to be prolonged indefinitely, but only until the peoples under tutelage are capable of managing their own affairs.[75]

The suggestion that a people should be denied independence until such time as Western powers considered them sufficiently 'civilised' is markedly distasteful.[76] Indeed, a 'civilisational' logic that is at best patronising and at worst an exercise of power as pernicious as imperialism pervaded the mandate system.[77] As Tzouvala discusses, the creation of the mandates system incorporated and modulated the pre-twentieth-century logic of the 'civilised' versus the 'uncivilised' world to create a new form of gatekeeper to the international community: before the former

[69] Matz, 'Civilization and the Mandates System' (n 68) 72.

[70] ibid 73.

[71] Tzouvala, *Capitalism as Civilisation* (n 5) 101. For an account of the events in South Africa and Namibia which precipitated these difficulties, see Pedersen, *The Guardians* (n 67) 216–220. It is highly indicative of the difficulty of establishing the difference between sovereignty and a class C mandate that Matz resorts to drawing the line as one 'between imperium and dominium': see Matz, 'Civilization and the Mandates System' (n 68) 73 (references omitted).

[72] In its *Legal Consequences for States of the Continued Presence of South Africa in Namibia (South West Africa) notwithstanding Security Council Resolution 276 (1970)*, Advisory Opinion, (1971) ICJ Reports 16. For discussion, see ch 4, s II.

[73] Q Wright, *Mandates under the League of Nations* (Chicago, University of Chicago Press, 1930) 11 (footnotes omitted).

[74] MD Callahan, *A Sacred Trust: The League of Nations and Africa 1929–1946* (Brighton, Sussex Academic Press, 2004) 17.

[75] The League of Nations, *Mandates System* (n 24) 23.

[76] For discussion of the ways in which the discourse of 'civilisation' was employed to mediate personality in the international community, see Tzouvala, *Capitalism as Civilisation* (n 5) *passim*, eg 51–55.

[77] ibid esp 88–128.

colonies could become members of the community – that is, before they could achieve independence – they would need to be 'civilised'; to be 'developed', in the parlance of the League. This Tzouvala names this the 'logic of improvement'.[78] And yet the system also incorporated the other axis of the civilisational dialectic, as identified by Tzouvala: the 'logic of biology'. The colonies and their peoples were, to some degree, inherently different, backward, lesser:

> The basic structure of the mandate enacted the idea that mandated territories could at least, in theory, reach capitalism and modernity. However, they were not able to do so endogenously, but only through a period of subjugation and supervision by international actors. The Eurocentric idea that there was something inherent in Western culture, religion or racial composition (and their various combinations) that enabled or even necessitated the transition to capitalism, modernity and global domination was entrenched in the very structure of the Mandate System, as was its mirror image of the stationary East that could only be transformed through external guidance and coercion.[79]

As Tzouvala and others have identified, the 'institutionalisation' (to use Tzouvala's term) of the pre-twentieth-century logic of civilisation in the architecture of the post-war international order embedded in that order a form of ongoing imperialism, albeit of a less overt kind than that practised in the eighteenth and nineteenth centuries.[80] Moreover, there was a marked tendency for the (already somewhat minimal) protections of the mandates system to be disregarded when it suited the interests of the European powers,[81] and there is thus more than a slight sense that the system – at least at its worst moments – amounted to little more than paying lip service to the principles which apparently underpinned it.

Nevertheless, there can be no doubt that a declaration that these territories were to be guided towards independent statehood was powerful. However cynical may have been the intention in establishing and running the mandates system, the members of the League's Permanent Mandates Commission (PMC) – the body that administered the mandates system – became, as Susan Pedersen puts it, the 'inadvertent architects of a world they had not imagined'.[82] In small movements, each of which seemed the logical corollary of the one before, a new reality emerged. There was, as Rodríguez-Santiago notes, no intention at the moment of the drafting of the League Covenant to create anything more extensive or

[78] For a brief definition of what Tzouvala understands by the terms 'logic of improvement' and its counterpart, the 'logic of biology', see ibid 2 and discussion *passim*.

[79] ibid 98 (references omitted).

[80] ibid eg 127–28. For a similar observation from a different perspective, see Chimni, 'Grotian Moments and Decolonization' (n 11); and further BS Chimni, *International Law and World Order: A Critique of Contemporary Approaches*, 2nd edn (Cambridge, Cambridge University Press, 2017); Anghie, *Imperialism* (n 3).

[81] Both Usha Natarajan and Tzouvala discuss the – quite horrifying – example of the British mandate over Iraq: U Natarajan, 'Creating and Recreating Iraq: Legacies of the Mandate System in Contemporary Understandings of Third World Sovereignty' (2011) 24 *Leiden Journal of International Law* 799, 807–11; Tzouvala, *Capitalism as Civilisation* (n 5) 120–27.

[82] Pedersen, *The Guardians* (n 67) 407.

powerful than a gradual movement towards independence that would remain the discretion of the PMC and the mandatory powers.[83] In particular, no right to self-determination at the behest of the people of the territory was envisaged. Institutionalising the movement to independence within a structure, however, regularised it. By 1931, the PMC produced a report for the League Council laying down the conditions which, in its opinion, should exist in a mandate territory before that territory should be granted independence.[84] Those criteria can, of course, serve as a barrier just as easily as they offer a gateway – a yardstick that can be used to indicate the ways in which a prospective new state does *not* measure up. Moreover, the PMC did not have the capacity to make demands of the mandatories in most cases, so the conditions were 'merely suggestions', and were not capable of creating a legal threshold.[85] Nevertheless, the mandatories' duty to report to the PMC contributed to a sense that territories should be prepared for their eventual independence and, in turn, '[t]he notion that the eventual independence of dependencies was inevitable and expedient tended to the notion that it was *a right*'.[86] As Pedersen argues,

> The League helped make the end of empire imaginable, and normative statehood possible, not because the empires willed it so, or the Covenant prescribed it, but because that dynamic of internationalization changed everything – including how 'dependent peoples' would bid for statehood, what that 'statehood' would henceforth mean, and whether empires would think territorial control essential to the maintenance of global power.[87]

The League of Nations did not live up to its promise. It failed to prevent the outbreak of war between two of its members, Japan and China, in 1931, and, through its silence, condoned Mussolini's action in Abyssinia (in modern-day Ethiopia) in 1936.[88] Following the Second World War, the League of Nations was replaced with the United Nations. In many ways, however, the mandates system was to prove stronger than the League. Callahan notes that when Japan pulled out of the League in 1935 it maintained its mandates, retained its seat on the PMC and continued to send the proper reports and representatives to the Commission.[89] Thus when the UN Charter was negotiated in 1945 it was not only the practical provisions on the administration of the mandate territories that were to be re-created in the trusteeship system; many of the ideas of self-government and self-determination that the mandates system had engendered found textual expression in the new system.

[83] Rodríguez-Santiago, 'Evolution of Self-Determination' (n 67) 213.

[84] Grimal, *Decolonization* (n 16) 18; see also Tzouvala, *Capitalism as Civilisation* (n 5) 110–11. The criteria included (paraphrased): (a) a settled government capable of delivering essential services; (b) the capability to maintain its territorial integrity; (c) the capability to maintain public peace within the territory; (d) adequate financial resources for governmental functions; and (e) a body of law and judicial organisation sufficient to ensure the rule of law.

[85] Grimal, *Decolonization* (n 16) 18.

[86] Wright, *Mandates* (n 73) 12 (emphasis added).

[87] Pedersen, *The Guardians* (n 67) 406.

[88] D Rothermund, *Decolonization: The Routledge Companion* (London, Routledge, 2006) 50.

[89] Callahan, *Sacred Trust* (n 74) 44–45.

IV. The United Nations and the Trusteeship System

On 26 June 1945, the delegates to the San Francisco Peace Conference concluded the Charter of the United Nations, and replaced the League's mandates system with a system of trusteeship. Although the systems were not identical, many of the mandates system's central features were incorporated into the trusteeship system with only minor changes. Unlike the mandates system, however, the trusteeship system was given a textual foundation in the UN Charter: Chapters XI and XII are devoted to the system in general, while Chapter XIII sets out the powers and remit of the Trusteeship Council. In that sense, the trusteeship system began life in an institutionally stronger position than did the mandates system: rather than being an afterthought – a 'bolt on' to the League, however central it became to that body's activities – administering the trusteeship system was to be one of the core functions of the new United Nations, on par with the maintenance of international peace and security. Nevertheless, the mandates system was not universally popular among the states represented at the San Francisco conference, and the trusteeship system as set down in the Charter neither realised the pre-Conference hopes of expansion and development of those who saw it as toothless and insufficient, nor effected the rollback of the mandates systems that would have sufficed to appease its detractors: as Dietmar Rothermund observes, while the system which emerged lacked the ambition of Roosevelt, who 'wanted to put all colonies … under a regime of international trusteeship to prepare them for independence', those who hoped, as Churchill did, 'that the old mandate system would be abolished after the war so that the respective territories could be added to the colonies of the mandatory powers',[90] had to reconcile themselves to a strengthened system, and one with an increased oversight capacity.[91]

The anaemic textual basis of the mandates system can be contrasted directly with the full and thorough expression of the principles and powers associated with trusteeship in the Charter. While the principles that underpinned the mandates system were largely unwritten and were often vague, the Charter codified the principles applicable to the trusteeship system, and made several significant changes to the language of the system which point to a more explicit focus on the ultimate independence of trust territories.[92] Not only did the Charter create an obligation on the trustee progressively to develop the infrastructure and institutions of the trust territory towards the self-government or independence of the population,[93] but Article 76 signalled the relevance of self-determination in that endeavour: the 'freely expressed wishes of the peoples concerned' are declared to be relevant to the development towards either self-government or independence.

[90] Rothermund, *Decolonization* (n 88) 51.

[91] ibid 51; Art 87(c) of the Charter of the United Nations and Statute of the International Court of Justice (San Francisco, 26 June 1945).

[92] Art 76–76(b) UN Charter (n 91).

[93] D Rauschning, 'Article 76' in B Simma et al (eds), *The Charter of the United Nations: A Commentary*, vol 2, 3rd edn (Oxford, Oxford University Press, 2012) 1852.

Care must be taken not to overemphasise the significance of these developments in the logic and stated goals of the system; though in parallel, they should not be unduly minimised. Some scholars have, perhaps overenthusiastically, identified the conclusion of the Charter as a clear and determined break with the imperial past. Plainly, as Sundhya Pahuja and others have comprehensively demonstrated, it was not.[94] The Charter did not demand the independence of even trust territories, recognising 'self-government' as a second viable end-state – something that, it is clear, was understood contemporaneously as compatible with a continuing colonial relationship.[95] Still less did it demand the independence of those colonies that were not subject to a trust.[96] And it is true to say, as Tzouvala does, that the Charter's reference to self-determination in the colonial context represented 'a principle and not a right'.[97]

Certainly, it is not possible 'to argue that the UN Charter and the international order that emerged in the immediate aftermath of the Second World War were inherently anti-imperialist'.[98] But equally, it would be an unfairly harsh appraisal that did not recognise elements of advancement in the system. That the seats on the Trusteeship Council were to be filled by states' representatives gave visibility to the Council's processes, and brought international politics to bear on decolonisation.[99] Similarly, there is no trusteeship equivalent of the class C mandates – 'in their practical effect not far removed from annexation'[100] – and the capacity of all trust territories to achieve independence or self-government was thus (tangentially) recognised. In that sense, and adopting Tzouvala's vocabulary, we could say that here the 'logic of improvement' perhaps began to obtain something of an upper hand over the 'logic of biology'.[101]

[94] For discussion of the ways in which colonial thinking is embedded in the Charter, see S Pahuja, *Decolonising International Law: Development, Economic Growth and the Politics of Universality* (Cambridge, Cambridge University Press, 2011) 30–31 and *passim*; and further Tzouvala, *Capitalism as Civilisation* (n 5) 129–38. For analysis of the ways in which patterns of imperialism continue to influence the contemporary international order, see influentially BS Chimni, 'International Institutions Today: An Imperial Global State in the Making' (2004) 15 *European Journal of international law* 1, *passim*, eg 1-6; BS Chimni, 'Capitalism, Imperialism, and International Law in the Twenty-First Century Symposium' (2012) 14 *Oregon Review of International Law* 17, *passim*, eg 27–32; and further Chimni, *International Law and World Order* (n 80).

[95] United Nations, *Documents of the United Nations Conference on International Organization, San Francisco, 1945*, vol 10 (New York, United Nations Information Organization, 1945) 440; and discussion in Tzouvala, *Capitalism as Civilisation* (n 5) 132–133. As Rothermund notes, self-government is conceived in a way more closely analogous to devolution than to independent statehood: Rothermund, *Decolonization* (n 88) 52.

[96] As Mazower observes, the colonial powers 'went away from San Francisco confident that the new world body was consistent with continued imperial rule': Mazower, *Governing the World* (n 10) 253.

[97] Tzouvala, *Capitalism as Civilisation* (n 5) 131.

[98] ibid 133.

[99] Mazower, *Governing the World* (n 10) 253.

[100] *Namibia* (n 72) para 45.

[101] Note that, as Tzouvala defines them, both the logics of improvement and biology are aspects of the standard of civilisation, albeit standing in ever-shifting relation and priority to each other (Tzouvala refers to a 'persistent' and 'fundamental argumentative oscillation between "improvement" and

Finally, and of most significance for this study, that the self-determination of the trust territories' inhabitants was relevant in determining the destiny of the territories gave the principle a central position within the process. In itself, the Article 76(2) reference to 'the freely expressed wishes of the peoples concerned' was not revolutionary. The article declares that (one of) the 'basic objectives of the trusteeship system … shall be':

> to promote the political, economic, social, and educational advancement of the inhabitants of the trust territories, and their progressive development towards self-government or independence as may be appropriate to the particular circumstances of each territory and its peoples and the freely expressed wishes of the peoples concerned, and as may be provided by the terms of each trusteeship agreement.[102]

The article certainly gives a prominence to the 'wishes of the peoples concerned', but hardly makes them determinative: self-determination is one factor to be considered alongside the 'particular circumstances' of the territory, and is subordinated to whatever stipulations may form part of the trusteeship agreement. As Tzouvala notes, at the time of its drafting the Article 76 reference to self-determination amounted to little more than a principle of the process, and certainly did not create a legal right.[103] Nevertheless, by placing self-determination at the centre of the process, it is likely that the Charter went some way towards enabling the norm development which was to follow from its implementation in the period 1945–c.1960.[104] Beyond these incremental developments, however, there is one respect in which the Charter was far more radical than the League: the Charter purported to give certain protections to the rights and entitlements also of the populations of colonial (non-self-governing) territories that were not the subject of a trust. While Chapter XII of the Charter laid down the principles to be applied specifically to the trusteeship system, Chapter XI sets down principles for the administration of all non-self-governing territories:

> Members of the United Nations which have or assume responsibilities for the administration of territories whose people have not yet attained a full measure of self-government recognise the principle that the interest of the inhabitants of these territories are paramount.[105]

Article 73 defines several aims that the states involved must pursue in the interests of the inhabitants. Prominently placed among these is the obligation to develop self-government in the territories.[106] As Rothermund notes, the Charter

"biology'"). Increasing priority being given to 'improvement' over biology', therefore, indicates a change to the functioning of, rather than an escape from, the standard of civilisation: Tzouvala, *Capitalism as Civilisation* (n 5) 4–5, and *passim*.

[102] Art 76(2) UN Charter (n 91).

[103] Tzouvala, *Capitalism as Civilisation* (n 5) 131.

[104] See generally below, esp s V.C.

[105] Art 73 UN Charter (n 91).

[106] Art 73(b) UN Charter (n 91).

is careful to refer only to 'self-government', and not to 'self-determination' or to 'independence'.[107] Nevertheless, for the first time it had been declared (and, by the colonial powers, accepted) that the powers had certain obligations vis-a-vis their colonies. Other provisions, too, point to an emerging sense that the colonies and the trust territories were of a kind. While the mandates system applied only to those territories stripped from the defeated central powers in the aftermath of the First World War, the trusteeship system was designed to apply to the existing mandated territories, territories 'detached from enemy states as a result of the Second World War' and even 'territories voluntarily placed under the system'.[108] This expansion explicitly made the system relevant to colonies held by states in their own capacities. While states were under no obligation to place colonies into the trusteeship system, it was nevertheless made clear that there was no difference in kind between the colonies stripped from the defeated powers in both wars, and the colonies held by the victors. This declaration of equivalency between the former mandates and other colonies naturally contributed to a sense that the same principles should apply to each.

While being appropriately cautious not to extrapolate backwards from the decolonisation era to imply a cause or breakpoint in the creation of the trusts system, nevertheless certain of the developments represented in that system compared to the mandates which it replaced were meaningful advancements. It did not, in itself, set in train the decolonisation process – as discussed, the Charter stops short of creating a right to independence, even for those territories under international trusteeship – but the greater centrality given to self-determination and the explicit equation of trust and other non-self-governing territories as of a kind did set the stage for what followed. As Pahuja puts it, developments of this kind 'meant that international law could provide a structure by which the heterogeneous movements for decolonisation could be smoothed into a coherent story':[109] in other words, the developments 'provid[ed] the vocabulary and conceptual tools for colonised peoples to articulate their aspirations and to render them intelligible in the international legal and political arena'.[110] Having set the stage, if minimally, what was missing was the actors; and it would be through the agency of the colonised peoples themselves – along with allies in former colonies – rather than by the colonial powers that the script would be written.

V. Self-Determination in the Law of the United Nations

From minimal – if not inauspicious – beginnings, in practice many trust territories did achieve independence within a few decades of the creation of the UN.

[107] Rothermund, *Decolonization* (n 88) 52.
[108] Art 77(a–c) UN Charter (n 91).
[109] Pahuja, *Decolonising International Law* (n 94) 45.
[110] Tzouvala, *Capitalism as Civilisation* (n 5) 133.

Between 1945 and c.1960, the practice of the UN and its members was ultimately to institute independence as the goal of trusteeship, and to extend that principle to apply to all non-self-governing territories. Over time, therefore, a right to colonial self-determination capable of resulting in the formation of an independent state was to emerge.

The reasons why the first colonies in this period were able to gain independence post-war (despite, in some cases, campaigns with much longer roots) were various, and need not detain us here.[111] Suffice it to say, in the main these early successes were the result neither of the beneficence of the West, nor because the colonial powers had come to believe that international law compelled them to confer sovereignty on their possessions.[112] Once independences had begun to take place, however, they gathered their own momentum. As Jansen and Osterhammel note, that momentum was in part a matter of pure practicality: with the independence of India, for example, the British Empire in Asia 'forfeited its geopolitical coherence'.[113] Lacking that source of resources and troops, as well as a base for its operations, it became far harder for the British Empire to sustain its other colonies in the region, in particular in the face of increasing domestic opposition. As this domino effect (so to speak) took hold and more and more new states emerged from former colonial possessions, the development started to look a lot like state practice. In parallel, though, there was a political momentum: as the balance shifted in the General Assembly, the newly independent states were quick to see the advantage of their numbers in voting on resolutions.[114] A series of resolutions made progressively stronger statements on decolonisation and self-determination for colonial peoples,[115] adding an (at least nascent) *opinio iuris* to the accelerating, and increasingly aligned, practice of states.

This section tracks the process of norm development through the work of the UN General Assembly over the period from 1945 to the Declaration on Friendly Relations in 1970. Through the Assembly's most significant resolutions – and above all, perhaps, resolution 1514 (XV) – and the preparatory work on the international human rights covenants, this section will show the progress of the colonial form of self-determination to a moment of crystallisation as a customary norm, but will also highlight the ways in which two other forms of self-determination – polity based and remedial self-determination – also wove through the work of the UN during this period. Indeed, despite little in the way of recent expression, the

[111] For an excellent history of the period, see Jansen and Osterhammel, *Dekolonisation* (n 8); and further Holland, *European Decolonization* (n 6); E Luard, *A History of the United Nations: The Age of Decolonization, 1955–1965*, vol 2 (London, Macmillan, 1989).

[112] In the case of India, for example, the British Empire offered a promise to the leadership of the Indian National Congress in the course of the Second World War that India would be permitted to decide its own fate after the war's conclusion, in return for continued Indian support. See Jansen and Osterhammel, *Dekolonisation* (n 8) 53–56ff.

[113] Jansen and Osterhammel, *Dekolonisation* (n 8) 53–54.

[114] Mazower, *Governing the World* (n 10) 254–55ff.

[115] See below, ss V.A–D.

polity-based form was given a central position in the legal order of the post-1945 world, quickly becoming a keystone of that system and – plausibly – acquiring the status of a norm *ius cogens*. Section V.B considers the international human rights covenants and their preparatory materials; section V.C examines resolution 1514 (XV); and section V.D looks at the Friendly Relations declaration. First, though, section V.A begins the survey with an examination of the text of the UN Charter.

A. The Charter of the United Nations

There can be no doubting the importance of the Charter of the United Nations for modern international law. As Christian Tomuschat has observed, '[t]he present-day world order rests entirely on the Charter',[116] and some authors have even characterised the Charter as a constitution of the international community.[117] Its particular status and normative force are based not only on the fundamental organisational principles of the international system with which it deals, but also on its status as a treaty of universal application. Uniquely among treaties, all acknowledged states have accepted the obligations it imposes as a matter of conventional international law; indeed, the list of the Charter's parties is sometimes taken to be a definitive list of the states of the world.[118] The legal status of references to self-determination in the Charter and the forms of self-determination they invoke are, however, uncertain.

i. Article 1(2): Self-Determination as a Purpose of the United Nations

The most significant Charter statement of self-determination is Article 1(2), which declares that:

> The Purposes of the United Nations are:
>
> ...

[116] C Tomuschat, 'Foreword' in C Tomuschat (ed), *The United Nations at Age Fifty: A Legal Perspective* (The Hague, Kluwer Law International, 1995) ix.

[117] B Fassbender, 'The United Nations Charter as Constitution of the International Community' (1998) 36 *Columbia Journal of Transnational Law* 529; and discussion in A O'Donoghue, *Constitutionalism in Global Constitutionalisation* (Cambridge, Cambridge University Press, 2014) 178–80.

[118] Some authors go so far as to argue that UN membership is now constitutive of statehood. See, inter alia, J Dugard, *Recognition and the United Nations* (Cambridge, Grotius Publications, 1987) 79; M Sterio, 'A Grotian Moment: Changes in the Legal Theory of Statehood' (2010–11) 39 *Denver Journal of International Law and Policy* 209; J Dugard, 'What Is a State in International Law? How Is This to Be Determined?' in N Blokker, D Dam-de Jong and V Prislan (eds), *Furthering the Frontiers of International Law: Sovereignty, Human Rights, Sustainable Development: Liber Amicorum Nico Schrijver* (Leiden, Brill/Nijhoff, 2021) 109–10; and *contra* NL Wallace-Bruce, *Claims to Statehood in International Law* (New York, Carlton Press, 1994) 59–60. Possible exceptions to this rule include the Republic of China (Taiwan), Vatican City, the Cook Islands, Kosovo and Palestine.

> 2. To develop friendly relations among nations based on respect for the principle of equal rights and self-determination of peoples, and to take other appropriate measures to strengthen universal peace.[119]

The status of Article 1 of the Charter is among the least certain of the Charter provisions, and it remains unclear whether it constitutes a binding obligation on the Member States, or merely imposes obligations on the organisation.[120] A textual approach to the article suggests, in the first place, that these are purposes of the organisation, and not of the members. It is addressed to the organisation, and not to the Member States, as clearly demonstrated by Article 1(4), which lists as a purpose '[t]o be a centre' for the facilitation of efforts towards those ends of the organisation.[121] The part clearly refers to a body (singular) which is the subject of the obligation, and as such the provision cannot apply to a multitude of actors. It may also be observed, with Rüdiger Wolfrum, that the language of the article 'is more appropriate for political objectives rather than for legally binding obligations'.[122]

In their respective analyses of the Charter, both Hans Kelsen and Antonio Cassese conclude that Article 1 creates no obligations on UN Members. Kelsen begins his analysis with the first purpose listed, that of maintaining international peace and security. The emphasis of the provision, in Kelsen's opinion, is preventative:[123] its focus is on the pacific settlement of international disputes.[124] As such, it is institutional in focus, centring on the infrastructure created by the Charter with a view to the maintenance of peace – the General Assembly, the Security Council and the ICJ.[125] Article 1 therefore sets down the 'function[s] of the Organization', while the 'corresponding' 'obligation[s] of the Members' can be found in Article 2.[126]

Kelsen also argues that Article 1 could not create legal rights.

> [I]t is highly problematic to refer in a legal instrument to rights without referring to the corresponding duties, since legally there exists no right of an individual without a corresponding duty on another individual; and if the right is a 'freedom,' not without a corresponding duty of the government.[127]

According to Kelsen, not only does the Charter not stipulate *which* rights individuals should have, or *who* should have the responsibility for ensuring that those

[119] Art 1(2) UN Charter (n 91).
[120] R Wolfrum, 'Article 1' in B Simma et al (eds), *The Charter of the United Nations: A Commentary*, vol 1, 3rd edn (Oxford, Oxford University Press, 2012) 108; E Chadwick, *Self-Determination in the Post-9/11 Era* (London, Routledge, 2011) 7.
[121] Art 1(4) UN Charter (n 91).
[122] Wolfrum, 'Article 1' (n 120) 108.
[123] H Kelsen, *The Law of the United Nations: A Critical Analysis of Its Fundamental Problems* (London, Stevens & Sons, 1951) 15.
[124] ibid 15; Art 1(4) UN Charter (n 91).
[125] Kelsen, *Law of the United Nations* (n 123) 15.
[126] ibid 15.
[127] ibid 29.

rights are respected and fulfilled, but it also fails to provide any form of redress for individuals whose rights are breached.[128] Indeed, the Statute of the ICJ specifically excludes the possibility that individuals could have standing before it.[129] Kelsen concludes that '[a]ll the formulas concerned establish purposes or functions of the Organisation, not obligations of the members'.[130] Cassese agrees, and he argues that self-determination 'was envisaged primarily as a programme or aim of the Organization … the Charter did not impose direct and immediate legal obligations on Member States in this area'.[131] Rather than imposing what may have become highly burdensome obligations on states, it 'merely laid down [the] many *lofty goals of the Organization*. The threat to State interests was thus minimized.'[132]

There are, therefore, many textual indications that Article 1 does not impose obligations on the Member States. Nevertheless, indications from the drafting of the Charter in San Francisco are more ambiguous, with some elements suggesting an intention to create binding effects. During the San Francisco conference, the categorisation of the statements reflecting the values of the Charter and the organisation as preambular, purposes (Article 1) or principles (Article 2) was discussed by Subcommittee I/1/A.[133] Although it is clear that the subcommittee understood the three parts as having a differing emphasis,[134] it appears that the subcommittee did not draw the sharp distinctions between the parts that conventional understanding has done, finding that all parts of the Charter (including the preamble) were capable of creating judiciable rights:

> The provisions of the Charter are, in this case, as in any other legal instrument, indivisible. They are equally valid, binding and operative. … May the understanding of these remarks dispel any doubts and quiet any apprehensions as to the validity and value of the Charter, whether called Preamble, Chapter I or Chapter II.[135]

There are some indications, also, that the subcommittee may have anticipated a wider role for the purposes than simply as a set of standards pertaining to the organisation. The Rapporteur stated that:

> The Purposes form the *raison d'être* of the Organisation. They are the aggregation of the common ends on which our minds, one and all, met; hence the object of our Charter, the signatories of which collectively **and severally** subscribe to.[136]

[128] ibid 29–33.
[129] ibid 32–33; Art 34(1) of the Statute of the International Court of Justice (San Francisco, 26 June 1945).
[130] Kelsen, *Law of the United Nations* (n 123) 29.
[131] Cassese, *Self-Determination of Peoples* (n 57) 43.
[132] ibid 43 (original emphasis).
[133] 'Report of the Rapporteur to Subcommittee I/1/A to Committee I/1' in US Department of State, *The United Nations Conference on International Organization; San Francisco, California, April 25 to June 26, 1945: Selected Documents* (United States Government Printing Office, 1946) 476.
[134] ibid 478.
[135] ibid 478.
[136] ibid 478 (italics in original, bold emphasis added).

Even if Article 1 may have been capable of creating legal rights for states, however, other elements of the drafting process speak against the suggestion that it actually did so. When the Secretariat was asked to justify the choice of the term 'peoples' in Article 1, it responded that:

> The interpretation of 'peoples' is even wider [than that of states or nations], for it reflects 'the idea of "all mankind" or "all human beings"'.[137]

As such, it seems that even were Article 1(2) able to create obligations for the states parties of the Charter, any such 'right' of self-determination on the part of 'all [hu]mankind' would be so broad and nebulous as to be virtually meaningless.

However, another view is possible, which draws from Hans Kelsen's analysis of the Charter and the structure of its obligations. Although Kelsen did not explicitly apply his analysis to self-determination in Article 1(2), he remarked on the close links between Articles 1 and 2 of the Charter, with many of the provisions existing both as obligations upon the organisation in the former, and the parties in the latter, and it may be that this dualism squares the Article 1 circle.[138] Article 1 is a mirror, and its reference to self-determination is paralleled (albeit not by name) in the Article 2(1) guarantee of the equality of Member States and the Article 2(4) prohibition on intervention. In its political form the right of self-determination attaches to the population of a state as a whole, and guarantees a choice over the *form* of government – a choice which belongs to that population alone.[139] Any external interference with that choice is inimical to the principle underpinning the right, and is illegitimate. Self-determination stands as an affirmation that no one people's interests may be considered superior to another's, such that the first can dictate the terms of the latter's national life. The principle thus guarantees both the equality of peoples (and thus the equality of polities) and the prohibition on intervention, which the Charter expresses as rights of 'peoples' (Article 1(2)) and as corresponding duties of States (Articles 2(1) and 2(4)). This appears, therefore, to meet Kelsen's criterion of a true legal right; that is to say, one which carries with it a corresponding duty and a potential remedy.[140]

However, the Charter appears to create such a right only in relation to one part of the political self-determination norm. As discussed above, political self-determination has both inward- and outward-facing aspects, which respectively stand for the principle that the individuals who comprise a social-political system should not be excluded from the determination of the form which that system will take (sometimes referred to as popular sovereignty), and the principle that no others who are outside the system should substitute their judgment for that of the individuals within it (non-interference). Only the second of these, the

[137] J Duursma, *Fragmentation and the International Relations of Micro-states: Self-Determination and Statehood* (Cambridge, Cambridge University Press, 1996) 14, citing Rapporteur, 'Report to Subcommittee' (n 133).

[138] Kelsen, *Law of the United Nations* (n 123) 15.

[139] See above, ch 1, s III.a.

[140] Kelsen, *Law of the United Nations* (n 123) 29.

outward-facing aspect of the right, appears to have achieved the status of a true right under the Charter, having been equipped with a corresponding duty (the Article 2(4) prohibition on intervention) and a sanction or remedy (the application of international law, and possible action under the Security Council's Chapter VI and VII powers). It is likely therefore that only this outward-facing aspect of political self-determination was established as a true legal right.[141]

ii. Self-Determination Elsewhere in the Charter

Other than in Article 1, self-determination appears in the Charter in two guises: in relation to the trusteeship system (discussed above)[142] and in Article 55. Article 55 appears in Chapter IX of the Charter, referring to international economic and social cooperation, and (similar to Article 1) sets out the principles applying to the organisation's work in the economic and social field:

> With a view to the creation of conditions of stability and well-being which are necessary for peaceful and friendly relations among nations based on respect for the principle of equal rights and self-determination of peoples, the United Nations shall promote:
>
> 1. higher standards of living, full employment, and conditions of economic and social progress and development;
> 2. solutions of international economic, social, health, and related problems; and international cultural and educational cooperation; and
> 3. universal respect for, and observance of, human rights and fundamental freedoms for all without distinction as to race, sex, language, or religion.[143]

Here, the self-determination reference seems to align closely with that in Article 1. The language is identical – 'friendly relations among nations based on respect for the principle of equal rights and self-determination of peoples' – and it seems clear, therefore, that the principle invoked is intended to be the same: that the work of the UN in the field of economic and social cooperation should respect and uphold national independence and the freedom of polities from political interference. That obligation – at least insofar as they act in consort with the UN in this area of its work – is then generalised to the Member States, in the Article 56 provision that '[a]ll Members pledge themselves to take joint and separate action in co-operation with the Organization for the achievement of the purposes set forth in Article 55'.[144]

Although of restricted scope, the recognition of political self-determination in Articles 1 and 55 of the Charter is of great importance, and may represent a significant turning-point. As I have argued,[145] the political form of self-determination is best established species of the self-determination genus, with roots as a legitimacy

[141] Chadwick, *Post-9/11 Era* (n 120) 10.
[142] See Arts 73 and 76(2); and further above, s IV.
[143] Art 55(1–3) UN Charter (n 91).
[144] Art 56 UN Charter (n 91).
[145] See ch 1, s III.A.

claim in the American and French revolutionary declarations of the eighteenth century.[146] Before its inclusion in the Charter, however, there was no suggestion that the principle was of a legal – as opposed to a political and moral – character. Notwithstanding several precursor attempts to create an effective norm, prior to 1945 there remained no (strong) legal prohibition on war, political coercion or on the acquisition of territory (colonial or otherwise) though the use of force.[147] The institution of a prohibition on interference, which the Charter attempts to establish, is significant both as the fulcrum between the old order and the new, and because it was the principle of (polity-based) self-determination that the drafters chose to centre within this new order. Subsequent developments were to reinforce both the status of the Charter and the importance of the non-interference norm within the post-1945 legal order, and would cement the place of polity-based self-determination as one of its foundation stones. In parallel, the practice of the UN was to continue to develop the colonial norm of self-determination, and would eventually see it transposed into legal form. In the following sections, I refer to the practice of the organisation relating to the human rights covenants (section V.B), the Declaration on the Granting of Independence to Colonial Countries and Peoples (section V.C) and the Declaration on Friendly Relations (section V.D), each a milestone in the development of these forms of self-determination.

B. The International Human Rights Covenants

The international human rights covenants are a pair of twinned treaties which, together, form what is arguably the General Assembly's – and the UN's – most significant contribution to human rights law.[148] Although less ambitious in key respects than the Universal Declaration on Human Rights, and marred – in the view of many states involved in the drafting[149] – by a split that (artificially, in their

[146] See ch 2, s II.

[147] Although note Josephson's argument that the role of the Kellogg–Briand pact as a forerunner to these developments should not be unduly minimised: H Josephson, 'Outlawing War: Internationalism and the Pact of Paris' (1979) 3 *Diplomatic History* 377. Lesaffer argues that we should look further back still, noting that 'although it cannot be denied that 19th-century international law conceded to states the right to resort to force and war, this right was conditional and restricted': R Lesaffer, 'Aggression before Versailles' (2018) 29 *European Journal of International Law* 773, 776 and *passim*.

[148] International Covenant on Economic, Social, and Cultural Rights (New York, 16 December 1966); International Covenant on Civil and Political Rights (New York, 16 December 1966). The Covenants were adopted and opened for signature together, annexed to UN General Assembly Resolution 2200 (XXI) A, 16 December 1966.

[149] See, for example, the (unsuccessful) proposed amendment by Chile, intended to reverse the decision to split the corpus of human rights between two covenants. Chile: Amendment to draft resolution A of the Third Committee (A/2112), General Assembly 6th Session, Agenda Item 29, UN Doc No A/2115. See further, statements of support of the amendment by Mexico (at para 11), USSR (at paras 42, 46–47), Saudi Arabia (at para 48) and Egypt (at para 56), in the course of debate in plenary session: UNGA, 6th Session, Official Record of the 375th Plenary Meeting, 5 February 1952, UN Doc No A/PV.375. The Chilean amendment was narrowly defeated by twenty-nine votes against to twenty-five in favour, with four abstentions: see UNGA, 375th Plenary Meeting, para 66.

view) separates economic, social and cultural rights from civil and political rights, the adoption of the covenants was a landmark in human rights law, and in the development of the General Assembly. More significantly for this study, it was also a landmark in self-determination. Here, self-determination for the first time finds expression as a legal right proclaimed by international treaty.

Self-determination appears in the twinned covenants – the International Covenant on Economic, Social and Cultural Rights (ICESCR), and the International Covenant on Civil and Political Rights (ICCPR) – in a provision common to both treaties, and which appears in both as their Article 1. It is the only substantive right or principle that finds expression in both instruments, and certainly is given an exceptional prominence thereby. There have long been debates, however, concerning the ambit of the term as it appears in the covenants,[150] and debated, too, is the question of whether, given its segregation from the other rights proclaimed by each instrument, the states parties to the covenants intended to create a legal right.[151] In order to answer those questions, this section considers first the resolutions which form the *travaux préparatoires* of the covenants, before section V.B.ii turns to a textual analysis of the common first article of the covenants itself.

i. The Preparatory Documents: Resolutions 421 (V), 545 (VI) and 1188 (XII)

In the years that followed the adoption of the Charter, the status of self-determination as a legal norm was increasingly acknowledged. One important recognition of the growing significance and status of self-determination in the minds of states came in the course of preparing the international covenants on human rights and, as a milestone in that process, resolution 421 (V). Resolution 421 (V) was an omnibus resolution, consisting of eight parts (A–H).[152] It covers a huge range of themes relating to the drafting of the covenants, including a decision to include an article in the covenants recognising the equality of the sexes;[153] a request to the Economic and Social Council to consider the modalities for the application of the covenants to the sub-units of federal states;[154] and setting the timeframe for the further stages of drafting the covenants.[155] It also, in a brief paragraph in its part D, requested that the Commission on Human Rights 'study ways and means which would ensure the right of peoples and nations to

[150] For an account of these discussions, see P Macklem, 'Self-Determination in Three Movements' in Tesón (ed), *The Theory of Self-Determination* (n 67).

[151] For an account of these discussions, see J Crawford, 'Outside the Colonial Context' in WJA Macartney (ed), *Self-Determination in the Commonwealth* (Aberdeen, Aberdeen University Press, 1988) 4–5. Crawford ultimately disagrees with that contention.

[152] UN General Assembly Resolution 421 (V) A–H, 4 December 1950.

[153] UNGA Res 421 E, para 7a.

[154] UNGA Res 421 C, para 5.

[155] UNGA Res 421 A, para 2; G, para 9; H, para 10.

self-determination, and to prepare recommendations'.[156] That statement, in itself, neither gives an indication of the ambit of any self-determination principle, nor took a decision to include self-determination (in some form) in the covenants. Nevertheless, that the General Assembly chose to incorporate a provision on self-determination into this key preparatory document was significant, and certainly set the direction of travel. The passage relating to self-determination closed by deciding that the recommendations of the commission be 'considered by the General Assembly at its sixth session' in 1952 and, indeed, that session produced a further – and more elaborated – resolution dealing with self-determination.

Returning to self-determination in the context of the covenants at its sixth session, the General Assembly passed resolution 545 (VI),[157] by which it decided to include 'an article on the right of all peoples and nations to self-determination in reaffirmation of the principle enunciated in the Charter' in the international covenants on human rights, which were then being drafted.[158] This resolution has a dual significance. Not only can this statement assist in interpreting the reference to self-determination in the covenants, but it can also aid in interpreting the Charter. The resolution is an example of the subsequent practice of the organisation, and indicates the interpretation of the Charter reference to self-determination to which the Member States present collectively subscribed.[159] As the resolution stated, the General Assembly decided 'to include in the International Covenant or Covenants on Human Rights an article on the right of all peoples and nations to self-determination in reaffirmation of the principle enunciated in the Charter'.[160] Having thus tied the resolution to the statement in Article 1(2), the Assembly went on to say that

> This article shall be drafted in the following terms: 'All peoples shall have the right to self-determination', and shall stipulate that all States, including those having responsibility for the administration of Non-Self-Governing Territories, should promote the realization of that right.[161]

It is clear that the states involved in the drafting of resolution 545 considered that the ambit of the right spoken of in paragraph 1 was to be identical to the contours of self-determination as that term appears in the Charter. It is less clear, however, which form of self-determination they understood the Charter as having proclaimed.

Resolution 545 refers to non-self-governing territories, and it is therefore tempting to conclude that the reference here is to colonial self-determination. It seems clear, however, that these references to self-determination are more

[156] UNGA Res 421 D, para 6.
[157] UN General Assembly Res 545 (VI), 5 February 1952.
[158] UNGA Res 545.
[159] A Aust, *Modern Treaty Law and Practice*, 2nd edn (Cambridge, Cambridge University Press, 2007) 241–43; see also A Bianchi, 'Law, Time, and Change: The Self-regulatory Function of Subsequent Practice' in G Nolte (ed), *Treaties and Subsequent Practice* (Oxford, Oxford University Press, 2013).
[160] UNGA Res 545, para 1.
[161] UNGA Res 545, para 1.

complex, with no clear ideational separation between the forms being appreciated by the participants. Thus, the injunction is addressed to 'all States … [to] promote the realization of that right … and that States having responsibility for the administration of Non-Self-Governing Territories should promote the realization of that right in relation to the peoples of such territories'.[162] The structure of this injunction (of 'all … and …') implies that while self-determination in the colonial context is emphatically included, it does not exhaust the situations to which self-determination applies. Rather, there are indications in the drafting process that (at least some of) the states present understood resolution 545's reference to self-determination as invoking other principles. While Mexico, for example, and Saudi Arabia clearly understood the reference as pertaining to decolonisation alone,[163] the Soviet Union focused in its remarks on the rights of internal minorities to the maintenance of their language and culture,[164] and Poland, while acknowledging the relevance to peoples living under colonialism, implied that the term has a wider sphere of application.[165] In parallel, Aureliu Cristescu identifies an attempt by some states to ensure that the inclusion of the right to self-determination in the covenants could 'not be confused with the rights of minorities'.[166] Rather, Cristescu extracts from the debates a principle with two elements: domestically it 'signified the people's right to self-government and from the external point of view their independence'.[167] In other words, according to Cristescu's reading of the process, the ambit of the right that was to be included in the covenants encompassed the twin inward-facing and outward-facing dimensions of the polity-based self-determination norm which was sketched above as finding expression in Article 1(2) of the Charter.

A further intervention during the drafting process by the General Assembly, in the form of its resolution 1188 (XII),[168] seemed to confirm that it has a compound character. Resolution 1188 did not, in fact, form a direct part of the drafting process of the covenants, and as such is only indicative. Nevertheless, the General Assembly in the second preambular paragraph recalled 'its resolution 545 (VI) of February 1952 in which it decided to include' self-determination in the covenants, which indicates a conceptual connection – if nothing stronger – between the documents. In the operative part of resolution 1188, the General Assembly noted the importance of self-determination in two different contexts. Certainly,

[162] UNGA Res 545, para 1.
[163] UNGA, 375th Plenary Meeting, paras 8–9, 54–55.
[164] UNGA, 375th Plenary Meeting, para 44.
[165] UNGA, 375th Plenary Meeting, para 95.
[166] A Cristescu, *The Right to Self-Determination: Historical and Current Development on the Basis of United Nations Instruments: Study Prepared by Aureliu Cristescu, Special Rapporteur of the Sub-Commission on Prevention of Discrimination and Protection of Minorities* (New York, United Nations, 1981) 5; citing UN General Assembly, 6th Session, Third Committee, Official Record of the 397th meeting, 21 January 1952, para 5.
[167] Cristescu, *Historical and Current Development* (n 166) 5; citing UNGA Third Committee, 397th meeting, para 5.
[168] UN General Assembly Resolution 1188 (XII), 11 December 1957.

it reaffirmed that 'Member States having responsibility for the administration of Non-Self-Governing Territories shall promote the realization' of self-determination in those territories,[169] but alongside that provision also declared that 'Member States shall, in their relations with one another, give due respect to the right of self-determination'.[170] Both principles it cast as having 'international importance' deriving from 'the purposes and principles of the Charter of the United Nations'.[171]

The declaration that 'Member States' are under an obligation deriving from the principles and purposes of the Charter to 'give due respect to the right of self-determination' 'in their relations with one another' supports the interpretation given above, that the Article 1(2) Charter reference to self-determination is to polity-based self-determination. As discussed above, that principle guarantees the internal integrity of political processes, requiring that polities – here understood to mean states – must be allowed to pursue their internal political development without external interference by other states or communities. It is political self-determination which stands behind, and is given expression in, the guarantee of non-intervention.[172] As will be argued in the following section, that dual-purpose understanding of self-determination is expressed in the covenants. Beyond this, however, the remarks on the polity-based form, and in particular its non-intervention aspect – foreshadows the Declaration on Friendly Relations, discussed below.[173]

ii. Self-Determination in International Treaty Law: The Human Rights Covenants

Through the international human rights covenants (the ICCPR and ICESCR), the rights proclaimed in the Universal Declaration of Human Rights (UDHR) are rendered enforceable. In addition to transposing the substance of the UDHR from declaration of the General Assembly to the plane of treaty obligations, the covenants give further specification and definition to the UDHR's broad statements of principle, and also create an institutional architecture for the interpretation and monitoring of the covenants, in the form of the Economic and Social Council and Human Rights Committee, respectively.

Although, as noted above,[174] numerous states were dissatisfied with the decision taken to divide them, the covenants formalise the division of the corpus of human rights into two families: economic, social and cultural; and civil and political. There are numerous differences between the framing and architecture of the two covenants, which have been exhaustively discussed in the literature. While the ICCPR demands that states 'respect and ensure to all individuals within

[169] UNGA Res 1188, para 1b.
[170] UNGA Res 1188, para 1a.
[171] UNGA Res 1188, para 1.
[172] See above, ss V.A and V.A.i.
[173] See below, s V.D.
[174] See above, n 149, and accompanying text.

[their territories] the rights' contained in that covenant, the ICESCR contains the softer injunction that they 'take steps … with a view to achieving progressively the full realization of the rights', for example.[175] Similarly, while the ICCPR provides for a dedicated committee (the Human Rights Committee) and a state-to-state complaints procedure, the role of monitoring of the ICESCR is given to the (existing) Economic and Social Council and there is no procedure by which states can complain of each other's breaches.[176] Nevertheless, the covenants come together in at least one important respect.

The covenants have a common first article, which provides that:

> 1. All peoples have the right of self-determination. By virtue of that right they freely determine their political status and freely pursue their economic, social and cultural development.
>
> …
>
> 3. The States Parties to the present convention, including those having responsibility for the administration of Non-Self-Governing and Trust Territories, shall promote the realization of the right of self-determination, and shall respect that right, in conformity with the provisions of the Charter of the United Nations.[177]

The article certainly refers – at least in part – to the decolonisation context, and contains a restatement of the right of non-self-governing peoples to colonial self-determination.[178] As discussed above and in the following section in relation to resolution 1514 (XV),[179] it is increasingly clear that in the years leading up to the adoption of the covenants, colonial self-determination was established as a legal right of colonial peoples under customary international law. That colonial self-determination is included in the covenants as a precept of human rights law is, therefore, important and significant, but not legally innovative.

It may be, however, that colonial self-determination does not exhaust the reference in common Article 1. In addition to the dual meaning given to self-determination in the drafting process as discussed in the previous section, there are textual indications that the article refers to colonial self-determination as one aspect of a broader category of meanings within the scope of the provision. To begin with, the article begins with a general statement of self-determination, which is then only secondarily applied to the peoples of non-self-governing territories. The reference in Article 1(1) is not limited to colonial circumstances, but rather refers to the right of 'all peoples' to self-determination. Moreover, the major focus is on their right to 'freely determine their political status and freely pursue their economic, social and cultural development'.[180] Such language is more appropriate

[175] Compare Art 2(1) of respectively the ICESCR and ICCPR (n 148).
[176] Compare Part IV of respectively the ICESCR and ICCPR (n 148).
[177] Article 1(1–3) ICESCR/ICCPR (n 148).
[178] Macklem notes that the state representatives drafting the Covenants certainly had the colonial context firmly in mind. Macklem, 'Three Movements' (n 150) 94–95.
[179] See above s IV; and below s V.C.
[180] Art 1(1) ICESCR/ICCPR (n 148).

to a right to polity-based self-determination, or the right of a population to institute the political and economic system of their choosing without outside interference. That interpretation is consistent with the Charter, and accords with the account of the practice of the General Assembly in the process of preparing the covenants, in particular resolutions 545 and 1188. It also accords with the interpretation of Article 1 by the Human Rights Committee in its General Comment 12, in which it refers for the need for states' reports on the implementation of article 1(1) to include a description of 'the constitutional and political processes which in practice allow the exercise of this right'.[181] That it is regarded by the Committee as having an internal and continuing application clearly indicated that it is has a life beyond the decolonisation context.

A further indication that the covenants did – and were intended to – secure and strengthen the right of states to polity-based self-determination has been highlighted by Idriss Fofana.[182] Fofana refers to the place of the covenants within a wider debate concerning the right of states to expropriate the property of non-nationals within their territories. Although by the middle of the 1960s more and more former colonies were gaining independence, significant imbalances remained between the former colonies and the former colonial powers. Not only were the former colonisers significantly more economically developed (often to the direct detriment of their former colonies), but the newly independent states often found themselves locked into specific trading relationships, distributions of property and economic systems as a result of both national and international law. Guha Roy and Georges Abi-Saab, key intellectual figures in understanding and seeking to dismantle these persistent power imbalances, not only argued that the newly independent states should have an opportunity to reimagine their economic and political systems post-independence, but conceptualised their right to do so as an aspect of the right to (polity-based) self-determination: 'A nation's ability to adopt the social and economic system of its choice and to pursue economic independence from a former colonial power, they argued, were core elements of self-determination.'[183] The covenants were – understood as a part of this history – one move in a longer game comprising also the General Assembly's declaration on Permanent Sovereignty over Natural Resources,[184] and the Charter of the Economic Rights and Duties of States.[185] These documents sought to substantiate the principle in the covenants: that it is for the state and its people to

[181] Human Rights Committee, General Comment 12 (1984), para 4.

[182] I Fofana, 'Afro-Asian Jurists and the Quest to Modernise the International Protection of Foreign-Owned Property, 1955–1975' (2020) 23 *Journal of the History of International Law/Revue d'histoire du droit international* 80, esp 97–105.

[183] ibid 103.

[184] UN General Assembly Resolution 1803 (XVII) ('Permanent Sovereignty over Natural Resources'), 14 December 1962.

[185] Charter of Economic Rights and Duties of States, annexed to UN General Assembly Resolution 3281 (XXIX), 12 December 1974.

make fundamental decisions concerning the organisation of their shared political life, including the basis and functioning of their economic systems. It is not for international law – or international society more broadly – either to dictate those choices or to lock states and their peoples into relationships of domination established prior to their independence.[186] Polity-based self-determination as it appears in the covenants was, in this sense, aligned with colonial self-determination, but went beyond it: where colonial self-determination was, by the definition of the time, satisfied, polity-based self-determination took over to support and enhance the independence of the postcolonial states, as well as all other states vulnerable to economic domination, whether or not they fell within the rubric of 'saltwater' colonies.

That the formulation of the right to political self-determination in the covenants was more than a mere restatement of the Charter can be seen, too, in that it seems to have corrected an imbalance within the right. Prior to the conclusion of the covenants, as noted above,[187] political self-determination was vulnerable to the challenge that an obligation without a corresponding remedy cannot be a legal obligation, properly so called.[188] Although the outward-facing aspect of polity-based self-determination – guaranteeing non-interference – had achieved the status of an enforceable right under the Charter, polity-based self-determination remained a 'half-right'. Its internal facet – guaranteeing the equality of population groups in determining the form of a state's governance – lacked an enforceable remedy or sanction. The covenants may have remedied that lack, by creating a right to political self-determination that is enforceable against states parties as a matter of treaty law.[189] In that way the covenants may have facilitated the emergence of polity-based self-determination as a full right opposable to the states parties.

It is also significant that the article is common to both covenants. Rather than being a right of the same kind as those enumerated in the covenants, its verbatim inclusion in both documents suggests that it was seen as having a different, and more basic, character. These are matters which, it seems to declare, come prior to the subdivision of human rights into rights of a civil and political or economic social and cultural character. To that extent it receives a treatment different even to the right to life, which appears in the list of civil and political rights only. There can hardly be a more eloquent indication of the fundamental character that the norm of polity-based self-determination was understood to possess.

[186] Fofana, 'Afro-Asian Jurists' (n 182) 103–05. Ultimately, these developments succeeded in limiting the scope of international review of expropriations, and Fofana highlights the significance of the agency of postcolonial states in 'defin[ing] and expand[ing] the content of the right of self-determination while cementing its status as a fundamental norm of the modern international public order' (105).

[187] See above, nn 127–32, and accompanying text.

[188] Kelsen, *Law of the United Nations* (n 123) 29.

[189] Although Crawford notes some remaining ambiguity on this point, he concludes that there is 'no basis for excluding Article 1 in principle from the complaints procedures'. Crawford, 'Outside the Colonial Context' (n 151) 4–5.

At the same time, however, it seems equally clear that the reference to self-determination was not boundless: at the least, it was not understood as giving rise to a right of secessionary self-determination. The Article 1(1) proclamation that '[a]ll peoples have the right to self-determination' must be interpreted in light of the meaning given to the term 'peoples' which, it seems clear, was understood to mean the population of states and of colonised territories, and not sub-state or minority groups. Reference to the *travaux préparatoires* yields several statements by individual states which support that conclusion, and which were not contradicted by other interpretations. In the course of the debates, for example, Venezuela stressed that:

> In paragraph 1 of the article, [Venezuela] understood the term 'peoples' in the most general and unqualified sense, and therefore as not applicable to racial, religious, or other groups or minorities. … [Self-determination means] freedom for all peoples and nations to manage their affairs in all respects without the intervention of another people or nation.[190]

It can be concluded, therefore, that the covenants concerned primarily political and secondarily colonial self-determination, and did not institute a right to secessionary or remedial self-determination.

C. Resolution 1514 (XV)

Resolution 1514 (XV), the '[d]eclaration on the granting of independence to colonial countries and peoples',[191] represented a significant departure from the General Assembly's previous references to self-determination. As Cristescu observes, the declaration 'represents one of the most significant contributions the United Nations has made to developing the concept of the right of self-determination'.[192] For the first time, the General Assembly sought not only to restate, but to *develop* the law on self-determination under the Charter.

The declaration had, as discussed in section V.B.i, been preceded by a series of resolutions that made increasingly confident statements on self-determination.[193] In its ancestry, too, it could count assertions of the principle that relations between a colonised people and its coloniser should be mediated by self-determination in the General Assembly's practice in relation to specific situations.[194] But these had

[190] UN General Assembly, 10th Session, Third Committee, Official Records of the 646th meeting, para 42; see also Interpretive Declaration of the Republic of Indonesia to the ICCPR made on the occasion of Indonesia's accession to the ICCPR, 23 February 2006, www.treaties.un.org.

[191] UN General Assembly Resolution 1514 (XV), 14 December 1960.

[192] Cristescu, *Historical and Current Development* (n 166) para 39.

[193] In addition to those resolutions in the context of the human rights covenants, see also UN General Assembly resolution 637 (VII) A–C, 16 December 1952, which can be read as a precursor to resolution 1514 (XV).

[194] See, for example, its resolution on Morocco: UN General Assembly Resolution 612 (VII), 19 December 1952.

hitherto always been partial and circumspect: on one side, specific and situational; on the other, dualistic and expressive of broad principles rather than legal norms. Resolution 1514 is strikingly different: this is a General Assembly confident of its position, firm in its resolve and being boldly led – almost for the first time, at least so ambitiously – by its new majority of postcolonial states.

Self-determination as formulated in the declaration refers exclusively to the colonial form. The preamble identifies those to whom the right would apply as 'dependent peoples',[195] and declares that 'an end must be put to colonialism'.[196] The operative paragraphs condemn '[t]he subjection of peoples to alien subjugation, domination and exploitation',[197] and mandate action in respect of 'Non-Self-Governing Territories or all other territories which have not yet attained independence'.[198] It was also clear that the principles applied could not be employed outwith the colonial context. The declaration specifically excludes their application in other cases, stating that:

> Any attempt aimed at the partial or total disruption of the national unity and the territorial integrity of a country is incompatible with the purposes and principles of the Charter of the United Nations.[199]

Although, in this way, the remit of the declaration is clearly confined only to the colonial form of self-determination, in two respects implications can be drawn from the declaration that reveal aspects of the other forms. First, it can be seen that the declaration regards colonial and secessionary self-determination as unrelated concepts. There is an understandable tendency to connect these forms of self-determination, which often result in similar outcomes (namely, the removal of a territory from the control of a state power and its establishment as a new state or its integration with another state). It was the view of the General Assembly, however, that these are separate ideas, hence the declaration's fulsome endorsement of the colonial form, while secession was declared unlawful.

Secondly, the declaration demonstrates one of the respects in which the colonial form and the secessionary forms of self-determination differ. The focus of the colonial form is colonial territories, and not the specific group or mix of peoples which inhabit them. Albeit with notable exceptions, the intention of the declaration-writers was that colonial territories would transition to statehood without modifications to the borders which had been applied to them by the colonising states. As the representative of Kenya in 2022 eloquently recounted to the Security Council (in a debate on the Russian invasion of Ukraine):

> Kenya and almost every African country were birthed by the ending of empire. Our borders were not of our own drawing. They were drawn in the distant colonial

[195] UNGA Res 1514, preamble.
[196] UNGA Res 1514.
[197] UNGA Res 1514, para 1.
[198] UNGA Res 1514, para 5.
[199] UNGA Res 1514, para 6.

> metropoles of London, Paris and Lisbon with no regard for the ancient nations that they cleaved apart.
>
> Today across the border of every single African country live our countrymen with whom we share deep historical, cultural and linguistic bonds. At independence, had we chosen to pursue States on the basis of ethnic, racial or religious homogeneity, we would still be waging bloody wars these many decades later. Instead, we agreed that we would settle for the borders that we inherited.[200]

This principle, *uti possidetis iuris*, has even been formulated as a legal rule: that colonial territories *may not* contest their colonial boundaries.[201] Leaving aside the legal status of any independent rule of *uti possidetis*, the strong statement in the Declaration that 'the partial or total disruption of the national unity and the territorial integrity of a country is incompatible' with the Charter may indicate that, as a matter of how the norm is conceived, the colonial norm of self-determination does not have as its subjects 'peoples' in the sense of minorities or population groups, but rather the whole people of defined territories. As such, it stands in sharp contrast to the secessionary form, which – by definition – has as its subjects subnational groups.

Although a partial right to colonial self-determination had been established through the mandate and trusts systems – as they developed – it was in this resolution that the ambit of that right was extended from trust territories to all non-self-governing territories. It speaks in absolutes: the 'subjection of peoples to alien subjugation' is a 'denial of fundamental human rights' and 'is contrary to the Charter';[202] '[i]mmediate steps' must be taken to transfer powers to the populations of non-self-governing territories 'without any conditions or reservations' and 'in accordance with their freely expressed will and desire';[203] the aim of the declaration is to bring about the 'end of colonialism in all its manifestations'.[204] No longer are self-government and independence equally weighted: 'all powers' must be transferred to those 'territories which have not yet attained independence'.[205] It seems clear, too, that the declaration was more than a political statement, and was capable of contributing to the formation of custom as an expression of the *opinio iuris* of states. The resolution mandates action formulated in specific and absolute terms, requiring '[i]mmediate steps' to grant non-self-governing territories independence.[206] It demands action by the trustee powers, an action within the General Assembly's competence under the trust system.[207] The resolution also

[200] Statement of Mr Kimani, Representative of Kenya, UN Security Council, 8970th Meeting, 21 February 2022, Provisional Verbatim Record, UN Doc No S/PV.8970, 8–9.

[201] For discussion, see A Peters, 'The Principle of *Uti Possidetis Juris*: How Relevant Is It for Issues of Secession?' in C Walter, A von Ungern-Sternberg and K Abushov (eds), *Self-Determination and Secession in International Law* (Oxford, Oxford University Press, 2014).

[202] UNGA Res 1514, para 1.

[203] UNGA Res 1514, para 5.

[204] UNGA Res 1514, preamble.

[205] UNGA Res 1514, para 5.

[206] UNGA Res 1514, para 5.

[207] *Namibia* (n 72) paras 71–72.

attracted widespread support, passing by eighty-nine votes in favour with nine abstentions and no state voting against, and it appears that those Member States involved in the drafting of the declaration accepted its significance and regarded it as a law-creating document:

> It was considered that the Declaration revitalized the spirit of the Charter, restored strength to the Charter provisions on self-determination and gave a new sense of reality and greater validity to the Universal Declaration of Human Rights. The new Declaration would be an epoch-making document, on an equal footing with the Charter and the Universal Declaration.[208]

These contemporaneous factors seem sufficient to produce a declaration *capable* of crystallising a customary norm of colonial self-determination, and thus to extend the ambit of the norm beyond trust and mandate territories to all non-self-governing peoples.[209] It also seems clear, as will be discussed in the following chapters, that such a norm did, in fact, arise in this period. Although the courts have been wary of ascribing definitive effect to any single instrument or development, it seems clear, too, that resolution 1514 played a significant role. In its *Chagos* Advisory Opinion – discussed in further detail in chapter six – the ICJ referred to the 'defining moment in the consolidation of State practice on decolonisation' represented by resolution 1514, and noted the 'clear relationship between resolution 1514 (XV) and the process of decolonization following its adoption'.[210] The Court continued by noting that although 'formally a recommendation, [1514] has a declaratory character with regard to the right to self-determination as a customary norm, in view of its content and the conditions of its adoption'.[211] Although, therefore, one must remain cautious in placing emphasis on any single development, it seems abundantly clear both that a fully fledged legal right of self-determination for colonial territories and peoples arose in this period, and that resolution 1514 certainly played a – if not 'the' – defining role.

Equally clearly, however, in formulating resolution 1514, the General Assembly and its Member States did not intend – and sought actively to avoid – extending the recognition therein to any other form of self-determination. To the extent that any other form of self-determination is mentioned, it was secessionary self-determination that is addressed, and is so in the form of a rejection of secessionary self-determination's applicability. As such, it did not affect the extent or legal status of self-determination in its other forms.

[208] Cristescu, *Historical and Current Development* (n 166) para 41.

[209] It should be noted, however, as Tesón does, that the crystallisation of this right did not bring an end to definitional questions concerning its ambit. Prior to the collapse of the Berlin Wall, he argues, the right of non-self-governing peoples to self-determination was conceived as a right applying to the colonies of the European powers, and no equivalent right was considered to apply to states, nations or minorities within the USSR, for example. FR Tesón, 'Introduction: The Conundrum of Self-Determination' in Tesón (ed), *The Theory of Self-Determination* (n 67) 3.

[210] *Legal Consequences of the Separation of the Chagos Archipelago from Mauritius in 1965*, Advisory Opinion, (2019) ICJ Reports 95, para 150.

[211] *Chagos* (n 210) para 152.

D. Declaration on Friendly Relations

In 1970 the UN General Assembly agreed resolution 2625 (XXV).[212] The resolution approved the Declaration on Principles of International Law Concerning Friendly Relations and Co-operation among States in accordance with the Charter of the United Nations (Declaration on Friendly Relations), the text of which was annexed to the resolution. It is on par only with resolution 1514 (XV) as one of the most significant documents on self-determination produced under the auspices of the United Nations,[213] in that the declaration not only materially developed the law on self-determination, but it cemented its legal status.

The declaration is customary in its entirety. In the *Case Concerning Military and Paramilitary Activities In and Against Nicaragua*, the ICJ declared the Declaration to be customary international law, holding that the Declaration was more than a mere 'reiteration or elucidation' of the Charter,[214] but that 'the adoption by States of this text afford[ed] an indication of their *opinio juris* as to customary international law on the question'.[215] In its advisory opinion on *Kosovo* the Court cited its judgment in *Nicaragua*, confirming that the Declaration 'reflects customary international law'.[216] The Court did not confine its comment to a section of the Declaration, nor point to such a limit in the *Nicaragua* judgment, and should be interpreted as a recognition of the status of the Declaration as a whole.[217] It is also clear, as the Court apprehended when it examined the text of the Declaration during the proceedings in *Nicaragua*, that the obligations found in the Declaration go beyond those of the Charter. The Declaration was therefore not merely a source of law, but a source of new law.

At first sight the Declaration appears simply to restate those forms of self-determination that, as discussed above, already existed in the law of the Charter and of the United Nations. Here, though, the separation between the colonial and polity-based forms of self-determination is no longer a matter of subtext: it is clear and explicit.[218] The Declaration re-emphasises the right of colonial peoples to self-determination and reiterates the conviction that 'subjection of peoples to alien subjugation, domination and exploitation constitutes a violation

[212] UN General Assembly Resolution 2625 (XXV), 24 October 1970.

[213] Declaration on Principles of International Law concerning Friendly Relations and Co-operation among States in accordance with the Charter of the United Nations, annexed to UNGA Res 2625.

[214] *Military and Paramilitary Activities in and Against Nicaragua (Nicaragua v United States of America)*, Merits, Judgment, (1986) ICJ Reports 14, para 188.

[215] *Nicaragua* (n 214) para 191.

[216] *Accordance with International Law of the Unilateral Declaration of Independence in Respect of Kosovo*, Advisory Opinion, (2010) ICJ Reports 403, para 80.

[217] This interpretation has been confirmed in *Legal Consequences of the Separation of the Chagos Archipelago from Mauritius in 1965*, Separate Opinion of Judge Cançado Trindade, (2019) ICJ Reports 156, para 27.

[218] In this regard, recall resolution 1188 (XII), which exhibited the same separation, and can be read as a precursor to the Declaration: see above, s V.B.ii.

of [self-determination], as well as a denial of fundamental human rights, and is contrary to the Charter'.[219] It also restates the rights of peoples to polity-based self-determination:

> [A]ll peoples have the right freely to determine, without external interference, their political status and to pursue their economic, social and cultural development, and every State has the duty to respect this right in accordance with the provisions of the Charter.[220]

Once more, it seems clear that 'peoples' was understood to mean the populations of states, and not sub-state groups. The declaration itself excludes the application of the principle to break up the state in very definite terms:

> Nothing in the forgoing paragraphs shall be construed as authorizing or encouraging any action which would dismember or impair, totally or in part, the territorial integrity or political unity of sovereign and independent States.[221]

It therefore seems clear that no right to secessionary self-determination was created by the Declaration.

This 'safeguard clause' may have another significance, however. Perhaps surprisingly, the clause does not provide states with an absolute protection against secession, but only a limited one. The clause forbids actions that would break up

> sovereign and independent States conducting themselves in compliance with the principle of equal rights and self-determination of peoples described above, and thus possessed of a government representing the whole people belonging to the territory without distinction as to race, creed or colour.[222]

This clause excludes from its protection colonial states that do not represent the people of the territory without distinction; it excludes entities that have not yet achieved statehood and independence; and (most significantly) it does not protect states that deny their populations' rights to internal self-determination, access to government, or full and equal participation in the states' political lives. It would be possible to interpret the statement as expressive of a legal lacuna – as indicating that while it may be that no permissive rule enabling secession exists, that peoples living in states which do not respect the rights of the whole population to political self-determination are at least *not actively prohibited* from seceding on remedial grounds. However, there are also those who have argued that the Declaration's safeguard clause amounts to recognition of a legal right to remedial

[219] Declaration on Friendly Relations (n 213).

[220] ibid. This statement is recalled by the Declaration on Aggression, the preamble of which '[r]eaffirm[s] the duty of States not to use armed force to deprive peoples of their right to self-determination, freedom and independence, or to disrupt territorial integrity'. See UN General Assembly Resolution 3314 (XXIX), 14 December 1974.

[221] Declaration on Friendly Relations (n 213).

[222] ibid.

self-determination, and it may be that this conclusion is correct: that proposition has received support from states in their legal submissions to the ICJ (for example, in the *Kosovo* advisory proceedings);[223] has been argued by academic commentators;[224] and has even found expression in the separate opinions of ICJ Judges.[225] In my view this latter stance, that the Declaration's safeguard clause represents an – at least nascent – recognition of a remedial right to self-determination is to be preferred.[226] Even if, however, it cannot be maintained that a right of *legal* character arose as a result of the safeguard clause, certainly the Declaration seems expressive of a view that an attempt to secede in extremis by a people denied basic human rights or participation in the political life of the polity is *legitimate* from a moral-political point of view.

The law on self-determination still largely reflects that set down in the Declaration. Resolution 2625 is, to date, the last of the significant statements made by the General Assembly on self-determination and, although the legal scheme has been clarified and refined by case law both prior to the Declaration's adoption and subsequently, the basic position remains that posited by the declaration in 1970.[227] Colonial self-determination is well-established as a legal right attaching to non-self-governing peoples, and the principle that the wishes of the inhabitants of a territory should be of great weight in determining the future status of that territory may now have some application beyond the strict definition of a colonised people. Of less certain application is the principle of remedial self-determination, which while it received some endorsement in the Declaration, is still of uncertain status. The same cannot be said of the secessionary form, which was rejected entirely. Perhaps of most significance, though, was the Declaration's treatment of political self-determination. That form of self-determination was strongly reasserted, and the importance of the principle for the modern international legal system was made clear both in the Declaration's statement that 'peoples have the right freely to determine, without external interference, their political status', and that states which fail to 'conduct[] themselves in compliance with the

[223] See, for example, Written Statement of the Netherlands, *Kosovo* Advisory Opinion, paras 3.6–3.7; Written Statement of Estonia, *Kosovo* Advisory Opinion, para 2.1; Written Statement of Finland, *Kosovo* Advisory Opinion, para 8; Written Statement of Poland, *Kosovo* Advisory Opinion, paras 6.8–6.9; Written Comment of Switzerland, *Kosovo* Advisory Opinion, para 60; Written Statement of Germany, *Kosovo* Advisory Opinion, 32–37.

[224] Cassese, *Self-Determination of Peoples* (n 57) 108–19; Duursma, *Fragmentation* (n 137) 25; M Sterio, *The Right to Self-Determination under International Law: 'Selfistans,' Secession, and the Rule of the Great Powers* (London, Routledge, 2013) 12–13; Rodríguez-Santiago, 'Evolution of Self-Determination' (n 67) 235.

[225] *Accordance with International Law of the Unilateral Declaration of Independence in Respect of Kosovo*, Separate Opinion of Judge Cançado Trindade, (2010) ICJ Reports 523, paras 175–81; *Accordance with International Law of the Unilateral Declaration of Independence in Respect of Kosovo*, Separate Opinion of Judge Yusuf, (2010) ICJ Reports 618, paras 11–12. Judge Cançado Trindade also made remarks which, although less direct, should in my view be understood as reaffirming that principle in Separate Opinion of Cançado Trindade, *Chagos* (n 217) para 86.

[226] Although note that the ICJ has cast doubt on that contention. For discussion, see below, ch 5, s II.B.

[227] Duursma, *Fragmentation* (n 137) 25.

principle of equal rights and self-determination of peoples' or are not 'possessed of a government representing the whole people belonging to the territory without distinction as to race, creed or colour' do not automatically receive the strong endorsement of their territorial integrity from which compliant states benefit.[228] These powerful statements demonstrate again the vitally important position which the principle of political self-determination occupies in the post-Charter legal world.

VI. Conclusion

This chapter has considered the development of the norm of colonial self-determination, beginning at the end of the long nineteenth century, in the rhetoric of the First World War. It has traced the idea as it developed from a mere promise of convenience, through its gradual institutionalisation in the mandates and trusts systems, and its eventual fruition in the practice of the General Assembly. In particular, it laid emphasis on the General Assembly's resolution 1514 (XV) as being capable of crystallising the self-determination idea as a norm of customary international law and, indeed, it has subsequently been confirmed by the ICJ that a customary law right did emerge in that period.[229]

As it developed, colonial self-determination did not have the stage to itself, however. As this chapter has shown, in the Charter and subsequent practice of the UN there are also important roles for polity-based and remedial self-determination. Although this latter, after its exertions in the age of revolution, may have been content with a walk-on part – during this period its only significant outing was in resolution 2625 (XXV) – polity-based self-determination very nearly stole the show. Long relegated to a role as a principle of political philosophy, the Charter placed polity-based self-determination at the heart of the post-1945 international order. Its expression in Article 1(2) of the Charter gives voice to the UN's founding principle – that it should be for each polity to govern its own affairs without the fear of armed intervention, or foreign interference – and is mirrored in the Article 2(4) prohibition on the threat or use of force and the Article 2(7) guarantee of non-intervention. Through its resolutions, the human rights covenants, and not least the Declaration on Friendly Relations, that principle of polity-based self-determination was to be given ever greater prominence as the defining idea of the age.

Although the importance – and legal status – of the polity-based form of self-determination are evident, matters are less clear in relation to other forms

[228] Emerson points to the Declaration on Non-Intervention (UNGA Res 2131 (XX)) as a statement of similar principles: R Emerson, 'Self-Determination' (1971) 65 *American Journal of International Law* 459, 465–66.

[229] For discussion, see ch 6.

of self-determination. In order to clarify the legal nature of the different forms of self-determination – as well as to track more recent developments – attention now turns to the legal sphere. In the following three chapters, I discuss the case law of the ICJ, together with other relevant courts and tribunals. Chapter four considers a sweep of judgments between c.1970 and 2010, with an eye primarily to colonial and secondarily to polity-based self-determination. Chapters five and six then give deeper attention to the ICJ's two most recent – and most detailed – discussions of self-determination, in the form of the *Kosovo* and *Chagos* advisory opinions.

4

Judicial Treatments of Self-Determination 1945–2004

Self-determination holds a special place in international adjudication. Although only a tiny minority of claims to self-determination have been the direct subject of judicial processes, self-determination claims have been at the root of some of the most significant cases to have come before international courts and tribunals – including the *East Timor* case before the ICJ,[1] as well as its *Kosovo* and *Chagos Archipelago* advisory opinions.[2] Not only have these – and other – self-determination cases made particularly noteworthy contributions to the development of international law, but cases concerning self-determination have made up a significant proportion of cases before the Court. Self-determination has been at the heart of nine individual judgments or advisory opinions of the ICJ,[3] a figure similar to the number of occasions on which the Court has addressed the use of force, diplomatic protection and immunities, and second only to questions of boundary delimitation.[4] That it has been such a (comparatively) frequent subject of disputes before the Court gives an indication of self-determination's centrality to the international legal order.

Beyond the ICJ context, too, self-determination has been the subject of influential consideration by quasi-judicial international processes such as the Badinter

[1] *East Timor (Portugal v Australia)*, Judgment, (1995) ICJ Reports 90.

[2] *Accordance with International Law of the Unilateral Declaration of Independence in Respect of Kosovo*, Advisory Opinion, (2010) ICJ Reports 403; *Legal Consequences of the Separation of the Chagos Archipelago from Mauritius in 1965*, Advisory Opinion, (2019) ICJ Reports 95. The *Kosovo* and *Chagos* advisory opinions are the subject of chs 5 and 6, respectively.

[3] The relevant cases are: the *International Status of South West Africa* Advisory Opinion (1950); the joined *South West Africa* cases (1966); the *Namibia* Advisory Opinion (1971); the *Western Sahara* Advisory Opinion (1971); the *East Timor* case (1995); the *Construction of a Wall* Advisory Opinion (2004); and the aforementioned *Kosovo* and *Chagos* advisory opinions, of 2010 and 2019, respectively. In addition, self-determination is a relevant matter in, but not central to, a further four cases: *Right of Passage* (1960), *Northern Cameroons* (1963), *Military and Paramilitary Activities* (1986), and *Certain Phosphate Lands* (1992). See also discussion in TD Musgrave, *Self-Determination and National Minorities* (Oxford, Clarendon Press, 1997) 77–90.

[4] Wolfgang Alschner and Damien Charlotin identify 126 unique judgments of the ICJ and its predecessor, the Permanent Court of international Justice (PCIJ). See W Alschner and D Charlotin, 'The Growing Complexity of the International Court of Justice's Self-Citation Network' (2018) 29 *European Journal of International Law* 83. Of these, approximately a fifth concern land or maritime boundary delimitation, making this by far the most common subject to be brought before the Court.

Commission,[5] by regional human rights bodies[6] and by domestic courts.[7] One of the most important insights to be gleaned from these decisions is the sheer importance of self-determination and adjacent questions for the international system, for constitutional orders, and for the day-to-day lives of individuals and communities. They also, however, reveal a great deal about the idea of self-determination and its four forms. This chapter will build upon the analysis of the development of the various norms and concepts of self-determination in contemporary international law in the previous chapters, and will apply the same four-part taxonomy of self-determination claims to judicial and quasi-judicial considerations of self-determination. In so doing it will permit a greater focus on the legal status of the various strands of the self-determination idea. I first survey the *Namibia* Advisory Opinion of the ICJ (1971), before considering its advisory opinion in *Western Sahara* (1975), the opinions of the Badinter Commission (1992–93), the judgment in *East Timor* (1995), the African Commission on Human and People's Rights decision in *Katanga* (1995), the Canadian Supreme Court's judgment in *Reference Re Secession of Quebec* (1998) and the advisory opinion in *Wall* (2004). The chapter then sets the stage for consideration of the ICJ's two most recent – and perhaps most significant – opinions on self-determination, the *Kosovo* (2010) and *Chagos* (2019) advisory opinions which, together with their attendant consequences, are the subjects of chapters five and six, respectively. First, however, section I considers the value of a focus on courts for an enquiry into the nature and legal status of self-determination.

I. Courts and Self-Determination

As was observed in chapter one,[8] questions of self-determination are among the most politically charged matters governed – or, as the case may be, not governed – by international law. In this highly specialised context, legal, political and moral appeals to legitimacy are densely interwoven, often without clear distinctions between them. That remains the case whether on the part of individuals and communities seeking to invoke self-determination's protection, ministries of foreign affairs seeking to respond to self-determination claims in a neighbouring state, or states parties drawing up declarations in the UN General Assembly. In the previous chapters, such statements and sources were used to chart the development of distinct kinds of legitimacy appeal under the self-determination category – namely, polity-based, secessionary, remedial and colonial self-determinations. With respect to only one of these forms, that of polity-based

[5] See below, s IV.
[6] See below, s VI.
[7] See below, s VII.
[8] See above, ch 1, s II.A.

self-determination, is it possible unequivocally to say that a legal norm of self-determination developed on the basis of these international statements and instruments: in the post-1945 legal order the right of peoples (here defined as the populations of whole-state units) to polity-based self-determination has acquired fundamental significance. This polity-based form of self-determination is the source of the prohibition on intervention, and as such is fundamental to the contemporary legal order: although the principle has often been breached, those breaches generally attract a strong international reaction and, as such, reinforce rather than eroding the legal status of the norm. It may even be possible to argue – and I would concur – that the polity-based form of self-determination has acquired a *ius cogens* character.[9]

The status of self-determination's other forms is far less clear, both because of the inherently tangled nature of the political, legal and moral arguments in this field, and because of the conceptual confusion that attends the self-determination question. For both of these reasons, while the legal status of self-determination's forms was sometimes an active question in drafting the documents issued by the political organs of the United Nations, the documents concerned generally speak of self-determination in the abstract, without distinguishing between its forms, and references to it are often vague and imprecise.

References to self-determination in court decisions are no less affected by the lack of conceptual clarity surrounding self-determination: it is no more common to find an articulated distinction between self-determination forms by judges than it is in political declarations. Nevertheless, a separation between forms of self-determination, albeit often subtextual, is easier to find in the decisions of courts because of the nature of the judicial function. In court cases, in contrast to political declarations, the right to self-determination is operationalised: courts, by their nature, deal with specificities in seeking to apply the correct interpretation of the law to the facts. As such, the standard tools of judicial reasoning – application, distinction, analogy and precedent – help to separate cases and ideas with similar ratios from those that understand themselves differently. It will be argued that over the sweep of cases dealing with self-determination, it is even possible to find the beginnings of recognition – albeit inchoate and incompletely theorised – of the forms of self-determination discussed here.

Given this aspect of the judicial function, it is perhaps surprising that both national and international courts have tended to avoid ruling on the status and scope of the various forms of self-determination (with the exception of colonial self-determination), and that such rulings, where made, are characterised by paucity of detail and a dearth of argumentation. Nevertheless, certain principles may be discerned which assist in an analysis of self-determination.

This chapter examines the major decisions of national and international courts – as well as the Badinter Arbitration Commission, which is discussed here as a

[9] See below, s VIII.

quasi-judicial body – in the post-Charter era. I begin the survey in 1971 with the ICJ's advisory opinion in *Namibia*. Although this was its first substantive assessment of self-determination principles, it would not be true to say that this is the first matter in which the Court was faced with a request with relevance for self-determination. A word on the preceding cases is therefore in order. The first case concerning matters of self-determination was submitted to the ICJ's predecessor – the Permanent Court of International Justice (PCIJ) – in the form of the advisory request in *Status of Eastern Carelia*.[10] Early in the post-Charter era the ICJ, too, was confronted with an advisory request on a self-determination-adjacent question, in *International Status of South-West Africa* (1950),[11] and a further case concerning the South-West Africa mandate territory was swiftly forthcoming in the form of the 1966 conjoined *South West Africa* cases, in which Ethiopia and Liberia sought to enforce elements of the mandate against South Africa.[12] In the interim, the Court in 1963 declined jurisdiction in the case concerning *Northern Cameroons*, between Cameroon and the United Kingdom.[13] With the exception of the 1950 *South-West Africa* Advisory Opinion none of these cases produced a judgment on the merits, and the 1950 opinion was concerned primarily with the change in legal regime resulting from the end of the mandate system with the

[10] *Status of Eastern Carelia* (1923) PCIJ, Series B, No 5, 7. The Court was asked to render an advisory opinion on the legal obligations on Finland and Russia under the Treaty of Dorpat which, among other matters, provided for 'the national right of self-determination' for the territory of Eastern Carelia, which at that time was split between Russian and Finnish territory (Treaty of Dorpat, concluded 14 October 1920, in force 1 January 1921, Art 10). The Court declined to give an opinion on the dispute because Russia had not given its consent to the jurisdiction of the Court (28), but it also observed that '[t]he question whether Finland and Russia contracted on the terms of the Declaration as to the nature of the autonomy of Eastern Carelia is really one of fact'. This should perhaps be taken as an indication that the Court considered that the reference to self-determination was a treaty-specific right, the content of which was to be determined by reference to the intention of the parties, and was not an incorporation of an autonomous international law standard or right. But see *contra* Rodríguez-Santiago, who argues that the inclusion of the right to self-determination in the treaty amounts to an expression of *opinio iuris*, and demonstrates that the states concerned considered themselves bound by the emerging international norm: E Rodríguez-Santiago, 'The Evolution of Self-Determination of Peoples in International Law' in FR Tesón (ed), *The Theory of Self-Determination* (Cambridge, Cambridge University Press, 2016) 216–217.

[11] *International Status of South-West Africa*, Advisory Opinion, (1950) ICJ Reports 128.

[12] *South West Africa (Ethiopia v South Africa; Liberia v South Africa)*, Second Phase, (1966) ICJ Reports 6. The Court concluded that it had no jurisdiction to hear the complaints by Ethiopia and Liberia that South Africa was failing to implement the mandate over the territory of South West Africa. The Court ruled that the supervision of the mandates was a matter for the League of Nations Council alone, and declined to accept the argument by Ethiopia and Liberia that the mandates system generated a right of supervision *erga omnes* or *erga omnes partes* (as we would today characterise it). See esp paras 33–35, 70–71, and *passim*.

[13] *Case Concerning the Northern Cameroons (Cameroon v United Kingdom)*, Preliminary Objections, Judgment of 2 December 1963, (1963) ICJ Reports 15. The Court declined to exercise jurisdiction for lack of object (p.33–34), noting that 'it may pronounce judgment only in connection with concrete cases where there exists at the time of the adjudication an actual controversy [… t]he Court's judgment must have some practical consequences'. In this case, the Court held that the integration of Northern Cameroons into Nigeria and the end of the mandate had deprived the case of its object (see also further p.35–36).

dissolution of the League of Nations and the establishment of the United Nations' trusts system. As such, the Court was not called upon to consider whether a self-determination right accrued to the population of the mandate territory.[14]

In the years which followed, however, various of the forms of self-determination began to acquire legal force, and it is in this period that judicial interpretations of self-determination have become increasingly important. Fernando Tesón asserts that '[i]n none of its opinions on self-determination did the Court depart from the restrictive view that only former colonies … had the right to self-determination'.[15] A different view will be presented here. In contrast to Tesón's statement, it will be argued that the Court has implicitly or explicitly recognised several forms of self-determination, and has accepted a customary law status for at least two forms: colonial and polity-based self-determination. Nor are such developments insignificant. As Hugh Thirlway restrainedly concludes: 'it is universally accepted, if not self-evident, that every decision the Court hands down will have an influence (to put it no higher) on how the law in the relevant field will thereafter be understood'.[16]

II. Advisory Opinion on *Namibia (South West Africa)*

In its advisory opinion on the *Legal Consequences for States of the Continued Presence of South Africa in Namibia (South West Africa)* of 1971,[17] the ICJ was confronted for the third time with a question relating to the former German colonial territory of Namibia (South West Africa). Already the subject of an advisory opinion in 1950[18] and conjoined contentious cases filed by Ethiopia and Liberia against South Africa in 1966,[19] the Court's advisory opinion in 1971 again related to the proper conduct of South Africa in its administration of the territory. On this occasion, the Court was responding to an advisory request from the Security Council, which asked the Court to assess the legal consequences for states of South Africa's continued presence in Namibia, in light of its resolution of 30 January 1970.[20] In the course of its opinion, the Court made a number of

[14] *South West Africa* AO (n 11). This case is discussed further in relation to the ambit of the trusts system in Chapter III, section 4.

[15] FR Tesón, 'Introduction: The Conundrum of Self-Determination' in Tesón (ed), *The Theory of Self-Determination* (n 10) 2, fn 5.

[16] H Thirlway, *The International Court of Justice* (Oxford, Oxford University Press, 2016) 202. On this point, see further Hernández, who provides a summary of academic and judicial opinion on the ability of the Court consciously to develop international law: GI Hernández, *The International Court of Justice and the Judicial Function* (Oxford, Oxford University Press, 2014) 90ff.

[17] *Legal Consequences for States of the Continued Presence of South Africa in Namibia (South West Africa) notwithstanding Security Council Resolution 276 (1970)*, Advisory Opinion, (1971) ICJ Reports 16.

[18] *South West Africa* Advisory Opinion (n 11).

[19] *South West Africa* Cases (n 12).

[20] UN Security Council Resolution 276 (1970), 30 January 1970.

important statements affirming the international nature of the governance of trust territories, as well as confirming that the ultimate independence of the territories is that system's telos. In these statements, an embryonic form of what was to become the norm of colonial self-determination can be seen.

The events leading to the 1970 advisory request are complex, but have their root in the racist apartheid policies of South Africa's minority government in the post-Second World War era.[21] Prior to 1915, the territory of modern-day Namibia was occupied by Germany, one of a small number of German territorial possessions in Africa.[22] Those territories, as discussed above,[23] were stripped from Germany following the First World War, and formed the majority of the mandate system territories under the League of Nations. By a decision of 17 December 1920, the Council of the League of Nations granted the mandate over the former German South West Africa to South Africa, 'to exercise it on behalf o[f] the League of Nations'.[24] The mandate granted was class C; that is to say, a mandate applying to those territories considered farthest away from the level of development necessary for independence.[25] Such C-mandates were to be governed 'as an integral portion' of the territory of the mandatory state[26] but on conditions remaining distinct from annexation: the mandatory exercises control over the territory 'on behalf of the League of Nations and in accordance with' the provisions of the mandate,[27] including that it 'shall promote to the utmost the material and moral well-being and the social progress of the inhabitants'.[28] In its 1950 advisory opinion on the *International Status of South-West Africa*, the ICJ confirmed that the conditions of the mandate continued to apply despite the disappearance of the League of Nations, with the United Nations exercising the supervisory authority of the former League.[29]

[21] For a summary of the events that form the background to the Court's opinion, see Musgrave, *National Minorities* (n 3) 80–84; J Dugard, 'The Opinion on South-West Africa ("Namibia"): The Teleologists Triumph' (1971) 88 *South African Law Journal* 460; E Gordon, 'Old Orthodoxies amid New Experiences: The South West Africa (Namibia) Litigation and the Uncertain Jurisprudence of the International Court of Justice' (1971) 1 *Denver Journal of International Law and Policy* 65.

[22] For a history of Germany's occupation of Namibia, as well as an account of numerous crimes and abuses committed against the population, see M Goldmann, '„Ich bin Ihr Freund und Kapitän". Die deutsch-namibische Entschädigungsfrage im Spiegel intertemporaler und interkultureller Völkerrechtskonzepte' in P Dann, I Feichtner and J von Bernstorff (eds), *(Post-)Koloniale Rechtswissenschaft* (forthcoming).

[23] ch 3, s III.

[24] Council of the League of Nations, Mandate for German South-West Africa (17 December 1920), www.archives.ungeneva.org.

[25] The League of Nations, *The Mandates System: Origin – Principles – Application* (Geneva, Series of League of Nations Publications, 1945); see also N Matz, 'Civilization and the Mandate System under the League of Nations as Origin of Trusteeship' (2005) 9 *Max Planck Yearbook of United Nations Law* 47, 72–73.

[26] Mandate for South-West Africa (n 24) Art 2; The League of Nations, *Mandates System* (n 25).

[27] Mandate for South-West Africa (n 24), Preamble.

[28] ibid Art 2. For further discussion of the mandates and the differences between classes A, B and C mandates, see ch 3, s III.

[29] *South West Africa* Advisory Opinion (n 11) 12–12, 19.

In the years following the replacement of the League by the United Nations, South Africa began to construct its infamous system of apartheid. Despite vociferous international objection by African states and others,[30] South Africa sought also to apply apartheid principles to the governance of Namibia. In a succession of resolutions, the General Assembly added its voice to those demanding an end to apartheid both in South Africa and in Namibia,[31] calls that went unheeded. Finally, on 27 October 1966, the General Assembly adopted resolution 2145 (XXI), by which it terminated the South African mandate over South West Africa, and placed the territory under the administration of an international committee of Member States of the General Assembly, whose task it would be to exercise the direct responsibility of the United Nations towards the territory and its people.[32] South Africa refused to comply with the termination of the mandate, and continued to exercise control over Namibia, prompting a further series of resolutions both by the General Assembly and the Security Council, condemning its actions. In its resolution 276 (1970) – the subject of the Court's opinion – the Security Council '[d]eclare[d] that the continued presence of the South African authorities in Namibia is illegal' and consequently that all of South Africa's actions in Namibia 'after the termination of the Mandate are illegal and invalid'.[33] It further '[c]all[ed] upon all States, particularly those which have economic and other interests in Namibia, to refrain from any dealings with the Government of South Africa which are inconsistent with paragraph 2'. It was the legal effects of that exhortation, together with the effects of the illegality as a whole, on third states which were the subject of the advisory request to the Court.[34]

South Africa contended that the determination made in resolution 2145 (XXI) – by which the General Assembly decided to terminate South Africa's mandate in Namibia – was beyond the Assembly's competence. According to it, therefore, it retained title over Namibia, and there was no illegality in relation to which the Security Council could require all states to take action. Among the arguments advanced by South Africa was the claim that class C mandates – including South West Africa – were transferred to the mandatory powers on terms 'not far removed from annexation',[35] and it was in the course of rejecting this proposition that the Court made its remarks on self-determination. It held that all categories of mandates were underpinned by a consistent set of principles.[36] Prominent among these was the idea that such territories were held on 'trust' – that no matter what their current state of development, the people of the territories have 'a potentiality

[30] Including the aforementioned attempt by Ethiopia and Liberia to bring South Africa before the ICJ to complain of its failure to fulfil the terms of its mandate: *South West Africa* Cases (n 12).

[31] See eg UN General Assembly Resolution 2074 (XX), 17 December 1965; UN General Assembly Resolution 2144 (XXI), 26 October 1966, Part B.

[32] UN General Assembly Resolution 2145 (XXI), 27 October 1966, paras 4–6.

[33] UNSC Res 276 (1970), para 2.

[34] UN Security Council Resolution 284 (1970), 29 July 1970.

[35] *Namibia* (n 17) para 45.

[36] ibid paras 45–46; AW Rovine, 'The World Court Opinion on Namibia' (1972) 11 *Columbia Journal of Transnational Law* 203, 206.

for independent existence', and that mandatories should provide the 'help and guidance necessary to enable them to arrive at the stage where they would be "able to stand by themselves"'.[37] There was, therefore, both in general and in the particular case of the mandate for South West Africa, a 'rejection of the notion of annexation'.[38] These foundational principles of the system had not lapsed on the transposition of the mandate system (under the League of Nations) to the United Nations.[39]

More significantly for present purposes, the Court found that 'the subsequent development of international law in regard to non-self-governing territories, as enshrined in the Charter of the United Nations, made the principle of self-determination applicable to all of them'.[40] It went on to call it 'obvious[]' that the 'sacred trust' principle 'continued to apply to League of Nations mandated territories', but declared further that '[t]he concept of the sacred trust was confirmed and expanded to all "territories whose people have not yet attained a full measure of self-government"'.[41] Referring explicitly to both the Charter and to resolution 1514 (XV) (the Declaration on the Granting of Independence to Colonial Countries and Peoples),[42] the Court declared that '[t]hese developments leave little doubt that the ultimate objective of the sacred trust was the self-determination and independence of the peoples concerned'.[43] Significantly, the Court did not consider it necessary to show that self-determination was the governing principle of the mandates system when it was enacted, or when the Namibian mandate was concluded: 'subsequent development[s]' in the international legal system 'made the principle of self-determination applicable to all' non-self-governing territories.[44] In effect, the Court was making the determination here that colonial self-determination was emerging as a result of the conclusion of the Charter, as well as the near-unanimous passage of resolution 1514.[45] Colonial self-determination had at least acquired the status of an interpretative principle, capable of modulating the implementation of other

[37] *Namibia* (n 17) para 45; Rodríguez-Santiago, 'Evolution of Self-Determination' (n 10) 214; Anon, 'The United Nations, Self-Determination and the Namibia Opinions' (1972–73) 82 *Yale Law Journal* 533, 539–40.

[38] *Namibia* (n 17) para 50; OJ Lissitzyn, 'International Law and the Advisory Opinion on Namibia' (1972) 11 *Columbia Journal of Transnational Law* 50, 56–57.

[39] *Namibia* (n 17) paras 78, and further 55–83; 'The Namibia Opinions' (n 37) 535–36.

[40] ibid para 52; see further Musgrave, *National Minorities* (n 3) 84–85; Rodríguez-Santiago, 'Evolution of Self-Determination' (n 10) 226.

[41] *Namibia* (n 17) para 52.

[42] For discussion, see ch 3, s V.C.

[43] *Namibia* (n 17) para 53.

[44] ibid para 52.

[45] K Samuel, 'Can Religious Norms Influence Self-Determination Struggles, and with What Implications for International Law?' in D French (ed), *Statehood and Self-Determination: Reconciling Tradition and Modernity in International Law* (Cambridge, Cambridge University Press, 2013) 304. Lissitzyn, too, argues that the Advisory Opinion 'comes close to affirming the existence of a legal right of self-determination in general international law (and not only in the law of the Charter)': Lissitzyn, 'International Law and the Advisory Opinion on Namibia' (n 38) 58. But see, *contra*, Macklem, who argues that this is better understood as an example of self-determination in the context of foreign occupation: P Macklem, 'Self-Determination in Three Movements' in Tesón (ed), *The Theory of*

rules of international law as they applied to territories within the compass of the League of Nations/United Nations system, and it is significant that the Court ascribed such a strong interpretative role to self-determination, with the effect that colonial self-determination conditions the interpretation of the mandate agreement, despite the mandate agreement pre-dating the developments to which the Court referred. Nevertheless, the Court did not fully explore the ambit of the colonial self-determination idea, and it is not clear from the Court's opinion whether or not it by this point regarded colonial self-determination as a self-standing right applicable to all colonial territories. The Court would be called upon to return to that point less than five years later, in its advisory opinion on *Western Sahara*.

III. The *Western Sahara* Advisory Opinion

In 1975 the ICJ handed down its advisory opinion on *Western Sahara* in response to a question posed by the General Assembly.[46] At the time of the resolution, the territory of Western Sahara had been under the control of Spain since at least 1884, with some Spanish presence in the territory and the wider region since the late fifteenth century. Western Sahara was at that time an extremely sparsely populated territory (with a population density in 1970 of approximately 0.2 inhabitants per square kilometer), with little water availability but considerable mineral wealth, predominantly phosphates. Although under Spanish control, the territory was claimed by Morocco, Mauritania and Algeria, and there were vehement disagreements concerning both to which state the territory should belong, as well as the means for reaching that decision.[47]

The decolonisation of the Spanish holdings in northern Africa – including Western Sahara – was actively before the UN for a decade leading up to the advisory request to the ICJ. In resolutions from 1965 onwards, the UN General Assembly called for the decolonisation of the territories, but applied different principles to each of them. In addition to Western Sahara, the Spanish territory of Ifni was under consideration (the enclaves of Ceuta and Melilla were not included in the resolutions, and remain Spanish to this day). Whereas Western Sahara was to be granted

Self-Determination (n 10) 104. In the typology used here, the Advisory Opinion would therefore, on Macklem's view, be best seen as a reference to political self-determination. In light of the Court's prominent references to the 'sacred trust' associated with the mandates system, as well as its references to resolution 1514, it is my view that Macklem unduly stresses the occupation context, which here (unlike at other points in the Court's opinion) was a secondary concern of the Court.

[46] *Western Sahara*, Advisory Opinion, (1975) ICJ Reports 12. For a summary of the events leading up to and following the case, see S Simon, 'Western Sahara' in C Walter, A von Ungern-Sternberg and K Abushov (eds), *Self-Determination and Secession in International Law* (Oxford, Oxford University Press, 2014); EH Riedel, 'Confrontation in Western Sahara in the Light of the Advisory Opinion of the International Court of Justice of 16 October 1975. A Critical Appraisal' (1976) 19 *German Yearbook of International Law* 405.

[47] For the background to the decolonisation process and advisory request, see generally TA Marks, 'Spanish Sahara – Background to the Conflict' (1976) 75 *African Affairs* 3.

self-determination and a referendum on its future status, Ifni was confirmed to be Moroccan, and its decolonisation was to be completed by returning the territory to that state.[48] In its resolution 2428 (XXIII), the General Assembly specifically referenced the 'difference in nature of the legal status' of the two territories, as well as the different 'processes of decolonization envisaged' by the General Assembly for them.[49] On 16 December 1969, as foreseen by the General Assembly, Spain transferred control over Ifni to Morocco. Western Sahara, however, remained a more controversial matter.

By 1973, Spain had committed itself to holding an independence referendum in Western Sahara in communications to the elected representatives of its people, and was taking steps progressively to develop its internal organs of governance.[50] Mauritania and Algeria supported the principle of self-determination by the inhabitants of Western Sahara, but the holding of a referendum was staunchly opposed by Morocco, which maintained that the legitimate way to dispose of the territory would be to (re)integrate it into Morocco, as Ifni had been.[51] Faced with this controversy, the General Assembly passed resolution 3292 (XXIX), by which it transmitted the request for an advisory opinion to the ICJ. Morocco, Mauritania and Nigeria all voted in favour of the resolution – along with a total of eighty-seven Member States – with no votes against. Forty-three states abstained, among them Spain.[52]

The key question for the Court to answer was whether Western Sahara was, at the time of its colonisation by Spain, *terra nullius*. Secondly, and if it answered the first question negatively, the Court was asked to assess what legal ties existed between Western Sahara and either Morocco or Mauritania prior to its colonisation.[53] The strong implication of that question, and one which gave rise to extensive discussion both before the Fourth Committee and in the opinions of the Judges, was that if Western Sahara was not *terra nullius* at the time of its colonisation, then the proper means of decolonisation would be to return it to its former sovereign. In other words, according to the contention of Morocco and Mauritania, the people of Western Sahara should be entitled to no self-determination if, reaching back to the 1880s and before Spanish colonisation, ties equivalent to sovereignty could be established. In the words of the representative of Kenya in the debate before the Fourth Committee, '[t]he United Nations was indeed being asked to treat [the inhabitants of Western Sahara] as chattels and not as people'.[54] Kenya's was not the

[48] UN General Assembly Resolution 2072 (XX), 16 December 1965; UN General Assembly Resolution 2229 (XXI), 20 December 1966.

[49] UN General Assembly Resolution 2428 (XXIII), 18 December 1968, preamble; referencing UN General Assembly Resolution 2354 (XXII), 19 December 1967.

[50] Marks, 'Spanish Sahara' (n 47) 9.

[51] ibid 11–12.

[52] UN General Assembly Resolution 3292 (XXIX), 13 December 1974; UNGA Voting Records, www.digitallibrary.un.org/record/651029?ln=en.

[53] UN General Assembly Resolution 3292 (XXIX), 13 December 1974, para 1.

[54] Question of Spanish Sahara, UN General Assembly, 29th Session, Fourth Committee, Official Record of the 2131st Meeting, 11 December 1974, Agenda Item 23 at para 46 (Mr Njenga, Kenya).

only delegation to object: numerous states noted their concern that the resolution as drafted represented a retrograde step in the development of self-determination.[55]

A similar concern, albeit in a different form, was clearly felt by the Judges of the Court, as revealed by their declarations and separate opinions. Judge Ignacio-Pinto put the concern succinctly:

> My objection to the Advisory Opinion is due to the fact that I consider that ... the questions as put are, as it were, loaded questions, leading in any case to the answer awaited in this particular instance, namely the recognition of rights of sovereignty of Morocco on the one hand and of Mauritania on the other over some part or other of Western Sahara.[56]

Judges Petrén, Gros, Dillard and de Castro raised similar concerns.[57] As Judge Dillard complained:

> [A] literal reading of the two questions appeared to compel the conclusion that if the answer to the first question was that Western Sahara was *not terra nullius* then by necessary implication there *must* have been legal ties between the territory and that of the two interested States.[58]

The Judges thus seemed concerned that the drafting of the question was designed in such a way as to manipulate the Court into reaching the conclusion desired by Morocco and Mauritania. But of equal concern, it seems, to certain of its members was the implication of the question that self-determination is a subsidiary means for the disposal of a decolonised territory. As Judge Dillard put it, the case raised a background question that – despite the best efforts of the drafters – could not be avoided: 'To what extent, if any, does the right of self-determination limit the possible policy choices open to the General Assembly?'[59] In grappling with this aspect the Court, as Mark Janis observes, went far beyond the scope of the question posed by the General Assembly.[60]

The Court rejected the implied binary choice posed by the General Assembly's question. It agreed that Western Sahara was not *terra nullius* prior to its colonisation by Spain in 1884,[61] but instead of proceeding along the lines apparently laid

[55] See Question of Spanish Sahara (n 54), remarks of Argentina (para 22), Equatorial Guinea (paras 50–51), Costa Rica (para 57), United States of America (paras 63–64), Venezuela (paras 85–87), Trinidad and Tobago (para 111), Yemen (para 114).

[56] *Western Sahara*, Declaration of Judge Ignacio-Pinto, (1975) ICJ Reports 78, 78.

[57] *Western Sahara*, Separate Opinion of Judge Petrén, (1975) ICJ Reports 104, 113; *Western Sahara*, Declaration of Judge Gros, (1975) ICJ Reports 69, 70, 74–75; *Western Sahara*, Separate Opinion of Judge Dillard, (1975) ICJ Reports 116, 116–24; *Western Sahara*, Separate Opinion of Judge de Castro, (1975) ICJ Reports 127, 131–33.

[58] Separate Opinion of Judge Dillard, *Western Sahara* (n 57) 124.

[59] Separate Opinion of Judge Dillard, *Western Sahara* (n 57) 122.

[60] MW Janis, 'The International Court of Justice: Advisory Opinion on the Western Sahara' (1976) 17 *Harvard Journal of International Law* 609, 618–19; see also Riedel, 'Confrontation in Western Sahara in the Light of the Advisory Opinion of the International Court of Justice of 16 October 1975' (n 46) 419–22.

[61] *Western Sahara* (n 46) paras 81–83.

for it (that it must therefore have been under the sovereignty either of Morocco or Mauritania), it concluded that the territory had been under the control of its inhabitants.[62] Although personal, religious, and other ties existed between the peoples of Western Sahara and each of these other entities, the Court

> has not found legal ties of such a nature as might affect the application of resolution 1514 (XV) in the decolonization of Western Sahara and, in particular, of the principle of self-determination through the free and genuine expression of the will of the people of the Territory.[63]

On the face of it, this is a somewhat ambiguous statement.[64] Certainly, the Court here reasserted the rights of the people of Western Sahara to self-determination, but on the wording of this statement it remained plausible to interpret the opinion as ratifying the contention that historical title would prevail over self-determination as the means of disposal for territories such as Western Sahara, had such title existed.[65] That may have been Judge Boni's interpretation of paragraph 162 of the opinion: in a fascinating separate opinion, Judge Boni notes first that he voted in favour of the Court's opinion, before revealing that he disagreed with the majority's conclusions in key respects. 'In strict logic', he concedes, 'I should have voted "no" to the second question', given his conclusion that '[t]he legal ties between [Western Sahara and Morocco] were thus not only religious … but also political, and had the character of territorial sovereignty'.[66] In other words, Judge Boni disagreed with the majority in the case on the core substance of the second question posed by the General Assembly, but had chosen to vote directly against his own opinion. He states as his reason his full agreement with the principle endorsed by the Court, that of 'obligatory consultation of the inhabitants of Western Sahara on their future',[67] noting that one cannot 'reasonably reproach the Court for having adopted such an attitude'.[68] What is not explicitly stated in the opinion is what the result of the reverse finding would have been, but – together with his idiosyncratic vote – it may be indicative that Judge Boni took care to refute the contention that

[62] ibid paras 129, 149–150.

[63] ibid para 162.

[64] But see, *contra*, Smith, who sees none of this ambiguity. Smith argues that '[t]he right of a colonized people to self-determination could not have been expressed more clearly'. JJ Smith, 'Western Sahara: The Failure and Promise of International Law' (2011) 69 *Advocate Vancouver* 179, 182 (footnotes omitted); see also Janis, 'The International Court of Justice: Advisory Opinion on the Western Sahara' (n 60) 618.

[65] Duursma argues that the context suggests that a finding by the Court that historical title existed over Western Sahara would have precluded the exercise of the population's self-determination. J Duursma, *Fragmentation and the International Relations of Micro-States: Self-Determination and Statehood* (Cambridge, Cambridge University Press, 1996) 61–62. For further discussion of historical title in the Advisory Opinion, see GJ Levy, 'Advisory Opinion on the Western Sahara' (1975–76) 2 *Brooklyn Journal of International Law* 289; MA Smith, Jr, 'Sovereignty over Unoccupied Territories – The Western Sahara Decision' (1977) 9 *Case Western Journal of International Law* 135.

[66] *Western Sahara*, Separate Opinion of Judge Boni, (1975) ICJ Reports 173, 173.

[67] ibid 173–74.

[68] ibid 173.

historical title would have prevailed.[69] Similarly, Judge Dillard took care to address this point in his separate opinion, declaring 'almost self-evident' that 'the existence of ancient "legal ties" … can only have a tangential effect in the ultimate choices available to the people': 'It is for the people to determine the destiny of the territory and not the territory the destiny of the people.'[70] Although the Court was less direct in its statements, in my view the reasoning of the majority supports the same conclusion: even had historical ties of sovereignty between Western Sahara and either of Morocco or Mauritania been found to exist, nevertheless the people of Western Sahara would have been entitled to self-determination. The Court treated self-determination not as a *choice* available to the General Assembly in the absence of a countervailing legal principle; rather, the Court was at pains to stress that self-determination had become a right of colonised peoples under international law.

The Court began citing its previous decision in *Namibia*, and repeated its finding that following the adoption of the UN Charter and resolution 1514 (XV), there is 'little doubt that the ultimate objective of the sacred trust was the self-determination and independence of the peoples concerned', developments it characterised as customary law.[71] It then cited the Declaration on Friendly Relations as further authority for the existence of a right to self-determination,[72] and concluded that fact that the General Assembly had on certain occasions set in train decolonisation processes without first consulting the inhabitants of the territories concerned should not be taken to cast doubt on the legal nature of the self-determination norm. Rather, those cases related to the applicability criteria of the norm (ie whether the population is a 'people') or the practicalities of implementing it: no referendum is necessary where the view of the people is already clear, for example.[73] Finally, it turned to the circumstances of Western Sahara, and confirmed that the General Assembly had not established an alternative pathway to decolonisation for Western Sahara through its prior practice, or the recourse to the Court. The process 'envisaged by the General Assembly', the Court said, 'is one which will respect the right of the population of Western Sahara to determine their future political status by their own freely expressed will'.[74] As Elizabeth Rodríguez-Santiago argues, the Court's straightforward application of the principles demonstrates that 'at that point, the right to self-determination for the peoples of the non-self-governing territories was, in the eyes of the Court, something already consolidated in the positive law'.[75]

[69] ibid 174.

[70] Separate Opinion of Judge Dillard, *Western Sahara* (n 57) 122

[71] *Namibia* (n 17) para 53; cited in *Western Sahara* (n 46) para 55. See also M Dawidowicz, 'Trading Fish or Human Rights in Western Sahara? Self-Determination, Non-Recognition and the EC–Morocco Fisheries Agreement' in French (ed), *Statehood and Self-Determination* (n 45) 254–55; Riedel, 'Confrontation in Western Sahara in the Light of the Advisory Opinion of the International Court of Justice of 16 October 1975' (n 46) 423–24.

[72] *Western Sahara* (n 46) para 58.

[73] ibid para 59.

[74] ibid para 70.

[75] Rodríguez-Santiago, 'Evolution of Self-Determination' (n 10) 227.

While this confirmation that self-determination had acquired a legal character is significant, it remained limited. It is clear that in the Court's view the right thus established was to colonial self-determination,[76] and the Court gave no opinion either on the way in which that right should be implemented,[77] or whether other forms of the norm had also acquired legal status.[78] Although it was implied by the Court that the principle of self-determination as posited in the Charter may have broader applications, its presence in resolution 1514 (XV) represented its incarnation as a tool 'for the purpose of bringing all colonial situations to a speedy end'.[79] It is an indication of that situational specificity that, as Laurence Hanauer notes, the self-determination norm applied by the Court in *Western Sahara* was a right which attached to the *territory* of Western Sahara, as a former colonial possession, and not to a particular *people*:

> Ethnically and historically, the Sahrawi 'nation' is a modern construct. … Organised along tribal and familial lines, no supratribal authority or state structure existed until the 1970s. Until twenty to thirty years ago, therefore, no Sahrawi 'nation' could be said to exist; a nomadic herder would have claimed to belong to his tribe but would not have been familiar with the idea of a Western Saharan national identity.[80]

This observation reveals something significant about the idea of colonial self-determination, and further reinforces its categorisation as a sui generis form of the idea which has its roots primarily in a political consensus rather than in the wider self-determination genus. For all that the Court referred to decolonisation processes without a 'people',[81] in decolonisation processes – and particularly in colonial Africa, a continent of straight lines drawn in European capitals – it is rare to find a territory occupied by a single 'people'. Instead, the principle *uti possidetis* has been taken as paramount.[82] Whereas in other cases of self-determination the people are primary, and give rise to the claim; in colonial self-determination, it is the claim which constructs the people.[83]

[76] Musgrave, *National Minorities* (n 3) 86; LL Herman, 'Western Sahara Advisory Opinion, ICJ Reports 1975, p 12 – An Analysis of the World Court Judgment in the Western Sahara Case' (1976–77) 41 *Saskatchewan Law Review* 133, 135; LS Hanauer, 'The Irrelevance of Self-Determination Law to Ethno-National Conflict: A New Look at the Western Sahara Case' (1995) 9 *Emory International Law Review* 133, 145; Riedel, 'Confrontation in Western Sahara in the Light of the Advisory Opinion of the International Court of Justice of 16 October 1975' (n 46) 426.

[77] F Wooldridge, 'The Advisory Opinion of the International Court of Justice in the Western Sahara Case' (1979) 8 *Anglo-American Law Review* 86, 106–07.

[78] ibid 117.

[79] *Western Sahara* (n 46) para 55.

[80] Hanauer, 'The Irrelevance of Self-Determination Law to Ethno-National Conflict' (n 76) 134.

[81] *Western Sahara* (n 46) para 59: 'in certain cases the General Assembly has dispensed with the requirement of consulting the inhabitants of a given territory. Those instances were based … on the consideration that a certain population did not constitute a "people" entitled to self-determination.'

[82] A Peters, 'The Principle of *Uti Possidetis Juris*: How Relevant Is It for Issues of Secession?' in Walter, von Ungern-Sternberg and Abushov (eds), *Self-Determination and Secession in International Law* (n 46).

[83] The question of Western Sahara remains on the General Assembly's agenda (see eg UN General Assembly Resolution 71/106, 6 December 2016). As Naldi notes, this is arguably one of the remaining

IV. Badinter Arbitration Commission

On 25 June 1991, Slovenia and Croatia each declared its independence from the Socialist Federal Republic of Yugoslavia.[84] These declarations were to sound the death knell for the Yugoslav state, which had at that point been in a period of decline for some time. Further declarations of independence swiftly followed: Macedonia on 17 September 1991, Kosovo on 19 October 1991, and Bosnia and Herzegovina on 22 September 1992. These declarations precipitated a prolonged and bloody conflict in the Balkans, in which many atrocities were committed.

On 27 August 1991, in an attempt to halt the already fierce conflict and to bring some stability to the region, the European Community and its Member States initiated a peace conference on Yugoslavia, and with it an arbitration commission which was to provide advice and guidance to the Conference on questions of international law. The Commission was chaired by Robert Badinter, and has ubiquitously become known as the Badinter Commission. From 11 January 1992 to 13 August 1993 the Badinter Commission delivered fifteen opinions on a range of matters concerning the current status of the various Yugoslav republics, the rules relating to the apportionment between them of assets and debts, and the permissibility of their recognition by the European Community. In the course of these proceedings the Commission also made some observations on the rights of these communities to self-determination.

It should be noted, to begin with, that at the time in question Yugoslavia was, according to the Commission's estimation, 'in the process of dissolution'.[85] This finding formed the background to the entirety of the Commission's work, and enabled many other of its conclusions. These declarations of independence were not, as the Commission characterised it, cases of attempted secession from an effective territorial sovereign; but rather were the products of an inevitable disintegration. Applying the principle *uti possidetis iuris*, the Commission gently

areas of the world in which the decolonisation process is still incomplete. Despite the actions of the General Assembly and the judgment of the Court the people of Western Sahara are yet to meaningfully exercise their right to self-determination. See G Naldi, 'Western Sahara: Suspended Statehood or Frustrated Self-Determination?' (2005) 13 *African Yearbook of International Law* 11; see also J Soroeta Liceras, *International Law and the Western Sahara Conflict* (Wolf Legal Publishers, 2014); P Epstein, 'Behind Closed Doors: "Autonomous Colonization" in the Post United Nations Era – The Case for Western Sahara' (2009) 15 *Annual Survey of International and Comparative Law* 107.

[84] V Meier, *Yugoslavia: A History of Its Demise*, tr S Ramet (London, Routledge, 1999) xvii, 110–37.

[85] Opinions of the Badinter Commission (1992) 31 ILM 1494, 1497 (Opinion No 1). Maogoto ascribes this conclusion to the Commission's finding that Yugoslavia 'no longer performs the functions of a state', and draws an interesting parallel with Somalia: JN Maogoto, 'Somaliland: Scrambled by International Law?' in French (ed), *Statehood and Self-Determination* (n 45) 212. Radan contests the finding, however, arguing that a close analysis of Opinions Nos 3 and 11 shows that Opinion No 3 was rendered 'in the context of secession and not the dissolution of a state'. P Radan, 'Post-Secession International Borders: A Critical Analysis of the Opinions of the Badinter Arbitration Commission' (2000) 24 *Melbourne University Law Review* 50, 54ff (footnotes omitted).

endorsed the upgrading of the former internal, regional boundaries of the state into external frontiers.[86] Although there was a self-determination element to the opinions of the Commission – the Commission refused to endorse the recognition of Bosnia-Herzegovina by the European Community because of the lack of a referendum demonstrating the will of the people of the territory to be an independent state[87] – its primary discussion of self-determination concerned the irredentist desire of the Serbian minority in Croatia and in Bosnia-Herzegovina.[88] Despite its tacit endorsement of the self-determination of the republics within their former federal boundaries, here the Commission declared that 'self-determination must not involve changes to existing frontiers at the time of independence (*uti possidetis juris*) except where the States concerned agree otherwise'.[89] Rather, it interpreted the right of those communities to self-determination as an extensive guarantee of their rights qua a minority community, declaring their rights to recognition of their identity, to identify themselves as a community and to choose their nationality.[90] This right to self-determination was interpreted, in direct contrast to the secession idea, as being an exceptionally strong right, and was described as having peremptory character.[91]

The Commission's treatment of self-determination was modest and restrained, but nonetheless significant. In placing emphasis on the failure of Yugoslavia's territorial sovereignty it evoked (consciously or unconsciously) the opinion of the Jurists in the Åland Islands dispute, who found that secessionary self-determination had acquired the status of a weak right, which could overcome territorial integrity only where a state is incompletely constituted and thus imperfectly sovereign.[92] The Commission also stressed the importance of internal administrative boundaries, however, interpreting the right of peoples to independent statehood as applying only within pre-existing regions and territories.[93] This may have been an attempt to constrain the application of the principle and to engineer 'un-revolutionary

[86] Badinter Commission (n 85) 1497–99 (Opinion No 2); A Pellet, 'The Opinions of the Badinter Arbitration Committee: A Second Breath for the Self-Determination of Peoples' (1992) 3 *European Journal of International Law* 178, 180; Peters, '*Uti Possidetis*' (n 82) 103–06.

[87] Badinter Commission (n 85) 1501–03 (Opinion No 4); Pellet, 'Second Breath' (n 86) 178.

[88] Badinter Commission (n 85) 1497–99 (Opinion No 2).

[89] ibid 1498 (Opinion No 2); see also the remarks of the Commission on the matter in Opinion No 3, 1499–1500, which Mégret interprets as the Commission's 'insist[ance] that there was no right to secede': F Mégret, 'The Right to Self-Determination: Earned, Not Inherent' in Tesón (ed), *The Theory of Self-Determination* (n 10) 51.

[90] Badinter Commission (n 85) 1498 (Opinion No 2). As Pellet discusses, it is not clear whether the Commission considered 'nationality' to bear the same meaning as 'citizenship', but the statement is nevertheless significant: Pellet, 'Second Breath' (n 86) 179–80.

[91] Badinter Commission (n 85) 1498 (Opinion No 2). For criticism of the Commission's reasoning on this point, see M Pomerance, 'The Badinter Commission: The Use and Misuse of the International Court of Justice's Jurisprudence' (1998–99) 20 *Michigan Journal of International Law* 31, 50–53.

[92] See ch 2, s III.C.

[93] See further Peters, '*Uti Possidetis*' (n 82); Pomerance, 'The Badinter Commission' (n 91) 50–57.

revolutions', of the kind identified in other contexts by David Armitage.[94] But whatever the motivation, it re-emphasises that the secessionary form of self-determination – if a right of legal character at all – remained a very weak right which would apply only in limited circumstances.

By contrast, its strong interpretation of the political self-determination idea – guaranteeing the rights of minority communities and enabling (at the least) individuals to self-identify with various national communities within states – speaks of an expansive interpretation of the self-determination idea. Here, again, one finds a tacit endorsement of the division of self-determination into different norms with different statuses. While the Commission found that secessionary self-determination operated only within limited circumstances, it referred to the 1966 International Human Rights Covenants as authority for a norm of political self-determination which offers extensive protections to self-identifying minorities, which it characterised as a rule of peremptory character under international law.[95] That the Commission highlighted – and ascribed such a high status to – the protection of minorities as an aspect of polity-based self-determination is a manifestation of a wider turning point. While the (near-exclusive) focus of judicial fora in the foregoing years had been on colonial self-determination, in the coming years polity-based self-determination was to receive increasing judicial attention. That shift is clear in the ICJ's judgment in the preliminary objections phase of *East Timor*.

V. *East Timor*

Just two years after the final Badinter Commission opinion, the idea of self-determination again came before the ICJ in the case concerning *East Timor*. Although the Court's decision in *East Timor* came at the preliminary objections stage and resulted in a finding that it lacked jurisdiction over the complaint (as a result of the *Monetary Gold* rule[96]), it nevertheless made significant remarks on self-determination and its status in international law. The Court reaffirmed its finding made in the *Namibia* and *Western Sahara* advisory opinions that certain forms of self-determination had acquired legal status, and even proclaimed the principle to have acquired a high status in the international legal system.[97]

Despite its brevity – the Court's consideration of self-determination is cursory at best – the *East Timor* case may be the most significant judgment on the subject

[94] D Armitage, *The Declaration of Independence: A Global History* (Cambridge, MA, Harvard University Press, 2007) 65.

[95] Badinter Commission (n 85) 1498 (Opinion No 2).

[96] For discussion of the *Monetary Gold* rule, see T Sparks, 'Reassessing State Consent to Jurisdiction: The Indispensable Third Party Principle before the ICJ' (2022) 91 *Nordic Journal of International Law* 216.

[97] *East Timor* (n 1) paras 28–29.

handed down by any court. Its great importance lies in the Court's determination that the

> assertion that the right of peoples to self-determination, as it evolved from the Charter and from United Nations practice, has an *erga omnes* character, is irreproachable. … [I]t is one of the essential principles of contemporary international law.[98]

This is a statement of particular significance. In making it the Court confirmed that self-determination has acquired a legal status: a right cannot be of *erga omnes* character unless it first possesses the character of a legal right. It is also clear that it is a right of exceptionally high status: all members of the international community have a legal interest in its protection and fulfilment. It is not immediately clear, however, to which form or forms of the idea the Court refers.

As has been concluded above,[99] the UN Charter and practice have given rise to three forms of the right: a right to self-determination by non-self-governing peoples, a right to polity-based self-determination, and, as a corollary of the polity-based form, a right to remedial self-determination. Of these, the colonial and the polity-based forms have been concluded to be firmly established as rights of legal status, while the status of the corollary right, remedial self-determination, is less clear. A fourth form of the idea, that of secessionary self-determination, remains of doubtful legal status, notwithstanding the opinions of the Badinter Commission which – evoking the Åland Islands matter – appeared to recognise a limited role for the norm where sovereignty is imperfect.[100] Of these, the circumstances of the case do not support the conclusion that either remedial or secessionary self-determination are implicated in the Court's statement, but the choice between the political and colonial forms is less clear.

The dispute which Portugal brought before the ICJ in *East Timor* concerned Australia's recognition (as Portugal saw it) of Indonesia's illegal annexation of East Timor in 1975.[101] During the course of 1975 the civil and military authorities of Portugal, the then colonial power, were in the process of withdrawing from the territory, and in December 1975 left East Timor altogether. Overlapping slightly with the Portuguese departure, on 7 December Indonesia intervened militarily in East Timor, swiftly gaining effective control of the territory. Its occupation was

[98] *East Timor* (n 1) para 29. It is interesting to note that the Opinions of the Badinter Commission were not cited, even though the Court's judgment clearly falls within the same intellectual territory.

[99] See ch 3, s V.

[100] See above, s IV; and further ch 2, s III.C.

[101] The Court summarised the history of the dispute in paras 11–18 of the Judgment; see also C Chinkin, 'East Timor: A Failure of Decolonization' (1999) 20 *Australian Yearbook of International Law* 35; R Kavanagh, 'Oil in Troubled Waters: The International Court of Justice and East Timor' (1996) 18 *Sydney Law Review* 87; DC Turack, 'Towards Freedom: Human Rights and Self-Determination in East Timor' (2000) 1 *Asia-Pacific Journal on Human Rights and Law* 55; N Bhuta, 'Great Expectations – East Timor and the Vicissitudes of Externalised Justice' (2001) 12 *Finnish Yearbook of International Law* 165.

widely condemned (including as an infringement on the rights of the Timorese population to self-determination) by states, the Security Council[102] and the General Assembly.[103] During this period East Timor continued to be listed as a non-self-governing territory under Chapter XI of the Charter.[104]

On 15 December 1978 Australia announced that, although it objected to the means by which Indonesia had acquired control over the territory, it would begin negotiations with Indonesia over the delimitation of the continental shelf in the 'Timor Gap' between East Timor and Australia. The negotiations yielded a treaty creating a Zone of Cooperation for the joint exploration and exploitation of the subsurface resources of the area, which was concluded in December 1989. Portugal brought an application before the ICJ, arguing that by concluding the treaty, Australia had infringed the rights of the Timorese population to self-determination, including their sovereignty over natural resources.[105]

The Court found that it had no jurisdiction to hear the case, because to do so would involve determining the rights of a state not party to the proceedings (Indonesia).[106] Portugal, however, had submitted that because the rights breached by Australia – the rights of the Timorese population to self-determination – were of an *erga omnes* character, Portugal was entitled to 'require [Australia], individually, to respect them regardless of whether or not another State had conducted itself in a similarly unlawful manner'.[107] This argument was ultimately unsuccessful, but it was in the course of rejecting this ground for jurisdiction that the Court held that self-determination has an *erga omnes* character, and that 'it is one of the essential principles of contemporary international law'.[108] This context implies, but does not clearly demonstrate, which form(s) of the idea it was to which the Court referred.[109]

[102] UN Security Council Resolution 384 (1975), 22 December 1975; UN Security Council Resolution 389 (1976), 22 April 1976.

[103] UN General Assembly Resolution 3485 (XXX), 12 December 1975; UN General Assembly Resolution 31/53, 1 December 1976; UN General Assembly Resolution 32/34, 28 November 1977; UN General Assembly Resolution 33/39, 13 December 1978; UN General Assembly Resolution 34/40, 21 November 1979; UN General Assembly Resolution 35/27, 11 November 1980; UN General Assembly Resolution 36/50, 24 November 1981; UN General Assembly Resolution 37/30, 23 November 1982.

[104] The situation was complicated further because Indonesia claimed to be acting in furtherance of the self-determination of the East Timorese population, and in direct accordance with their wishes. As Clark notes, this claim does not stand up to scrutiny: RS Clark, 'The "Decolonization" of East Timor and the United Nations Norms on Self-Determination and Aggression' (1980–1981) 7 *Yale Journal of World Public Order* 2, 11–19.

[105] *East Timor* (n 1) para 19.

[106] ibid para 28. For discussion of the Court's previous case-law on indispensable third-parties and its decision in this case, see Kavanagh, 'ICJ and East Timor' (n 101) 90–92.

[107] *East Timor* (n 1) para 29.

[108] ibid para 29.

[109] For an excellent summary which highlights the complexities of determining which form of self-determination was at issue in the case, see MC Maffei, 'The Case of East Timor before the International Court of Justice – Some Tentative Comments' (1993) 4 *European Journal of International Law* 223, 228–30.

In the first place, it is clear that despite the withdrawal of the colonial power (Portugal) East Timor was still considered during this time to be a non-self-governing territory for the purposes of the decolonisation provisions of the UN Charter.[110] An interpretation of the judgment as referring primarily to colonial self-determination is suggested, too, by the Court's references to its previous statements in *Namibia* and *Western Sahara*, both of which dealt with the colonial form of the norm.[111] However, the context appears to be more appropriate to polity-based self-determination: in particular, the context seems appropriate to the role of polity-based self-determination as a guarantor against intervention in the internal affairs of states and polities which is expressed in Article 2(4) of the Charter and in the Declaration on Friendly Relations, as well as the rights of states and polities to dispose freely of their natural resources as expressed in the Friendly Relations Declaration and common Article 1 of the international human rights covenants. In fact, elements of both the political and the colonial forms of the right can be seen throughout the history of the situation, and elements of both norms were referenced by many of the states participating in the debates before the General Assembly.[112] This practice cannot be collapsed to a reference to a single form, and the statement by the Court of the high status to be attributed to self-determination could therefore be understood as a reference to either the colonial or political forms.

The plot thickens through reading the separate and dissenting opinions: it may be that (part of) the reason for the disagreements within the Court was the different interpretation of the source and extent of self-determination adopted by different members of the bench. The opinions of Judges Oda and Weeramantry can be contrasted to demonstrate the difference in interpretation. Neither Judge was analysing self-determination in accordance with the four-part typology employed here, and there is thus no sharp separation between the forms (and their associated sources) to be found in the pages of the opinions. Nevertheless, it seems clear that for Judge Oda (who voted with the majority) the centre of gravity of the self-determination norm at issue lay in the colonial form,[113] while Judge Weeramantry (who dissented) gave primacy to sources which pertain to the polity-based form.[114]

[110] Musgrave, *National Minorities* (n 3) 88–90; R Burchill, 'The ICJ Decision in the Case Concerning East Timor: The Illegal Use of Force Validated?' (1997) 2 *Journal of Armed Conflict Law* 1, 5ff.

[111] See also Chinkin, Simpson and Rodríguez-Santiago, all of whom characterise the question as one of colonial self-determination: Chinkin, 'East Timor' (n 101) 53; G Simpson, 'Judging the East Timor Dispute: Self-Determination at the International Court of Justice' (1993–94) 17 *Hastings International and Comparative Law Review* 323, 335; Rodríguez-Santiago, 'Evolution of Self-Determination' (n 10) 227; and *contra* Charney, who comments that a non-intervention lens seems more apposite: JI Charney, 'Self-Determination: Chechnya, Kosovo, and East Timor' (2001) 34 *Vanderbilt Journal of Transnational Law* 455, 465.

[112] See extensive citations to this practice in the Counter Memorial of the Government of Australia, 1 June 1992, paras 100–40.

[113] *East Timor (Portugal v Australia)*, Separate Opinion of Judge Oda, (1995) ICJ Reports 107, paras 9–12, 15, 19.

[114] *East Timor (Portugal v Australia)*, Dissenting Opinion of Judge Weeramantry, (1995) ICJ Reports 139, 193–97, esp 194–95.

Understood as a territory to which the colonial norm applies, East Timor was undergoing a process of decolonisation which was interrupted by Indonesia's invasion. Notwithstanding that Indonesia purported to hold a consultative process (although one that was neither free nor fair) to ratify its action, in order for Australia's action to be problematic that invasion would need to be understood as illegal and as having precluded a true self-determination process on the part of the East Timorese people. Although one can (and the judges did) disagree about whether the *Monetary Gold* principle should be engaged by such a chain of reasoning, it is clear that Australia's wrongful act (if such there be) would need to be understood as perpetuating an illegal state of affairs that was created by another's (Indonesia's) action.[115]

By contrast, understood as a polity within the meaning of the UN Charter, the international human rights covenants, and resolution 2526, no such finding of prior illegality was necessary. Judge Weeramantry relied upon Article 55 of the Charter – self-determination in the context of economic cooperation – and the Article 56 duty of States to cooperate with the United Nations to achieve the Article 55 aims. That self-standing duty to cooperate obviated, in Judge Weeramantry's view, the need for a finding of prior illegality on the part of Indonesia.[116]

Here, again, greater conceptual clarity concerning the nature and forms of self-determination could have added greater clarity to the judgment and facilitated a more productive debate within the Court. Leaving aside that debate, however, it seems most appropriate to read the references to self-determination in the judgment as references to the colonial form: at the least, such an interpretation is implied by the separate opinions of those Judges voting with the majority, to the extent that they can be taken as representative of their colleagues.[117] Nevertheless, and as Judge Weeramantry's opinion demonstrates, the circumstances of the case could apply equally comfortably to the polity-based form, and the sparse treatment of the concept in the pages of the majority's opinion could support either interpretation.[118] Although its ambit should – most likely – be understood as limited to the colonial form of the idea, the judgment in *East Timor* nevertheless represents a very significant advance in understanding self-determination. The right of colonial peoples to determine their future political status is confirmed

[115] Separate Opinion of Judge Oda, *East Timor* (n 113) paras 19–20, and foregoing; *East Timor (Portugal v Australia)*, Separate Opinion of Judge Ranjeva, (1995) ICJ Reports 129, 131–32; *East Timor (Portugal v Australia)*, Separate Opinion of Judge Vereshchetin, (1995) ICJ Reports 135, 135–38; *East Timor (Portugal v Australia)*, Dissenting Opinion of Judge Skubiszewski, (1995) ICJ Reports 223, paras 156–61, 163. See also the opinion of Judge Shahabuddeen, who discusses the application of *Monetary Gold* without making direct reference to self-determination: *East Timor (Portugal v Australia)*, Separate Opinion of Judge Shahabuddeen, (1995) ICJ Reports 119, *passim*.

[116] Dissenting Opinion of Judge Weeramantry, *East Timor* (n 114) 194–95, 197.

[117] Separate Opinion of Judge Oda, *East Timor* (n 113); Separate Opinion of Judge Ranjeva, *East Timor* (n 115); Separate Opinion of Judge Vereshchetin, *East Timor* (n 115) 137–138. Judge Shahabuddeen's opinion does not indicate which form of self-determination is (in his view) at issue.

[118] *East Timor* (n 1) paras 11–18, 29.

to be a principle of exceptionally high status in the international legal order. *East Timor* confirms *Western Sahara* in interpreting colonial self-determination as a legal right pertaining to non-self-governing peoples, and extends that finding to conclude that colonial self-determination is of *erga omnes* character.[119]

VI. *Katangese Peoples' Congress v Zaire*

The same year as the *East Timor* decision, 1995, also produced a decision by the African Commission on Human and People's Rights in response to a communication brought by the Katangese Peoples' Congress against Zaire.[120] Katanga was – and remains[121] – a region of (what is now known as) the Democratic Republic of Congo (DRC). Katanga is the most-south-easterly part of the DRC, and encompasses a significant part of the state's mineral wealth. Following the DRC's independence from Belgium in 1960, the (European) settler population in Katanga – supported by mining companies and with a veneer of legitimacy supplied by alliance with elite sections of the Katangese population[122] – sought the province's independence from the new republic. Although initially supported by the former African colonial powers and by apartheid South Africa, who feared the anticolonialism and social-reformist agenda of the DRC government under Patrice Lumumba, international powers withdrew their support for the secession following Lumumba's murder by the Katangese authorities in 1961.[123] With the decisive assistance of UN Peacekeeping forces (ONUC),[124] Katanga was returned to the control of the DRC in 1963.[125]

Having failed in its military attempt to break away, secessionary elements in Katanga adopted an alternative strategy. In 1992, the Katangese Peoples' Congress – a secessionist political movement – filed a suit before the African Commission of Human and Peoples' Rights, alleging a breach of Article 20 of the African Charter

[119] Rodríguez-Santiago rhetorically asks whether the Court's 'equation – *inalienable* plus *fundamental human right* plus erga omnes *character* plus *essential principle of international law* – [could] be interpreted as an intention of the Court to rank self-determination as a jus cogens norm?' Rodríguez-Santiago, 'Evolution of Self-Determination' (n 10) 228 (emphasis in original). She does not immediately answer the question, but argues that the Court's later *Wall* decision shows that the Court did indeed intend to imply an *ius cogens* status for self-determination (230). For discussion of *Wall*, see below s VIII.

[120] *Katangese Peoples' Congress v Zaire*, African Commission on Human and Peoples' Rights, Communication no 75/92 (1995).

[121] In the political reorganisation of Congo in 2015, Katanga was subdivided into four provinces: Haut-Katanga, Haut-Lomami, Lualaba and Tanganyika.

[122] G Nzongola-Ntalaja, *The Congo from Leopold to Kabila: A People's History* (New York, Zed Books, 2002) 99–101; T Lumumba-Kasongo, 'Why Katanga's Quest for Self-Determination and Secession Failed' in R Berekereab (ed), *Self-Determination and Secession in Africa: The Post-Colonial State* (Abingdon, Routledge, 2015) 178.

[123] Nzongola-Ntalaja, *Leopold to Kabila* (n 122) 101.

[124] Established under UN Security Council Resolution 143 (1960), 14 July 1960; see also UN Security Council Resolution 145 (1960), 22 July 1960.

[125] Lumumba-Kasongo, 'Katanga's Quest' (n 122) 177.

on Human and Peoples' Rights (ACHPR) which provides for the 'inalienable' right of peoples to self-determination, to free determination of their political status, and of their right to existence;[126] to the right of colonised peoples to independence;[127] and the right of peoples to the assistance of states parties to the Charter in cases of 'foreign domination, be it political, economic or cultural'.[128] The Congress alleged that as a popular liberation movement, it was entitled to the support of the states parties to the Charter, to recognition of the independence of Katanga, and to the evacuation of Zaire (DRC) from the territory.[129]

In other words, the Congress sought a declaration that the Banjul Charter offered sub-state groups a right to secessionary self-determination. Leaving aside the – rather doubtful – legitimacy of the Congress's claim to be able to speak on behalf of the Katangese people,[130] this was a claim to a right of secession based on a conviction of national separateness: a pure secessionary claim. Indeed, on the wording of the Banjul Charter, it is an understandable confusion: Article 20(1) of the Charter proclaims the 'right to existence' of '[a]ll peoples'. 'They shall have', it declares, 'the unquestionable and inalienable right to self-determination'.[131] The Commission disabused the Congress of that confusion in a 1995 judgment that was brief, but nonetheless intriguing.

The Commission began by recognising that '[a]ll peoples have a right to self-determination',[132] and although it noted the existence of controversy over the definition of 'people', it seems to have accepted that the people of Katanga met this criterion.[133] However, the Commission found that no right to secessionary self-determination attached to Katanga. Like the jurists in the Åland Islands dispute and the Badinter Commission, it prioritised the sovereignty and territorial integrity of Zaire, holding that the form of self-determination exercised by a people must be 'fully cognisant' of 'sovereignty and territorial integrity'.[134]

It is tempting to conclude that the Commission thus confined self-determination to a colonial meaning. Certainly, it is that context that seems most in accordance with the Banjul Charter and the remainder of Article 20, where the decolonial context is explicit.[135] The Commission clearly did not do so, however: such a judgment would have resulted in a simple proclamation that Katanga, as an entity not subject to colonial domination, was not entitled to self-determination. Instead, the Commission explicitly recognised Katanga's self-determination, but held that

[126] Art 20(1) African Charter on Human and Peoples' Rights (Banjul Charter) (Nairobi, 27 June 1981).
[127] Art 20(2) Banjul Charter (n 126).
[128] Art 20(3) Banjul Charter (n 126).
[129] *Kantanga v Zaire* (n 120), para 1.
[130] As Lumumba-Kasongo notes in relation to a predecessor entity, the Conakat, the pro-secession movement in Katanga, often amounted to little more than 'the voice of white settlers through African mouths': Nzongola-Ntalaja, *Leopold to Kabila* (n 122) 100.
[131] Art 20(1) Banjul Charter (n 126).
[132] *Kantanga v Zaire* (n 120), para 3.
[133] ibid paras 3–6.
[134] ibid paras 4–5.
[135] Art 20(2–3) Banjul Charter (n 126).

its self-determination must be exercised in a way 'compatible with the sovereignty and territorial integrity of Zaire'.[136] In other words, the Commission appeared to recognise a right of polity-based self-determination for Katanga.

The Commission also went further, however, and then drew an explicit connection between polity-based self-determination and remedial secession. It implied that secession may be lawful when employed as a final resort to remedy abuses. The Commission noted that self-determination may be exercised through 'selfgovernment [*sic*], local government, federalism, confederalism, unitarianism, or any other form of relations that accords with the wishes of the people',[137] and held that:

> In the absence of concrete evidence of violations of human rights to the point that the territorial integrity of Zaire should be called into question and in the absence of evidence that the people of Katanga are denied the right to participate in Government … the Commission holds the view that Katanga is obliged to exercise a variant of self-determination that is compatible with the sovereignty and territorial integrity of Zaire.[138]

In other words, self-determination must first be exercised internally, but where political self-determination is denied, secession may result as the application of the remedial form of self-determination.[139] The subject-matter of this brief statement was to be further discussed (although the *Katanga* judgment was not referenced) in the judgment of the Supreme Court of Canada in its *Reference Re: Secession of Quebec*.

VII. *Reference Re Secession of Quebec*

In the case concerning the *Reference Re Secession of Quebec* the Supreme Court of Canada considered whether Quebec could legally separate itself from Canada by its unilateral act, both under the Canadian constitution and under general international law.[140] By contrast to the prior decisions of the ICJ, therefore, the case dealt not with colonial self-determination, but with the secessionary and remedial

[136] *Kantanga v Zaire* (n 120), para 6.
[137] ibid para 4.
[138] ibid para 6.
[139] Simon draws a somewhat more minimal interpretation, that in the absence of 'a showing of denial of internal self-determination and group harms, Katanga lost its secessionist bid'. TW Simon, 'Remedial Secession: What the Law Should Have Done, from Katanga to Kosovo' (2011) 40 *Georgia Journal of International and Comparative Law* 105, 157. In the opinion of the present author, the formula 'in the absence of … then …' clearly implies the possibility of a reverse holding, and it is therefore reasonable to draw the conclusion given above: that the Commission implicitly recognised that the presence of abuses (presumably to a sufficient threshold) overcomes territorial integrity and permits remedial secession.
[140] *Reference Re Secession of Quebec* (1998) 2 SCR 217. For a summary of the background to the dispute, see P Bienvenu, 'Secession by Constitutional Means: Decision of the Supreme Court of Canada in the Quebec Secession Reference' (1999–2000) 21 *Journal of Public Law and Policy* 1.

forms. Despite being the judgment of a national court, the *Quebec* decision has proven to be at least as influential in the understanding and development of self-determination as the prior jurisprudence of the ICJ. The *Quebec* decision has proven to be a gravitational judgment; one that is regularly cited both by learned publicists and states as highly persuasive authority when dealing with questions of self-determination and secession.[141]

The Court's answer to whether secessionary self-determination could apply to the situation of Quebec was emphatic:

> It is clear that international law does not specifically grant component parts of sovereign states the legal right to secede unilaterally from their 'parent' state.[142]

Similarly, the Court stated definitively that, whatever its legal status, remedial self-determination would not apply to Quebec.[143] That conclusion was reached despite the Court claiming that it made no determination on the status of remedial self-determination.[144] It is on this basis, as a proof that Quebec could not avail itself of remedial secession *even were it to exist as a legal right*, that the Court stated that:

> [T]he international law right to self-determination only generates, at best, a right to external self-determination in situations of former colonies; where a people is oppressed, as for example under a foreign military occupation; or where a definable group is denied meaningful access to government to pursue their political, economic,

[141] J Crawford, *The Creation of States in International Law*, 2nd edn (Oxford, Clarendon Press, 2006) 119–20; Written Comment of Argentina, *Kosovo Advisory Opinion*, para 48; Written Comment of Cyprus, *Kosovo Advisory Opinion*, paras 154–155; Written Comment of the Czech Republic, *Kosovo Advisory Opinion*, 7; Written Comment of Finland, *Kosovo Advisory Opinion*, para 8; Written Comment of Norway, *Kosovo Advisory Opinion*, para 5; Written Comment of Russia, *Kosovo Advisory Opinion*, paras 84–86. For an explanation of why certain judgments and other forms of interpretation of law acquire this kind of gravitational status, see A Bianchi, 'The Game of Interpretation in International Law: The Players, the Cards, and Why the Game Is Worth the Candle' in A Bianchi, D Peat and M Windsor (eds), *Interpretation in International Law* (Oxford, Oxford University Press, 2015).

[142] *Quebec* (n 140) para 111.

[143] Summers argues that the conclusions of the Court, although they do not support the existence of a right to secede where political self-determination is denied would amount to a finding of the opposite: that there can be no right to secede (irrespective of whether there is in any other circumstances) where a state complies with the requirements of political self-determination. See J Summers, 'The Internal and External Aspects of Self-Determination Reconsidered' in French (ed), *Statehood and Self-Determination* (n 45).

[144] *Quebec* (n 140) para 135. Nevertheless, many authors hold that the Court *did* in fact implicitly acknowledge the existence of a legal rule permitting remedial secession. Bienvenu, for example, draws attention to the Court's finding that the denial of the legality of unilateral secession under international law is 'implicit in the exceptional circumstances required for secession to be permitted' (*Quebec* (n 140) para 112). Bienvenu appears to take this as a recognition of the legality of secession *in extremis*, stating that '[t]he Court has *no difficulty* in finding that … self-determination only equates with a right to external self-determination' in extreme circumstances: Bienvenu, 'Secession by Constitutional Means' (n 140) 56 (emphasis added); D Raič, *Statehood and the Law of Self-Determination* (The Hague, Kluwer Law International, 2002) 331; see also van der Vyver, who seems to feel sufficiently strongly that the Court recognised remedial secession that he considers it necessary to rebut that finding: JD van der Vyver, 'Self-Determination of the Peoples of Quebec under International Law' (2000) 10 *Transnational Law and Policy* 1, 22–26.

> social and cultural development. In all three situations, the people in question are entitled to a right to external self-determination because they have been denied their ability to exert internally their right to self-determination.[145]

In so doing the Court relied on the same principles as the earlier judgment of the African Commission of Human and Peoples' Rights in *Katanga*,[146] although it neither mentioned nor cited that judgment. It is significant to note, therefore, that two courts operating in different legal systems independently came to similar conclusions.

The parallels between the judgments are striking. The Commission gave broad statements that 'in the absence of … violations of human rights *to the point that the territorial integrity*' of the state should be compromised, and that unless 'the people of Katanga are denied the right to participate in Government',[147] self-determination could not be exercised through secession.[148] The Canadian Supreme Court stated in greater detail that it considered the threshold for remedial secession to be very high: except in cases of colonisation, the Court held that 'only' oppression akin to a people being 'under foreign military occupation', or the denial of a 'definable group' to 'access to government' would justify remedial self-determination.[149] In other words, under the framework mooted by the Canadian Supreme Court, remedial self-determination would only apply where there are exceptionally grave abuses against a definable population group within a state, and which amount to a manifest denial of that group's political self-determination.

While it is debatable whether the Canadian Supreme Court was correct to posit such a high threshold, it clearly stated its position that its discussion of the threshold requirement is hypothetical given that the issue did not arise in the case.[150] Indeed, the Court declined to make a determination on whether remedial self-determination exists *at all*.[151] Nevertheless, the Court's judgment is routinely cited by both commentators and states as a judicial finding that remedial secession applies only in exceptional circumstances, and there can be little doubt that it has contributed to a developing *opinio iuris* on behalf of states that remedial self-determination is a right of very limited application.[152]

[145] *Quebec* (n 140) para 138; see also K MacMillan, 'Secession Perspectives and the Independence of Quebec' (1999) 7 *Tulane Journal of International and Comparative Law* 333, 359–61; RM Hanna, 'Right to Self-Determination in In Re Secession of Quebec' (1999) 23 *Maryland Journal of International Law and Trade* 213, 234–36.

[146] *Katanga* (n 120).

[147] ibid para 4 (emphasis added).

[148] ibid para 6.

[149] *Quebec* (n 140) para 138.

[150] ibid para 135; see also R Rayfuse, 'Reference Re Secession of Quebec from Canada: Breaking Up Is Hard to Do' (1998) 21 *University of New South Wales Law Journal* 834, 841–43.

[151] *Quebec* (n 140) para 135; Mégret describes the judgment as a 'passing recognition' of the idea of remedial secession in an otherwise 'lukewarm' international reception of the idea: Mégret, 'Earned, Not Inherent' (n 89) 52.

[152] See, inter alia JD Ohlin, 'The Right to Exist and the Right to Resist' in Tesón (ed), *The Theory of Self-Determination* (n 10) 72–73; Macklem, 'Three Movements' (n 45) 113–14.

VIII. The *Wall* Advisory Opinion

Israel will remove Yasser Arafat, President of the Palestinian Authority 'in a manner and at a time of our choosing'. So said the Government of Israel on 9 September 2003, following a spate of suicide attacks against Israel and its citizens, and amid a campaign of extrajudicial killings by Israel targeting the leadership of Palestinian groups.[153] International consternation at this open threat against an elected official led Pakistan, South Africa, Sudan and Syria to submit a draft resolution to the Security Council which '*Demand[ed]* that Israel … desist from any act of deportation and cease any threat to the safety of the elected President of the Palestinian Authority'. The draft resolution also reiterated the Council's demand for an end to 'all acts of violence, including all acts of terrorism', and noted its support for the ongoing diplomatic efforts by the 'Quartet' to reach a negotiated end to the conflict.[154] Although supported by a majority of members of the Council, including China, France and Russia, and with the United Kingdom abstaining, the resolution was defeated by the negative vote of the United States.[155]

Although precipitated by the failure of the Security Council to respond to the threat against President Arafat – and, yet again, meaningfully to act on the Israeli/ Palestinian conflict more broadly – the US veto of 16 September 2003 was to set in train a sequence of events that branched off in quite a different direction.

On 17 September 2003, the President of the UN General Assembly received a letter from the Permanent Representative of Sudan. On behalf of the Arab Group, Sudan requested that the General Assembly resume sitting in its tenth emergency special session, called to address the increasingly troubling situation in Israel/Palestine, as well as the repeated failure of the UN Security Council to agree a resolution dealing with the security aspects.[156] In response to the request, the General Assembly held emergency special sessions on 19 September, 20–21 October and 8 December 2003, and adopted a series of resolutions. At its sitting on 19 September, the General Assembly voted on – and adopted – a resolution almost identical to that rejected by the Security Council on the negative vote of the United States.[157] It then went further, however, and at its sitting on 21 October 2003 adopted a resolution which, by 144 votes to 4 (with 12 abstentions) '*Demand[ed]* that Israel stop and reverse the construction of the wall in the Occupied Palestinian Territory', and requested that the Secretary General

[153] UN Security Council, 4824th Meeting, 15 September 2003, Provisional Verbatim Record, UN Doc No S/PV.4824, Statement of Mr Terje Roed-Larsen, Special Coordinator for the Middle East Peace Process and Personal Representative of the Secretary-General, 4.

[154] Draft Resolution of Pakistan, South Africa, Sudan and Syrian Arab Republic, 16 September 2003, UN Doc No S/2003/891.

[155] UN Security Council, 4828th Meeting, 16 September 2003, Provisional Verbatim Record, UN Doc No S/PV.4828, 2.

[156] Letter Dated 17 September 2003 from the Permanent Representative of Sudan to the United Nations addressed to the President of the General Assembly, UN Doc No A/ES-10/237.

[157] UN General Assembly Resolution ES-10/12, 19 September 2003.

report on Israel's compliance with that instruction.[158] On 24 November 2003, the Secretary General submitted his report to the General Assembly, in which he concluded that Israel 'has not stopped or reversed the ongoing construction of the Barrier', and as such had 'not complied with th[e] demand' in resolution ES-10/13.[159] The Assembly met again on 8 December 2003, when it was faced with a draft resolution with a single operative paragraph: to submit an advisory request to the Court, asking it to opine on the 'legal consequences arising from the construction of the wall being built by Israel, the occupying Power, in the Occupied Palestinian Territory'.[160]

Israel's construction of what is variously known as the 'West Bank barrier', 'security fence' or 'apartheid wall'[161] had been a major source of tension in the region since construction began in 2002. By the autumn of 2003, according to contemporaneous analysis conducted by the UN Office for the Coordination of Humanitarian Affairs, 180 km of a planned length of 687 km had been completed.[162] Although the line of the wall in certain areas follows the so-called 'green line' – the armistice line between Israeli and Palestinian territory established in 1949 – in many cases the proposed line of the wall departs from the line, deviating into the West Bank.[163] In 2003, the UN's analysis estimated that following completion approximately 14.5 per cent of the West Bank (excluding East Jerusalem) would lie between the wall and the green line, amounting to 85,000 hectares and the homes of 274,000 Palestinians.[164] Although Israel has consistently referred to the wall as a temporary security measure,[165] construction of the wall has resulted in the confiscation and demolition of Palestinian homes, farms and other infrastructure,[166] the destruction of crop trees and other agricultural land,[167] and the construction of significant physical infrastructure along the route. In places, the wall is comprised of an eight-metre-high concrete barrier,[168] while elsewhere it consists of a complex of fences, ditches, and roads measuring 50–70 (and sometime up to 100) metres deep.[169] Protestations of the temporary nature of the barrier aside, therefore, the

[158] UN General Assembly Resolution ES-10/13, 21 October 2003.

[159] Report of the Secretary-General prepared pursuant to General Assembly resolution ES-10/13, 24 November 2003, UN Doc No A/ES-10/248, paras 3, 28.

[160] UN General Assembly Resolution ES-10/14, 8 December 2003.

[161] Other names include: 'separation fence', 'separation wall' and 'separation barrier', among others. In its decision the ICJ adopted the (more neutral) terminology of 'wall' employed by the General Assembly in its request for an Advisory Opinion (see n 160). I adopt that terminology here.

[162] UN Office for the Coordination of Humanitarian Affairs, 'OPT: New Wall Projections', 9 November 2003, www.reliefweb.int/report/occupied-palestinian-territory/opt-new-wall-projections.

[163] ibid. The UN OCHA estimated that approximately 89 per cent of the route of the wall departs from the green line.

[164] ibid.

[165] Report of the Secretary General (n 159), para 29.

[166] UN Office for the Coordination of Humanitarian Affairs, 'OCHA Humanitarian Update Occupied Palestinian Territories 16 Dec 2003–19 Jan 2004', 19 January 2004, www.reliefweb.int/report/occupied-palestinian-territory/ocha-humanitarian-update-occupied-palestinian-territories-16-0.

[167] ibid.

[168] United Nations Development Programme, 'Human Development Report 2009/10, Occupied Palestinian Territory: Investing in Human Security for a Future State', January 2010, 63.

[169] Report of the Secretary General (n 159), para 9.

wall has frequently attracted concerns that its construction amounts to an annexation of Palestinian territory by Israel.

In 2004 the ICJ replied to the request of the General Assembly, giving its advisory opinion on the *Legal Consequences of the Construction of a Wall in the Occupied Palestinian Territory*.[170] In a wide-ranging examination, the Court opined that the construction of the wall contravened both international human rights law and international humanitarian law.[171] Significantly, it also held that the construction of the wall represented a breach of the Palestinian people's right to self-determination. It should be noted at the outset, however, that whether the Palestinian people's right to self-determination gave rise to a right to independence or statehood was beyond the scope of the question presented by the General Assembly and was not discussed.

Recalling its prior judgments on self-determination, the ICJ confirmed that self-determination had acquired the status of a legal right under international law. States have parallel obligations under the Declaration on Friendly Relations, to 'refrain from any forcible action which deprives peoples … of their right to self-determination',[172] and under the common Article 1 ICCPR/ICESCR, to 'promote the realization of [the right to self-determination] and to respect it'.[173] In other words, states are under a negative obligation to refrain from depriving peoples of their right to self-determination, as well as a positive obligation to promote its realisation. The Court found that the construction of the wall violated both obligations. It found, first, that the construction of the wall 'would be tantamount to *de facto* annexation',[174] implying a breach of the negative obligation not to deprive; and that its construction violates the state's positive obligation by 'imped[ing] the exercise by the Palestinian people of its right to self-determination, and is therefore a breach of Israel's obligation to respect that right'.[175] The negative obligation to refrain from depriving peoples of their right and the positive obligation to promote its realisation were also held to apply to other states. The Court confirmed

[170] *Legal Consequences of the Construction of a Wall in the Occupied Palestinian Territory*, Advisory Opinion, (2004) ICJ Reports 136.

[171] For a summary of the legal issues discussed by the Court, see A Bianchi, 'Dismantling the Wall: The ICJ's Advisory Opinion and its Likely Impact on International Law' (2004) 47 *German Yearbook of International Law* 343.

[172] Declaration on Friendly Relations, annexed to UN General Assembly Resolution 2625 (XXV), 24 October 1970, in *Wall* (n 170) para 88.

[173] *Wall* (n 170) para 88.

[174] ibid para 121; S Verhoeven, 'Advisory Opinion on the Legal Consequences of the Construction of a Wall in the Occupied Palestinian Territories' (2004) 6 *International Law Forum du droit international* 106, 108; CE Foster, 'Legal Consequence of the Construction of a Wall in the Occupied Palestinian Territory: The Advisory Opinion of the International Court of Justice, Human Security and Necessity' (2005) 2 *New Zealand Yearbook of International Law* 51, 77.

[175] *Wall* (n 170) para 122; see also 'Legal Consequences of the Construction of a Wall in the Occupied Palestinian Territory: Advisory Opinion, 9 July 2004' (2005) 54 *ICLQ* 1003. For an analysis of the separate and dissenting opinions in the case, and in particular the question of whether every impediment to self-determination amounts to a breach of the norm, see S Akram and M Lynk, 'The Wall and the Law: A Tale of Two Judgments' (2006) 24 *Netherlands Quarterly of Human Rights* 61, 77–78.

that third states are under an *erga omnes* obligation to refrain from recognising the 'illegal situation resulting from the construction of the wall', and to withhold 'aid or assistance in maintaining the situation'.[176] More surprisingly, the Court also held that all states are under the parallel positive obligation to promote the realisation of self-determination.[177]

Although the Court stated clearly that a right to self-determination exists under international law, and that the corresponding obligations apply both to Israel and to third states, the form of the right engaged is less clear. Although the Court referred to its case law on colonial self-determination, it does not appear that the Court considered that Palestine had a right to self-determination as a former mandate or as a non-self-governing territory.[178] By contrast, the Court laid emphasis on Palestine's status as an occupied territory,[179] and it seems likely, therefore, that the Court relied principally on the right of the Palestinian people to political self-determination in making its decision. The construction of the wall by Israel effected the de facto annexation of (parts of) the territory, prejudicing the ability of the Palestinian peoples, as a unit, to determine the form and manner of their political integration and future governance.[180]

What is significant is that this was the first occasion on which the Court clearly addressed a norm of self-determination outwith a colonial context.[181] It is not entirely clear whether the majority in the case appreciated that, in employing the term, it was stepping beyond the ambit of its previous precedents,[182] but certainly that point was not lost on certain of the separate opinion-writers.[183] In her separate opinion, Judge Higgins notes her broad agreement with the conclusions of the Court, but states a degree of reservation concerning its reasoning on certain points; among them its reasoning on self-determination. She notes the longstanding practice of the General Assembly on self-determination in the colonial context – as discussed above, amply confirmed by the Court – but that a more recent body of practice on 'post-colonial' self-determination has also emerged, relating to 'circumstances where peoples are subject to "alien subjugation, domination, and

[176] *Wall* (n 170) para 159.

[177] ibid 159. It was this point which led Judge Kooijmans to dissent on para 3D of the *dispositif*.

[178] ibid para 88.

[179] ibid para 78.

[180] Samuel, 'Religious Norms' (n 45) 304; C Waters, 'South Ossetia' in Walter, von Ungern-Sternberg and Abushov (eds), *Self-Determination and Secession in International Law* (n 46) 184–85.

[181] As Orakhelashvili notes, this was an 'innovative' application of self-determination 'outside the colonial context': A Orakhelashvili, 'Legal Consequence of the Construction of a Wall in the Occupied Palestinian Territory: Opinion and Reaction' (2006) 11 *Journal of Conflict and Security Law* 119, 122; see also Foster, 'Wall Advisory Opinion' (n 174) 76.

[182] Although note, as discussed above, the slight question mark in relation to *East Timor*: see above, n 114, and accompanying text.

[183] See, in particular, *Legal Consequences of the Construction of a Wall in the Occupied Palestinian Territory*, Separate Opinion of Judge Higgins, (2004) ICJ Reports 206, paras 29–30; and further *Legal Consequences of the Construction of a Wall in the Occupied Palestinian Territory*, Separate Opinion of Judge Kooijmans, (2004) ICJ Reports 219, para 33.

exploitation'", as the Friendly Relations declaration has it.[184] 'The Court has for the very first time', she says, 'without any particular legal analysis, implicitly also adopted this second perspective.'[185] Judge Kooijmans, too, seemed to acknowledge that the norms concerned were non-identical, noting that in the '*East Timor* case the Court called the rights of peoples to self-determination in a colonial situation a right *erga omnes*'.[186] These opinions seem to confirm that the *East Timor* finding was, indeed, understood as limited to a colonial context.

That distinction, however, seems to have been (somewhat) lost on the majority of the Court. The Court refers to self-determination outwith a colonial context, and refers to those documentary sources that were found in chapter three to give shape to the polity-based form of self-determination: the Charter, the human rights covenants and the Friendly Relations Declaration.[187] In the same breath, however, it also cites to its own case law relating to colonial self-determination: in *Namibia*, *Western Sahara* and *East Timor*.[188] In particular, it makes important use of its *East Timor* precedent, relying wholly on the authority of that judgment for its finding that '[t]he Court indeed made it clear that the right of peoples to self-determination is today a right *erga omens* (see *East Timor* …)'.[189] As discussed above, there is every reason to believe that the Court was correct in making that finding (namely, that the polity-based form of self-determination is a norm of *erga omnes* status), but understanding the mismatched context nevertheless imbues it with an additional significance. Whether the Court understood it as such or not, this was no mere restatement of its *East Timor* precedent, but a novel finding applying that same high status to a separate norm. What is more, it is highly likely that the non-equivalence of the norm as applied in *East Timor* and that at issue before the Court in *Wall* will have been discussed in the deliberation room: it is a prominent aspect of Judge Higgins's separate opinion, and as such will have been read (and perhaps debated) by the Court as a whole in formulating its advisory opinion.

The primary significance of the advisory opinion is often seen as the ICJ's confirmation that Israel's legal status in the Palestinian territories is that of an occupying power. Nevertheless, an equally important aspect of the opinion was its contribution to the development of self-determination. Israel was declared to be under an obligation to cease construction of the wall, to dismantle those sections already constructed[190] and to return lands seized for the purpose of constructing the wall.[191] Other states, meanwhile, are under parallel obligations to refrain

[184] Separate Opinion of Judge Higgins, *Wall* (n 183) para 29, citing the Friendly Relations Declaration (n 172).
[185] ibid para 30.
[186] Separate Opinion of Judge Kooijmans, *Wall* (n 183) para 33.
[187] *Wall* (n 170) para 88; and further ch 3, ss V.A–D.
[188] *Wall* (n 170) para 88; and further above ss II, III and V.
[189] *Wall* (n 170) para 88.
[190] ibid para 151.
[191] ibid para 153.

from recognising the situation created by the wall, to refrain from enabling its construction and to take steps to bring the impediment to the exercise of the Palestinians' political self-determination to an end.[192] Not only does the advisory opinion amount to a reaffirmation of the non-interference aspect of political self-determination, therefore, but it confirms that it exists as a right *erga omnes* in both its positive and negative aspects.[193]

IX. Conclusion

The sheer number of judgments relating to the international law on self-determination before international, domestic and regional courts is testament to its significance in the international legal order. There are few subjects that have come as frequently before international courts, and probably none that have consistently produced judgments and opinions with such far-reaching import for the international legal system. Self-determination is, in many ways, a microcosm of that system: in these judgments, we see the development of international law.

In the judgments and opinions surveyed here, self-determination as it exists in the international legal order is uncovered and analysed, but is also actively developed. As in previous chapters, it is clear that the self-determination norm that can be unearthed in the pronouncements of international courts is a creature of precedent. Each judgment builds on those that have gone before including, in some instances, in ways that are quite unhelpful: the ICJ's references in *Wall* to its previous decision in *East Timor*, for example, show no awareness that the forms of self-determination at issue in the two cases are different (in *Wall*, polity-based self-determination; in *East Timor*, colonial self-determination). Nevertheless, over the course of the judgments discussed here, various forms of self-determination – and above all the colonial and polity-based forms – were found by the courts to have high status in the international legal system: norms *erga omnes*, and possibly even norms *ius cogens*.

Yet simultaneously, in these judgments we can discern a norm that is highly uncertain of itself. Courts seem to be split between wishing bullishly to assert the high status and key role of self-determination within the international legal

[192] ibid para 159; and further I Scobbie, 'Unchart(er)ed Waters?: Consequences of the Advisory Opinion on the Legal Consequences of the Construction of a Wall in the Occupied Palestinian Territory for the Responsibility of the UN for Palestine' (2005) 16 *European Journal of International Law* 941, 945–48.

[193] Rodríguez-Santiago goes further, arguing that the 'whole approach by the Court' together with the reference to a right of *erga omnes* status suggests that the Court 'was under the understanding that it was dealing with a *jus cogens* norm.' Rodríguez-Santiago, 'Evolution of Self-Determination' (n 10) 230. By contrast the present author does not feel that the text of the Advisory Opinion, for all that it demonstrates that the Court considered the right to political self-determination to be a norm of high status, supports such a far-reaching conclusion.

system, and pulling back from it as something dangerous and uncontrollable; between wanting to say more, and wanting to say nothing at all. That trend reached its apogee in 2010 with the ICJ's advisory opinion in *Kosovo*, which highlights not only the damaging conceptual consequences of failing to distinguish adequately between different forms of self-determination, but which has also given rise to a deeply concerning set of practical consequences. The next chapter analyses the Court's opinion, together with an event explicitly based on that precedent: the Russian invasion of Crimea in 2014.

5

The *Kosovo* Advisory Opinion

In 2010, the ICJ issued its advisory opinion on the *Accordance with International Law of the Unilateral Declaration of Independence in Respect of Kosovo*.[1] The opinion has rightly been seen as highly significant, and a great deal of ink has been expended in analysing its many facets.[2] Nevertheless, the analytical framework

[1] *Accordance with International Law of the Unilateral Declaration of Independence in Respect of Kosovo*, Advisory Opinion, (2010) ICJ Reports 403.

[2] See, inter alia, N Beal, 'Defending State Sovereignty: The ICJ Advisory Opinion on Kosovo and International Law' (2012) 21 *Transnational Law & Contemporary Problems* 549; T Burri, 'The Kosovo Opinion and Secession: The Sounds of Silence and Missing Links' (2010) 11 *German Law Journal* 881; T Christakis, 'The ICJ Advisory Opinion on Kosovo: Has International Law Something to Say about Secession?' (2011) 24 *Leiden Journal of International Law* 73; E Ćirković, 'An Analysis of the ICJ Advisory Opinion on Kosovo's Unilateral Declaration of Independence' (2010) 11 *German Law Journal* 895; J Crawford, 'Kosovo and the Criteria for Statehood in International Law' in M Milanović and M Wood (eds), *The Law and Politics of the Kosovo Advisory Opinion* (Oxford, Oxford University Press, 2015); H Hannum, 'The Advisory Opinion on Kosovo: An Opportunity Lost, or a Poisoned Chalice Refused?' (2011) 24 *Leiden Journal of International Law* 155; P Hilpold, 'The International Court of Justice's Advisory Opinion on Kosovo: Perspectives of a Delicate Question' (2009) 14 *Australian Review of International and European Law* 259; R Howse and R Teitel, 'Delphic Dictum: How Has the ICJ Contributed to the Global Rule of Law by its Ruling on Kosovo?' (2010) 11 *German Law Journal* 841; M Jovanović, 'After the ICJ's Advisory Opinion on Kosovo: The Future of Self-Determination Conflicts' (2012) 3 *Annals of the Faculty of Law in Belgrade – International Edition* 292; DH Meester, 'The International Court of Justice's Kosovo Case: Assessing the Current State of International Legal Opinion on Remedial Secession' (2010) 48 *Canadian Yearbook of International Law* 215; M Milanović and M Wood (eds), *The Law and Politics of the Kosovo Advisory Opinion* (Oxford, Oxford University Press, 2015); R Muharremi, 'A Note on the ICJ Advisory Opinion on Kosovo' (2010) 11 *German Law Journal* 867; A Orakhelashvili, 'The International Court's Advisory Opinion on the UDI in Respect of Kosovo: Washing Away the "Foam on the Tide of Time"' (2011) 15 *Max Planck Yearbook of United Nations Law* 65; A Pellet, 'Kosovo – The Questions Not Asked: Self-Determination, Secession, and Recognition' in M Milanović and M Wood (eds), *The Law and Politics of the Kosovo Advisory Opinion* (Oxford, Oxford University Press, 2015); A Peters, 'Does Kosovo Lie in the Lotus-Land of Freedom?' (2011) 24 *Leiden Journal of International Law* 95; A Peters, 'Has the Advisory Opinion's Finding that Kosovo's Declaration of Independence Was Not Contrary to International Law Set an Unfortunate Precedent?' in M Milanović and M Wood (eds), *The Law and Politics of the Kosovo Advisory Opinion* (Oxford, Oxford University Press, 2015); M Sterio, 'The Case of Kosovo: Self-Determination, Secession, and Statehood under International Law' (2010) 104 *American Society of International Law Proceedings* 361; M Vashakmadze and M Lippold, '"Nothing but a Road towards Secession"? – The International Court of Justice's Advisory Opinion on Accordance with International Law of the Unilateral Declaration of Independence in Respect of Kosovo' (2010) 2 *Göttingen Journal of International Law* 619; M Weller, 'Modesty Can Be a Virtue: Judicial Economy in the ICJ Kosovo Opinion?' (2011) 24 *Leiden Journal of International Law* 127; M Weller, 'The Sounds of Silence: Making Sense of the Supposed Gaps in the Kosovo Opinion' in M Milanović and M Wood (eds), *The Law and Politics of the Kosovo Advisory Opinion* (Oxford, Oxford University Press, 2015); R Wilde, 'International Court of Justice Advisory Opinion on the Consistency of Kosovo's Declaration of Independence with Principles of Self-Determination and International Administration' (2011) 105 *American Journal of International Law* 301.

for self-determination presented here – as well as subsequent events in Ukraine – makes a reassessment of the advisory opinion a valuable exercise.

The political circumstances surrounding the General Assembly's request to the Court – and the Court's answer – inevitably marked the *Kosovo* opinion as a lightning rod for controversy, and such it proved. In the guise of the General Assembly's question on the legality of the unilateral declaration of independence, the Court was presented for the first time with an opportunity to rule directly on the legality of secession, and in particular to examine those forms of self-determination that can result in the separation of a territory from a state: remedial and secessionary self-determination. Perhaps precisely because of the controversial nature of the subject matter, however, the Court chose not to do so. Rather, there seems to have been a studious – if ultimately unsuccessful – attempt on the part of the Court to say nothing at all: despite a growing, if very tentative, consensus on the legality of remedial secession in the years that preceded the opinion, the Court made a choice to disregard these fledgling legal principles in favour of a reassertion of the *Lotus* dogma.[3] In so doing, the Court removed the question of secession from the ambit of law altogether, and relegated it to the sphere of power politics. Subsequent events in Crimea – and Ukraine more broadly – beg the question of whether the Court's choice ultimately contributes to, or rather detracts from, the authority of international law.

In order to interrogate these aspects of the opinion, the text of the *Kosovo* Advisory Opinion will first be examined (sections I and II), and it will be argued that the Court's treatment of sovereignty, self-determination and *ius cogens* – all facilitated by its (mis)interpretation of the General Assembly's question – demonstrated a desire on the part of the Court to avoid substantive engagement with questions relating to secession. Finally, section III turns to the Russian invasions of Ukraine as recent examples of conflicts in which self-determination principles – and the judgment of the Court in *Kosovo* – were explicitly invoked.

I. The Advisory Opinion

Although, as the previous chapter has discussed, a number of its judgments had examined self-determination and connected matters in greater or lesser detail, in its 2010 advisory opinion on the *Accordance with International Law of the Unilateral Declaration of Independence in Respect of Kosovo* the ICJ was, for the first time, called upon to decide a question that placed secession and self-determination at the heart of its decision.[4] The General Assembly asked: 'Is the unilateral declaration

[3] *The Case of the SS 'Lotus'*, 1927 PCIJ Series A, No 10.

[4] *Kosovo* (n 1). For a summary of the factual background to the opinion, see J Summers, 'Kosovo' in C Walter, A von Ungern-Sternberg and K Abushov (eds), *Self-Determination and Secession in International Law* (Oxford, Oxford University Press, 2014).

of independence by the Provisional Institutions of Self-Government of Kosovo in accordance with international law?'[5] According to one point of view, the advisory opinion was the most significant statement of the law of self-determination yet achieved,[6] but from other perspectives the opinion has been viewed as, variously, a culpable example of judicial law-making,[7] a narrow answer to a narrow question,[8] poor judicial reasoning,[9] 'institutional cowardice'[10] or something of a damp squib.[11] By contrast, it will be submitted here that the advisory opinion represents a strange dichotomy. In side-stepping questions of self-determination and choosing to render no opinion on significant issues, the Court failed to provide guidelines for future conduct and, crucially, created a legal regime which cannot be successfully implemented in practice. It has been suggested by, for example, Christian Tams, that these *lacunae* in the Court's opinion were a creditable recognition that its function is not to make, but to apply, law.[12] However, while it may be true to say that no law relevant to the questions existed – particularly in relation to remedial secession – the Court's avoidance of the question of *whether or not* relevant legal rules exist amounts to a failure of the judicial function, and represents a choice not to apply relevant and applicable international law even if some should be found. Indeed, that the Court failed to apply putative legal standards has retrospectively cast doubt on the validity of those standards. In doing so the Court has not only failed to resolve, but has increased the uncertainty in this already vague area of international law.

A. The Background to the Opinion

The events that led to the General Assembly's advisory request to the Court are well known. Nevertheless, before beginning to analyse the opinion it is valuable to

[5] *Kosovo* (n 1) para 1; UN General Assembly Resolution 63/3, 8 October 2008.

[6] T Beta, 'K Albanians Hail ICJ Decision as Big Victory' *B92* (22 July 2010) www.b92.net/eng/news/politics.php?yyyy=2010&mm=07&dd=22&nav_id=68621.

[7] Leonid Slutsky, first deputy Chairman of the Russian State Duma's International Affairs Committee stated that the Court's ruling 'could be likened to Pandora's box'. See N Makarova, 'UN Court Ruling Doesn't Change Moscow's Stance on Kosovo' *RT* (5 August 2010) https://on.rt.com/11n5.

[8] See eg C Tams, 'The Kosovo Opinion' *EJIL:Talk!* (6 August 2010) www.ejiltalk.org/the-kosovo-opinion/; C Borgen, 'The Kosovo Advisory Opinion, Self Determination, and Secession' *Opinio Juris* (23 July 2010) www.opiniojuris.org/2010/07/23/the-kosovo-advisory-opinion-self-determination-and-secession/.

[9] See eg J Vidmar, 'The Kosovo Opinion and General International Law: How Far-Reaching and Controversial Is the ICJ's Reasoning?' (11 October 2010) www.haguejusticeportal.net/index.php?id=12110.

[10] M Blake, 'Civil Disobedience, Dirty Hands, and Secession' in FR Tesón (ed), *The Theory of Self-Determination* (Cambridge, Cambridge University Press, 2016) 167. Blake ultimately dismisses the charge of moral cowardice, concluding that 'the modesty of this decision is worth celebrating, rather than lamenting' (168).

[11] See eg D Jacobs, 'The Kosovo Advisory Opinion: A Voyage by the ICJ into the Twilight Zone of International Law' *The Hague Justice Portal* (12 October 2010) http://www.haguejusticeportal.net/index.php?id=12131; J Cerone, 'The World Court's Non-Opinion' *Opinio Juris* (25 July 2010) www.opiniojuris.org/2010/07/25/the-world-court%E2%80%99s-non-opinion/.

[12] Tams, 'The Kosovo Opinion' (n 8).

recall certain aspects, in particular because of the decisive role which the specific factual circumstances of the unilateral declaration of independence played in the Court's opinion.

Kosovo has a deep-rooted significance in the history and mythology of Serbia. Although the Slavic peoples had settled the Balkans in the late sixth century,[13] and a Slavic-Serbian kingdom has arisen in the region around modern-day Serbia in the ninth,[14] it is the late fourteenth century which holds the imagination of Serbian nationalists. As the Ottoman Empire waxed, on 28 June 1389 on the 'Field of Blackbirds' – a battlefield located in modern-day Kosovo – Serbian forces met those of the Ottoman Sultan. The battle was fought to a standstill, with both armies destroyed and both commanders – Serbian Prince Lazar Hrebeljanović and Ottoman Sultan Murad Hüdavendigâr – killed. It is said in Serbian national mythology that Prince Lazar chose 'God over victory', and the Field of Blackbirds has been remembered as 'the cradle of the Serbian nation: a place where Serbian blood was shed for national identity, and a place where some of the oldest artefacts of the Serbian Orthodox Church were erected and remain'.[15] In the years that followed, numerous events of significance for Serbian nationalists have taken place – or have been timed to coincide – with the anniversary of the battle on the Field of Blackbirds. In 1876, Serbia declared war on the Ottoman Empire on the 28th of June; a war that, in 1878 at the Congress of Berlin, was to lead to Serbia's recognition as an independent State. In 1921, the 28th of June was the date chosen for the proclamation of the revised Constitution of the Kingdom of Serbs, Croats and Slovenes, the state that in 1929 was to be christened Yugoslavia. And perhaps most strikingly, it was on 28 June 1914 that self-proclaimed Yugoslav nationalist Gavrilo Princip fired the shot which killed Archduke Franz Ferdinand of Austro-Hungary, triggering the slide into the First World War.

The 28th of June, too, was the date chosen for the Gazimestan speech, delivered by Slobodan Milošević at the Gazimestan monument on the Field of Blackbirds in 1989. Neither the location nor the timing was accidental: Milošević returned to the Field on the 600th anniversary of the battle as part of a carefully calculated plan to inflame Serbian nationalism.[16] Yet when Milošević stood in Kosovo on the Field of Blackbirds he stood in what was, as it had been throughout the twentieth century, a region in which the majority of the population was Kosovar Albanian.[17]

[13] JVA Fine, *The Early-Medieval Balkans: A Critical Survey from the Sixth to the Late Twelfth Century* (Ann Arbor, MI, University of Michigan Press, 1991) 25–29. Fine notes that the presence of the Albanian people in the modern-day region of Kosovo likely predated the arrival of the Slavic peoples, with the Albanians tracing their ancestry to the pre-Roman Illyrian peoples (9–10, 304). He also notes, however, that there has been extensive mixing between the different peoples in the region, and that ethnic or 'bloodline' distinctions between the different national groups are largely illusory (12).

[14] ibid 141–42.

[15] HH Perritt Jr , *The Road to Independence for Kosovo: A Chronicle of the Ahtisaari Plan* (Cambridge, Cambridge University Press, 2010) 16.

[16] ibid 26.

[17] ibid 18. Perritt notes that whether there is a racial distinction between the Slavic Serbian people and the Albanian peoples is disputed, but certainly there are linguistic differences (16); and further

For the years of Tito's – Josip Broz's – rule, Yugoslavia had been held together by a mixture of authoritarianism, Tito's extraordinary charisma, and most of all by his careful statecraft.[18] Tito's careful intention was to build a multi-ethnic Yugoslavian state, in which multiple ethnic and religious identities could be accommodated alongside an overarching Yugoslavian identity.[19] After his death in 1980, however, no such subtlety remained: following a period of political instability brought about by the lack of an obvious successor, Milošević swept to power. The vehicle he chose to carry his ambition was Serbian nationalism.[20] When Milošević stood before the Gazimestan monument on the Field of Blackbirds in 1989 it was to rally the Serbian people against Kosovar Albanians. In the months leading up to and following the Gazimestan speech, Milošević replaced ethnic Albanians with Serbs in positions of authority in industry, education and public administration; and on 23 March 1989 had compelled the Kosovan Assembly effectively to abolish itself, rolling back Kosovan autonomy in favour of direct rule by Belgrade.[21] Protests in Kosovo were met with police batons and gunfire, with estimates placing the death toll as high as 140 Kosovar Albanians killed.[22] Gradually, in the face of resurgent Serbian nationalism and as joblessness and economic hardship hit Kosovar Albanian families deprived of work by Milošević's policies, waves of protests and repression coalesced into organised resistance, and further into guerrilla insurgency.[23]

Although a much earlier date could be mentioned – and many have been suggested[24] – the dissolution of Yugoslavia was set unambiguously in train when, on 25 June 1991, Slovenia and Croatia each declared its independence.[25] The long-threatened split swiftly tore the region apart along ethnic lines: Albanians,

Fine, *Early-Medieval Balkans* (n 13) 26–26. Post the arrival of Christianity with the Roman empire, most Slavic Serbian peoples have adopted Orthodox Christianity (Fine, ibid 27–28, 290ff), while the majority of Albanians are Muslim, Islam having arrived in modern-day Albania with the Ottoman invasion in the late fourteenth century (see SP Ramet, *Nihil Obstat: Religion, Politics, and Social Change in East-Central Europe and Russia* (Durham, NC, Duke University Press, 1998) 209ff). Although in other areas, as in Croatia and Bosnia, there was extensive mixing between the communities, Perritt notes that mixed marriages between Kosovar Albanians and Serbian Slavs in Kosovo were 'virtually unknown', with the two groups living 'similarly but separately in tiny villages' (Perritt, 17).

[18] SL Woodward, *Balkan Tragedy: Chaos and Dissolution after the Cold War* (Washington, DC, The Brookings Institution, 1995) 45ff; Perritt, *Road to Independence* (n 15) 18–22; V Meier, *Yugoslavia: A History of its Demise*, tr S Ramet (London, Routledge, 1999) 2–3.

[19] D McGoldrick, 'The Tale of Yugoslavia: Lessons for Accommodating National Identity in National and International Law' in S Tierney (ed), *Accommodating National Identity: New Approaches in International and Domestic Law* (The Hague, Martinus Nijhoff, 2000) 16–17; Perritt, *Road to Independence* (n 15) 18.

[20] Perritt, *Road to Independence* (n 15) 24–25; L Sell, *Slobodan Milosevic and the Destruction of Yugoslavia* (Durham, NC, Duke University Press, 2003) 39–54. As Sell notes (72): 'There is no evidence that Milosevic as a young man displayed much interest in Serb national traditions.'

[21] Sell, *Milosevic* (n 20) 87; Perritt, *Road to Independence* (n 15) 25–26.

[22] Sell, *Milosevic* (n 20) 87–88.

[23] Perritt, *Road to Independence* (n 15) 26–29.

[24] Perritt, for example, tells a story reaching back at least to the beginning of the twentieth century: ibid 15–18.

[25] Meier, *Yugoslavia* (n 18) 110–37. This history is also briefly discussed in relation to the Badinter Arbitration Commission in ch 4, s IV.

Bosniacs, Croats and Slovenes – along with numerous smaller groups – sought to remove themselves from the control of a Serbian-dominated state. A spate of independence declarations[26] rapidly reduced the Yugoslavian state's effective territorial scope from its previous position dominating a huge swath of the Balkans, to modern-day Serbia, Montenegro and Kosovo. The ethnic conflict which followed has been characterised by the ICJ as including instances of genocide and ethnic cleansing,[27] and has seen numerous international criminal convictions for genocide, ethnic cleansing and crimes against humanity.[28]

Although Kosovo was not the site of any single event that has acquired the same historical salience as Srebrenica, for example, the region was subject to many of the horrific acts of repression and violence which characterised the conflict. It also sought to declare its independence in this period: an independence referendum organised by the Albanian political opposition on 19 October 1991 produced an overwhelming vote in favour of secession, but Kosovo did not gain any effective political autonomy.[29] Perhaps it was the significance of Kosovo to the Serbian nationalist psyche that meant its secession was unthinkable, or perhaps Kosovo's smaller size and geographical proximity made it an easier proposition than retaining Bosnia, Croatia or Slovenia. Whatever the cause, Kosovo was never allowed a breath of free air. Political and cultural repression was rampant – the use of Albanian in the print and broadcast media was restricted, with Albanian-language media outlets forced to close; Albanians were prevented from teaching in schools and universities; policing was extreme, with midnight house searches, beatings and enforced disappearances[30] – and when armed resistance began, it was met with scorched earth tactics.[31] Milošević intended not only to quash the insurgency, but also to reshape the demographic profile of Kosovo: a deliberate policy of expulsions – as well as the ongoing violence – led by the autumn of 1998 to the displacement of at least 250,000 Kosovan civilians.[32]

Milošević's brutal military response to the activities of the newly formed Kosovo Liberation Army (KLA) did not, contrary to contemporaneous

[26] Croatia and Slovenia on 25 June 1991; Macedonia on 17 September 1991; Kosovo on 19 October 1991; Bosnia and Herzegovina on 22 September 1992.

[27] *Application of the Convention on the Prevention and Punishment of the Crime of Genocide (Bosnia and Herzegovina v Serbia and Montenegro)*, Merits, Judgement, (2007) ICJ Reports 43, para 471(5), and further 278–97. The Court considered allegations of genocide further in *Application of the Convention on the Prevention and Punishment of the Crime of Genocide (Croatia v Serbia)*, Merits, Judgement, (2015) ICJ Reports 3, paras 154–66.

[28] See, for example, the ICTY's judgment in *Prosecutor v Radovan Karadžić*, Judgment of 24 March 2016, ICTY Case No IT-95-5/18-T. Karadžić was found guilty on ten of eleven counts, including genocide, murder as a crime against humanity, and hostage-taking as a war crime. More than ninety individuals have been convicted and sentenced before the ICTY.

[29] Perritt, *Road to Independence* (n 15) 26.

[30] ibid 27–28.

[31] See, for example, Perritt's account of the raid by Serbian forces on the Jasari family compound in Prekaz in 1998, in which fifty-seven family members (including infant children and the elderly) were killed: ibid 36ff; and further Human Rights Watch, *Under Orders: War Crimes in Kosovo* (New York, Human Rights Watch, 2001) 47–50.

[32] Human Rights Watch, *Under Orders* (n 31) 47.

expectations, suppress the insurgency: instead, the KLA strengthened its position, and what began as a guerrilla operation slowly acquired more conventional outlines, with the KLA even at points controlling portions of the territory.[33] With the balance of force on the two sides seemingly at a stalemate, atrocities against the civilian populations on both sides were increasingly committed. Nevertheless, and despite diplomatic concern in East and West, it was not until the end of 1998 and the start of 1999 that the escalating ferocity of the conflict triggered meaningful engagement by the international community. By the autumn of 1998, a series of UN Security Council resolutions were passed under Chapter VII of the Charter,[34] culminating in resolution 1199 of 23 September 1998, which '[d]emand[ed] that all parties groups and individuals immediately cease hostilities and maintain a ceasefire in Kosovo',[35] and urged the involvement of states in the activities of the Kosovo Diplomatic Observer Mission.[36]

The UN's demand for a ceasefire was not respected, and further atrocities continued to be committed, such as the massacre committed at Abri të Epërme/Gornje Obrinje against Kosovar Albanian civilians on 26 September 1998, just a few days after resolution 1199 was passed.[37] A further ceasefire agreement – between Milošević and US envoy Richard Holbrooke, who brought with him the threat of NATO involvement – was concluded in October 1998 and held for a while, though imperfectly, allowing the deployment of the observer mission.[38] Provocations continued by militia groups on both sides, each seeking to induce the other to break the ceasefire under the eyes of the observer mission,[39] and a key turning point was reached on 15 January 1999, when the world was shocked by the massacre at Račak/Reçakut. Probably provoked by the killing of three Serbian policemen in a KLA ambush a few days previously, government forces killed – having by some accounts first tortured – more than forty Kosovar Albanians.[40] Partly in response, the Rambouillet Conference was swiftly convened, bringing together representatives of the Serbian government and the Kosovan opposition, as well as the participation of France and the United Kingdom (which co-sponsored the talks), the Austrian presidency of the European Union, Russia and the United States.

[33] It is important to note that human rights abuses and violations of the laws of war were also committed on the Kosovar Albanian side: Human Rights Watch has documented numerous instances of disappearances and, at least in some cases, evidence of extrajudicial killings of Kosovan Serb civilians: ibid 50–53.

[34] See UN Security Council Resolution 1160 (1998), 31 March 1998, preamble; UN Security Council Resolution 1199 (1998), 23 September 1998, preamble. Note that the USSR voted in favour of Resolution 1199, as did all other members of the Council except China, which abstained.

[35] UNSC Res 1199, para 1.

[36] UNSC Res 1199, paras 8–10. The observer mission was the product of an agreement between Milošević and Boris Yeltsin in June 1998.

[37] Human Rights Watch, *Under Orders* (n 31) 54–55.

[38] ibid 54–56; Perritt, *Road to Independence* (n 15) 39.

[39] Human Rights Watch, *Under Orders* (n 31) 56. There was a documented attack by armed men in December 1998 at the Panda Café in Pec, for example, in which six Serbian youths were killed. The KLA denied that it was behind the attack.

[40] OSCE, *Kosovo: As Seen, As Told* (November 1999); Human Rights Watch, *Under Orders* (n 31) 57–58.

The talks were unsuccessful, with the Milošević government refusing to sign the resulting agreement because, it said, it failed to respect Kosovo's status as an integral part of Yugoslavia.[41] Holbrooke met Milošević in Belgrade on 23 March in a final attempt to reach an agreement, but left without success. On 24 March 1999, notoriously without waiting for authorisation from the Security Council, NATO commenced a strategic bombing campaign intended to degrade the capacities of Milošević's forces in Kosovo.[42]

On 9 June 1999, battered by NATO's bombing campaign, in the face of waning Russian support, and fearful of a ground invasion, the good offices of UN envoy Martti Ahtisaari prevailed, and Milošević signed the Kumanovo Accord, an agreement with NATO for the deployment of an international force to Kosovo.[43] The agreement was swiftly followed by UN Security Council resolution 1244, which added the force of Chapter VII of the UN Charter to the Accord, decided the mandate for the international security presence in Kosovo, and authorised the UN Secretary-General to establish an international civil presence to administer the region.[44] Henry Perritt Jr. has described the deployment as the establishment of 'the United Nations' first colony',[45] and while the appellation is perhaps hyperbolic, it contains an important truth: with the deployment, the international forces together had the effect of excluding all practical markers of sovereignty on the part of Yugoslavia. Policing and security, justice and the courts system, coordination of humanitarian relief, the return of refugees, and establishing provisional institutions of government: all functions of public life were subsumed either by KFOR (the NATO security mission), or UNMIK (the UN's interim civil administration), later supported also by EULEX, or the European Union Rule of Law Mission in Kosovo. The sole remaining marker that Yugoslavia – and later Serbia – had of its sovereignty over Kosovo, during this period, was a name on a map.[46]

By the time the members of the Assembly of Kosovo, the prime minister and the president met, on 17 February 2008, to adopt Kosovo's declaration of independence, Kosovo had been under international authority for more than eight years. Although Serbia retained formal sovereignty it had not, during this time, exercised effective control over the territory of Kosovo for all of that time, a fact that was to prove important. The individuals present (including, significantly, the president, who was not entitled to vote in the Assembly) did not act within the framework of the Provisional Institutions of Self-Government of Kosovo, but rather constituted themselves as a form of constitutional assembly – '[c]onvened in an extraordinary

[41] Human Rights Watch, *Under Orders* (n 31) 58–59.

[42] Perritt, *Road to Independence* (n 15) 47; Human Rights Watch, *Under Orders* (n 31) 59.

[43] Military and Technical Agreement between the International Security Force ('KFOR') and the governments of the Federal Republic of Yugoslavia and the Republic of Serbia (Kumanovo, 9 June 1999). See further Perritt, *Road to Independence* (n 15) 51.

[44] UN Security Council Resolution 1244 (1999), 10 June 1999, paras 2, 5, 7–11.

[45] Perritt, *Road to Independence* (n 15) 51.

[46] ibid 51–78.

meeting', as the Declaration had it.[47] By a vote of 109 members of the 120-member Assembly, they stated that:

1. We, the democratically-elected leaders of our people, hereby declare Kosovo to be an independent and sovereign state. …
2. We declare Kosovo to be a democratic, secular and multi-ethnic republic, guided by the principles of non-discrimination and equal protection under the law. We shall protect and promote the rights of all communities in Kosovo and create the conditions necessary for their effective participation in political and decision-making processes.[48]

Serbia's reaction was immediate, and furious. Belgrade denounced the declaration as illegal and argued that it was null and void. The Declaration, Serbia argued, contravened Security Council resolution 1244 (by which the international presence in Kosovo was established), the preamble of which '[r]eaffirm[ed] the commitment of all Member States to the sovereignty and territorial integrity of [Serbia]'.[49] Serbia could not, however, take any forceful or police action to prevent the secession or to reassert its authority over Kosovo without breaching the ceasefire line and engaging the international forces in the territory, and this is did not do. Rather, Serbia pursued a diplomatic strategy and when, in October 2008, the UN General Assembly adopted resolution 63/3 – by which it submitted the advisory request to the Court – it was on a proposal by Serbia.

The General Assembly asked the Court a single, and apparently straightforward, question, but one that was weighted with complexities:

> Is the unilateral declaration of independence by the Provisional Institutions of Self-Government of Kosovo in accordance with international law?[50]

Marko Milanović points out that although 'everybody concerned claimed that the question was clear, narrow, and precisely defined', it was in fact anything but. He argues that 'practically every single word in the question required interpretation, and in fact allowed for several possible interpretations'.[51] In the course of the Court's decision, not only those complexities in the wording of the question but also the many intricacies of the (especially recent) history of Kosovo were to play a determining role. Section II embarks on an analysis of the different thematic areas of the Court's opinion as they relate to self-determination, but first the specificities of the question and history of the situation demand a caveat.

[47] Kosovo Declaration of Independence, reproduced in *Kosovo* (n 1) para 74.
[48] ibid para 75.
[49] Remarks of President Tadić, UN Security Council, 5839th Meeting, 18 February 2008, Provisional Verbatim Record, UN Doc No S/PV.5839, 4; UNSC Res 1244, preamble.
[50] UNGA Res 63/3.
[51] M Milanović, 'Arguing the Kosovo Case' in Milanović and Wood (eds), *The Law and Politics of the Kosovo Advisory Opinion* (n 2) 30 (footnotes omitted).

B. A Caveat

Before criticising the Court's decision, it is important to acknowledge that there were certain matters that the Court did not, and arguably some that it *could* not, address. It is worth noting, first, that the direct subject matter of the Advisory Opinion was not self-determination, but rather the legality of the declaration of independence.[52] Indeed, the Court clearly stated its view that an assessment of whether international law contained a right of self-determination (of whatever form) would be beyond the scope of the General Assembly's question.

> The Court is not required by the question it has been asked to take a position on whether international law conferred a positive entitlement on Kosovo unilaterally to declare its independence or, *a fortiori*, on whether international law generally confers an entitlement on entities situated within a State unilaterally to break away from it. Indeed, it is entirely possible for a particular act – such as a unilateral declaration of independence – not to be in violation of international law without necessarily constituting the exercise of a right conferred by it. The Court has been asked for an opinion on the first point, not the second.[53]

Nor, to the disappointment of some,[54] did the Court consider whether Kosovo had achieved statehood, and whether third states were obliged either to recognise Kosovo as an independent state or to refrain from doing so.[55]

The coherence of the Court's reasoning on the first point is doubtful – after all, while the absence of a prohibition may demonstrate that the declaration of independence was lawful, it is equally possible to demonstrate its legality by showing the existence of a permissive rule. Concurrently, although the absence of a prohibition can demonstrate the legality of an act,[56] the reverse cannot be maintained. Were the Court to find a prohibition on secession (in the form of territorial integrity, for example), it would nevertheless be necessary to show that no permissive rule qualified that prohibition.[57] In other words, had the Court found evidence for

[52] Although see *contra* Milanović, 'Arging the Kosovo Case' (n 51) 30.
[53] *Kosovo* (n 1) para 56.
[54] See eg Borgen, 'Kosovo Advisory Opinion' (n 8); Tams, 'The Kosovo Opinion' (n 8).
[55] *Kosovo* (n 1) para 51; and further D Müller, 'The Question Question' in Milanović and Wood (eds), *The Law and Politics of the Kosovo Advisory Opinion* (n 2) 120–22.
[56] *Lotus* (n 3); GI Hernández, *The International Court of Justice and the Judicial Function* (Oxford, Oxford University Press, 2014) 263–276, esp 264–66. Hernández discusses the significance of the *Kosovo* Opinion for the structure of international law and the continuing relevance of the *Lotus* principle. He notes that the Court's Opinion in *Kosovo* has had the effect of 'resuscitating *Lotus*', commenting that '[d]iscarding all intermediate views, the Court arguably took the view that international law was a gapless legal order, but it did so in the most straightforward manner, adhering to the binary conception of international law in the mould of the *Lotus* judgment, and not, for example, examining the possibilities of negative permissions and prohibitions and of legal neutrality' (265, footnotes omitted). See also Müller, 'The Question Question' (n 55) 130–32.
[57] See *contra* Rodríguez-Santiago, who argues that 'however absurd the Court's reasoning might seem, there was no contradiction in it': E Rodríguez-Santiago, 'The Evolution of Self-Determination of Peoples in International Law' in Tesón (ed), *The Theory of Self-Determination* (n 10) 232.

a prohibition its (supposedly value-neutral) methodological approach would no longer have been adequate to answer the question posed by the General Assembly.

The Court's interpretation of the question posed thus appears teleological – as if the answer informs the question. In his Declaration, Judge Simma is highly scathing about this restrictive reading:

> Under these circumstances, even a clearly recognized positive entitlement to declare independence, if it existed, would not have changed the Court's answer in the slightest.[58]

Peter Hilpold, too, is critical of the Court's decision to focus purely on prohibitive rules. He comments that:

> Unlike the situation prevailing a century ago, international law is now far more dense and no longer regulates state behaviour primarily by prohibitive rules. State interaction is far too complex [for] such an approach to be sufficient.[59]

In excluding international law rights from its analysis the Court did not merely give a strict answer to a narrow question; such a narrow interpretation of the question necessitated an alteration of the question, and not 'only in a linguistic sense, but in fact deeply modifying its meaning.'[60] Simma concludes that the Court's restrictive interpretation 'significantly reduces the *advisory* quality of this Opinion'.[61]

While the Court's decision that the question did not require an examination of the consequences of the declaration is also (in my view) regrettable, its decision here is more reasonable.[62] Whereas it is arguable that a full consideration of the legal issues necessitated an examination of whether the declaration had any effect (as will be argued below, the Court's failure to decide whether the declaration of independence was effective is one of the most damaging legacies of the opinion), the Court was at least arguably correct in its holding that the question

[58] *Accordance with International Law of the Unilateral Declaration of Independence in Respect of Kosovo*, Declaration of Judge Simma, (2010) ICJ Reports 478, para 8.

[59] Hilpold, 'Delicate Question' (n 2) 287; see also Orakhelashvili, 'Kosovo Advisory Opinion' (n 2) 73.

[60] Hilpold, 'Delicate Question' (n 2) 288–89; see also A Nollkaemper, 'The Court and its Multiple Constituencies: Three Perspectives on the Kosovo Advisory Opinion' in Milanović and Wood (eds), *The Law and Politics of the Kosovo Advisory Opinion* (n 2) 224; but see, *contra*, Pellet, who argues that the 'Court strictly kept to the question asked – and rightly so': Pellet, 'The Questions Not Asked' (n 2) 269.

[61] Declaration of Judge Simma, *Kosovo* (n 58) para 10 (original emphasis).

[62] Although see, *contra*, Müller, who declares that 'the limited and narrow way the Court understood the scope of the question certainly constituted a proper way to navigate around the very delicate and controversial issues' that a wider interpretation would have raised: Müller, 'The Question Question' (n 55) 123. For a different perspective, see Nollkaemper, who offers a perceptive political evaluation of why the Court may have chosen to interpret the question in this way. He examines the different constituencies that the Court responds to in any given case, and argues that 'a wider discussion of the question of whether the declaration was in accordance with international law would have required the Court to pronounce on highly controversial questions of secession and self-determination. By doing so, it would inevitably have divided its constituencies in a manner that would likewise have endangered its stature. The result of its decision to duck these two questions was that the Court in the short term only served the interests of Kosovo and its supporters; however, this is better understood as a side effect of its decision to serve its longer-term interests than as a strategic decision to serve this particular constituency over all others.' Nollkaemper, 'Multiple Constituencies' (n 60) 221ff.

'd[id] not ask whether or not Kosovo ha[d] achieved statehood',[63] but instead focused solely on the legality of the *act* of declaring independence. Although the Court's decision to exclude these considerations is, therefore, disappointing, their inclusion would have necessitated a (further) strained reinterpretation of the General Assembly's question. It would, therefore, not be appropriate overly to criticise the Court for this omission.

II. The Court's Decision

Although the Court's conclusions were narrow, they were not insignificant. As previously stated, the Court chose to construe the question as one phrased entirely in the negative. In other words, on the premise that any action not prohibited is permitted,[64] the Court considered that a sufficient answer could be given by asking a more limited question: does international law prohibit declarations of independence?

The Court's answer was that international law contains no 'prohibition on declarations of independence'.[65] Although it held that a declaration could be rendered unlawful by a connection to certain illegal acts (such as an illegal use of force),[66] it decided that no norm of general application prohibits declarations of independence. By contrast, many states had argued that 'a prohibition of unilateral declarations of independence is implicit in the principle of territorial integrity',[67] arguing that territorial integrity is inviolable, and that the state's right to territorial integrity forbids secession. The Russian Federation, for example, argued that:

> The Declaration of independence sought to establish a new State though separation of a part of the territory of the Republic of Serbia. It was therefore, *prima facie*, contrary to the requirement of preserving the territorial integrity of Serbia.
>
> Territorial integrity is an unalienable attribute of a State's sovereignty.[68]

Azerbaijan, likewise, stated:

> International law is unambiguous in not providing for a right of secession from independent States. Otherwise, such a fundamental norm as the territorial integrity of States would be of little value were a right to secession under international law be recognised as applying to independent States.[69]

[63] *Kosovo* (n 1) para 51.

[64] See the Declaration of Judge Simma, who described the Court's line of reasoning as 'obsolete': Declaration of Judge Simma, *Kosovo* (n 58) para 3; and further Hernández, *Judicial Function* (n 56) 264–66.

[65] *Kosovo* (n 1) para 84.

[66] ibid para 81.

[67] ibid para 80.

[68] Written Statement of Russia, *Kosovo Advisory Opinion*, paras 76–77 (footnotes omitted).

[69] Written Statement of Azerbaijan, *Kosovo Advisory Opinion*, para 24.

Similar arguments were advanced by Argentina,[70] China,[71] Iran,[72] Romania[73] and Spain.[74]

Despite this strongly expressed argument, the Court referred to obligations on states to respect the territorial integrity of other states in the UN Charter and the Declaration on Friendly Relations, and a statement to the same effect in the Helsinki Final Act, and concluded that states alone are bound by the international law prohibition on any action which violates territorial integrity, holding that 'the scope of the principle of territorial integrity is confined to the sphere of relations between States'.[75] In other words: territorial integrity, according to the Court, operates as an *obligation* of states vis-a-vis each other, but does not exist as a *right* of states in the abstract or which could be opposed to other actors.

This finding has attracted significant criticism, including by Judge Koroma in his Dissenting Opinion,[76] and, indeed, the Court's reasoning on this point is

[70] 'The aim of the principle of territorial integrity is to protect a quintessential element of the State – its territory – whereby any modification of a State's territorial sovereignty must take place in accordance with international law, mainly through the consent of the interested State. As a corollary of the sovereign equality of State, the principle of the respect of territorial integrity is a fundamental principle of international law. The 1970 Declaration on Principles of International Law Concerning Friendly Relations lists as one of the elements of the equal sovereignty of States the principle that "[t]he territorial integrity and political independence of the State are inviolable".' Written Statement of Argentina, *Kosovo Advisory Opinion*, para 70 (footnotes omitted).

[71] 'In the exercise of the right to self-determination, the territorial integrity of a sovereign State should be respected rather than undermined. A series of important international and regional documents, while affirming the right of self-determination, all provide for respect for State sovereignty and territorial integrity. The above principle is also reflected in State practices.' Written Statement of China, *Kosovo Advisory Opinion*, 5.

[72] 'The Islamic Republic of Iran believes that the principle of territorial integrity prevails both between and within states. It might falsely be argued that the principle of territorial integrity applies solely *between states* in their relations, ie only *states* are obliged to respect territorial integrity of the other states and not to encroach on the territory of their neighbors and other states.' Written Statement of Iran, *Kosovo Advisory Opinion*, para 3.1 (emphasis in original).

[73] 'The principles of territorial integrity and of the inviolability of frontiers have an absolute character. This means that no changes to a State's territory or to its frontiers can occur except in those cases when the State concerned consents to that end.

'Therefore, the territorial integrity of States can not be affected as a result of a unilateral right of secession, which is not recognized as such by international law … but only as a result of a mutual agreement between or among the parties involved.' Written Statement of Romania, *Kosovo Advisory Opinion*, paras 97–98.

[74] 'Taking into account the nature of the UDI and its intended effects, it seems obvious that the legal standards of reference should be found in the rules that regulate the sovereignty and territorial integrity of the State, especially in the form of the *principle of the sovereignty equality of States*, solemnly proclaimed in the Charter of the United Nations, in Resolution 2625 (XXV) of the General Assembly and reaffirmed in a large number of international instruments with a general scope, especially the Helsinki Final Act. Undoubtedly, this is a basic principle of contemporary international law, which constitutes one of the basic tenets of the existing politico-legal system and which contributes decisively to guaranteeing peace and security in international relations.' Written Statement of Spain, *Kosovo Advisory Opinion*, para 13 (emphasis in original).

[75] *Kosovo* (n 1) para 80.

[76] *Accordance with International Law of the Unilateral Declaration of Independence in Respect of Kosovo*, Dissenting Opinion of Judge Koroma, (2010) ICJ Reports 467, paras 21–23: 'The truth is that international law upholds the territorial integrity of a State. One of the fundamental principles of contemporary international law is that of respect for the sovereignty and territorial integrity of States. This principle entails an obligation to respect the definition, delineation and territorial integrity of an

flawed and cursory.[77] It is startling, first, that the Court considered it sufficient to refer to three documents (one of which – the Helsinki Final Act – is at best soft law) in reaching the central conclusion of the opinion. As a matter of logic, the fact that the UN Charter (a treaty between states), does not seek to impose an obligation on non-state actors is not determinative of the non-existence of such an obligation. Indeed, Jovanović cites a number of examples of other international documents that appear to recognise an obligation to respect territorial integrity opposable to non-state actors,[78] and the opinion that territorial integrity is to be characterised as a right of states appears to be entirely orthodox.[79]

In other words, the Court either identified or caused a not insignificant shift in the meaning of territorial integrity. While there are, in my opinion, good reasons to approve of the shift the Court here presaged,[80] that the Court's conclusion may have been desirable from a policy point of view does not absolve it of the need to provide adequate reasoning for its finding.[81] It is submitted here that the Court's incomplete and unsatisfying treatment of territorial integrity is the result of its overall approach to the judgment. Following its insistence that the question posed by the General Assembly required only a negative treatment, the Court could only, with any consistency, treat territorial integrity as a negative concept. This it did uncritically rather than, as would have been more appropriate, giving a reasoned appraisal of the change in the meaning of the concept. Whatever its reason, instead of considering whether territorial integrity exists as a positive *right of states*, the Court construed it as a negative *obligation* on the part of other states. Given that it found no evidence of a similar, express obligation applying to non-state actors,[82] it declared that no such norm operated to prevent the impairment of a state's territorial integrity. By contrast, a more rigorous analysis of the idea would not only

existing State' (para 21). See also Beal, 'Defending State Sovereignty' (n 2); Jovanović, 'After Kosovo' (n 2).

[77] Weller lists this as an example of one of the 'major determinations by the Court which are stated, but not supported by a deeper analysis of their legal basis'. Weller, 'Sounds of Silence' (n 2) 188.

[78] Jovanović, 'After Kosovo' (n 2) 300–02.

[79] See, inter alia, MG Kohen, 'Introduction' in MG Kohen (ed), *Secession: International Law Perspectives* (Cambridge, Cambridge University Press, 2006) 6; Rodríguez-Santiago, 'Evolution of Self-Determination' (n 57) 234–35; see also support for this position in A Pellet, 'The Opinions of the Badinter Arbitration Committee: A Second Breath for the Self-Determination of Peoples' (1992) 3 *European Journal of International Law* 178, 180; but note the different view expressed in Pellet, 'The Questions Not Asked' (n 2) 274–75, where he argues that the Court was correct to hold that territorial integrity applies only between States.

[80] Elements of this argument are made in: T Sparks, 'Statehood in an Era of Sinking Islands' in T Jafry (ed), *Routledge Handbook of Climate Justice* (Abingdon, Routledge, 2019); and further T Sparks, 'Towards a Human-Centred International Law: Self-Determination and the Structure of the International Legal System' (thesis, Durham University, 2017) http://etheses.dur.ac.uk/12408/.

[81] And further: the right shift if made with inadequate justification can be damaging to, rather than expressive of, the emancipatory potential of law. As discussed below, the result of the Court's paucity of reasoning here was not to correct the law, but rather to remove the question from the ambit of law entirely. See below, s III.

[82] ALthough note, again, that Jovanović argues that sufficient evidence for the contrary finding was available, had the Court sought it a little harder: Jovanović, 'After Kosovo' (n 2) 300–02.

have resulted in a richer and more intellectually honest opinion, but would have retained an important principle: that international law is capable of regulating such conflicts. By contrast, as will be argued, the Court has effectively removed the question of secession from the ambit of law entirely, retaining only some limited regulation of the conduct of the parties in the course of secession conflicts.

A. The Court's Treatment of *Ius Cogens*

In the course of the proceedings, the Court heard the argument that previous resolutions of the Security Council, for example on Southern Rhodesia,[83] demonstrated that a general prohibition on declarations of independence exists.[84] In reviewing those resolutions, however, the Court concluded that the Security Council's decision to condemn any individual declaration was due to that declaration's connection to another, substantively illegal, act or situation.[85] The Court concluded, in a statement of general significance, that:

> [T]he illegality attached to the declarations of independence thus stemmed not from the unilateral character of these declarations as such, but from the fact that they were, or would have been, connected with the unlawful use of force or other egregious violations of norms of general international law, in particular those of a peremptory character (*jus cogens*).[86]

It may be inferred from the Court's reasoning that a declaration of independence connected with an 'egregious' violation of a general international law norm would be illegal. What, though, is an 'egregious' violation of a general international law norm? And in particular: what relation does the term 'egregious violations' have to the norms *ius cogens* which the Court mentions in its next breath? The Court gives only a single example (the use of force), and its further guidance on this pivotal question is ambiguous. Indeed, a literal interpretation of the English and French texts suggest different results.[87]

It is the English text of the opinion that is authoritative, according to the *despotif*.[88] In its English version, the Court indicates that a declaration of independence would be rendered illegal if it is 'connected with' an 'egregious violation[]' of a 'general international law' norm, 'in particular those of a peremptory character'. Leaving aside the question of what it means that a declaration is 'connected with' a violation – a major uncertainty with which the text does not assist – it is necessary to clarify which norms would engage the reasoning here. To begin with, it is strongly implied in the text that 'norms of general international law' is a category

[83] UN Security Council Resolution 216 (1965), 12 November 1965.
[84] *Kosovo* (n 1) para 81.
[85] ibid para 81.
[86] ibid para 81.
[87] I am obliged to Gleider Hernández for bringing this disparity to my attention, and for his assistance in interpreting the French text. Any errors are mine alone.
[88] *Kosovo* (n 1) para 122.

that is broader than *ius cogens* norms. Peremptory norm breaches may be *particularly* apt to engage the rule, but any breach of a general international law norm which is 'egregious' would suffice. It may be, indeed, that there is no restriction on the category of norms here: that *any* norm, if its breach is sufficiently 'egregious', could render a connected declaration illegal.

The counterpart to that conclusion is, if anything, even more puzzling. The English text suggests a deliberate focus not on the *status* of the norm, but on the degree and severity of the violation. No different rule appears to be applied to *ius cogens* violations than to any other norm of general international law: it is only 'egregious' violations that count. In other words, the formulation suggests that a minor, transitory or incidental breach of international law – even of a *ius cogens* norm – will have no effect on the legality of a declaration of independence. But that, surely, cannot have been the message the Court intended: we could, from a moral or a political view, acknowledge that the consequences of some *ius cogens* violations are more serious than others (or better: *even* more serious). But the same ability to qualify such violations does not make sense from a legal point of view: all violations of *ius cogens* norms are, by definition, serious; all equally impermissible. To suggest that certain breaches may, on occasion, be overlooked would call the concept as a whole into question. Yet if read literally the English text would suggest that *only* certain violations of *ius cogens* norms – those that are classified as 'egregious' – would result in the illegality of a declaration of independence.

Although it is the English text that is, officially, authoritative, we can nevertheless have regard to the French text as an aid to interpretation. Here, though questions remain, some of odd implications of the English text are not reproduced. Here, the Court employs a (visually) very similar phrase:

> La Cour relève cependant que, dans chacun de ces cas, le Conseil de sécurité s'est prononcé sur la situation telle qu'elle se présentait concrètement lorsque les déclarations d'indépendance ont été faites; l'illicéité de ces déclarations découlait donc non de leur caractère unilatéral, mais du fait que celles-ci allaient ou seraient allées de pair avec un recours illicite á la force ou avec d'autres violations graves de normes de droit international général, en particulier de nature impérative (*jus cogens*).[89]

While the English phrase 'in particular' implies a subset of a larger category, the French phrase 'en particulier' perhaps connotes 'specifically' or 'in extension'. The French text thus implies that the Court was seeking to refer solely to *ius cogens* norms, and that the resultant limitation on unilateral declarations of independence is much narrower than suggested by the English text. Based on the French text, we should perhaps understand the Court to have indicated that a declaration will be rendered illegal if connected to 'egregious violations of norms of general international law [ie of norms *ius cogens*]'. In other words, the categories of 'egregious violations of international law' and 'violations of *ius cogens* norms' are identical.

[89] ibid para 81.

How, then, should a future Court approach the question? The reader is left with a choice between an extremely broad English text, and one which seems to understand the concept of *ius cogens* in some rather surprising ways; and a French translation which, for all that it makes more intuitive sense, does not match the authentic text.[90] Nor can clarification be gleaned from the separate and dissenting opinions. The Court's observations on *ius cogens* feature only in the separate opinion of Judge Cançado Trindade, who approves the conclusions of the Court on this point, but argues that the Court should also have taken cognisance of violations of *ius cogens* norms committed against Kosovo.[91] The Court's language ('in particular'/'en particulier'), though, is preserved in Cançado Trindade's opinion (where, again, the English text is the original), meaning that the opinion cannot aid the choice between interpretations. A further, if secondary, guide to interpretation may perhaps be found in academic commentary, which appears to read the Court's statement as a reference to *ius cogens* norms alone. Alexander Orakhelashvili, for example, reports that a declaration would 'constitute a nullity if an argument were to succeed that the proclamation of the UDI by itself constitutes, or is contingent upon, a breach of a *ius cogens* rule'.[92] Dov Jacobs and Miodrag Jovanović employ similar interpretations.[93]

The clustering of academic opinion around the interpretation suggested by the French text indicates that this interpretation may be successful in any future application, but an inherent ambiguity remains given that the English text is, officially, the authoritative expression. However problematic it may be, therefore, it may be that the (authentic) English text is given priority by some future bench. The choice between these interpretations is not minor or marginal, but on the contrary is highly significant for any future secession attempt. Under the interpretation as it is implied by the English text, a declaration of independence that is sufficiently closely 'connected' to the breach of any international law norm may be rendered illegal by that connection, if the violation meets some (undefined) severity threshold. The nature of the norm is not material: presuming the severity threshold is crossed, a breach of the international postal regulations could suffice. Less fancifully, it seems likely that, according to the English text, it is only in extremely limited circumstances that a group seeking to secede would be permitted to resort to forcible means to affect their separation, without that action invalidating their

[90] We can speculate that the French formulation may, in fact, have preceded the English, here: the fact that the English text was chosen as the authentic version does not preclude the possibility that the working language of the drafting committee (or the first formulation of this point) may have been French. The information that would allow a definite conclusion to be drawn is not normally released by the Court.

[91] *Kosovo* (n 1); *Accordance with International Law of the Unilateral Declaration of Independence in Respect of Kosovo*, Separate Opinion of Judge Cançado Trindade, (2010) ICJ Reports 523, paras 213–14.

[92] Orakhelashvili, 'Kosovo Advisory Opinion' (n 2) 101 (footnotes omitted).

[93] D Jacobs, 'International Court of Justice, Accordance with International Law of the Unilateral Declaration of Independence in Respect of Kosovo, Advisory Opinion of 22 July 2010: Case Comment' (2011) 60 *ICLQ* 799; Jovanović, 'After Kosovo' (n 2) 299–300.

declaration of independence.[94] By contrast, under the formulation found in the French text, the limits on the seceding group's actions are narrower, and more precise: international law will have nothing to say about the legality or otherwise of the act of declaring independence, up until the point that a norm *ius cogens* is breached.

Whatever the Court's intention, both interpretations can legitimately be maintained on the text(s) of the opinion. I submit that the French text should be preferred by any future Court or tribunal, given both its more natural wording and the fact that the implications of the English text would amount to a substantive revision of the *ius cogens* concept. The narrower scope of the French text is, too, more coherent when applied to non-state (or aspirant-state) actors, and is better able to guide conduct in this fraught and uncertain area of law. Having said that, however, given that a textual basis exists for the wider interpretation found in the (authoritative, after all) English text, it could be that a future decision-maker will choose to privilege that reading.

B. Remedial Self-Determination after *Kosovo*

The Court chose expressly not to consider remedial self-determination in the course of the Advisory proceedings. As discussed above, the Court held that the question of whether international law conferred a right upon the Kosovar people to separate from Serbia was beyond the scope of the question posed by the General Assembly.[95] In the course of the Opinion, however, the Court made certain remarks on the subject that were, nonetheless, significant. As has been discussed in this and in the previous chapter, the legal status of remedial self-determination remains unclear. There are, however, some indications that remedial self-determination may be in the process of emergence as a norm of customary international law.

The idea of remedial self-determination has a long historical pedigree, and has received renewed interest in the post-Charter era. As was discussed above, the 1776 American Declaration of Independence is best characterised as an appeal to remedial self-determination, and it is partly for this reason that the majority of declarations of independence of the long nineteenth century made substantially the same claim.[96] In more recent years, the General Assembly's Declaration on Friendly Relations may have made reference to the idea. Although the Declaration expressly excludes secession as an acceptable outcome to a self-determination

[94] Although here it is necessary to ask whether, and under what circumstances, the use of force by a non-state actor is regulated by international law. For an overview of this debate, see N Tsagourias, 'Non-State Actors in International Peace and Security: Non-State Actors and the Use of Force' in J d'Aspremont (ed), *Participants in the International Legal System: Multiple Perspectives on Non-state Actors in International Law* (London, Routledge, 2011).

[95] *Kosovo* (n 1) paras 82–83.

[96] See above, ch 2, ss II.A–III.

process, it implies that the prohibition on secession only operates where political self-determination is realised:

> Nothing in the foregoing paragraphs shall be construed as authorizing or encouraging any action which would dismember or impair, totally or in part, the territorial integrity or political unity of sovereign and independent States *conducting themselves in compliance with the principle of equal rights and self-determination of peoples* described above, and thus possessed of a government representing the whole people belonging to the territory without distinction as to race, creed or colour.[97]

This clause excludes from its protection colonial states that do not represent the people of the territory without distinction; it excludes entities that have not yet achieved statehood and independence; and (most significantly) it does not protect states that deny their population's right to internal self-determination, access to government, or full and equal participation in the state's political life.[98] While, as noted above, it is not clear that this amounts to a recognition of remedial self-determination,[99] it has been interpreted as doing so both by academics and a number of states,[100] and the Declaration was cited as the basis of remedial self-determination by Judges Cançado Trindade and Yusuf in their separate opinions.[101]

Remedial secession has also been discussed by two significant cases in recent years: *Katangese Peoples' Congress v Zaire*, and the *Reference Re: Secession of Quebec*.[102] Although the Court in *Quebec* explicitly refused to rule on the legal

[97] Declaration on Friendly Relations, annexed to UN General Assembly Resolution 2625 (XXV), 24 October 1970 (emphasis added). See further discussion in ch 3, s V.D.

[98] The same logic – although without reference to the Declaration – leads Pellet to conclude that there exists a right to remedial secession as the necessary corollary of the *ius cogens* (in his view) right to political self-determination. Pellet, 'The Questions Not Asked' (n 2) 272.

[99] As stated above, it may be that this statement amounts not to a recognition of a legal rule, but rather as recognition of a legal lacuna. In other words, that while the breakup of states which do properly protect the political self-determination of their populations is prohibited, no rule acts to prevent the breakup of states which do not do so. That would, on the reasoning of the Court in *Kosovo*, be something less than a permissive rule. See above ch 3, s V.D.

[100] The proposition is supported by the written submissions of a number of states to the Court in the course of the proceedings, as well as academic commentators. See, for example, Written Statement of Estonia, *Kosovo Advisory Opinion*, para 2.1; Written Statement of Finland, *Kosovo Advisory Opinion*, para 8; Written Statement of Germany, *Kosovo Advisory Opinion*, paras 32–37; Written Statement of the Netherlands, *Kosovo Advisory Opinion*, paras 3.6–3.7; Written Statement of Poland, *Kosovo Advisory Opinion*, paras 6.8–6.9; Written Comment of Switzerland, *Kosovo Advisory Opinion*, para 60; A Cassese, *Self-Determination of Peoples: A Legal Reappraisal* (Cambridge, Cambridge University Press, 1995) 108–19; J Duursma, *Fragmentation and the International Relations of Micro-States: Self-Determination and Statehood* (Cambridge, Cambridge University Press, 1996) 25; M Sterio, *The Right to Self-Determination under International Law: 'Selfistans,' Secession, and the Rule of the Great Powers* (London, Routledge, 2013) 12–13; V Epps, 'Self-Determination after Kosovo and East Timor' (1999–2000) 6 *ILSA Journal of International and Comparative Law* 445; Rodríguez-Santiago, 'Evolution of Self-Determination' (n 57) 235; C Tomuschat, 'Secession and Self-Determination' in MG Kohen (ed), *Secession: International Law Perspectives* (Cambridge, Cambridge University Press, 2006) 38–42.

[101] Separate Opinion of Judge Cançado Trindade, *Kosovo* (n 91) paras 175–81; *Accordance with International Law of the Unilateral Declaration of Independence in Respect of Kosovo*, Separate Opinion of Judge Yusuf, (2010) ICJ Reports 618, paras 11–12.

[102] For discussion, see ch 4, ss VI–VII.

status of remedial self-determination,[103] the Commission in *Katanga* does appear to have accepted the existence of the norm.[104]

Despite the affirmation of the legal status of the Friendly Relations Declaration elsewhere in its Opinion,[105] the Court referred neither to the Declaration nor to the Courts in *Quebec* or *Katanga* in its consideration of remedial secession, however, merely observing that

> Whether … the international law of self-determination confers upon part of the population of an existing State a right to separate from that State is, however, a subject on which radically differing views were expressed by those taking part in the proceedings and expressing a position on the question. Similar differences existed regarding whether international law provides for a right of 'remedial secession' and, if so, in what circumstances.[106]

Although the Court's remarks were purely incidental (the Court declared that 'it is not necessary to resolve these questions'[107]), they nevertheless cast doubt on the existence of a customary law right of remedial secession. It is probable that this finding does not – formally, at least – alter the legal situation pertaining to remedial self-determination, but it nevertheless changes the structure of the argument.[108] Although it was possible, following the Declaration, to argue that a norm of remedial secession was emerging or had emerged,[109] that position is now harder to maintain: despite its protestations that it was not considering the matter, the Court has effectively indicated that no uniform *opinio iuris* exists.[110] As with the question of territorial integrity, whether or not the Court's conclusion was correct (and, in my opinion, it was not in this instance) would not release the Court from the requirement to provide adequate reasoning for a statement that, as this does, has implications for the understanding of this area of law.

[103] See *Reference Re Secession of Quebec* (1998) 2 SCR 217, para 135.

[104] See *Katangese Peoples' Congress v Zaire*, African Commission on Human and Peoples' Rights, Communication no 75/92 (1995) para 6.

[105] See *Military and Paramilitary Activities in and Against Nicaragua (Nicaragua v United States of America)*, Merits, Judgment, (1986) ICJ Reports 14, which the Court cited as authority for the proposition that the Declaration is customary international law. In *Nicaragua* the ICJ declared the Declaration to be customary international law, holding that the Declaration was more than a mere 'reiteration or elucidation' of the Charter (para 188), but that 'the adoption by States of this text afford[ed] an indication of their *opinio juris* as to customary international law on the question' (para 191). Those holdings were reconfirmed by the Court in *Kosovo*, where it declared that the Declaration 'reflects customary international law': *Kosovo* (n 1) para 80. In the *Chagos* Advisory Opinion in 2019, Judge Cançado Trindade referred to the Court's *Kosovo* opinion as confirming the customary status of the Declaration: *Legal Consequences of the Separation of the Chagos Archipelago from Mauritius in 1965*, Separate Opinion of Judge Cançado Trindade, (2019) ICJ Reports 156, paras 27, 29.

[106] *Kosovo* (n 1) para 82.

[107] ibid 83.

[108] Summers, 'Kosovo' (n 4) 252–253.

[109] See, above nn 100–01, and accompanying text.

[110] Weller, 'Sounds of Silence' (n 2) 200–03.

C. Declarations of Independence after *Kosovo*

Proponents of an extensive international law right to secessionary self-determination may, at first sight, have regarded the *Kosovo* Advisory Opinion as a significant victory.[111] As Ralph Wilde puts it, '[a]ll substate groups in the world are now on notice that … no international law rule bars independence declarations'.[112] In truth, the Opinion is less favourable to secession than it appears, however: 'In reality … the principle of effectivity has been dominant.'[113]

While the Court held that declarations of independence are not prohibited by international law,[114] it did not ascribe to them any legal effect.[115] A declaration of independence is not therefore sufficient to realise the secession of an entity; it is also necessary for there also to be an effective displacement of statal authority.[116] In other words, in order to effect independence the declaration must reflect – or bring about – a factual situation. In submissions to the Court on behalf of the United Kingdom, James (later Judge) Crawford expressed the proposition in the following terms:

> Mr President, Members of the Court, I am a devoted but disgruntled South Australian. 'I hereby declare the independence of South Australia.' What has happened? Precisely nothing. Have I committed an internationally wrongful act in your presence? Of course not. Have I committed an ineffective act? Very likely. …
>
> The reason is simple. A declaration issued by persons within a State is a collection of words writ in water; it is the sound of one hand clapping. What matters is what is done subsequently.[117]

The Court seems to have accepted that logic entirely.

Notably, this was a logic that, tailored to its goals, was highly successful at exploiting the unique situation in which Kosovo found itself at the time of the declaration of independence, in February 2008. In the example of Kosovo, and to the extent that Kosovo now exists as a de facto independent entity, the declaration of independence *may* have succeeded in rendering future Serbian authority

[111] See eg Rodríguez-Santiago, who argues that the 'Court ended up validating not only these declarations but also the claims for unilateral separation that are always at the heart of them': Rodríguez-Santiago, 'Evolution of Self-Determination' (n 57) 233–234.

[112] Wilde, 'Kosovo's Declaration' (n 2) 304.

[113] Hilpold, 'Delicate Question' (n 2) 300; see also Orakhelashvili, 'Kosovo Advisory Opinion' (n 2) 79; Wilde, 'Kosovo's Declaration' (n 2) 306; Vashakmadze and Lippold, 'Road Towards Secession?' (n 2) 646–47.

[114] *Kosovo* (n 1) para 84. The Court's reasoning has caused Muharremi to question whether the ICJ has extended the *Lotus* principle to non-state actors, see Muharremi, 'Advisory Opinion on Kosovo' (n 2) 876.

[115] Vashakmadze and Lippold, 'Road Towards Secession?' (n 2) 646.

[116] 'Effective' is used in this section to refer to efficacy in establishing an area outside the control of the parent state, and not efficacy in establishing a *new* state, nor to 'effective control' in the sense of the term used in the Montevideo Convention.

[117] Remarks of Mr Crawford, Verbatim Record of the Public Sitting held on 10 December 2009, at 10 am, CR 2009/32, paras 5–6 (p 47).

over Kosovo illegitimate by replacing Serbia's authority-right with Kosovo's own authority-right. But that transfer was only possible because, at the time of the issuance of the declaration, Kosovo was under international administration – the United Nations' first colony, as Perritt characterised it.[118] Although it may have retained a de jure sovereignty, Serbia's de facto authority over Kosovo was, at that time, non-existent. Although the status of Kosovo remains uncertain, it is clear that the exceptional circumstances surrounding the declaration created a situation in which it had the *potential* to be effective.

Indeed, so carefully calibrated were the submissions – and the Court's findings – that it is difficult to envisage any other situation in which a unilateral secession, either as a result of a remedial or a secessionary claim to self-determination, could be effective under such a legal framework. Short of international intervention under a Security Council mandate (as in Kosovo), or perhaps where a state is undergoing collapse and is no longer able to exercise authority over its territory (as in the disintegration of Yugoslavia), the necessary lack of any effective exercise of the markers of sovereignty (de facto authority) is unlikely to be found. In all other cases, a secession movement must effectively displace the authority of the state but, as the Court has reaffirmed, it must do so without recourse to force.[119] No such limit is placed on the state, however, which is entitled to use force internally provided that it complies with the relevant provisions of international humanitarian law, human rights law and peremptory norms.[120] Mindia Vashakmadze and Matthias Lippold comment that 'the Opinion lacks practical value. Secessionist movements may interpret the Court's Advisory Opinion as favourable to their aspirations; however, the Court's Opinion does not give them a legal tool to realize those aspirations.'[121] The conclusion is correct but it is arguably necessary to go further. The Court has engineered a legal landscape in which unilateral secession is next to impossible.

What, then, is the legal status of the secessionary form of self-determination? The Court has provided no clear answer. Although it is clearly implied that no strong right of peoples to secessionary self-determination has emerged, the Court's reasoning could support either the mere absence of a prohibition, or the existence of a weak right of the kind implied by the Jurists in the Åland Islands dispute and by the Badinter Commission.[122] Nothing in the Court's judgment aids discrimination between these alternatives, and it is not even clear that the Court considered

[118] Perritt, *Road to Independence* (n 15) 51ff. For the context, see further *Kosovo* (n 1) paras 57–77; and discussion above, s I.A.

[119] *Kosovo* (n 1) para 81. In the case of a non-state actor, which cannot have recourse to self-defence, unlawful force must be interpreted as any use of force that is not authorised by the Security Council, whose practice confirms that it considers non-state actors to be subject to the prohibition on the use of force. See *Kosovo* (n 1) para 116, where that practice is cited by the Court.

[120] Consider, for example, the (unsuccessful) attempted secession of the Kurdish Autonomous Region of Iraq in 2014, discussed above, ch 1, ss I and II.A.

[121] Vashakmadze and Lippold, 'Road Towards Secession?' (n 2) 647.

[122] For discussion, see ch 2, s III.C and ch 4, s IV.

that there is a relevant distinction between them: as Judge Simma commented, the Court's espousal of the 'obsolete'[123] *Lotus* reasoning collapses the categories of '"tolerated" to "permissible" to "desirable"' and results in a situation where 'everything which is not expressly prohibited carries with it the same colour of legality'.[124] 'Under these circumstances', Simma comments, 'even a clearly recognized positive entitlement to declare independence, if it existed, would not have changed the Court's answer in the slightest.'[125] While it can be concluded, therefore, that secessionary self-determination is not prohibited by international law, the status of the concept remains unclear, and significant questions remain over whether – and, if so, in what circumstances – it can be effectively implemented outside of the context of international intervention or fatal state collapse.

D. Concluding Thoughts

For those who wished to see clarification of the legal status of the various forms of self-determination, the *Kosovo* Advisory Opinion is an opportunity missed. The Court's insistence on a negative characterisation of the question may have fulfilled its function, in that it has provided guidance to the General Assembly on the legal situation pertaining (specifically) to Kosovo, but it has done little to clarify the state of international law on secession and self-determination more broadly, and in some respects has added to the confusion surrounding this most contested of concepts. For example, despite a tentative coalescence of opinion around the idea that a right to remedial secession had crystallised in international law, and despite the Court's protestations that it was unnecessary to consider the subject, it has cast doubt on the idea. In parallel, the Court's negative methodology prevented an analysis of whether secessionary self-determination is not illegal merely because of the absence of a prohibition, or because a weak legal right exists that would have application is some cases. Whatever the reason, the finding that secessionary self-determination is not illegal had the potential to be a startling and far-reaching conclusion, but the Court's ancillary remarks on the subject have shown it to be primarily of rhetorical importance. Far from legalising secession, the Court has created a situation in which secession can legally take place only where the state's authority has already been displaced.[126] As Orakhelashvili has it, it is 'understandable that international law contains no prohibition on [Unilateral Declarations of Independence], for there can be little reason for prohibiting an act that on its own

[123] Declaration of Judge Simma, *Kosovo* (n 58) para 3.
[124] ibid para 8.
[125] ibid para 8.
[126] Mégret comments that: 'Normatively, this is arguably the worst possible result, an invitation to political adventurism that is not remotely constrained by normative ambition and ends up recognizing what is based on purely pragmatic grounds.' F Mégret, 'The Right to Self-Determination: Earned, Not Inherent' in Tesón (ed), *The Theory of Self-Determination* (n 10) 53.

can produce no legal effect'.[127] Of greater concern, however, as will be discussed in the next section, the Court's studied attempt to say as little as possible has had the inadvertent effect of reducing the ability of international law to regulate intra- and inter-state conflicts involving claims of secession. The Court has declared that territorial integrity does not apply to secession struggles, and has implied that no norm of international law is capable of resulting in a right of a people to secede. While, therefore, the people of a territory have no strong right to break away from a state, that state has no right to prevent them from so doing. Although the conduct of the parties in a secession conflict may, to a greater or lesser extent, still be regulated, no law applies to the act itself. It is understandable that the Court did not wish to engage in an analysis of a possible right to self-determination, whether remedial or not, and its standing in relation to sovereignty – to do so would ultimately have required it to determine that Kosovo either had or did not have a right to secede, and thus to make a determination relevant to its final status. The Court can be forgiven – even praised – for its reluctance to engage in such intensely political and contentious questions, but the better course in such circumstances is surely to decline the reference.[128] Instead the Court has produced a poorly (and teleologically) reasoned, equivocal Opinion that ultimately, to paraphrase Simma, has little '*advisory*' value.[129] This aspect of the Opinion will now be examined in relation to a recent example; the irredentist conflict in Crimea.

III. *Kosovo* Applied: Russian Rhetoric and the Invasions of Ukraine

Since the advisory opinion in 2010, there have been a number of occasions on which the after-effects of the *Kosovo* opinion have played out, often in very bloody ways. In September 2017, the Kurdish Autonomous Region of Iraq (KAR) sought to secede, for example. Although, at the time that the referendum was held, the KAR was not under the de facto administration of Iraq as a result of Iraq's (then) bitter conflict with the Islamic State militant group, the news of a vote in favour of secession provoked an immediate response from the Iraqi government. A brief, but fierce, conflict ensued, as Iraqi government forces and allied militia swept into the KAR to re-establish control over the region.[130] Within a month, the KAR

[127] Orakhelashvili, 'Kosovo Advisory Opinion' (n 2) 79.

[128] A course of action advocated by Vice-President Tomka and Judge Bennouna: *Accordance with International Law of the Unilateral Declaration of Independence in Respect of Kosovo*, Declaration of Vice-President Tomka, (2010) ICJ Reports 454, paras 2–9; *Accordance with International Law of the Unilateral Declaration of Independence in Respect of Kosovo*, Dissenting Opinion of Judge Bennouna, (2010) ICJ Reports 500, paras 1–26.

[129] Declaration of Judge Simma, *Kosovo* (n 58) para 10 (original emphasis).

[130] 'Iraq Kurds: Army Claims Full Control of Kirkuk Province' *BBC News* (20 October 2017) www.bbc.com/news/world-middle-east-41693143.

had been brought back under Iraqi de facto sovereignty (in addition to de iure), and the KAR's president had been forced to resign.[131] Although the opinion was not directly referenced by the major actors in Kurdistan, it is no great stretch to see *Kosovo* playing out in the KAR of 2017, the imprint of the advisory opinion stamped into the province with the tread of soldiers' boots. No great stretch, too, to see its mark on the (as it was widely seen) excessively violent response to the attempt to hold an independence referendum in the Spanish province of Cataluña, also in October 2017.[132] And there are other examples in which the afterlife of the advisory opinion can be even more clearly seen. In Russia's invasion of Crimea in 2014, for example, the advisory opinion was even expressly referenced as offering legal authority for the invasion, occupation and cession of the territory of Ukraine. The next sections make some remarks on Russia's invasions of Ukraine, with section III.A examining the 2014 invasion and annexation of Crimea, while section III.B gives some brief reaction to the February 2022 invasion of Ukraine that is, at the time of writing, still a very live conflict. The Crimea situation, one of the most contentious recent examples of the purported application of self-determination principles, not only serves the purpose of a case study, but has generated a great deal of comment and legal argumentation on the part of states. It thus provides a vivid demonstration of the divergence of self-determination law and state rhetoric in this highly politicised arena.

A. The 2014 Invasion

The facts surrounding the invasion of Crimea in 2014 remain in dispute.[133] Certain elements, however, are accepted by all sides. To begin with, it is clear that (whatever its roots) the conflict was sparked by a popular protest movement in Ukraine, which toppled the pro-Russia government of Viktor Yanukovych. In response, on 1 March 2014, pro-Russian militia took control of the Crimean Peninsula. On 16 March, the pro-Russian forces in Crimea held a referendum on the future of the province, which produced a vote in favour of union with Russia. Although Russia has claimed that the result was free and fair, doubt has been cast on the integrity of the referendum by others,[134] and minority communities in Crimea announced their intention to boycott the vote, over fears that Russia would manipulate the outcome.[135]

[131] 'Iraqi Kurdish Leader Massoud Barzani to Step Down' *BBC News* (29 October 2017) www.bbc.com/news/world-middle-east-41794083.

[132] 'Catalan Referendum: Clashes as Voters Defy Madrid' *BBC News* (1 October 2017) www.bbc.com/news/world-europe-41457238; S Jones and S Burgen, 'Catalan Referendum: Preliminary Results Show 90% in Favour of Independence' *The Guardian* (2 October 2017) www.theguardian.com/world/2017/oct/01/dozens-injured-as-riot-police-storm-catalan-ref-polling-stations.

[133] A timeline of events can be found here: 'Ukraine Crisis: Timeline' (*BBC News*, 13 November 2014) www.bbc.co.uk/news/world-middle-east-26248275.

[134] Security Council, Official Records, 69th Year, 7144th Meeting, 19 March 2014, Provisional Verbatim Record, S/PV.7144, e.g. 6–8.

[135] Y Bell, 'Russia "Will Fix" Crimea Referendum, Says Tatar Leader' *Reuters* (10 March 2014) https://retu.re/1kHOd5A.

On 18 March 2014, Crimea became a (de facto, at least) part of Russian territory when Russia ratified a treaty effecting the integration of the region.[136] The extent and influence of Russian military presence in Crimea during this period is disputed: according to Russia's account, its troops first entered Crimea following its formal incorporation of the region, but credible sources suggest that Russian troops may have been covertly operating in the province earlier, indeed perhaps from the very beginning of the conflict.[137]

i. Russia's Claim

The main ground advanced by Russia in support of its actions in Crimea and the Crimean referendum appears to have been remedial self-determination. Russia characterised the change of government in Ukraine as a 'coup d'état' instigated by foreign states, and claimed that the fall of the legitimate government led to 'anarchy', 'gross and mass violations of human rights' and other circumstances including 'persecution due to nationality, language and political convictions – all of this has made the existence of the Republic of Crimea within the Ukrainian state impossible'.[138] These circumstances, Russia claimed, resulted in an exceptional right to separate from Ukraine:

> It is clear that the achievement of the right to self-determination in the form of separation from an existing State is an extraordinary measure. However, in the case of Crimea, it obviously arose as a result of the legal vacuum created by the violent coup against the legitimate Government carried out by the nationalist radicals in Kyiv, as well as by their direct threats to impose their order throughout the territory of Ukraine.[139]

Notwithstanding that other states denied that any abuses had occurred against the Crimean population,[140] it is unlikely that the situation described would be sufficient to ground a right of the Crimean people to self-determination.

As discussed above, it is unclear whether international law now recognises a right to remedial self-determination. Although the right appears to have a textual basis in the Declaration on Friendly Relations and seemed, prior to 2010, to be gaining a significant degree of international acceptance,[141] the *Kosovo* opinion both suggested that the requisite *opinio iuris* was not present, and implied in its

[136] 'Putin Signs Crimea Annexation into Law' *Al Jazeera English* (22 March 2014) https://aje.io/tfvbz.
[137] C Marxsen, 'The Crimea Crisis: An International Law Perspective' (2014) 74 *Zeitschrift für ausländisches öffentliches Recht und Völkerrecht* 367, 367–70 and *passim*.
[138] Sergey Lavrov, Russian Foreign Minister, Address to State Duma of Russia, 20 March 2014.
[139] Mr Churkin, Permanent Representative of the Russian Federation to the UN Security Council, Security Council, Official Records, 69th Year, 7134th Meeting, 13 March 2014, Provisional Verbatim Record, S/PV.7134, 15.
[140] Security Council, Official Records, 69th Year, 7138th Meeting, Provisional Verbatim Record, S/PV.7138, 15 March 2014, 5ff.
[141] See above, s II.B.

approach that the existence of a right to remedial self-determination would, in any event, have been immaterial to a determination of the question of Kosovo's status.[142] It is doubtful, therefore, whether remedial secession would have been capable of grounding a Crimean secession.

Nevertheless, it is instructive to consider whether the situation in Crimea would qualify for the engagement of remedial secession, should such a norm have crystallised. Following the Declaration on Friendly Relations, a state conducting itself in accordance with the right of its inhabitants to political self-determination is entitled to the protection of its territorial integrity. In extension, a state that denies a portion of its population political self-determination is not entitled to such protection and it is, therefore, necessary to assess whether the situation in Ukraine infringed the rights of the people of Crimea to this form of self-determination. The Court in *Quebec* characterised this as a strenuous test. It held that nothing short of 'oppression' equivalent to foreign military occupation and denial of 'meaningful access to government' would be sufficient to show that political self-determination had been denied.[143] The African Commission on Human and Peoples' Rights held that the test would be met by 'violations of human rights' or denial 'of the right to participate in Government', although it, too, implied that there would be a threshold to be cleared, saying that it would be necessary to show that abuses occurred 'to the point that the territorial integrity of [the state] should be called into question'.[144]

It seems unlikely that the situation in Crimea met this high threshold. Although there is little doubt that the abuses described by Russia would, if true, have amounted to an imposition on the rights of the people of Crimea to self-determination, both courts cast secession as a final resort. Although it is likely that certain abuses (genocide is, perhaps, the example par excellence) are a sufficiently serious violation of the self-determination and human rights of a people to ground an instant right to remedial self-determination, it is unlikely that the abuses alleged by Russia fall within this category. These abuses probably did not ground a right to remedial self-determination partially because they had not yet actualised – fear of abuses is not sufficient; anticipatory remedial self-determination is a contradiction in terms – and because the Crimean population had not exhausted available avenues of recourse, such as the 2015 Ukrainian elections, which may have served to normalise the situation.

I would suggest, however, that in principle (and pending, in particular, issues of proof) the abuses described by Russia could have been sufficient to ground a right to remedial secession for the people of Crimea if not resolved through an internal process. The denial of political self-determination is a factual estate, and remedial secession is therefore contingent on the practical effect of its denial. The question in any given situation is not whether the state's actions are reprehensible,

[142] *Kosovo* (n 1) paras 56, 82–83.
[143] *Quebec* (n 103) para 138.
[144] *Katanga* (n 104), para 6.

but whether they have the effect of denying to a section of the population the right to politically self-determine. The abuses described by Russia certainly appear to have had the potential to produce such effects (if proven), but it is not possible to say whether they would, in practice, have done so.

ii. Crimea's Claim

By contrast, Crimea appears to have claimed for itself a right to secessionary self-determination. In its declaration of independence of 11 March 2014, the Crimean parliament stated that the *Kosovo* Advisory Opinion provides authority for their secession, as a unilateral declaration of independence does not violate any international norms.[145] While the ICJ made this finding, it did not, thereby, authorise secession.[146] On the contrary, the ICJ held that declarations of independence, in and of themselves, have no legal effect – a declaration of independence is only effective where the declaration is describing a fait accompli. It is likely that Russian military action in Crimea produced exactly such a fait accompli, but it is highly likely, too, that the Russian incursion would have rendered the declaration of independence unlawful, if it occurred prior to the de facto loss of Ukrainian control over Crimea. The ICJ held that a declaration of independence connected to an unlawful use of force would be illegal,[147] and two questions are therefore posed: (1) did Russia's intervention occur before the de facto separation of Crimea? And (2) if the intervention took place prior to that separation, was Russia's use of force justified by any other rule of international law? The latter question is, perhaps, the more straightforward: Russia claimed that it intervened in self-defence and with the consent of the (deposed) legitimate government of Ukraine, but it is clear that a number of States Members of the Security Council regarded Russia's actions as illegal,[148] as do most commentators.[149] The question of chronology is more difficult to

[145] 'Crimean Parliament Adopted a Declaration of Independence of the ARC and Sevastopol' (11 March 2014) www.rada.crimea.ua/news/11_03_2014_1; see also Peters, 'Unfortunate Precedent' (n 2) 291.

[146] *Kosovo* (n 1) para 81.

[147] ibid para 81.

[148] See eg Security Council, Official Records, 69th Year, 7124th Meeting, Provisional Verbatim Record, S/PV.7124, 1 March 2014; Security Council, Official Records, 69th Year, 7125th Meeting, Provisional Verbatim Record, S/PV.7125, 3 March 2014; Security Council, Official Records, 69th Year, 7134th Meeting, Provisional Verbatim Record, S/PV.7134, 13 March 2014; Security Council, Official Records, 69th Year, 7138th Meeting, Provisional Verbatim Record, S/PV.7138, 15 March 2014; Security Council, Official Records, 69th Year, 7144th Meeting, Provisional Verbatim Record, S/PV.7144, 19 March 2014.

[149] See Marxsen, 'Crimea Crisis' (n 137) and further; D Wisehart, 'The Crisis in Ukraine and the Prohibition of the Use of Force: A Legal Basis for Russia's Intervention?' *EJIL:Talk!* (4 March 2014) www.ejiltalk.org/the-crisis-in-ukraine-and-the-prohibition-of-the-use-of-force-a-legal-basis-for-russias-intervention/; Z Vermeer, 'Intervention with the Consent of a Deposed (but Legitimate) Government? Playing the Sierra Leone Card' *EJIL:Talk!* (6 March 2014) www.ejiltalk.org/intervention-with-the-consent-of-a-deposed-but-legitimate-government-playing-the-sierra-leone-card/; N Krisch, 'Crimea and the Limits of International Law' *EJIL:Talk!* (10 March 2014) www.ejiltalk.org/crimea-and-the-limits-of-international-law/.

address, for several reasons. It is, first, extremely difficult to pinpoint the moment at which Crimea ceased to be under the effective control of Ukraine. Secondarily, there is significant uncertainty surrounding the point at which Russian forces engaged. It is widely believed that Russian troops were covertly acting in Crimea long before Russia engaged openly, and it is conceivable that the actions of certain of the Crimean militia groups may have been attributable to Russia, if the threshold of effective control was met.[150] An adequate resolution to that question would require extensive evidence as part of a court process, but as an interim answer it certainly seems credible to believe that Russian troops were actively engaged on the territory of Ukraine prior to the declaration of independence. As such, the deceleration would be connected to an unlawful use of force.

A number of states argued, in addition, that the secession of Crimea was illegal because it was contrary to Ukrainian constitutional law. The objection runs, first, that Ukrainian constitutional law requires an all-Ukraine referendum to authorise an alteration of its territory, and secondly, that Crimea was not competent to call such a referendum.[151] Such an argument can have no consequences for the legality of Crimea's secession, however. The ICJ in *Kosovo* stated clearly that the legality of a declaration of independence under international law does not require an investigation of its legality under domestic law, a conclusion which must be correct. In answering the question posed by the General Assembly, the Court stated that there was no 'need to enquire into any system of domestic law'.[152] The issuing of a declaration of independence is an act carried out by a sub-state actor on the international plane. It is an *extra-constitutional* act, and its legality under domestic or constitutional law is, therefore, irrelevant to the question of its international legality.

Although certain of the arguments advanced by both sides in relation to the Crimean secession were clearly specious, it is nevertheless challenging to determine its legality under international law. Although there is, following *Kosovo*, no prohibition on a declaration of independence, such declarations lack legal effect. Simultaneously, the Russian use of force in Crimea may, subject to questions of chronology and extenuating circumstances, have deprived the declaration of legality. Although Russia claimed that its actions were justified in pursuance

[150] See eg 'Ukraine Crisis: Timeline' (n 133); 'Ukraine: Russia behind Airport Takeovers' *Al Jazeera* (28 February 2014) https://aje.io/dbp8n; O Iakymenko, 'Russian Ruse, Ukrainian Crisis' *Al Jazeera* (12 March 2014) https://aje.io/ym554; 'Russian Lawmaker Suggests Moscow Has Sent Troops to Crimea' *Reuters* (12 March 2014) http://reut.rs/1kN0mGv; 'Captured Russian Troops "in Ukraine by Accident"' *BBC News* (26 August 2014) www.bbc.co.uk/news/world-europe-28934213; 'Ukraine Crisis: Russian Troops Crossed Border, Nato Says' *BBC News* (12 November 2014) www.bbc.co.uk/news/world-europe-30025138.

[151] Security Council, Official Records, 69th Year, 7134th Meeting, Provisional Verbatim Record, S/PV.7134, 13 March 2014, Statement of Luxembourg (4); Statement of United States of America (6); Statement of United Kingdom (7); Statement of Australia (13).

[152] *Kosovo* (n 1) para 26. For discussion of this aspect of the Advisory Opinion, see AXM Ntovas, 'The Paradox of Kosovo's Parallel Legal Orders in the Reasoning of the Court's Advisory Opinion' in D French (ed), *Statehood and Self-Determination: Reconciling Tradition and Modernity in International Law* (Cambridge, Cambridge University Press, 2013).

of the Crimean people's right to remedial self-determination, it is far from clear that remedial self-determination exists as a norm of international law, and there remain significant questions as to whether any abuses eventuated and, if so, whether they met the threshold of the in extremis form. Three things only are clear following *Kosovo*: that the people of Crimea had no right to separate themselves from Ukraine, that Ukraine had no right to prevent them from doing so, and that the Crimean declaration of independence was, legally speaking, an irrelevance. International law, simply put, does not regulate the situation, but merely places limited restraints on the conduct of the parties. Such a conclusion has worrying implications for future international stability; fears which were revived when Russian forces again marched into Ukraine in 2022.

B. A Brief Note on the Events of 2022

At the time of writing this book, Russia is again engaged in military action against Ukraine. On 24 February 2022, Russian forces poured across Russia's border with Ukraine, as well as the border between Ukraine and (Russia's ally) Belarus. Despite predictions that Kyiv could fall within days, the Russian advance was first halted and then forced into retreat in the north of Ukraine, although the conflict has continued to intensify in the eastern regions. As I write, Russian forces appear to be on the verge of capturing Ukraine's last positions in the city of Mariupol, and reports of attacks targeted at civilians and civilian areas have acquired a horrific kind of ubiquity: so common that they have dropped off most newspaper front pages as no longer 'newsworthy'.

As a live and developing situation, there is a limited extent to which any analysis in these pages can be of value, doomed as it is to be out of date before this book appears in print. Nevertheless, it is worth noting that self-determination has not formed a major part of Russia's rhetoric in justifying its illegal invasion on this occasion.[153] That is not to say, however, that self-determination and norms adjacent to it have played no part: Among the justifications that Russia has put forward is a claim that the Donetsk and Luhansk oblasts of Ukraine – two provinces bordering Russia and with a high proportion of Russian-speakers – are now independent of Kyiv, and that it has the right to intervene in Ukraine in support of the right of (collective) self-defence under Article 51 of the UN Charter. In making this argument, notably, Russia seems to rely on its *recognition*

[153] As extensively discussed before the ICJ, Russia's primary – though not sole – justification is the argument that there is an ongoing genocide against Russian-speakers in Ukraine, and that Russia's intervention is intended to protect that population. As the Court has emphasised, no evidence has been advanced to support its claim of a genocide by the Kyiv government. See *Allegations of Genocide under the Convention on the Prevention and Punishment of the Crime of Genocide (Ukraine v Russian Federation)*, Provisional Measures, Order of 16 March 2022, ICJ General List No 182. See also the document submitted by Russia to the Court of 7 March 2022, in lieu of a formal submission; www.icj-cij.org/en/case/182/other-documents.

of Donetsk and Luhansk as independent as sufficient; it has not claimed that a self-determination process has been undertaken in either one.

However, that Russia has not (as yet) made a self-determination argument is not to say that it will not. If it succeeds in gaining – and retaining – control over Donetsk and Luhansk, it may seek a referendum to back up its Article 51 argument. It has been speculated, too, that it may seek to separate not only to Donetsk and Luhansk oblasts, but also those of Kherson and Zaporizhia, and thus to establish a land corridor along the northern shore of the Sea of Azov, connecting its Rostov oblast to Crimea. Here, too, it might seek to follow its 2014 playbook, and rely on the *Kosovo* statement that declarations of independence are not regulated by international law to provide a veneer of legality for its action – however spurious.

At present, this remains speculation. Nevertheless, and while it is not clear that the decision of the Court in *Kosovo* actively affected Russian policy (as opposed to merely shaping its rhetorical strategy), it must be regarded as distinctly possible that the lack of legal regulation in this area emboldened Russia's aggressive action in 2014 and 2022. At the least, the Court's approach made it easy for Russia to claim that these events fit the *Kosovo* precedent. As Anne Peters argues:

> [I]t is exactly the sparseness of the Opinion (and in particular the failure of the Court to pronounce itself on the underlying issue of secession instead of concentrating on the act of declaring independence) which allowed Crimea and Russia in 2014 to rely on the ICJ Opinion in order to justify the Crimean claim for self-determination and secession.[154]

While legal rules can be powerful tools for those who seek to wield them,[155] it is arguably the absence of legal rules (and the liberation of political and power-based approaches that come with that) that should be of greater concern.

IV. Conclusion

In 2010, the ICJ seemed to have been handed a question that it did not want to answer. Through a careful (mis)reading[156] of the question, the Court sought

[154] Peters, 'Unfortunate Precedent' (n 2) 299. To paraphrase Bianchi, this could be characterised as a somewhat pyrrhic victory for the Court in the 'interpretation game': A Bianchi, 'The Game of Interpretation in International Law: The Players, the Cards, and Why the Game Is Worth the Candle' in A Bianchi, D Peat and M Windsor (eds), *Interpretation in International Law* (Oxford, Oxford University Press, 2015).

[155] See, for example, Judge Koroma's warning that the Advisory Opinion 'will serve as a guide and an instruction manual for secessionist groups the world over', and Judge Skotnikov's warning that the opinion will have an 'inflammatory' effect: Dissenting Opinion of Judge Koroma, *Kosovo* (n 76) para 4; *Accordance with International Law of the Unilateral Declaration of Independence in Respect of Kosovo*, Dissenting Opinion of Judge Skotnikov, (2010) ICJ Reports 515, para 17.

[156] Declaration of Judge Simma, *Kosovo* (n 58) paras 8ff; and further Hilpold, 'Delicate Question' (n 2) 287; Orakhelashvili, 'Kosovo Advisory Opinion' (n 2) 73.

to avoid saying anything very much; a 'modesty' for which it was widely congratulated.[157] And yet the *Kosovo* opinion was far from 'modest', whatever its drafters may have believed: it was radical. Through its resurrection of *Lotus* – a doctrine previous benches had sought carefully to contain – and blithe attempt to wish away any question of the consequences of an independence declaration, the Court has had the effect of removing the question of secession from the ambit of international law almost entirely. This despite that (emerging) legal principles existed which could have served to offer a more principled way forward: despite being asked to consider remedial secession by states and members of the Bench, the majority chose not to devote any analytical space to the principle, merely casting doubt on its existence as a legal principle in passing. In so doing it diminished – rather than enhanced – the authority of international law, as the subsequent events in Ukraine (and perhaps also in Kurdistan and Cataluña) show all too clearly.

Perhaps the Court learnt from this experience that it is not apolitical minimalism that is most apt to maintain and build its authority in the international legal community, but rather bold and principled action. Certainly, it has taken a different, and much more forthright, approach in its most recent[158] encounter with self-determination. The next chapter turns its attention to the *Chagos Archipelago* Advisory Opinion, where the contrast to *Kosovo* could not have been more stark.

[157] See eg Blake, who argues that 'the modesty of this decision is worth celebrating': Blake, 'Dirty Hands' (n 10) 168; and further Tams, 'The Kosovo Opinion' (n 8); Borgen, 'Kosovo Advisory Opinion' (n 8).

[158] As of time of writing, May 2022.

6

The *Chagos Archipelago* Advisory Opinion

The ICJ had a further opportunity to consider self-determination in 2019: the request for an advisory opinion in *Legal Consequences of the Separation of the Chagos Archipelago from Mauritius in 1965*.[1] The request offered the Court little opportunity to reconsider its opinion in *Kosovo*, however; here a quite different form of self-determination was at issue. Whereas in *Kosovo* the Court sought strenuously to avoid questions of remedial and secessionary self-determination, *Chagos* was a return to safer ground and the colonial form of self-determination. Although the resulting opinion is not beyond criticism, it has offered a substantive and revealing treatment of colonial self-determination.

The chapter will proceed as follows. First, I briefly discuss the background and context of the advisory request, and will situate the questions asked of the Court within the long-running dispute between Mauritius and the United Kingdom. I then proceed to canvass the opinion as a whole, and will highlight points at which the Court has been both radical and tentative. The discussion will then focus on the Court's discussion of self-determination, and I will argue that although it has clarified the scope of colonial self-determination, there remained missed opportunities further to elucidate the category of self-determination as a whole. I will look to the individual opinions to explain these lacunae, and will identify again a persistent conceptual confusion, which impedes the satisfactory treatment of self-determination.

I. The Advisory Opinion

On 22 June 2017 Raymond Balé, Permanent Representation of the Congo to the United Nations, took the floor of the UN General Assembly to introduce draft resolution A/71/L.73 on behalf of the Group of African States.[2] That draft resolution was titled 'Request for an advisory opinion of the International Court

[1] *Legal Consequences of the Separation of the Chagos Archipelago from Mauritius in 1965*, Advisory Opinion, (2019) ICJ Reports 95.

[2] UN General Assembly, 71st Session, Official Record of the 88th Plenary Meeting, 22 June 2017, A/71/PV.88.

of Justice on the legal consequences of the separation of the Chagos archipelago from Mauritius in 1965', and a somewhat lopsided debate followed. The United Kingdom objected stridently, characterising the question as a bilateral dispute between Mauritius and the United Kingdom and maintaining that the advisory request would amount to a thinly veiled subversion of the principle of consent to international adjudication,[3] but few states came to its aid. With the exception of the United States, the vast majority of speakers noted their delegation's support for the resolution, and still more were notable by their absence.[4] Indeed, when the General Assembly voted only fifteen states objected to the request for an advisory opinion, with ninety-four voting in favour (the majority coming from Africa and Latin America), and an unusually-high sixty-five abstentions (including most of the European states).[5] Although falling just shy of an absolute majority,[6] the resolution was thus adopted by a large margin as General Assembly Resolution 71/292,[7] and the advisory request was accordingly sent to the Court.

Resolution 71/292 begins by recalling the General Assembly's resolution 1514 (XV), as well as its resolutions 2066 (XX), 2232 (XXI) and 2357 (XXII) on the separation of the Chagos Archipelago from Mauritius.[8] It noted in particular paragraph 6 of resolution 1514, discussed above,[9] which declares that '[a]ny attempt aimed at the partial or total disruption of the national unity and the territorial integrity of a country is incompatible with the purposes and principles of the Charter of the United Nations'. Having noted this practice, it decided to submit two questions to the ICJ under the advisory procedure:

(a) 'Was the process of decolonization of Mauritius lawfully completed when Mauritius was granted independence in 1968, following the separation of the Chagos Archipelago from Mauritius and having regard to international law, including obligations reflected in General Assembly resolutions 1514 (XV) or 14 December 1960, 2066 (XX) of 16 December 1965, 2232 (XXI) of 20 December 1966 and 2357 (XXII) or 19 December 1967?';

(b) 'What are the consequences under international law, including obligations reflected in the above-mentioned resolutions, arising from the continued

[3] For a full account, see P Webb, 'The United Kingdom and the Chagos Archipelago Advisory Opinion: Engagement and Resistance' (2021) 21 *Melbourne Journal of International Law* 726, 731–35.

[4] UNGA, 88th Plenary Meeting. It is intriguing to note, with Minas, that this loss in the General Assembly (and the absence of a European vote to support the UK) occurred at a time when the UK was occupied with Brexit, and was closely followed by the loss of the British seat on the Court: S Minas, 'Why the ICJ's Chagos Archipelago Advisory Opinion Matters for Global Justice – and for "Global Britain"' (2019) 10 *Transnational Legal Theory* 123, 135.

[5] UN General Assembly Voting Records, www.digitallibrary.un org/record/1290041.

[6] At the time of its adoption, the General Assembly had 193 voting members, meaning 97 are required for an absolute majority. However, only 174 states cast a vote (to adopt, to reject or to abstain) in relation to resolution 71/292, meaning the resolution comfortably achieved an absolute majority of those states present and voting.

[7] UN General Assembly Resolution 71/292, 22 June 2017.

[8] UN General Assembly Resolution 2066 (XX), 16 December 1965; UN General Assembly Resolution 2232 (XXI), 20 December 1966; UN General Assembly Resolution 2357 (XXII), 19 December 1967.

[9] See above, ch 3, s V.C.

> administration by the United Kingdom of Great Britain and Northern Ireland of the Chagos Archipelago, including with respect to the inability of Mauritius to implement a programme for the resettlement on the Chagos Archipelago of its nationals, in particular those of Chagossian origin?'.[10]

Hearings in the advisory process took place in the Hague from 3 to 6 September 2018, with the participation of twenty-one states and the African Union, and an additional ten states filed written statements. The Opinion was delivered on 25 February 2019, and by thirteen votes to one held that the process of decolonisation of Mauritius has not been lawfully completed,[11] that the United Kingdom 'is under an obligation to bring to an end its administration of the Chagos Archipelago as rapidly as possible',[12] and that all Member States should cooperate with the UN to complete the decolonisation of Mauritius.[13] It also found unanimously that it had jurisdiction to give the advisory opinion requested, and by twelve votes to two decided to comply with the request.[14] The following sub-sections will canvass the advisory opinion and analyse the reasoning of the Court, before section II turns to the Court's treatment of self-determination.

A. Jurisdiction and Discretion

Before the Court could consider the substantive questions posed by the General Assembly, it had first to establish its jurisdiction to answer the request made by resolution 71/292. That it could do so was not self-evident: it faced the weighty objection that in opining it would in effect be ruling on a bilateral dispute between the United Kingdom and Mauritius in the absence of the former's consent.[15] If sustained, that would amount to a 'compelling reason' for it to decline to exercise its jurisdiction over the request.[16] The Court thus seemed to be offered an ideal opportunity to sidestep the complex and political issues involved in the substantive questions if, as it did in *Kosovo*,[17] it was inclined to do so. Much has changed in the decade following the *Kosovo* opinion, however, and the Court did not take the easy way out. On the contrary, it delivered a brave and principled opinion that seemed entirely ready to engage with controversial and politically charged questions. That it did so is, moreover, particularly significant in the context of self-determination. As will be further discussed below, the objection that a dispute has

[10] UNGA Res 71/292.
[11] *Chagos* (n 1) para 183(3).
[12] *Chagos* (n 1) para 183(4).
[13] *Chagos* (n 1) para 183(5).
[14] *Chagos* (n 1) paras 183(1)–(2).
[15] A similar objection was raised in *Wall*: *Legal Consequences of the Construction of a Wall in the Occupied Palestinian Territory*, Advisory Opinion, (2004) ICJ Reports 136, paras 14–42.
[16] *Western Sahara*, Advisory Opinion, (1975) ICJ Reports 12, paras 32–33; *Interpretation of Peace Treaties with Bulgaria, Hungary and Romania*, First Phase, Advisory Opinion, (1950) ICJ Reports 65, 71.
[17] See above, ch 5, section I.B.

a bilateral character is likely to apply to most cases in which international concern regarding a self-determination claim results in a reference to the Court. A contrary finding on this point could, therefore, have severely restricted the potential of international adjudication in the context of future self-determination claims.

As has become common in advisory proceedings, the challenge made by the states opposed to the advisory request – here, the United Kingdom, the United States and others – centred not on the Court's jurisdiction but on the exercise of its discretion. As the Court recalled in paragraph 55 of its opinion, Article 65(1) of its Statute gives it the jurisdiction to consider a request for an advisory opinion on 'any legal question':

> The Court may give an advisory opinion on any legal question at the request of whatever body may be authorized by or in accordance with the Charter of the United Nations to make such a request.[18]

In order, then to establish its jurisdiction it had only to note that the General Assembly is competent to request an opinion – it is so under Article 96(1) of the Charter[19] – and to ask whether the question posed falls within the meaning of a 'legal' question. This it considered self-evident, holding baldly that 'a request from the General Assembly for an advisory opinion to examine a situation by reference to international law concerns a legal question'.[20] Having thus found that it had jurisdiction to consider the request, it had then to consider the propriety of its exercise of that jurisdiction.

The Court has long taken the view that the formulation in its Statute, that the 'Court *may* give an advisory opinion', invests it with a discretionary power.[21] Although in principle an answer to a request 'represents [the Court's] participation in the activities of the Organization' and 'should not be refused' lightly,[22] 'compelling reasons'[23] may lead it to decline to answer a question that is in all other respects properly put. Four reasons were put forward by some of the states participating in the proceedings as presenting 'compelling' grounds for declining the request, although all were ultimately judged to be unconvincing by a majority of the Bench: that the complexity of the factual issues at stake in the proceedings rendered the question unsuitable for determination through the non-adversarial advisory process; that any response by the Court would not in fact assist the General Assembly in the performance of its functions; that the question had already been settled by an Annex VII UNCLOS arbitral tribunal;[24] and that to

[18] Art 65(1) of the Statute of the International Court of Justice (San Francisco, 26 June 1945).

[19] Art 96(1) of the Charter of the United Nations (San Francisco, 26 June 1945).

[20] *Chagos* (n 1) para 58.

[21] Art 65(1) ICJ Statute (n 18) (emphasis added); *Chagos* (n 1) paras 63–64; see further H Thirlway, *The International Court of Justice* (Oxford, Oxford University Press, 2016) 67.

[22] *Interpretation of Peace Treaties* (n 16) 71.

[23] *Wall* (n 15) para 44.

[24] *Chagos Marine Protected Area Arbitration (Mauritius v United Kingdom)*, Arbitral Tribunal Constituted under Annex VII of the United Nations Convention on the Law of the Sea, Award of 18 March 2015, PCA Case no 2011–03.

answer the advisory request would compromise the principle of state consent to jurisdiction.[25] Only this fourth generated any meaningful degree of controversy in the Court, receiving substantial analysis and resulting in a split decision. Judge Tomka and Judge Donoghue voted against the Court's exercise of jurisdiction as a result of this objection, and appended respectively a declaration and a strongly expressed dissent to the opinion.

It is self-evidently true that the factual circumstances laid before the Court by way of the advisory request arose from the relations between (first) the United Kingdom and its Mauritian colony, and (later) between the United Kingdom and Mauritius. There exists a bilateral dispute between the United Kingdom and Mauritius concerning the Chagos Islands, which relates both to the propriety of the separation and the continuing status of the archipelago. What is more, Mauritius had been the primary instigator of the motion before the General Assembly;[26] the most recent of its attempts to bring its dispute with the United Kingdom before international fora.[27] Nevertheless, the Court found that it was possible to separate the bilateral UK–Mauritian dispute from the question asked by the General Assembly.[28] The bilateral dispute did not take up all of the available space, and it was appropriate in parallel for the Court to advise the general assembly on its work:

> The Court notes that the questions put to it by the General Assembly relate to the decolonization of Mauritius. The General Assembly has not sought the Court's opinion to resolve a territorial dispute between two States. Rather, the purpose of the request is for the General Assembly to receive the Court's assistance so that it may be guided in the discharge of its functions relating to the decolonization of Mauritius.[29]

By contrast, Judge Donoghue did not believe the questions could so easily be separated. '[T]he present request', she argued, 'places before the Court the lawfulness of past United Kingdom conduct, the present-day consequences of that conduct

[25] See GI Hernández, *The International Court of Justice and the Judicial Function* (Oxford, Oxford University Press, 2014) 79–82; H Thirlway, *The Law and Procedure of the International Court of Justice: Fifty Years of Jurisprudence*, vol I (Oxford, Oxford University Press, 2013) 843–50.

[26] Mauritius made the initial request for the inclusion in the agenda of the General Assembly's seventy-first session of a debate on a resolution requesting an advisory opinion: letter dated 14 July 2016 from the Permanent Representative of Mauritius to the United Nations addressed to the Secretary General, UN Doc No A/71/142; Summary Record of the 1st Meeting of the General Committee of the Seventy-First Session of the General Assembly, 19 October 2016, UN Doc No A/BUR/71/SR.1, para 23.

[27] See further, *Chagos Marine Protected Area Arbitration* (n 24).

[28] In so doing, it followed a path closely parallel to that it walked in *Wall* (n 15). Thirlway, commenting on that decision, goes so far as to argue that the Court 'tacitly abandoned' its previous position that the circumvention of consent would amount to a 'compelling reason' to decline a reference: Thirlway, *International Court of Justice* (n 21) 69; and further H Thirlway, *The Law and Procedure of the International Court of Justice: Fifty Years of Jurisprudence*, vol II (Oxford, Oxford University Press, 2013) 1723–25. Pratap argues that this abandonment occurred earlier, in the *Peace Treaties* case of 1950: *Interpretation of Peace Treaties* (n 16); D Pratap, *The Advisory Jurisdiction of the International Court of Justice* (Oxford, Clarendon Press, 1972) 157–58ff.

[29] *Chagos* (n 1) para 86.

for the rights of that State and the adjudication of sovereignty over territory.'[30] She continued:

> It is difficult to imagine any dispute that is more quintessentially bilateral than a dispute over territorial sovereignty. The absence of United Kingdom consent to adjudication of that bilateral dispute has been steadfast and deliberate. Mauritius was thwarted by this absence of consent, so took another route, pursuing the present request and thereby fulfilling the affirmation of its Foreign Minister in 2004 … that the State would use 'all avenues open to us in order to exercise our full sovereign rights over the Chagos Archipelago'. The delivery of this Advisory Opinion is a circumvention of the absence of consent.[31]

The dissent of Judge Donoghue discloses a vitally important debate, the outcome of which has the potential to shape the uses of the advisory procedure in the coming years and decades. Donoghue refers to the centrality of consent in the Court's contentious jurisdiction, and notes with concern the transformation of the advisory process into a 'fall-back mechanism to be used to overcome the absence of consent' where it is not given. Although she recognises that '[s]ome may find this to be a welcome development', she sees it as 'undermin[ing] the integrity of the Court's judicial function'.[32] Judge Tomka raised many of the same concerns. Although he does not – as Judge Donoghue seems to do – draw the conclusion that the request should therefore be wholly refused, he makes a strong call for judicial minimalism:

> The Court is thus willing to provide 'its advice' to the General Assembly on an issue which the latter had not considered for half a century, despite the undisputable role assigned to the General Assembly by the Charter of the United Nations in matters of decolonization. If one can accept this course of action, one must also exercise caution not to go further than what is strictly necessary and useful for the requesting organ. The Court must not forget that what looms in the background is a bilateral dispute over which the Court lacks jurisdiction.[33]

In other words; it should not be for the General Assembly alone to judge what will be useful to it. Rather, Tomka argued that the Court must consider the purposes to which the General Assembly is likely to put its answer, in assessing what information the General Assembly ought to receive. In a matter such as that placed before the Court by resolution 71/292, in his view, it should answer only to the extent strictly necessary to enable the General Assembly to pursue its functions.

By contrast, the Court seems to have accepted a different role for itself, although it is unclear whether this should be conceived to be broader or narrower than

[30] *Legal Consequences of the Separation of the Chagos Archipelago from Mauritius in 1965*, Dissenting Opinion of Judge Donoghue, (2019) ICJ Reports 261, para 18.

[31] ibid para 21 (references omitted).

[32] ibid para 23.

[33] *Legal Consequences of the Separation of the Chagos Archipelago from Mauritius in 1965*, Declaration of Judge Tomka, (2019) ICJ Reports 148, para 6 (references omitted).

that suggested by Tomka. Although it acknowledged that a dispute exists between Mauritius and the United Kingdom on the matters in question, it held that 'the fact that the Court may have to pronounce on legal issues on which divergent views have been expressed by Mauritius and the United Kingdom does not mean that, by replying to the request, the Court is dealing with a bilateral dispute'.[34] Although blandly stated, that proposition is not straightforward to maintain, in particular in light of the extensive and direct conclusions to which the Court comes.[35] Indeed, its conclusions were at least as significant as those usually expected from a contentious case: it considered the legality of the acts of an individual state, ruled on its current legal position, and made a determination of the demands of international law on its future conduct. That the Court was able to maintain that in doing so it was not 'circumventing the principle of consent',[36] therefore, implies one of three conclusions: it might be, first, that the Court construed its role to be significantly *narrower* than that contemplated by Judge Tomka; it could not substantively assess the usefulness of its answer to the General Assembly, and was therefore required to answer by its 'duty of cooperation' in the work of the organisation.[37] A second possibility would hold the Court's role to be becoming broader, perhaps even in the sense of *constitutionalising*; that the combined competences of the General Assembly and the Court itself are now capable of displacing the consent requirement.[38] Thirdly, it could be argued that as the requirement of consent to jurisdiction plainly does not operate within the advisory jurisdiction in terms comparable to its role in contentious cases, that previous cases have overstated the extent to which the absence of consent can provide a reason for the Court to decline a request.[39]

These questions are already attracting a burgeoning scholarly interest – and I have sought to address them elsewhere – but they need not be resolved for the

[34] *Chagos* (n 1) para 89.

[35] The Court finds that the decolonisation of Mauritius was unlawfully completed, because the separation of the archipelago took place in contravention of the norm of self-determination; and then held that the UK is 'under an obligation to bring an end to its administration of the Chagos Archipelago as rapidly as possible': *Chagos* (n 1) para 183.

[36] *Chagos* (n 1) para 90.

[37] Hernández, *Judicial Function* (n 25) 78–79; G Abi-Saab, 'On Discretion: Reflections on the Nature of the Consultative Function of the International Court of Justice' in L Boisson de Charzournes and P Sands (eds), *International Law, the International Court of Justice, and Nuclear Weapons* (Cambridge, Cambridge University Press, 1999) 48–49.

[38] This appears to be along similar lines to the position suggested by Thirlway, albeit that Thirlway offers a more restrained statement of the argument: Thirlway, *International Court of Justice* (n 21) 69; Thirlway, *Law and Procedure II* (n 28) 1724. Hernández describes this as a 'maximalist interpretation' of the Court's duty to respond to a request: Hernández, *Judicial Function* (n 25) 82.

[39] For a discussion of the nature of consent between the jurisdictions, see T Sparks, 'Reassessing State Consent to Jurisdiction: The Indispensable Third Party Principle before the ICJ' (2022) 91 *Nordic Journal of International Law* 216. Although see *contra* Pratap, who argues that the relevance of consent to the advisory function is, to begin with, the result of a deliberate choice by the Court to 'assimilate[] its advisory procedure to its contentious procedure and fully [to] treat[] it as a judicial function': Pratap, *Advisory Jurisdiction* (n 28) 154.

purposes of the present discussion.[40] It is possible briefly to observe, however, that the Court's reasoning appears better suited to the first possibility than the second. The Court lays emphasis – as it has consistently – on the fact that a request from the General Assembly 'in principle, should not be refused' because its answer 'represents its participation in the activities of the Organisation'.[41] As a result, 'only "compelling reasons" may lead the Court to refuse its opinion'.[42] That the Court so consistently and strongly asserts the limited circumstances in which it can refuse a request leads Georges Abi-Saab to question the characterisation of its advisory jurisdiction as discretionary at all. The form of words it uses – that of 'compelling reasons' – 'is intriguing, for what is compelling constrains or exerts compulsion which, by definition, negates choice. How can a course of action dictated by such "compelling reasons" then be considered as an exercise of discretion?'[43] This leads Abi-Saab to characterise the Court's facility to give advisory opinions not as a *right* conferred by the Statute – 'which is a power or faculty that its holder can exercise or not exercise, keep or abandon' – but instead as a *function*, for 'a function combines a power with a charge or obligation to exercise it in pursuit of a specific finality'.[44] It is this charge or obligation that Gleider Hernández names the Court's *duty of cooperation*,[45] and it seems certainly to be strongly felt by the Court.[46] Such a reading would explain why the Court felt able to disregard the fact that the decolonisation of Mauritius had not appeared on the General Assembly's agenda for approaching fifty years (a fact which appeared strongly pertinent to Judges Tomka and Donoghue), finding it sufficient to refer to the General Assembly's interest in the broad topic of decolonisation.[47]

Even a strong reading of the duty of cooperation remains less than fully satisfying as an explanation, however. The Court noted that a difference of views does not

[40] See, inter alia, Sparks, 'Reassessing Consent' (n 39); M Law, 'The Chagos Request: Does it Herald a Rejuvenation of the International Court of Justice's Advisory Function?' (2018) 9 *Queen Mary Law Journal* 25; B Kuźniak and D Kabat-Rudnicka, 'Advisory Opinion or Judgment? The Case of the Chagos Archipelago' (2021) 13 *Przegląd Prawniczy Uniwersytetu im. Adama Mickiewicza* 45; Z Crespi Reghizzi, 'The *Chagos* Advisory Opinion and the Principle of Consent to Adjudication' in T Burri and J Trinidad (eds), *The International Court of Justice and Decolonisation* (Cambridge, Cambridge University Press, 2021); FL Bordin, 'State Responsibility in Advisory Proceedings: Thoughts on Judicial Propriety and Multilateralism in the *Chagos* Opinion' in T Burri and J Trinidad (eds), *The International Court of Justice and Decolonisation* (Cambridge, Cambridge University Press, 2021). These questions will, no doubt, continue to provide material for a rich vein of further scholarship.

[41] *Chagos* (n 1) para 65; citing *Interpretation of Peace Treaties* (n 16) 71; *Difference Relating to Immunity from Legal Process of a Special Rapporteur of the Commission on Human Rights*, Advisory Opinion, (1999) ICJ Reports 62, para 29; *Wall* (n 15) para 44.

[42] *Chagos* (n 1) para 65; citing *Wall* (n 15) para 44; *Accordance with International Law of the Unilateral Declaration of Independence in Respect of Kosovo*, Advisory Opinion, (2010) ICJ Reports 403, para 30; see further Pratap, *Advisory Jurisdiction* (n 28) 161.

[43] Abi-Saab, 'On Discretion' (n 37) 49.

[44] ibid 44; see also discussion in Law, 'The Chagos Request' (n 40) 34–35.

[45] Hernández, *Judicial Function* (n 25) 78–79.

[46] Thirlway describes it as 'overriding': Thirlway, *International Court of Justice* (n 21) 68.

[47] *Chagos* (n 1) paras 87–88; FL Bordin, 'Reckoning with British Colonialism: The Chagos Advisory Opinion' (2019) 78 *Cambridge Law Journal* 253, 254.

suffice to bilateralise a dispute and that it has a duty to cooperate with the General Assembly, but its conclusion seemed to be motivated by another factor. It held that its opinion *would not* 'circumvent the principle of consent by a State to the judicial settlement of its dispute with another State', and that it 'therefore cannot, in the exercise of its discretion, decline to give the opinion on that ground'.[48] The formulation 'would not' does not imply that the principle of state consent has been overridden by a countervailing factor (such as a duty of cooperation), but rather that state consent was never engaged in the first place. However, the Court continued to maintain that the circumvention of consent would be a compelling reason to decline, a profession that now rings somewhat hollow. It would be reasonable to ask, given the context of this case, what circumstances then *would* be sufficient to engage the injunction that the advisory jurisdiction should not be used to circumvent the requirement of consent in contentious cases?[49]

I agree with the Court's substantive conclusion on this preliminary question of jurisdiction and propriety, but the reasoning the Court offers is not sufficient to explain its approach. Although the Court has treated this case as falling outwith the boundaries of its rule on the circumvention of consent, it seems by doing so to have shrunk the applicable area of that rule to such a degree that it has likely been rendered largely irrelevant to future cases. To that extent, it speaks of a similar ad hoc-ism to that identified in relation to the *Kosovo* Advisory Opinion, and which was strongly criticised in that case by Judge Simma.[50] Although the Court can, at least to some degree, continue to function through these ad hoc exceptions, redefinitions and circumscriptions, it would be better served in the long term by a substantial and reasoned engagement with the rules at issue. It is to be hoped, therefore, that future advisory opinions will offer a clear and compelling clarification of the role of consent in the advisory jurisdiction, and whether – and if so to what degree[51] – the integrity of the judicial function requires the advisory jurisdiction to be safeguarded from the encroachment of a 'constitutionalised' model of international justice.[52]

Seen specifically from the point of view of self-determination, however, the decision is procedurally helpful. In finding that consent does not bar an international request for an opinion on such a question, Court has here avoided placing a significant blockage in the path of the international treatment of self-determination claims. Most instances of self-determination concern the relationship between a state and a sub-state group; whether an oppressed minority (remedial), a region seeking independence (secessionary), or an overseas possession (colonial). Lacking standing in their own right, these groups' only routes to international

[48] *Chagos* (n 1) para 90.

[49] It is difficult to imagine a case that is, to a degree greater than this, a 'bilateral dispute'. See above, nn 26–27, and accompanying text; and further Sparks, 'Reassessing Consent' (n 39) 235–39, *passim*.

[50] See above ch 5, ss I.B ff.

[51] Pratap, *Advisory Jurisdiction* (n 28) 154.

[52] See further Sparks, 'Reassessing Consent' (n 39) 243–44.

adjudication of their claims are via a contentious claim by a sympathetic state, or (perhaps the more likely) an advisory request by a competent international body. Both will normally require a state to champion the cause of the sub-state group, as Mauritius has the Chagos Islanders, and any claim before a court that results is thus likely to be amenable to the charge that it is at heart a bilateral dispute. Although the reasons why remain somewhat shrouded, the Court has confirmed that in the advisory procedure the charge of bilateralism is at least not a trump card and will be narrowly construed. In so doing, it has ensured that international adjudication remains available in instances of self-determination.

B. The Substantive Questions 1: The Decolonisation of Mauritius

Having thus concluded both that it has jurisdiction to consider the request placed before it and that it would be appropriate for it to do so, the Court proceeded to examine the substantive questions asked by the General Assembly. In its first question, the General Assembly asked the Court to answer:

> Was the process of decolonization of Mauritius lawfully completed when Mauritius was granted independence in 1968, following the separation of the Chagos Archipelago from Mauritius and having regard to international law, including obligations reflected in General Assembly resolutions 1514 (XV) of 14 December 1960, 2066 (XX) of 16 December 1965, 2232 (XXI) of 20 December 1966 and 2357 (XXII) of 19 December 1967?[53]

As the Court identified, that question demands a time-limited enquiry. It must be answered according to the applicable rules of international law in the period between the separation of the archipelago from Mauritius in 1965 and the independence of Mauritius in 1968.[54] It thus proceeded to consider the state of the law of self-determination during those key years, emphasising that the form of self-determination to be considered is that applicable in the context of decolonisation.[55]

It began with the Charter, looking in particular to the provisions of Chapter XI concerning non-self-governing territories.[56] Those provisions establish a set of principles for the conduct of administering powers, including that the these powers are obliged to develop the self-government of those territories, a requirement the Court confirmed here.[57] But they stop short either of requiring the ultimate independence of those territories, or of creating rules of conduct

[53] UNGA Res 71/292.
[54] *Chagos* (n 1) para 140.
[55] ibid para 144.
[56] The provisions of the Charter are discussed in detail above, ch 3, ss IV–V.A.ii.
[57] *Chagos* (n 1) para 146.

for the independence process.[58] Rather, those provisions establish the *telos* of the regime applicable to non-self-governing territories:

> Having made respect for the principle of equal rights and self-determination of peoples one of the purposes of the United Nations, the Charter included provisions that would enable non-self-governing territories ultimately to govern themselves. It is in this context that the Court must ascertain when the right to self-determination crystallized as a customary rule binding on all States.[59]

The Court found a more concrete expression of the requirements of self-determination in the colonial context in the *Declaration on the Granting of Independence to Colonial Countries and Peoples*, the UN General Assembly's resolution 1514 (XV).[60] The Court held the adoption of that resolution to be a 'defining moment in the consolidation of State practice on decolonization'.[61] Although it is 'formally a recommendation' and is not binding qua a resolution of the General Assembly, 'it has a declaratory character with regard to the right to self-determination as a customary norm'.[62] Its high status is indicated by its wording. As discussed above, the resolution is phrased in imperative terms, and purports to require action of the states that are trustees over non-self-governing territories, an action within the competence of the General Assembly in relation at least to territories formally falling within the trusts system.[63] Relevant, too, were the overwhelming vote in favour of the resolution in the General Assembly, and the statements made by state representatives in the course of that debate.[64] The Court recalled that the resolution was adopted with eighty-nine votes in favour and nine abstentions, and no state voting against. Although telling in its own right, the Court buttresses that numerical calculus with the observation that a number of the states which cast their votes to abstain noted that they did so 'on the basis of the time required for the implementation of such a right'.[65]

An examination of the verbatim record of the General Assembly's session on 14 December 1960, indeed, finds support for that proposition, but also highlights the nuanced and complex nature of those statements. The US representative, for example, in explaining his delegation's abstention, highlights exactly the question of timing picked up by the Court. He cautioned that paragraph 3 of the resolution 'permits the interpretation that the question of preparation for independence is wholly irrelevant', or, in other words, that it risks creating a principle that is absolute

[58] See above, ch 3, ss IV and V.A.ii.
[59] *Chagos* (n 1) para 148.
[60] UN General Assembly Resolution 1514 (XV), 14 December 1960; for analysis, see above ch 3, s V.C.
[61] *Chagos* (n 1) para 150.
[62] ibid para 152.
[63] See above, ch 3, ss IV and V.C.
[64] *Chagos* (n 1) paras 152–53.
[65] ibid para 152.

and immediately actionable.[66] The representative of the UK referred in similar terms to paragraph 5, noting that it could be (in his view) misconstrued to mandate an immediate transfer of powers to non-self-governing territories.[67] However, the Unted Kingdom also noted its belief that paragraph 1 of the resolution – which declares that the 'subjection of peoples to alien subjugation, domination and exploitation' is contrary to the Charter[68] – 'is, I must assume, simply not applicable to the peoples in these territories for which we are responsible … the United Kingdom administration of dependent territories is conducted strictly in accord with the relevant provisions of the Charter'.[69] Even despite these caveats and debates over the resolution's scope of application, it is arguable that these statements amount to an *opinio iuris*, as discussed above.[70] The Court's conclusion, then, that the declaration could have had an immediate effect to crystallise the developing norm against colonial rule and in favour of the self-determination of non-self-governing peoples seems to be warranted. This, indeed, appears to have been the view of the resolution shared by the General Assembly at the time of its adoption.[71]

Resolution 1514 establishes and discloses two principles that the Court considered to be material to the question before it. First, that resolution 'affirms that "[a]ll peoples have the right to self-determination"'. It then makes self-determination the primary instrument of the end of colonialism, in its paragraph 5 demand that '[i]mmediate steps shall be taken, in Trust and Non-Self-Governing Territories or all other territories which have not yet attained independence, to transfer all power to the people of those territories … in accordance with their freely expressed will and desire'.[72] The Court found further support for this principle in the common first article to the International Covenant on Economic, Social, and Cultural Rights and the International Covenant on Civil and Political Rights,[73] in the General Assembly's *Principles which should guide Members in determining whether or not an obligation exists to transmit the information called for in Article 73e of the Charter of the United Nations*, annexed to resolution 1541(XV),[74] and in its advisory opinion in *Western Sahara*.[75]

[66] UN General Assembly, 15th Session, Official Record of the 947th Plenary Meeting, 14th December 1960, A/PV.947, para 149.

[67] UNGA, 947th Meeting, para 54.

[68] UNGA Res 1514 (XV), para 1.

[69] UNGA, 947th Meeting, para 149.

[70] See above, ch 3, s V.D.

[71] Bodin commends the Court for 'avoiding an excessively static approach to the formation of international custom' and comments that '[w]hile an international lawyer looking at the question the day after the Colonial Declaration was adopted might have been unsure as to whether self-determination was already a rule of customary international law, the way in which the principle was invoked and applied in the subsequent years sheds light on its evolution and emergence as a normative practice adhered to by states': Bordin, 'Reckoning with British Colonialism' (n 47) 255.

[72] UNGA Res 1514 (XV), paras 2, 5; *Chagos* (n 1) para 153.

[73] International Covenant on Economic Social and Cultural Rights and International Covenant on Civil and Political Rights (New York, 16 December 1966); for analysis, see above ch 3, s V.B.

[74] UNGA Res 1541; for analysis, see above ch 3, s V.C.

[75] *Western Sahara* (n 16) paras 36, 59; for analysis, see above, ch 4, s III.

Secondly, here referring also to the Declaration on Friendly Relations,[76] the Court referred to the injunction in paragraph 6 of Resolution 1514, that:

> Any attempt aimed at the partial or total disruption of the national unity and the territorial integrity of a country is incompatible with the purposes and principles of the Charter of the United Nations.[77]

Although familiar, this 'safeguard clause', as it is termed above, takes on a subtly new complexion in the Court's analysis here. The clause is bifunctional. In the analysis to this point it has been shown that a major purpose of the inclusion of the provision was to establish a division between the exercise of self-determination in colonial territories, and that by regions and sub-state units of independent states (or, in other words, between colonial and secessionary self-determination). In particular, its inclusion in principle 5 of the Declaration on Friendly Relations speaks to this purpose. There it is specified that the scope of the provision relates to 'the territorial integrity or political unity of *sovereign and independent* States'.[78] However, the preamble of that Declaration uses, as does paragraph 6 of Resolution 1514, a more general language:

> *Convinced* in consequence that any attempt aimed at the partial or total disruption of the national unity and territorial integrity of **a State or country** or at its political independence is incompatible with the purposes and principles of the Charter.[79]

Although the reference here is oblique, this appears to echo the 1514 application of the principle to territories as yet under colonial rule. It amounts to a strong interpretation of the principle *uti possedetis iuris*, and an affirmation of its application as a limit not only to the aspirations of peoples under colonial rule, but also to those powers which, having determined those boundaries, are not entitled to change them for their own purposes. The Court confirmed that this second reading of the safeguard clause is no mere afterthought, but rather was firmly intended during the drafting of resolution 1514. It remarks that the clause was included in the resolution '*in order to* prevent any dismemberment of non-self-governing territories',[80] and confirmed that:

> Both State practice and *opinio juris* at the relevant time confirm the customary law character of the right to territorial integrity of a non-self-governing territory as a corollary of the right to self-determination. No example has been brought to the attention

[76] Declaration on Friendly Relations, annexed to UN General Assembly Resolution 2625 (XXV), 24 October 1970; for analysis, see above ch 3, s V.D.

[77] UNGA Res 1514 (XV), para 6; *Chagos* (n 1) paras 153, 155.

[78] Declaration on Friendly Relations (n 76), principle 5 (emphasis added).

[79] ibid preamble (italics in original; bold emphasis added).

[80] *Chagos* (n 1) para 153. As Summers has demonstrated, for all that this conclusion is welcome, there are ample grounds to be sceptical about the Court's reasoning on this point: J Summers, 'Decolonisation Revisited and the Obligation Not to Divide a Non-Self-Governing Territory' (2018) 55 *Questions of International Law, Zoom Out* 147, 161–67. For an analysis of how this principle may apply to existing and future controversies, see J Trinidad, 'Self-Determination and Territorial Integrity in the Chagos Advisory Proceedings: Potential Broader Ramifications' (2018) 55 *Questions of International Law, Zoom Out* 61.

> of the Court in which, following the adoption of resolution 1514 (XV), the General Assembly or any other organ of the United Nations has considered as lawful the detachment by the administering Power of part of a non-self-governing territory, for the purpose of maintaining it under its colonial rule. States have consistently emphasized that respect for the territorial integrity of a non-self-governing territory is a key element of the exercise of the right to self-determination under international law.[81]

It concluded, therefore, that 'any detachment by the administering Power of part of a non-self-governing territory, unless based on the freely expressed and genuine will of the people of the territory concerned, is contrary to the right to self-determination'.[82]

In order, then to determine the legality of the separation of the Chagos Archipelago from Mauritius, the Court needed to answer two questions. First, whether the Chagos Archipelago was an integral part of the territory of Mauritius at the time of the separation in 1965; and secondly, whether the separation was effected in accordance with the self-determination ('freely expressed and genuine will') of the Mauritian people as a whole. The first was uncontroversial, and was answered affirmatively: in 1965, prior to the detachment, 'the Chagos Archipelago was clearly an integral part of that' territory.[83] In coming to that finding the Court relied on the original transfer of the Mauritius together with its dependencies (which included Chagos) to the British in the 1814 Treaty of Paris,[84] and that the United Kingdom consistently included the Chagos Archipelago as a sub-territory of the Mauritian non-self-governing territory in its reporting under Article 73 of the Charter.[85]

The Court then turned its attention to whether the separation could be said to have been effected in accordance with Mauritian self-determination, and this it answered negatively. Here there was, however, some small complexity as a result of the Lancaster House agreement of September 1965. Although the means by which that agreement was extorted can only be described as shameful,[86] it cannot be

[81] *Chagos* (n 1) para 160.

[82] ibid para 160.

[83] ibid para 160.

[84] Art VIII of the Definitive Treaty of Peace between his Britannic Majesty and his most Christian Majesty Louis XVIII (Paris, 30 May 1814). Translation in: E Baines, *History of the Wars of the French Revolution, from the Breaking Out of the War, in 1792, to the Restoration of a General Peace in 1815: Comprehending the Civil History of Great Britain and France, During that Period*, vol II (London, Longman, Hurst, Rees, Orme, and Brown, 1818) 343–46.

[85] Sir Lowry Cole's Despatch from Mauritius, List of Dependencies (British) of Mauritius (1826), FCO 31/3836 (19 September 1826); *Chagos* (n 1) para 28; see further Minas, 'Why the Chagos AO Matters' (n 4).

[86] In commenting on those events, Judge Robinson remarked that 'on that day British colonial relations reached a nadir. The intent to bully, frighten and coerce the Mauritian Premier was all too obvious. If one needs an explanation of what was meant in paragraph 1 of [Resolution 1514] by alien subjugation, domination and exploitation, one need look no further than the United Kingdom's treatment of the Mauritian Premier': *Legal Consequences of the Separation of the Chagos Archipelago from Mauritius in 1965*, Separate Opinion of Judge Robinson, (2019) ICJ Reports 294, para 93. Those events are described in Judge Robinson's separate opinion at paras 90–100, and in the judgment of the Court at paras 31–34 and 98–112. See also further discussion in S Motha, '"The Object Is to Frighten Him

avoided that the agreement appears to disclose a consent to the separation on the part of the Mauritian institutions of self-government. The Court (rightly) declined to take such a formal approach to the agreement, however, instead noting that 'heightened scrutiny' is appropriate to the question of consent to territorial separation, and that in any case it is 'not possible to talk of an international agreement, when one of the Parties to it … is under the authority of the [other]'.[87] Having thus decided to examine the circumstances in which the agreement was concluded, the Court came to the inevitable conclusion that neither the agreement nor the consequent detachment were 'based on the free and genuine expression of the will of the people concerned'.[88] Judge Robinson expanded on that conclusion in his separate opinion, giving a statement of the position which could be said to be more appropriate to the circumstances than the Court's (rather understated) conclusion:

> But the circumstances in which the Premier gave his 'consent' to the detachment of the Chagos Archipelago during his meeting with the British prime Minister were wholly antithetical and repugnant to the free expression of his own will. The general atmosphere was one of intimidation and coercion. Therefore any 'consent' to the detachment given by the Premier in those circumstances would not accord with what was required by the customary and peremptory norm of the right to self-determination.[89]

The Court thus found the detachment to have been 'unlawful', and concluded that the 'process of decolonization of Mauritius was not lawfully concluded' upon its independence in 1968.[90]

C. The Substantive Questions 2: The Consequences

Having thus answered the General Assembly's first question with the reply that the detachment of the Chagos Archipelago was unlawful, the Court turned its attention to the second question posed:

> What are the consequences under international law, including obligations reflected in the above-mentioned resolutions, arising from the continued administration by the United Kingdom of Great Britain and Northern Ireland of the Chagos Archipelago, including with respect to the inability of Mauritius to implement a programme for the resettlement on the Chagos Archipelago of its nationals, in particular those of Chagossian origin?[91]

with Hope": Questioning the Tragic Emplotments of International Law and Decolonisation in the Chagos Archipelago' in S Chalmers and S Pahuja (eds), *Routledge Handbook of International Law and the Humanities* (London, Routledge, 2021).

[87] *Chagos* (n 1) para 172.

[88] ibid para 172.

[89] Separate Opinion of Judge Robinson, *Chagos* (n 86) para 94; see also *Legal Consequences of the Separation of the Chagos Archipelago from Mauritius in 1965*, Separate Opinion of Judge Sebutinde, (2019) ICJ Reports 270, paras 14–21; *Legal Consequences of the Separation of the Chagos Archipelago from Mauritius in 1965*, Declaration of Judge Gaja, (2019) ICJ Reports 267, para 2.

[90] *Chagos* (n 1) para 174.

[91] UNGA Res 71/292.

Although it noted that this second question need not be dependent upon the answer to the first, the Court recognised that there is a clear relationship between the two. Referring to its finding on the detachment, the Court declared that:

> [H]aving found that the decolonization of Mauritius was not conducted in a manner consistent with the right of peoples to self-determination, it follows that the United Kingdom's continued administration of the Chagos Archipelago constitutes a wrongful act entailing the international responsibility of that State .... It is an unlawful act of a continuing character which arose as a result of the separation of the Chagos Archipelago from Mauritius.[92]

The United Kingdom is, therefore 'under an obligation to bring an end to its administration of the Chagos Archipelago as rapidly as possible, thereby enabling Mauritius to complete the decolonization of its territory in a manner consistent with the right of peoples to self-determination'.[93]

Although the strong expression of these conclusions probably surprised some observers – certainly it did the present author – the Court's decision on these points is unimpeachable, and its forthright expression welcome.[94] It is now a commonplace, codified in the International Law Commission's (ILC's) Articles on the Responsibility of States for International Wrongful Acts (ARSIWA), that it is a corollary of a state's responsibility for an internationally wrongful act that it must 'cease that act, if it is continuing'.[95] As Robert Kolb points out, this is no more than the necessary consequence of the breach of the primary obligation:

> This duty [to cease] is automatic because it is inherent in the primary obligation: if the latter is still in force, it requires certain conduct of the States bound; therefore, when conduct which is contrary to the obligation occurs, it has to be discontinued.[96]

Such has been the Court's approach in those cases that have come before it in which continuing acts have been at issue,[97] and it has applied the same approach

[92] *Chagos* (n 1) para 177 (references omitted).

[93] *Chagos* (n 1) para 178.

[94] Note, however, the criticism by Hilpold that the Court failed to consider reparations: P Hilpold, '"Humanizing" the Law of Self-Determination – The Chagos Island Case' (2022) 91 *Nordic Journal of International Law* 189, 205.

[95] International Law Commission, 'Articles on the Responsibility of States for Internationally Wrongful Acts' (ARSIWA), *Report of the International Law Commission on the Work of its 53rd Session*, 2001, UN Doc No A/56/10(SUPP), 30, Art 30(a); see also *Jurisdictional Immunities of the State (Germany v Italy; Greece Intervening)*, Judgment, (2012) ICJ Reports 99, para 137.

[96] R Kolb, *The International Law of State Responsibility: An Introduction* (Cheltenham, Edward Elgar, 2017) 149. A similar (although distinct) point is made by Corten, when he observes that 'it is impossible to conceive of a legal order which does not impose on every author of a breach the obligation to cease that breach': O Corten, 'The Obligation of Cessation' in J Crawford, A Pellet and S Olleson (eds), *The Law of International Responsibility* (Oxford, Oxford University Press, 2010) 545; and further C Annacker, 'Part Two of the International Law Commission's Draft Articles on State Responsibility' (1994) 37 *German Yearbook of International Law* 206, 219–20; D Shelton, 'Righting Wrongs: Reparations in the Articles on State Responsibility' (2002) 96 *American Journal of International Law* 833, 839–40; A Hoque, 'Existence, Breach and Responses to the Breach of State Responsibility: A Critical Analysis' (2016) 53 *Journal of Law, Policy and Globalization* 136, 140.

[97] See, for example, *United States Diplomatic and Consular Staff in Tehran (United States of America v Iran)*, Judgment, (1980) ICJ Reports 3, para 95(3); and further Thirlway, *Law and Procedure II* (n 28) 1565–69.

here. If the wrongful act concerned can be construed as continuing, an obligation of cessation arises. Here, however, its reasoning leaves something to be desired. It is unclear, in the formulation adopted by the Court, *what* obligation it considers to be of a continuing character. It left unclear, too, why it is appropriate to deal with the events of 1965 under that rubric, rather than understanding the separation to be a single wrongful act that has been completed, to which an obligation of restitution would be more appropriate than one of cessation. In Article 14 ARSIWA, the ILC drew a distinction between continuing and non-continuing wrongful acts:

> 1. The breach of an international obligation by an act of a State not having a continuing character occurs at the moment when the act is performed, even if its effects continue.
> 2. The breach of an international obligation by an act of a State having a continuing character extends over the entire period during which the act continues and remains not in conformity with the international obligation.[98]

Therefore, to order cessation, the Court needed to conceive of the separation qua the administration of the territory, and thus as an act 'extend[ing] over the entire period during which the act continues', rather than as a single event having long-lasting effects, specifically the displacement of Mauritian sovereignty over the Chagos Archipelago.[99] The Court did not, however, explain this distinction, nor did it make clear on what basis it chose to conceive of the separation as a continuing administration.[100]

In his declaration, Judge Gaja offers a perspective on these lacunae. The United Kingdom's detachment of the territory was unlawful because it contravened the principle that the territorial integrity of colonial territories must not be infringed in the absence of self-determination, but that obligation in itself is an aspect of the larger obligation binding on the United Kingdom in its dealings with Mauritius, that of decolonisation. He reformulated the Court's opinion, arguing that 'the Court thus rightly stated that there continues to exist an obligation for the administering Power to decolonize the Chagos Archipelago'.[101] Judge Xue made a similar observation, albeit in a different context, when she noted that '[d]ecolonization is a process'.[102] It seems, thus, that the Court considered the United Kingdom's administration of the archipelago as being (in very broad terms) analogous to an occupation, and moreover that the administration formed a continuing chain of conduct from the separation of the territories, with which it is indissolubly connected. In so doing, it brought the conduct wholly within the ILC's definition

[98] ARSIWA (n 95), Art 14(1)–(2).

[99] For more on this distinction, see J Crawford, *State Responsibility: The General Part* (Cambridge, Cambridge University Press, 2013) 462–64.

[100] Shelton argues that the difficulty in distinguishing between a continuing and non-continuing violation is the result of a broader failure by the ILC to analyse the concept 'sufficiently in either the articles or the commentary to allow for predictable or consistent results': Shelton, 'Righting Wrongs' (n 96) 840–41 (references omitted).

[101] Declaration of Judge Gaja, *Chagos* (n 89) para 4.

[102] *Legal Consequences of the Separation of the Chagos Archipelago from Mauritius in 1965*, Declaration of Vice-President Xue, (2019) ICJ Reports 142, para 19.

of a wrongful act of a continuing character as one in which the breach 'extends over the entire period during which the act continues and remains not in conformity with the international obligation'.[103] Formulated in the terms used by Judges Gaja and Xue, I agree that the Court was correct to characterise the administration as a process rather than to conceive the separation as an event.

It is salient also to note at this point a final aspect of the Court's consideration of the consequences, which will be further developed in section II, below. The Court confirmed – which is unsurprising – that respect for the right to self-determination is an obligation *erga omnes*. It cited its previous decision to that effect in *East Timor*,[104] and held that as a result 'all States have a legal interest in protecting that right'.[105] Although it left it to the General Assembly to 'pronounce on the modalities required' to complete the decolonisation of Mauritius, it also held that 'all Member States must co-operate with the United Nations to put those modalities into effect'.[106]

That second element is politically striking, seeming to be aimed directly at the United States.[107] It is also, however, legally fascinating: here the Court appears to draw a conclusion – the requirement on all states to cooperate in bringing an illegal situation to an end – that is associated primarily with norms of *ius cogens* status.[108] It does not – or, at least, does not explicitly – make a finding that the norm of self-determination is peremptory in character, however. Rather, the paragraph containing the reference to cooperation begins with the phrase '[s]ince respect for the right to self-determination is an obligation *erga omnes*',[109] and concludes with a reference to resolution 2625 noting the 'duty' on all states 'to promote, though joint and separate action, realization of the principle of equal rights and self-determination of peoples'.[110] This brief statement could support any one of three intriguing conclusions. First, it may be that the obligation to cooperate to bring an end to the illegal situation derives from the *erga omnes* nature of the norm. Although this appears at first sight to collapse to an unacceptable degree the distinction between norms *erga omnes* and *ius cogens*,[111] it closely echoes the

[103] ARSIWA (n 95), Art 14(2).
[104] *East Timor (Portugal v Australia)*, Judgment, (1995) ICJ Reports 90, para 29; for analysis, see ch 4, s V.
[105] *Chagos* (n 1) para 180.
[106] *Chagos* (n 1) para 180.
[107] A Twyman-Ghoshal, 'State Co-Offending: The Case of the Recolonization of the Chagos Archipelago and the Forced Eviction of the Chagossians' (2021) 29 *Critical Criminology* 311, *passim*, eg 318–19.
[108] The requirement to cooperate to end an illegal situation arising from the breach of a *ius cogens* norm is codified in ARSIWA as resulting automatically from the breach of a peremptory norm: ARSIWA (n 95) Art 41(1). Note, however, Bordin's point that the Court drew conclusions only on the obligation to cooperate, and not on the (as Bordin sees it) stronger duty not to recognise, also contained in Art 41. Bordin argues that the Court's decision to refer only to *erga omnes* and not *ius cogens* enabled it to arrive at this halfway-house: Bordin, 'Reckoning with British Colonialism' (n 47) 256.
[109] *Chagos* (n 1) para 180.
[110] Declaration on Friendly Relations (n 76) principle 5.
[111] It is notable, for example, that most modern textbooks of international law continue to draw a distinction between norms applicable *erga omnes* and norms of *ius cogens* status on the basis that only

Court's previous advisory opinion in *Wall*. There the Court drew a similar conclusion concerning the obligation not to recognise an illegal situation – also noted as an aspect of *ius cogens* in Article 41 ARSIWA – as arising from the *erga omnes* character of self-determination.[112]

Secondly, it may be that the obligation to cooperate to bring an end to illegal situations arising from the breach of self-determination is understood as a *sui generis* aspect of the norm of self-determination itself. In other words, it may be that a breach of the self-determination norm entails *erga omnes* consequences not because it fits within any one of the international law doctrines which could in the normal course of events give rise to consequences of that kind, but rather as a specific corollary of some aspect of that norm itself. Some slight support for such a finding could be drawn from the Court's use (in both *Chagos* and *Wall*) of principle 5 of the Declaration on Friendly Relations, which proclaims that:

> Every State has the duty to promote, through joint and separate action, realization of the principle of equal rights and self-determination of peoples, in accordance with the provisions of the Charter, and to render assistance to the United Nations in carrying out the responsibilities entrusted to it by the Charter regarding the implementation of the principle.[113]

This second possibility is, ultimately, also unconvincing, however. Although the phrasing in *Chagos* is ambiguous, in *Wall* the Court clearly employs this passage to demonstrate the *erga omnes* character of the norm of self-determination. Rather than deriving from it any statement of a special or *sui generis* status of self-determination, it is used to buttress the Court's reference to its judgment in *East Timor*.

The final possibility is that the Court, in noting the duty to cooperate which flowed from the breach of self-determination, did in fact recognise that norm to be of *ius cogens* status. An appraisal of that possibility demands a detailed assessment of the Court's treatment of self-determination as a whole, and it is to that question that the next section turns.

II. Self-Determination in the *Chagos* Advisory Opinion

In the *Chagos* Advisory Opinion the Court was given another opportunity to return to its now-familiar topic of self-determination. Although much in its

the latter category entails substantive consequences. Norms *erga omnes*, by contrast, relate primarily to standing: to establishing which states have an interest in any given wrongful act. See, inter alia, GI Hernández, *International Law* (Oxford, Oxford University Press, 2019) 65; J Crawford, *Brownlie's Principles of Public International Law*, 9th edn (Oxford, Oxford University Press, 2019) 580–87; M Shaw, *International Law*, 8th edn (Cambridge, Cambridge University Press, 2017) 92–93.

[112] *Wall* (n 15) para 159.

[113] Declaration on Friendly Relations (n 76) principle 5; cited in *Chagos* (n 1) para 180; *Wall* (n 15) para 156.

analysis aligns closely with its pronouncements in forgoing cases, it broke new ground in its opinion on the date at which (colonial) self-determination crystallised as a customary rule, and had the opportunity to revisit its (somewhat inconclusive) references in *Wall* to a possible higher normative status of self-determination. This section will consider each in turn, before finally I assess (in section III) the Court's treatment of self-determination in light of the four-part typology of self-determination norms established in these pages. I argue that for all the progress made by the Court in this opinion a lack of conceptual clarity continues to inhibit a deeper and more satisfying engagement with self-determination.

A. The Crystallisation of Colonial Self-Determination

As has been discussed above (section I.B), whether a norm of self-determination had crystallised by the date of Mauritius's independence on 12 March 1968 was at the centre of the question the Court was asked to address by the General Assembly. This opinion of the Court gives the international community, therefore, a far clearer answer than any previous treatment of the subject to the question of when the norm of self-determination in the colonial context crossed the divide from making a claim of *right*, to making a claim of *law*. Although the Court was asked only to specify a date *by which* the crystallisation had occurred (ie that it could not have been later than 12 March 1968), its opinion also implies an earlier date. On the basis of its analysis, it is now possible to argue with reasonable confidence that a customary norm of colonial self-determination existed following the adoption of the General Assembly's resolution 1514 (XV).

The Court's analysis on this point accords closely with the examination of resolution 1514 and the other major documents and declarations of the General Assembly conducted in chapter three, above.[114] The Court described the adoption of resolution 1514 as 'a defining moment in the consolidation of State practice on decolonization', and it found 'a clear relationship between resolution 1514 (XV) and the process of decolonization following its adoption'.[115] It referred to its 'declaratory character',[116] its 'normative wording'[117] and the immediate action it mandates as key aspects supporting that contention.[118] It noted also the overwhelming majority in favour of its adoption in the General Assembly,[119] and the

[114] See ch 3, ss IV–V.

[115] *Chagos* (n 1) para 150. It may be that the Court's approach to resolution 1514 here lends support to Michael Scharf's theory of the 'Grotian Moment', an accelerated process of customary law formation that occurs at a time of fundamental change: MP Scharf, 'Grotian Moments: The Concept' (2021) 42 *Grotiana* 193. I have argued elsewhere that labelling the passage of resolution 1514 as a 'Grotian' development adds little from an analytical point of view, and could tend to (unnecessarily) pathologise the process of custom formation of which it was a part: T Sparks, 'Grotian Moments in the Law of Self-Determination: Law, Rhetoric, and Reality' 43 *Grotiana* 159, 183.

[116] *Chagos* (n 1) para 152.

[117] ibid para 153.

[118] ibid para 153.

[119] ibid para 152.

indications in the statements made both by states in favour and abstaining that they anticipated that legal effects would flow from its adoption.[120]

It was argued above that resolution 1514 was, indeed, a turning point in the development of a distinct norm of self-determination applicable to the colonial context. The groundwork for that shift had been laid with the adoption of the UN Charter, which employed self-determination as a key tool in the process of decolonisation of territories subject to a trusteeship arrangement under its Chapter XII.[121] Before the adoption of resolution 1514, however, neither the Charter nor subsequent decisions and declarations of the General Assembly had extended those principles to all non-self-governing territories.[122] No such timorousness can be seen in resolution 1514: it reflects both the growing power and confidence of the former colonies in the General Assembly, and an increasingly overwhelming international consensus that colonialism represents an evil to which 'an end must be put'.[123] It does so in absolute terms, employing strongly normative language to declare that 'all peoples *have* the right to self-determination',[124] that 'immediate steps *shall* be taken',[125] and that the disruption of territorial integrity '*is* incompatible' with the UN Charter.[126] Beyond these textual factors, the Court referred to the debate in the General Assembly on 14 December 1960, and the statements made both by supporting states and those abstaining do indeed appear to disclose at least a nascent *opinio iuris*.[127] To this may be added the observation that subsequent state practice also supports the contention that – to make no stronger claim – 1960 is of particular significance for the decolonisation story: the years 1960–1970 saw a remarkable uptick in the number of former colonies attaining independence, with a particular concentration of new states created in the early years of that decade.[128]

In summary, although the Court's judgment does not purport to establish a specific date on which a norm of colonial self-determination crystallised, it further buttresses the contention that resolution 1514 was instrumental in that process.[129]

[120] See above, nn 66–71, and accompanying text.
[121] Chapter XII of the UN Charter (n 19).
[122] UN General Assembly Resolution 543 (VI), 5 February 1952; UN General Assembly Resolution 545 (VI), 5 February 1952; UN General Assembly Resolution 637 (VII), 16 December 1952; UN General Assembly Resolution 1188 (XII), 11 December 1957.
[123] UNGA Res 1514 (XV), preamble.
[124] ibid para 2 (emphasis added).
[125] ibid para 5 (emphasis added).
[126] ibid para 6 (emphasis added).
[127] For a wider discussion, see J Summers, '*Chagos*, Custom and the Interpretation of UN General Assembly Resolutions' in Burri and Trinidad (eds), *The International Court of Justice and Decolonisation* (n 40). Summers particularly notes, at 24, that the Court in fact avoids framing its analysis in terms of *opinio iuris*.
[128] Armitage provides a useful table of declarations of independence: D Armitage, *The Declaration of Independence: A Global History* (Cambridge, MA, Harvard University Press, 2007) 146–55; see further AP Blaustein, J Sigler and BR Beede, *Independence Documents of the World*, vols 1 and 2 (Dobbs Ferry, NY, Oceana Publications, 1977).
[129] S Allen, 'Reflections on the Treatment of General Assembly Resolutions in the *Chagos* Advisory Opinion' in Burri and Trinidad (eds), *The International Court of Justice and Decolonisation* (n 40) 46.

It was concluded above that that declaration was indeed sufficient to crystallise the customary norm of colonial self-determination, a contention that is strengthened by the analysis conducted by the Court. Although crystallisation is (almost) always better conceived as a process rather than an event,[130] it is possible to conclude that a legal norm (properly so-called) of colonial self-determination emerged at the latest in 1960 as a result of the adoption of resolution 1514.

B. Self-Determination and *Ius Cogens*

That the normative status of self-determination has long been a matter of controversy among both Judges and scholars has already been extensively discussed in these pages. That long-running disagreement raised its head again in the *Chagos* Advisory Opinion, and it is clear from the separate opinions that strongly differing opinions existed between the Judges on that question. It is perhaps for this reason that the Court's opinion is (almost studiously) vague on that point, and very carefully does not advance beyond the comments – themselves open to numerous interpretations – it made in its opinion in *Wall*.[131] Although it is clear that the Court regards (some forms of) self-determination to be of *erga omnes* character, in both cases it appeared to accord legal consequences to the breach of self-determination that are associated with the breach of *ius cogens* norms.

The relevant passages in *Wall* have been extensively discussed in the academic literature. There the Court found that an obligation 'not to recognize the illegal situation' and 'not to render aid or assistance in maintaining' that situation arose from 'the character and importance of the rights and obligations involved'.[132] In *Chagos* the Court completed the trio, noting that 'since respect for the right to self-determination is an obligation *erga omnes*', the breach of the right to

[130] See the observation by Brunnée and Toope that '[l]ike all law, customary international law gels; it does not crystallise': J Brunnée and S Toope, 'International Law and the Practice of Legality: Stability and Change' (2018) 49 *Victoria University of Wellington Law Review* 429, 443. Although note also that a question-mark hangs over those instances described in the literature as 'instant custom'. The notion of 'instant' custom is commonly attributed to Bin Cheng: B Cheng, 'United Nations Resolutions on Outer Space: "Instant" International Customary Law?' (1965) 5 *Indian Journal of International Law* 23, *passim*, esp 35–40; see also, among many others, P Weil, 'Towards Relative Normativity in International Law?' (1983) 77 *American Journal of International Law* 413, 435; J Kammerhofer, 'Uncertainty in the Formal Sources of International Law: Customary International Law and Some of its Problems' (2004) 15 *European Journal of International Law* 523, 530–31. Compare this idea with that of the 'Grotian Moment', a term originally coined by Richard Falk, but which has been most fully developed by Michael Scharf. Although the 'Grotian Moment' speaks of an accelerated process of custom formation, it is nevertheless not usually considered to be 'instant': MP Scharf, 'Seizing the "Grotian Moment": Accelerated Formation of Customary Law in Times of Fundamental Change' (2010) 43 *Cornell International Law Journal* 439; Scharf, 'Grotian Moments' (n 115); and further T Sparks and M Somos, 'Grotian Moments: An Introduction' (2021) 42 *Grotiana* 179.

[131] *Wall* (n 15) para 159.

[132] *Wall* (n 15) para 159.

self-determination created the obligation on 'all Member States' to 'co-operate with the United Nations'.[133] The significance of these three particular *erga omnes* effects flowing from breach of the norm is unmistakable: these are the three consequences identified by the ILC as flowing from 'a serious breach' of an obligation of *ius cogens* character:

1. That 'States shall cooperate to bring to an end through any lawful means any serious breach within the meaning of article 40' (ie of a peremptory norm);
2. That '[n]o State shall recognize as lawful a situation created by a serious breach within the meaning of article 40'; and
3. '[N]or [may States] render aid or assistance in maintaining that situation'.[134]

Moreover, that these are the consequences that arise as a result of a *serious* breach of a peremptory norm seems additionally significant. A breach of a peremptory norm was defined by the ILC in Article 40(2) as 'serious' 'if it involves a gross or systematic failure by the responsible State to fulfil the obligation'.[135] The ILC elaborated in its commentary that

> The word 'serious' signifies that a certain order of magnitude is necessary in order not to trivialize the breach and it is not intended to suggest that any violation of these obligations is not serious or is somehow excusable. But relatively less serious cases of breach of peremptory norms can be envisaged, and it is necessary to limit the scope of this chapter to the more serious or systematic breaches.[136]

It is possible to disagree with the ILC's conclusion that the category of breaches of peremptory norms may be subdivided into 'serious' and 'relatively less-serious' breaches. Nevertheless, that the ILC sought to limit the application of the three consequences listed in Article 41 only to 'serious' breaches of peremptory norms strongly implies their exceptional nature. The breach of norms of lesser status does not entail *erga omnes* effects.[137]

Differing conclusions have been drawn by academic commentators from the Court's somewhat Delphic pronouncements in *Wall*. Iain Scobbie argues that the Court's intention was indeed to disagree with the ILC's strict limitation of the Article 41 consequences to 'serious breaches' of peremptory norms. Rather, in his view the opinion 'indicates that the Court as a whole thought that obligations

[133] *Chagos* (n 1) para 180.
[134] ARSIWA (n 95), Art 41(1)–(2).
[135] ibid Art 40(2).
[136] ibid commentary on Art 40, para 7.
[137] Although note Judge Higgins's opinion to the contrary. She noted that '[t]hat an illegal situation is not to be recognized or assisted by third parties is self-evident, requiring no invocation of the uncertain concept of "*erga omnes*"': Separate Opinion of Judge Higgins, *Legal Consequences of the Construction of a Wall in the Occupied Palestinian Territory*, Advisory Opinion, (2004) ICJ Reports 207, [38]; and *contra* C Chinkin, *Third Parties in International Law* (Oxford, Clarendon Press, 1993) 292–293.

erga omnes do impose substantive obligations on third states' in the event of their breach.[138] Andrea Bianchi, too, notes this possibility, but wonders also whether

> perhaps, more simply what the Court had in mind was *jus cogens* and it simply did not dare mention it, preferring to focus on the *erga omnes* character of the obligations underlying *jus cogens* norms.[139]

Bianchi does not firmly conclude the point, but it seems that he leans overall to this latter point of view. He notes that:

> It is at the very least curious that the Court, in determining the legal consequences for States of the construction of the wall, conformed strictly to Article 41 of the ILC's Articles on State Responsibility without mentioning peremptory norms, not least to distinguish its own approach from that of the ILC.[140]

Alexander Orakhelashvili shares that conclusion, arguing that as the notion of *erga omnes* would be incapable in and of itself of grounding effects of these kinds, '[t]he reference to the concept of *erga omnes* was unnecessary and th[u]s can be viewed as the implicit acknowledgement of the effect of peremptory norms'.[141] The conclusions that can be drawn from the *Chagos* opinion appear to run directly parallel.

These views, indeed, were mirrored in the separate opinions of the Judges in *Chagos*. Judge Iwasawa clearly understands the *erga omnes* obligation of cooperation as arising from the *erga omnes* nature of self-determination, and phrases his comment on this aspect of the Court's judgment as expressing a logical relationship ('[a]s the right of peoples to self-determination has an *erga omnes* character … it follows … that all Member States have an obligation to co-operate').[142] By contrast, Judges Sebutinde, Robinson and Cançado Trindade each strongly assert the peremptory character of self-determination.[143] Judge Sebutinde's opinion is representative, when she states that:

> In my view, the Court should have expressly recognized that in the context of decolonization, the rule requiring respect for the territorial integrity of a self-determination unit is now a peremptory norm. It lies at the heart of the right to self-determination.[144]

[138] I Scobbie, 'Unchart(er)ed Waters? Consequences of the Advisory Opinion on the Legal Consequences of the Construction of a Wall in the Occupied Palestinian Territory for the Responsibility of the UN for Palestine' (2005) 16 *European Journal of International Law* 941, 952.

[139] A Bianchi, 'Dismantling the Wall: The ICJ's Advisory Opinion and its Likely Impact on International Law' (2004) 47 *German Yearbook of International Law* 343, 382.

[140] ibid 383.

[141] A Orakhelashvili, 'Legal Consequence of the Construction of a Wall in the Occupied Palestinian Territory: Opinion and Reaction' (2006) 11 *Journal of Conflict and Security Law* 119, 133–34.

[142] *Legal Consequences of the Separation of the Chagos Archipelago from Mauritius in 1965*, Declaration of Judge Iwasawa, (2019) ICJ Reports 340, para 9.

[143] Separate Opinion of Juge Sebutinde, *Chagos* (n 89) paras 30–46; Separate Opinion of Judge Robinson, *Chagos* (n 86) paras 48–89; *Legal Consequences of the Separation of the Chagos Archipelago from Mauritius in 1965*, Separate Opinion of Judge Cançado Trindade, (2019) ICJ Reports 156, *passim*, esp para 118.

[144] Separate Opinion of Judge Sebutinde, *Chagos* (n 89) para 31.

She is later scathing in her description of the Court's hesitancy to find self-determination (in the form of the protection of territorial integrity) to have *ius ogens* status as a 'failure':

> Having failed to recognize the peremptory status of the territorial integrity rule in the context of decolonization, the Court has failed to properly articulate the consequences of the United Kingdom's internationally wrongful conduct.[145]

Judge Robinson's process, sources and conclusions are similar. He lists five factors which speak to the peremptory character of self-determination:

> (a) it is a norm of customary international law that has become a peremptory norm of general international law, which is recognized and accepted by States as a whole even without conventional obligation to do so;
> (b) it is a norm that reflects principles that have a moral and humanitarian underpinning, serving a wider public, communitarian purpose;
> (c) it is a norm that protects one of the most fundamental values of the international community, namely, the obligation to respect the inherent dignity and worth of the human person …
> (d) it is a norm that is universally applicable in that it applies to all States;
> (e) … the instruments referred to show the recognition and acceptance by States of the non-derogability of the norm.[146]

The instruments to which Judge Robinson refers in this last include the UN Charter,[147] the Declaration on Friendly Relations,[148] the 1966 Human Rights Covenants,[149] the UN Human Rights Committee's general comment no 12,[150] the 1993 Vienna Declaration,[151] the UN Declaration on the Rights of Indigenous Peoples,[152] and the work of the ILC under its work streams on the law of treaties and on peremptory norms of general international law.[153]

Although room for reasonable disagreement remains, I share this conclusion. The right to self-determination in the colonial context must now be regarded as a norm of customary international law of a peremptory character. That conclusion

[145] ibid para 45.

[146] Separate Opinion of Judge Robinson, *Chagos* (n 86) para 77.

[147] ibid para 71(a); UN Charter (n 19).

[148] Separate Opinion of Judge Robinson, *Chagos* (n 86) para 71(b); *Friendly Relations* (n 76).

[149] Separate Opinion of Judge Robinson, *Chagos* (n 86) para 71(d); ICESCR/ICCPR (n 73).

[150] Separate Opinion of Judge Robinson, *Chagos* (n 86) para 71(e); Human Rights Committee, General Comment No. 12: Article 1 (Right to Self-Determination), 13 March 1984.

[151] Separate Opinion of Judge Robinson, *Chagos* (n 86) para 71(f); Vienna Declaration and Programme of Action, World Conference on Human Rights, 25th June 1993.

[152] Separate Opinion of Judge Robinson, *Chagos* (n 86) para 71(g); *UN Declaration on the Rights of Indigenous Peoples*, annexed to UNGA Res 61/295, 13 September 2007, UN Doc no A/Res/61/295.

[153] Separate Opinion of Judge Robinson, *Chagos* (n 86) para 73(a)–(b); Third Report on Peremptory Norms of General International Law (*Jus Cogens*) by Dire Tladi, Special Rapporteur, 12th February 2018, ILC 70th Session, UN Doc No A/CN.4/714; ILC, 'Draft Articles on the Law of Treaties with Commentaries', *Report of the International Law Commission on the Work of its 18th Session*, 1966, UN Doc No A/CN.3/191, 187.

can be drawn from the strong (and effective) right to independence of colonial territories which emerged from the documents and practice of the UN General Assembly – of which resolution 1514 was the keystone – and the remarkable consistency with which the international community has condemned colonialism since at least the 1960s. Although a small number of territories remain on the list of the Committee of Twenty-Four as 'territories whose people have not yet attained a full measure of self-government' – at the time of writing, seventeen such territories are listed[154] – the majority of these should be regarded as complex cases, rather than as persisting examples of clear colonial rule.[155] And it is inconceivable that an attempt by a state to establish a new colonial relationship over any inhabited part of the Earth's surface would not be subject to vociferous international condemnation.[156]

Although the conclusion is most probably correct, however, the reasoning employed by these Judges continues to disclose a problematic definitional uncertainty concerning self-determination that reduces the authority and usability of their opinions. In continuing to treat self-determination as a unitary norm, these opinions fail to differentiate appropriately between sources which refer to different kinds of self-determination, and thus produce reasoning that is both over- and under-inclusive. It may be speculated, too, that a failure adequately to differentiate between different forms of self-determination at least contributes to the Court's reluctance properly to recognise the normative status of (in *Wall*) the polity-based and (in *Chagos*) the colonial forms. The following section will examine the reasoning of the Court and certain of the separate opinions, in order to demonstrate that the four-part typology of self-determination suggested by this book would provide analytical rigour to the debate on self-determination, and would allow the various norms thus distinguished to realise their emancipatory potential.

[154] See UN, 'Non-Self-Governing Territories', www.un.org/dppa/decolonization/en/nsgt#_edn2.

[155] For example, the Committee of Twenty-Four's list includes the Falkland Islands/Islas Malvinas, which are the subject of a sovereignty dispute between the UK and Argentina, and the French Pacific Ocean territory of New Caledonia, which in both 2018 and 2021 voted to reject independence and to remain a part of France with its current constitutional status: '"Tonight France Is More Beautiful": Macron Hails New Caledonia's Rejection of Independence' *France 24* (12 December 2021) https://f24.my/8DtY.T.

[156] Although note that as BS Chimni (influentially) and others have argued, such colonial relationships do continue to exist and be established, albeit in the less overt form of great power domination, economic coercion and the use of international law to establish patterns of neocolonialism: BS Chimni, *International Law and World Order: A Critique of Contemporary Approaches*, 2nd edn (Cambridge, Cambridge University Press, 2017); BS Chimni, 'International Institutions Today: An Imperial Global State in the Making' (2004) 15 *European Journal of International Law* 1. There is no doubt that Chimni and others in the TWAIL movement have identified something very significant here, but it is beyond the scope of this present treatment – these new patterns of domination are of a sufficiently different kind that they would not be possible to subsume under the 1960s norm of colonial self-determination. For discussion, see ch 3, s V.B.ii, and further I Fofana, 'Afro-Asian Jurists and the Quest to Modernise the International Protection of Foreign-Owned Property, 1955–1975' (2020) 23 *Journal of the History of International Law/Revue d'histoire du droit international* 80.

III. Disambiguation: A Continuing Failure of Definition

In this book I have established and defended a four-part typology of self-determination that distinguishes between the polity-based, remedial, colonial and secessionary forms of self-determination.[157] These, I have argued, have distinct intellectual histories, justification narratives and areas of application. Moreover, they have been differently received by international legal actors and are of differing legal status. The polity-based form of self-determination has achieved a high and privileged position within the international legal system, is one of the system's fundamental (or 'basic', 'intransgressible') principles, and certainly numbers amongst international law's norms *ius cogens*. By contrast, the secessionary form of self-determination has, with only a very few exceptions, rarely been applied by states, and almost certainly does not exist as a legal norm. It remains a claim on the political level – an invocation of a moral-political rightness – that has not yet crystallised as a right (properly so-called) substantiated by law, and indeed may never do so. It has been argued here that colonial self-determination has also acquired the status of a legal norm of peremptory character, but it remains both ideationally and in operation distinct from the polity-based form.

A key finding of the analysis to this point has been that the ideational and operational separation between the types of self-determination results not in a unitary norm of self-determination with four 'flavours' or spheres of application; rather it is necessary to understand these as four separate forms of self-determination. In consequence, it is no argument in favour of the legal status of colonial self-determination to point to the legal status of the polity-based form; any more than the legal sources of the colonial form can buttress a secessionary argument. Failing adequately to respect these differences muddies the waters, conflates the forms and risks sending dangerously mixed messages of the kind seen in *Kosovo*.[158] By contrast, a clear-sighted distinction between the forms and their sources facilitates a principled and compelling argument to be made concerning the legal status (or lack thereof) of each individual form, and preserves an appropriate separation between them. This part will examine first the separate opinions of Judges Robinson and Sebutinde in order to show that such a confusion concerning the nature and sources of self-determination's forms was a feature of their reasoning.[159]

[157] See ch 1, s III.D.

[158] See ch 5, ss II.D and IV. It is worth recalling Vashakmadze and Lippold's concern that the Court's equivocal and uncertain treatment of self-determination could represent a worst of all worlds: 'Secessionist movements may interpret the Court's Advisory Opinion as favourable to their aspirations; however, the Court's Opinion does not give them a legal tool to realize those aspirations': M Vashakmadze and M Lippold, '"Nothing but a Road towards Secession"? – The International Court of Justice's Advisory Opinion on Accordance with International Law of the Unilateral Declaration of Independence in Respect of Kosovo' (2010) 2 *Göttingen Journal of International Law* 619, 647.

[159] The opinions of Judges Robinson and Sebutinde are chosen because these, together with that of Judge Cançado Trindade, assert a peremptory status for self-determination, and therefore undertake a

It will then turn briefly to the Court's opinion and will identify a similar definitional uncertainty in its treatment of self-determination.

A. The Separate Opinions: Judges Robinson and Sebutinde

In their opinions, Judges Robinson and Sebutinde refer to a wide range of documentary and other sources in support of the proposition that 'self-determination' has acquired *ius cogens* status. Although many of these unquestionably refer to the colonial form of self-determination, and are manifestly well-suited to establish the legal status of that form, other sources referenced are appropriate only to the polity-based form and have no place in that enquiry. Thus, although Judge Robinson refers to resolution 1514, the Friendly Relations Declaration and the human rights covenants – all of which were found above to have relevance for colonial self-determination[160] – his opinion also refers to Article 1(2) of the UN Charter, the UN Declaration on the Elimination of All Forms of Racial Discrimination and the International Convention on the Suppression and Punishment of the Crime of Apartheid, which are more appropriate to the polity-based form.[161] It was argued above, for example, that the reference to self-determination in the Charter's Article 1(2) is a mirror to Articles 2(1) and 2(4), which establish respectively the sovereign equality of Member States of the organisation, and the prohibition on the threat or use of force 'against the territorial integrity or political independence of any State'.[162] Although the Charter does make reference to self-determination as a tool to be applied in the colonial context (in its Chapters XI and XII), it was argued that these fall some way short of establishing a legal right of universal application, let alone one of peremptory status. Rather, the development of that Charter-based principle into the modern norm of colonial self-determination was to occur as the result of a number of authoritative reinterpretations and mobilisations of that right, most notably in the human rights covenants and in resolution 1514 itself. In other words, to refer to the peremptory status of Article 1(2) of the UN Charter (which it certainly has) is to do no more than to invoke sovereign equality (a foundational principle of the international legal order) and the prohibition of aggressive force (itself a norm of *ius cogens* status).[163] It has no bearing on the status of the colonial – or any other – form of self-determination.

substantial analysis of the norm and its sources. While the opinions of Judges Robinson and Sebutinde proceed along similar lines – and thus may conveniently be analysed together – Judge Cançado Trindade's opinion adopts quite a different process and methodology and is excluded purely on practical grounds. Readers of that opinion will note that the conclusions drawn here apply, mutatis mutandis, also to Judge Cançado Trindade's reasoning.

[160] Separate Opinion of Judge Robinson, *Chagos* (n 86) para 71.

[161] ibid para 71; UN Charter (n 19); UN General Assembly Resolution 1904 (XVIII), 20 November 1963; International Convention on the Suppression and Punishment of the Crime of Apartheid (New York, 30 November 1973).

[162] This argument is set out in full above, ch 3, s V.A.i.

[163] Indeed, Judge Sebutinde explicitly draws parallels between self-determination and the prohibition on aggression in order to argue that the former is also of peremptory status: Separate Opinion of Judge Sebutinde, *Chagos* (n 89) para 43.

Similarly, Judge Sebutinde refers to the *Wall* Advisory Opinion as an indication of the peremptory status of self-determination.[164] Although the Court did, as discussed, give a strong nod in the direction of an *ius cogens* status for self-determination in that opinion, it seems highly unlikely that the reference made is to the colonial form.[165] As was noted above, the *Wall* opinion appears to be an example of polity-based self-determination. The Court did not lay emphasis on the status of Palestine as a former mandate or a non-self-governing territory; rather it seemed most concerned with its position as an occupied territory and the maintenance of its territorial integrity.[166] A similar observation applies to the Court's treatment of self-determination in *East Timor*,[167] although here the judgment can be understood to refer to the colonial form, notwithstanding that the polity-based form could equally – or more easily – have applied. It was argued above that although the Court's focus on intervention and on sovereignty over natural resources implies that it was the polity-based form of self-determination that was primarily implicated in the Court's reasoning, the complex history of the territory does not permit a clean separation.[168]

Regrettable in themselves, purely for reasons of analytical rigour, these misfiring references reduce the usability and authority of these opinions by making them both over- and under-inclusive. Over-inclusive because they include sources which pertain primarily (or wholly) to other forms of self-determination, they are simultaneously under-inclusive in that they do not therefore make a self-standing argument in favour of the peremptory status of colonial self-determination. Although it has been argued here that Judges Robinson and Sebutinde were entirely correct in drawing the conclusion that colonial self-determination is a norm *ius cogens*, the inclusion of sources appropriate to polity-based self-determination artificially simplifies that enquiry. The peremptory status of polity-based self-determination is indisputable; that of colonial self-determination still at present demands justification. The opinions thus risk treating the peremptory status of colonial self-determination as a matter too easy to establish, and so of failing to a put forward a fully conclusive argument in its favour.[169] The missing element in this examination, in my opinion, is an assessment of international principle, which

[164] ibid para 39; *Wall* (n 15).

[165] *Wall* (n 15) para 159; see above, s II.B.

[166] For analysis of this point, see ch 4, s VIII.

[167] Separate Opinion of Judge Sebutinde, *Chagos* (n 89) para 38; *East Timor* (n 104).

[168] *East Timor* (n 104) para 29; for analysis, see ch 4, s 5.

[169] Writing extrajudicially, Judge Sebutinde argued that '[c]haracterisations of the right to self-determination as a peremptory norm stretch back many decades and are now far too common to ignore'. She then cited numerous sources, including the ICJ, proceedings before the ILC, statements by UN Special Rapporteurs, and statement by States, and concludes that '[t]hese statements and instruments inexorably demonstrate that the right to self-determination is a rule of special importance in the international legal order': J Sebutinde, 'Is the Right to Self-Determination *Jus Cogens*: Reflections on the *Chagos* Advisory Opinion' in D Tladi (ed), *Peremptory Norms of General International Law (Jus Cogens): Disquisitions and Disputations* (Leiden, Brill/Nijhoff 2021), 405. Notwithstanding that I agree with the conclusion, this kind of reasoning risks obscuring that not all of these sources refer to the same form of self-determination.

has been squeezed out as apparently unnecessary by the sheer, beguiling weight of hard sources. By contrast, I prefer the view that a source-based approach to norms *ius cogens* will almost never be adequate on its own. Numerous academic commentators have noted the paucity of a purely source-based enquiry in the field of *ius cogens* whether, as Bruno Simma and Philip Alston show,[170] on practical grounds or, with Christopher Ford, as a result of the nature of the category:

> Ultimately, rules of *jus cogens* may derive from no conventional doctrinal 'source' other than the 'conscience' of the international community. … [*J*]*us cogens* defines what the international community, as a whole, finds unacceptable. No positivist state 'consent' can justify breaking a norm, short of a general agreement upon a rule displacing that norm.[171]

Along similar lines, Simma noted that:

> The conclusion I draw from this is, that, for the International Court, too, once recognition by the 'international community as a whole' can be established, the question from which formal source rules of peremptory law can flow is more or less irrelevant. … The reason why certain rules possess such peremptory quality is to be seen in the universal recognition that these rules consecrate values which are not at the disposal of individual States (any more).[172]

Thus in the case of norms as yet lacking an explicit and universal recognition as *ius cogens* it is not sufficient merely to point to an overwhelming weight of sources, or to remark on the centrality or importance of the norm for the international legal system as it exists. Rather, it must be shown that the norm has the character of expressing a facet of international conscience; that it is 'so basic, so important, that it is more than slightly artificial to argue that states are legally bound to comply with [it] simply because there exists an agreement between them to that effect'.[173] That assessment is and must be normative in character, and must not 'hid[e] ethical and political considerations behind the screen of objectivity of positive law rules derived directly or inductively from the will of States'.[174] To acknowledge the many and powerful arguments from principle and policy that have in actuality motivated (and continue to motivate) the prohibition on colonialism is no failure

[170] They comment that '[s]ettled practices of States as regards *jus cogens* are elusive to grasp, mainly because most, if not all, rules of *jus cogens* are prohibitive in substance; they are rules of abstention. How does one marshal conclusive evidence of abstentions? Abstentions *per se* mean nothing; they are meaningful only when considered in the light of the intention motivating them': B Simma and P Alston, 'The Sources of Human Rights Law: Custom, Jus Cogens, and General Principles' (1988–89) 12 *Australian Yearbook of International Law* 82, 103–04. Cutting through the heavy sarcasm, D'Amato seems to make a similar point: A D'Amato, 'It's a Bird, It's a Plane, It's Jus Cogens!' (1990) 6 *Connecticut Journal of International Law* 1.

[171] CA Ford, 'Adjudicating Jus Cogens' (1994–95) 13 *Wisconsin Journal of International Law* 145, 152.

[172] B Simma, 'From Bilateralism to Community Interest in International Law' (1994) 250 *Recueil des Cours* 217, 292.

[173] M Koskenniemi, 'The Pull of the Mainstream' (1990) 88 *Michigan Law Review* 1946, 1946–47.

[174] A Bianchi, 'Human Rights and the Magic of Jus Cogens' (2008) 19 *European Journal of International Law* 491, 495.

of legal reasoning; on the contrary, it is a recognition of the vitally important role law plays in (international) society, which both shapes and is shaped by its provisions. The separate opinions – and the case for a peremptory norm of colonial self-determination – would have been stronger for engaging more deeply and openly with these aspects.

B. The Court's Opinion

I suggest that in the Court's opinion, too, there is evidence of an ongoing failure of definition in the realm of self-determination's norms which restrict the potential of its analysis. This conclusion must, however, remain somewhat speculative: the reasoning offered by the Court on the status of self-determination is so thin that, as discussed above, it is challenging even to ascertain what status the Court intended to imply for it.[175] That lack of specificity may, in itself, be indicative, however: as was argued above, a reluctance to accord any particular status to self-determination is commonplace among courts and scholars, and I suggested that this reluctance derives from a failure to separate self-determination's forms. The idea of self-determination as a unitary norm encourages a homogenisation, wherein those manifestations that are viewed as more useful or acceptable are nevertheless treated with suspicion, hedged with caveats and restricted, for fear of an inadvertent transfer of the colour of legitimacy to the other forms. If this is a single norm, then it becomes more difficult to say that it is illegal in some situations and legal in others; it becomes more difficult to draw the dividing line between its acceptable and unacceptable applications; and there is a presumption that legality in one sphere will bleed over into other areas of the norm's application. Evidence of such attitudes can be seen in the practice of states in relation to self-determination, and instances in which states, courts and others have been reluctant to accept the legality or applicability of self-determination principles – perhaps because they fear the resultant presumption of legality that will reflect onto other areas of self-determination's application – have been highlighted in the discussion above.[176]

It may be that it is a fear of such spillover effects that has led the Court, here, studiously to avoid any comment on the nature or status of self-determination that goes beyond the remarks it made in *Wall*. Like in *Wall*, the Court has raised the somewhat dissonant prospect of an obligation under Article 41 ARSIWA being triggered by a norm as a result of its character as an obligation *erga omnes*, but it declined to clarify that relationship further. More tellingly still, the Court did so on the basis of the same sources cited in *Wall*; its previous judgment in *East Timor* and

[175] See above, s II.B.

[176] See, for example, Court's reluctance to engage adequately with remedial self-determination in *Kosovo*, ch 5, s II.B. Summers comments that 'states can always agree on the right [self-determination] in a general form, while disagreeing on its specific implications': Summers, 'Interpretation of Resolutions' (n 127) 27 (footnotes omitted).

the injunction on states 'to promote, through joint and separate action, realization of the principle of equal rights and self-determination of peoples' contained in resolution 2625.[177] That paragraph, however, is far more appropriate to a conclusion on the nature of polity-based self-determination than that of the colonial form. As such, it was more appropriately deployed in *Wall*'s examination of polity-based self-determination than in *Chagos*. It may be, too, that the fear of saying too much helps to explain the Court's failure to engage with the human rights tragedy at the centre of this case, as eloquently identified and critiqued by Peter Hilpold.[178] An understanding of self-determination that recognises the separate character of its forms would therefore be much to be welcomed, both from the point of view of analytical rigour, and because it would release the Court from an artificial fear of unintended spillover effects.

C. Final Thoughts

Although the *Chagos* opinion represents a much more satisfying engagement with self-determination than any judgment by an international court to date, I have argued that conceptual uncertainty continues to restrict the ability of courts and others adequately to treat self-determination. That uncertainty means that self-determination, rather than appropriately being divided into four forms with different sources, scopes and status, is seen as being unitary in character. The conflation detracts from the analytical rigour of self-determination analyses. As was seen in the opinions of Judges Robinson and Sebutinde, inquiries into self-determination tend to be both over- and under-inclusive where self-determination is seen as unitary. Of equal concern, that conflation raises the spectre of unintended and unwarranted spillover effects, in which the assertion of a (higher) legal status for self-determination in one of its aspects (the polity-based or colonial forms) has the effect of (apparently) supporting also a legal character for (for example) the secessionary form.

Although I have criticised the lack of differentiation between self-determination's forms found in the separate opinions of Judges Robinson and Sebutinde, these remain inspiring opinions. While it is to be regretted that the Judges characterise self-determination as a unitary norm, in so doing they follow the vast majority of treatments of the norm to this point in international law. In every other respect these opinions are a model of international adjudication as it should be: rigorous, brave and principled. In their treatment of the legal sources of self-determination and decolonisation they mobilise the true authority and emancipatory potential of law, and demonstrate the power of combining forensic

[177] *Chagos* (n 1) para 180.

[178] Hilpold, '"Humanizing" Self-Determination' (n 94) 201–02, 206–11; for an account of that human tragedy, see Motha, 'Tragic Emplotments' (n 86).

legal analysis with a full and present regard for the human consequences of law. It is to be hoped that in future opinions of this type will benefit additionally from an appropriately disaggregated view of self-determination, which can only lend support and weight to that analysis.

IV. Conclusion

The *Chagos* Advisory Opinion promises a coming of age by the ICJ. While in the past it has often sought to construct its authority by carefully stepping around controversial questions and avoiding conclusions with significant political implications, in *Chagos* it has met those political questions head on. Whether this change of attitude evidences a belief on the part of the Court that it now has sufficient authority to speak confidently, or a strategy on its part to set aside deference in favour of building its authority through bravery, probity, and a manifest commitment to the emancipatory potential of law, it is in either case much to be welcomed. Still more so are the separate opinions of Judges Robinson and Sebutinde, which offered a vision of a powerful and principled model of international adjudication that keeps the human factor always in centre-view, without sacrificing any degree of analytical rigour.

Aside from promising a bright future for international adjudication, the *Chagos* opinion makes a substantive contribution to the law of self-determination. Although there remain gaps and missed opportunities – this chapter has referred in particular to an ongoing definitional confusion concerning self-determination's forms – the Court has established more precisely than previous treatments the point in time at which colonial self-determination emerged as a legal norm (at the latest with the adoption of resolution 1514 in 1960), and it has strongly implied that that norm has in the modern day acquired a peremptory status. I concur entirely with both of those conclusions, notwithstanding that the argument here has highlighted that a more rigorous separation between the polity-based and colonial forms of self-determination would have enabled the Court to go further, in particular in relation to this latter. Future judgments must address this continuing uncertainty, and in so doing will allow the potential of the various forms of self-determination to be realised.

7

Interregnum

Since at least 1320 – and likely long before – some form of self-determination idea has been a motive force in the world. It has had a world-making effect in at least two great 'moments' – in the 'age of revolution' of the long nineteenth century, which owed its intellectual structure to the American and French declarations of 1776 and 1789; and the decolonisation era, the core of which was the period 1945–1970. And beyond these time periods, it continues to construct and reconstruct the world around us in smaller – but by no means insignificant – ways.

Whether ideationally or in practical terms, there is no denying the significance of self-determination. Few subjects have attracted more attention from international law scholars; have been at the heart of more international court judgments; or have been proclaimed with greater gravitas by the General Assembly. And beyond these markers, there is something instinctively important about self-determination. As discussed above, the search for the origin of self-determination's story – the first self-determination precedent – is fascinating and instructive, but it would perhaps be yet more noteworthy if we were to find no connection between the early declarations; if the drafters in 1320, 1581 and 1776 had independently generated a set of ideas sufficiently similar that we now capture them under the same term. One can think of only a very few other concepts that have so lit the world.

And yet, amid this similarity, this book has told a story of difference. I have argued that self-determination cannot be adequately captured either as a unitary norm ('self-determination'), or under the framework of the 'internal' and 'external' expressions of self-determination that scholars have sought to apply to it. Those terms, as I argued in Chapter I, are incoherent: by basing our analytical framework on the *effect* of a (successful) self-determination claim, scholars routinely conflate different self-determination claims and narratives. Focusing on this superficial similarity, we miss more significant differences: for example between claims which make a remedial claim (a secession as a last resort in the face of a serious and persistent denial of human or civil rights), and that of a group which claims a right to a state purely on the basis of its separate sense of itself. Moreover, the internal/external distinction produces a framework that is not capable of making principled distinctions between claims, even where such distinctions are to be found in international law as it is practised: what I have termed colonial self-determination, notwithstanding that it is unambiguously lawful (indeed, is a norm *ius cogens*), is lumped together with remedial and secessionary claims under the crude heading of 'external' self-determination.

By contrast, in this book I have argued that self-determination – as it is currently understood by international law – must be subdivided into four forms:

- *Polity-based self-determination*: a claim on the part of a people of a political society (a polity) that they form a single political unit, and should be treated as such for the purposes of the governance of their shared social and political life. Within that are the twin corollary claims that all individuals within a given society should have the opportunity to participate in its governance on the basis of equality, and that only those individuals within a given society should do so: external interference in its sociopolitical life is illegitimate.
- *Secessionary self-determination*: an identity-based claim to secession and independence that treats the separate character of a group as sufficient justification for its independent nationhood. The same principle can also ground a claim on the part of a group with a single identity but which is split between several entities to unify itself within a single state, either through parallel secessions and unification, or irredentism.
- *Remedial self-determination*: a claim by a group that has suffered a severe abuse of its rights vis-a-vis other groups within a state, and seeks autonomy, secession or irredentism as a remedy of last resort.
- *Colonial self-determination*: a claim by a colonial possession or other non-self-governing territory to independence and self-government. Generally, the idea has been applied to 'saltwater' colonial territories, or those separated from the municipal state by an ocean.

As I have argued in these pages, it is appropriate to term these ideas 'forms' rather than 'norms' of self-determination, given that they are of different legal status. Of the four forms, only polity-based and colonial self-determinations have acquired the status of legal norms under international law: secessionary self-determination is certainly not the subject of a positive entitlement (although it is not actively prohibited – see chapter five), and the legal status of remedial self-determination is unclear. Those forms that have gained recognition in international law have, however, acquired a high status: colonial self-determination is certainly of *erga omnes* and likely *ius cogens* status (see chapters three and six), while polity-based self-determination has been embedded in the post-Charter legal order as the fundamental organising principle of the international community.

I have argued that the term 'self-determination' stands in relation to the individual forms in a manner similar to that of genus to species in taxonomy. 'Self-determination' is a category of ideas, not an idea in itself, and certainly not a norm of law. Although it designates a group of concepts which all share significant common features – and so are related in much the same way that lions are related to snow leopards – it is itself only a marker for those similarities. To refer to 'self-determination' without specifying one or other of the forms tells the reader virtually nothing.

With that framework in mind, I have in this book retold the story of self-determination from 1320 to the present day.[1] I first considered the historical origins and prehistory of the self-determination idea (chapter two) and, while I noted that the vocabulary of self-determination (as a term of political theory) would have been alien to the drafters of any self-determination declaration before c.1920, I argued that ideas that are recognisably of a similar kind could be discerned as early as the Declaration of Arbroath in 1320 and Plakkaat van Verlatinghe in 1581. Whether or not those documents were an influence on the 1776 American Declaration of Independence and the Déclaration des droits de l'homme et du citoyen of 1789, it is certain that these eighteenth-century declarations were instrumental in shaping the age of revolution, as Hobsbawm dubs it, that followed them.[2]

The age of revolution, the first great self-determination moment, was born largely of the remedial form of self-determination: across Latin America, Europe and elsewhere, a wave of independence movements proclaimed their right to throw off someone else's sovereignty on the grounds of the long abuses suffered at the hands of their erstwhile rulers. As the long nineteenth century came to a fiery end in the brutality of the First World War, however, another form of self-determination began to take shape. As chapter three discussed, in the wartime promises of the European combatants, together with the growing strength of home-grown independence movements, the first murmurings of what was to become the next great independence moment began to grow. With the end of the war, the mandates system of the League of Nations gave textual expression to a principle – not yet a norm – of self-determination in the context of governing the colonies of the defeated powers, albeit one that was still weak and subordinated to other political considerations. As that system developed into the trusts system of the United Nations, and more significantly still in the practice of an increasingly confident General Assembly, with a swelling majority of postcolonial Member States, colonial self-determination developed from a principle to a norm, and over time acquired a high status.

Chapter four then switched its focus to self-determination as it has been understood before courts. In the years post-1945 there are few subjects which have more frequently been discussed before the ICJ, and there are significant

[1] Or at least: until the events of 24 February 2022 (briefly discussed in ch 5), the consequences of which – for self-determination, Europe, the world and most importantly for Ukraine – are yet to play out. As discussed above, at the time of writing Russia has not actively invoked self-determination in its 2022 invasion of the eastern Oblasts of Ukraine (as it did – albeit spuriously – in Crimea in 2014), but it may yet do so. Its rhetoric around genocide (already provisionally rejected by the ICJ) may be an attempt to lay the groundwork for a 'remedial' secession of Donetsk and Luhansk. Nevertheless, and irrespective of whether Russia invokes remedial self-determination, the conflict in Ukraine *is* a self-determination conflict: Ukraine's sovereignty, statehood and ability to choose its future direction – in sum, its polity-based self-determination – and Russia's refusal to accept its right to do so, is at the heart of the conflict.

[2] EJ Hobsbawm, *The Age of Revolution: Europe 1789–1848* (London, Weidenfeld & Nicolson, 1962).

treatments, too, by the African Commission on Human and Peoples' Rights and Supreme Court of Canada,[3] as well as by the quasi-judicial Badinter Arbitration Commission.[4] I discussed the ICJ's judgments and opinions in *Namibia*,[5] *Western Sahara*,[6] *East Timor*[7] and *Wall*,[8] which establish without question the growing significance of self-determination – in one form or another – during this period. In *East Timor* the Court proclaimed 'self-determination' to be a norm of *erga omnes* character, and declared that 'it is one of the essential principles of contemporary international law'.[9] In *Wall*, albeit implicitly, the Court ascribed to Israel's breach of self-determination the consequences that would normally be expected to flow from the breach of a norm *ius cogens*.[10]

In coming to those findings, however, the ICJ showed little awareness of the different norms of self-determination with which it was dealing. As recourse to the separate and dissenting opinions helped to demonstrate, alongside a close reading of the majority opinion, in *East Timor* it is likely it was the colonial form of self-determination that was primarily under consideration by the Judges, while in *Wall* the Court was faced with a question better related to the polity-based form. The mismatch of sources, circumstances and conclusions in these cases indicated the ways in which the conceptual confusion afflicting self-determination reduces the rigour and analytical value of judicial treatments of its forms. However, that trend was amplified in the Court's 2010 *Kosovo* advisory opinion (chapter five).[11]

In *Kosovo* the Court seemed at pains, more than anything else, to say nothing at all. With Judge Simma,[12] it was noted that the Court chose materially to reinterpret the General Assembly's question so as to bring it within the ambit of the so-called *Lotus* principle. In so doing, the Court appeared (as I have argued) to be motivated by a desire to avoid what I have termed 'spillover' legitimacy: that is to say, the impression that if 'self-determination' is lawful in one situation or factual context, then it must be legal in different circumstances. These 'spillover' legitimacy concerns are the direct consequence of the conceptual confusion besetting self-determination and the inadequate delimitation between its forms. In the

[3] *Katangese Peoples' Congress v Zaire*, African Commission on Human and Peoples' Rights, Communication no 75/92 (1995); *Reference Re Secession of Quebec* (1998) 2 SCR 217.

[4] Opinions of the Badinter Commission (1992) 31 ILM 1494.

[5] *Legal Consequences for States of the Continued Presence of South Africa in Namibia (South West Africa) notwithstanding Security Council Resolution 276 (1970)*, Advisory Opinion, (1971) ICJ Reports 16.

[6] *Western Sahara*, Advisory Opinion, (1975) ICJ Reports 12.

[7] *East Timor (Portugal v Australia)*, Judgment, (1995) ICJ Reports 90.

[8] *Legal Consequences of the Construction of a Wall in the Occupied Palestinian Territory*, Advisory Opinion, (2004) ICJ Reports 136.

[9] *East Timor* (n 7) para 29.

[10] *Wall* (n 8) para 159.

[11] *Accordance with International Law of the Unilateral Declaration of Independence in Respect of Kosovo*, Advisory Opinion, (2010) ICJ Reports 403.

[12] *Accordance with International Law of the Unilateral Declaration of Independence in Respect of Kosovo*, Declaration of Judge Simma, (2010) ICJ Reports 478, paras 8–10.

Kosovo proceedings, concerns of this type led the Court to adopt a minimalist approach that, far from containing the damaging consequences of a liberalisation of secession (as the Court seemed to see it), unleashed them. The Court denied that any prohibition on declarations of independence existed in international law, and ignored the question of secession entirely; relying rather on the 'unique' circumstances of Kosovo at the time of the declaration and placing the emphasis on the effective displacement of Serbian sovereignty over the province. In so doing, it cast secession as a matter outwith the ambit of international law: secession is a fact of which international law will take note if it is successful, and will treat as an entirely internal matter if it is not. Simultaneously, the Court refused adequately to examine remedial self-determination, but in passing cast doubt on the development of an international law norm.[13]

Beyond the perpetuation of conceptual confusion, however, the *Kosovo* opinion had damaging real-world consequences: as chapter five discussed, the *Kosovo* advisory opinion's focus on practical consequences (ie whether the erstwhile sovereign's authority over the territory in question *actually* was displaced) created a precedent capable of being invoked in the context of the Russian invasion and annexation of Crimea in 2014.[14] Spurious though that justification may have been, and although it is not clear to what extent the existence of a convenient precedent actually shaped Russia's actions (as opposed to merely shaping its rhetorical strategy), nevertheless that the Court's opinion was capable of being (mis)used in this way should be a cause for concern – and doubly so given the events of 2022. The Court effectively removed secession from the ambit of legal rules (and so liberated political and power-based approaches in the place of principled regulation), something that should be of great concern to all those interested in a stable and peaceful international order, irrespective of one's views on the rights and wrongs of secession.

In these circumstances, the *Chagos* advisory opinion of 2019 – the subject of chapter six – can be seen as a spectacular return to form.[15] *Chagos* has given us a glimpse of international adjudication at its best: brave, principled, unyielding to great power interests. Certainly, it will have facilitated matters that the Court here was on the more familiar ground of the colonial norm of self-determination, and that its subject matter was among the worst of the copious abuses of the British Empire. However commodious the circumstances, however, few observers expected an advisory opinion that would be so forthright in identifying and condemning both the historical and current abuses of the United Kingdom and the United States. In the course of the opinion, the Court was faced with the task of identifying whether colonial self-determination had emerged as a legal rule by the time of the detachment of Chagos from Mauritius in 1965. It found that

[13] See ch 5, s II.B.

[14] See ch 5, s III.A.

[15] *Legal Consequences of the Separation of the Chagos Archipelago from Mauritius in 1965*, Advisory Opinion, (2019) ICJ Reports 95.

it had done so, and laid particular significance on the UN General Assembly's resolution 1514 (XV) – the Declaration on the Granting of Independence to Colonial Countries and People – of 1960.[16] Although the Court was criticised by some of its members for failing to go further – Judges Cançado Trindade, Robinson and Sebutinde all used their separate opinions to argue strongly that colonial self-determination is a norm *ius cogens* – the advisory opinion in *Chagos* should overall be warmly welcomed.

Nevertheless, here too the conceptual confusion concerning self-determination continued to afflict the advisory opinion. Both in the majority opinion, and in the separate opinions of Cançado Trindade, Robinson and Sebutinde, sources most appropriately considered as relating to the colonial form of self-determination are discussed alongside – and with insufficient differentiation from – sources relating to the polity-based form. Although there were not, as in *Kosovo*, negative practical consequences arising from this lack of conceptual clarity, it does tend to reduce the rigour and authority of the opinions to some extent. Perhaps, too, the reluctance of the majority to declare colonial self-determination to be a norm *ius cogens* – as Cançado Trindade, Robinson and Sebutinde so persuasively urged the Court to do – can be attributed to the same 'spillover' legitimacy concerns that have been identified elsewhere.

Whatever the effects on any specific case or claim, in this book I have argued that the failure to differentiate between different forms of self-determination has a warping effect on its forms. Rather than being understood as a unitary or binary norm, self-determination must be understood as a category – a genus – with only minimal content of its own. Rather, and in particular when treated at the level of international law, it is necessary to differentiate between specific *forms* of self-determination – the species – which while ideationally related remain things in themselves: that one form of self-determination is given the status of a legal norm need have no necessary effect on any of the other species that form part of the self-determination genus. In this book, I have identified four such forms: the polity-based, colonial, remedial and secessionary self-determinations.

So far, so good. But here we do not reach a conclusion, merely an interregnum. Although the conceptual clarity of the framework proposed here – or so I argue – makes it possible to draw rational distinctions between different claims to self-determination at both the conceptual level and the level of international law, that is only half the story. Once it is possible to draw distinctions, we need to know which distinctions to draw. Should colonial self-determination be a norm of *ius cogens* status? How should international law treat the aspect of polity-based self-determination which demands internal political equality within states? What would be the arguments in favour or against recognising a remedial self-determination right, and under what conditions? And how should international

[16] UN General Assembly Resolution 1514 (XV), 14 December 1960.

law react to attempts to secede purely on the grounds of the separate sense of self of the group involved? In all of this, how can the emancipatory potential of law be best realised, balancing as it must between the demands of separateness and togetherness inherent in national and international societies that are, and will always be, associations of minorities?[17]

This book has not engaged with such questions, but I hope it has enabled them. Answering them will be the task of scholars, courts and others in the coming years. For one thing is certain: the idea of self-determination that has lit the world since at least 1320 shows no sign of going away.

[17] I borrow this phrase from John le Carré: J le Carré, *Smiley's People* (Pan Books, 1980) 92.

BIBLIOGRAPHY

Abi-Saab G, 'On Discretion: Reflections on the Nature of the Consultative Function of the International Court of Justice' in L Boisson de Charzournes and P Sands (eds), *International Law, the International Court of Justice, and Nuclear Weapons* (Cambridge, Cambridge University Press, 1999).

Akram S and Lynk M, 'The Wall and the Law: A Tale of Two Judgments' (2006) 24 *Netherlands Quarterly of Human Rights* 61.

Allen S, 'Reflections on the Treatment of General Assembly Resolutions in the *Chagos* Advisory Opinion' in T Burri and J Trinidad (eds), *The International Court of Justice and Decolonisation* (Cambridge, Cambridge University Press, 2021).

Alschner W and Charlotin D, 'The Growing Complexity of the International Court of Justice's Self-citation Network' (2018) 29 *European Journal of International Law* 83.

Alsop V, *Melius Inquirendum, or a Sober Inquiry into the Reaonings of the Serious Inquiry: Wherein the Inquirers Cavils against the Principle, His Calumnies against the Preachings and Practices of the Non-Conformists Are Examined and Refelled* (1679).

Alstyne RW van, 'Woodrow Wilson and the Idea of the Nation State' (1961) 37 *International Affairs* 293.

Alves AA and Moreira JM, *The Salamanca School* (New York, Bloomsbury, 2009).

Ambar S, 'Woodrow Wilson: Impact and Legacy' (Miller Center of Public Affairs, University of Virginia, 2016).

Amato A D', 'It's a Bird, It's a Plane, It's Jus Cogens!' (1990) 6 *Connecticut Journal of International Law* 1.

Anghie A, *Imperialism, Sovereignty and the Making of International Law* (Cambridge, Cambridge University Press, 2004).

Anghie A, 'Bandung and the Origins of Third World Sovereignty' in L Eslava, M Fakhiri and V Nesiah (eds), *Bandung, Global History, and International Law: Critical Pasts and Pending Futures* (Cambridge, Cambridge University Press, 2018).

Annacker C, 'Part Two of the International Law Commission's Draft Articles on State Responsibility' (1994) 37 *German Yearbook of International Law* 206.

Armitage D, 'The Contagion of Sovereignty: Declarations of Independence since 1776' (2005) 52 *South African History Journal* 1.

Armitage D, *The Declaration of Independence: A Global History* (Cambridge, Mass, Harvard University Press, 2007).

Armitage D, '1320, 1776, and All That: A Tale of Two "Declarations"' (Forthcoming) 101 *Scottish Historical Review*.

Armstrong P, *Stirling Bridge and Falkirk 1297–98: William Wallace's Rebellion* (Hailsham, Osprey Publishing, 2003).

Arnade P, *Beggars, Iconoclasts, and Civic Patriots: The Political Culture of the Dutch Revolt* (Ithaca, NY, Cornell University Press, 2008).

Ascherson N, *Stone Voices: The Search for Scotland* (London, Granta Books, 2014).

Aspremont J d' and Singh S, 'Introduction: The Life of International Law and its Concepts' in J d'Aspremont and S Singh (eds), *Concepts for International Law: Contributions to Disciplinary Thought* (Cheltenham, Edward Elgar, 2019).

Aust A, *Modern Treaty Law and Practice*, 2nd edn (Cambridge, Cambridge University Press, 2007).

Austin J, *The Province of Jurisprudence Determined* (Cambridge, Cambridge University Press, 1995).

Baines E, *History of the Wars of the French Revolution, from the Breaking Out of the War, in 1792, to the Restoration of a General Peace in 1815: Comprehending the Civil History of Great Britain and France, During That Period*, vol II (London, Longman, Hurst, Rees, Orme, and Brown, 1818).

Bak McKenna M, 'The Referendum on Catalan Self-Determination: Long Shots and Legal Flair' *Völkerrechtsblog* (27 September 2017).

Barbour J, *The Bruce: Edited and with an Introduction by AAM Duncan* (Edinburgh, Canongate Books, 2010).

Barrow GWS, *Robert Bruce and the Community of the Realm of Scotland* (Berkeley, University of California Press, 1965).

Baxter R, *Richard Baxter's Catholick Theologie: Plain, Pure, Peaceable, for Pacification of the Dogmatical Word-Warriours* (London, Nevill Simmons, 1675).

Beal N, 'Defending State Sovereignty: The ICJ Advisory Opinion on Kosovo and International Law' (2012) 21 *Transnational Law & Contemporary Problems* 549.

Beaulac S, 'The Westphalian Legal Orthodoxy – Myth or Reality' (2000) 2 *Journal of the History of International Law/Revue d'histoire du droit international* 148.

Belda Plans J, *Grandes Personajes del Siglo de Oro Español* (Madrid, Ediciones Palabra, 2013).

Berman HR, Lyons O and Falk RA, 'Indigenous Peoples and the Right to Self-Determination' (1993) 87 *Proceedings of the Annual Meeting of the American Society of International Law* 190.

Berman N, 'Sovereignty in Abeyance: Self-Determination and International Law' (1988) 7 *Wisconsin International Law Journal* 51.

Bhuta N, 'Great Expectations – East Timor and the Vicissitudes of Externalised Justice' (2001) 12 *Finnish Yearbook of International Law* 165.

Bianchi A, 'Dismantling the Wall: The ICJ's Advisory Opinion and its Likely Impact on International Law' (2004) 47 *German Yearbook of International Law* 343.

Bianchi A, 'Human Rights and the Magic of Jus Cogens' (2008) 19 *European Journal of International Law* 491.

Bianchi A, 'Textual Interpretation and (International) Law Reading: The Myth of (in) Determinacy and the Genealogy of Meaning' in P Bekker, R Dolzer and M Waibel (eds), *Making Transitional Law Work in the Global Economy – Essays in Honour of Detlev Vagts* (Cambridge, Cambridge University Press, 2010).

Bianchi A, 'Law, Time, and Change: The Self-regulatory Function of Subsequent Practice' in G Nolte (ed), *Treaties and Subsequent Practice* (Oxford, Oxford University Press, 2013).

Bianchi A, 'The Game of Interpretation in International Law: The Players, the Cards, and Why the Game Is Worth the Candle' in A Bianchi, D Peat and M Windsor (eds), *Interpretation in International Law* (Oxford, Oxford University Press, 2015).

Bienvenu P, 'Secession by Constitutional Means: Decision of the Supreme Court of Canada in the Quebec Secession Reference' (1999–2000) 21 *Journal of Public Law and Policy* 1.

Binder G, 'The Case for Self-Determination' in R McCorquodale (ed), *Self-Determination in International Law* (Aldershot, Ashgate Dartmouth, 2000).

Blake M, 'Civil Disobedience, Dirty Hands, and Secession' in FR Tesón (ed), *The Theory of Self-Determination* (Cambridge, Cambridge University Press, 2016).

Blaustein AP, Sigler J and Beede BR, *Independence Documents of the World*, vols 1 and 2 (Dobbs Ferry, NY, Oceana Publications, 1977).

Bordin FL, 'Reckoning with British Colonialism: The *Chagos* Advisory Opinion' (2019) 78 *Cambridge Law Journal* 253.

Bordin FL, 'State Responsibility in Advisory Proceedings: Thoughts on Judicial Propriety and Multilateralism in the *Chagos* Opinion' in T Burri and J Trinidad (eds), *The International Court of Justice and Decolonisation* (Cambridge, Cambridge University Press, 2021).

Borgen C, 'The *Kosovo* Advisory Opinion, Self Determination, and Secession' *Opinio Juris* (23 July 2010).

Breeze DJ, *The Stone of Destiny: A Symbol of Nationhood* (Edinburgh, Historic Scotland, 1997).

Brunnée J and Toope S, 'International Law and the Practice of Legality: Stability and Change' (2018) 49 *Victoria University of Wellington Law Review* 429.

Buchanan A, 'Secession, Self-Determination, and the Rule of International Law' in J McMahan and R McKim (eds), *The Morality of Nationalism* (Oxford, Oxford University Press, 1997).

Buchanan A, 'Theories of Secession' (1997) 26 *Philosophy & Public Affairs* 31.
Buchanan A, 'Democracy and Secession' in M Moore (ed), *National Self-Determination and Secession* (Oxford, Oxford University Press, 1998).
Buchheit L, *Secession: The Legitimacy of Self-Determination* (New Haven, CT, Yale University Press, 1978).
Burchill R, 'The ICJ Decision in the Case Concerning East Timor: The Illegal Use of Force Validated?' (1997) 2 *Journal of Armed Conflict Law* 1.
Burri T, 'The *Kosovo* Opinion and Secession: The Sounds of Silence and Missing Links' (2010) 11 *German Law Journal* 881.
Callahan MD, *A Sacred Trust: The League of Nations and Africa 1929–1946* (Brighton, Sussex Academic Press, 2004).
Campos AS, 'Francisco Suárez's Conception of the Social Contract' (2019) 75 *Revista Portuguesa de Filosofia* 1195.
Campos AS, 'The Idea of the Social Contract in the History of "Agreementism"' (2019) 24 *The European Legacy* 579.
Cannon J, 'Edinburgh, Treaty Of, 1328' in R Crowcroft and J Cannon (eds), *The Oxford Companion to British History*, 2nd edn (Oxford, Oxford University Press, 2015).
Carpenter D, *The Struggle for Mastery: Britain 1066–1284* (London, Penguin Books, 2004).
Carroll S, *Martyrs and Murderers: The Guise Family and the Making of Europe* (Oxford, Oxford University Press, 2011).
Carroll S, 'The Rights of Violence' (2012) 214 *Past & Present* 127.
Cassese A, *Self-Determination of Peoples: A Legal Reappraisal* (Cambridge, Cambridge University Press, 1995).
Cerone J, 'The World Court's Non-Opinion' *Opinio Juris* (25 July 2010).
Chadwick E, *Self-Determination in the Post-9/11 Era* (London, Routledge, 2011).
Chambers R (ed), 'Alexander III', *A Biographical Dictionary of Eminent Scotsmen*, vol I, 2nd edn (Glasgow, Blackie and Son, 1857).
Charney JI, 'Self-Determination: Chechnya, Kosovo, and East Timor' (2001) 34 *Vanderbilt Journal of Transnational Law* 455.
Cheng B, 'United Nations Resolutions on Outer Space: "Instant" International Customary Law?' (1965) 5 *Indian Journal of International Law* 23.
Chimni BS, 'International Institutions Today: An Imperial Global State in the Making' (2004) 15 *European journal of international law* 1.
Chimni BS, 'The Past, Present and Future of International Law: A Critical Third World Approach' (2007) 8 *Melbourne Journal of International Law* 499.
Chimni BS, 'Capitalism, Imperialism, and International Law in the Twenty-First Century Symposium' (2012) 14 *Oregon Review of International Law* 17.
Chimni BS, *International Law and World Order: A Critique of Contemporary Approaches*, 2nd edn (Cambridge, Cambridge University Press, 2017).
Chimni BS, 'The Grotian Tradition, Grotian Moment, and Decolonization: A TWAIL Perspective' (2021) 42 *Grotiana* 252.
Chinkin C, *Third Parties in International Law* (Oxford, Clarendon Press, 1993).
Chinkin C, 'East Timor: A Failure of Decolonization' (1999) 20 *Australian Yearbook of International Law* 35.
Christakis T, 'The ICJ Advisory Opinion on Kosovo: Has International Law Something to Say about Secession?' (2011) 24 *Leiden Journal of International Law* 73.
Ćirković E, 'An Analysis of the ICJ Advisory Opinion on Kosovo's Unilateral Declaration of Independence' (2010) 11 *German Law Journal* 895.
Clark RS, 'The "Decolonization" of East Timor and the United Nations Norms on Self-Determination and Aggression' (1980–81) 7 *Yale Journal of World Public Order* 2.
Cobban A, *National Self-Determination* (Oxford, Oxford University Press, 1944).
Cobban A, *The Nation State and National Self-Determination*, 2nd edn (London, Collins, 1969).

Conte GB, *Latin Literature: A History*, ed DP Fowler and GW Most, tr JB Solodow (Baltimore, MD, Johns Hopkins University Press, 1994).
Cooper TM, 'The Numbers and the Distribution of the Population of Medieval Scotland' (1947) 26 *Scottish Historical Review* 2.
Corbet J, *A Humble Endeavour of Some Plain and Brief Explication of the Decrees and Operations of God, about the Free Actions of Men: More Especially of the Operations of Divine Grace* (London, Tho. Parkhurst, 1683).
Corten O, 'The Obligation of Cessation' in J Crawford, A Pellet and S Olleson (eds), *The Law of International Responsibility* (Oxford, Oxford University Press, 2010).
Cowan EJ, *The Declaration of Arbroath, 1320: 'For Freedom Alone'* (Edinburgh, Birlinn, 2020).
Crawford J, 'Outside the Colonial Context' in WJA Macartney (ed), *Self-Determination in the Commonwealth* (Aberdeen, Aberdeen University Press, 1988).
Crawford J, *The Creation of States in International Law*, 2nd edn (Oxford, Clarendon Press, 2006).
Crawford J, *State Responsibility: The General Part* (Cambridge, Cambridge University Press, 2013).
Crawford J, 'Kosovo and the Criteria for Statehood in International Law' in M Milanović and M Wood (eds), *The Law and Politics of the Kosovo Advisory Opinion* (Oxford, Oxford University Press, 2015).
Crawford J, *Brownlie's Principles of Public International Law*, 9th edn (Oxford, Oxford University Press, 2019).
Crespi Reghizzi Z, 'The *Chagos* Advisory Opinion and the Principle of Consent to Adjudication' in T Burri and J Trinidad (eds), *The International Court of Justice and Decolonisation* (Cambridge, Cambridge University Press, 2021).
Cristescu A, *The Right to Self-Determination: Historical and Current Development on the Basis of United Nations Instruments: Study Prepared by Aureliu Cristescu, Special Rapporteur of the Sub-Commission on Prevention of Discrimination and Protection of Minorities* (New York, United Nations, 1981).
Cummings-Bruce N, 'UN Sounds Alarm Over Killings in Idlib as Syria Cease-Fire Collapses' *New York Times* (9 August 2019).
Dalrymple D, *Annals of Scotland from the Accession of Robert I. Surnamed Bruce, to the Accession of the House of Stewart* (Edinburgh, Balfour & Smellie, 1779).
Dawidowicz M, 'Trading Fish or Human Rights in Western Sahara? Self-Determination, Non-Recognition and the EC–Morocco Fisheries Agreement' in D French (ed), *Statehood and Self-Determination: Reconciling Tradition and Modernity in International Law* (Cambridge, Cambridge University Press, 2013).
Davies JR and Broun D, 'The Manuscripts of the Declaration' in D Broun et al (eds), *The Dynamic Edition of the Declaration of Arbroath*.
Derrida J, 'Force of Law: The "Mystical Foundation of Authority"' in *Acts of Religion*, ed G Anidjar (London, Routledge, 2013).
Dugard J, 'The Opinion on South-West Africa ("Namibia"): The Teleologists Triumph' (1971) 88 *South African Law Journal* 460.
Dugard J, *Recognition and the United Nations* (Cambridge, Grotius Publications, 1987).
Dugard J, 'What Is a State in International Law? How Is This to Be Determined?' in N Blokker, D Dam-de Jong and V Prislan (eds), *Furthering the Frontiers of International Law: Sovereignty, Human Rights, Sustainable Development: Liber Amicorum Nico Schrijver* (Leiden, Brill/Nijhoff, 2021).
Duke A, 'A Legend in the Making: News of the "Spanish Inquisition" in the Low Countries in German Evangelical Pamphlets, 1546–1550' (1997) 77 *Nederlands Archief voor Kerkgeschiedenis/Dutch Review of Church History* 125.
Dunbar AH, *Scottish Kings: A Revised Chronology of Scottish History, 1005–1625*, 2nd edn (Edinburgh, David Douglas, 1906).
Duncan AAM, *The Kinship of the Scots, 842–1292: Succession and Independence* (Edinburgh, Edinburgh University Press, 2016).
Duursma J, *Fragmentation and the International Relations of Micro-states: Self-Determination and Statehood* (Cambridge, Cambridge University Press, 1996).

Dworkin R, *Taking Rights Seriously* (London, Duckworth, 2005).
Edelstein D, 'What Was the Terror?' in D Andress (ed), *The Oxford Handbook of the French Revolution* (Oxford, Oxford University Press, 2015).
Emerson R, 'Self-Determination' (1971) 65 *American Journal of International Law* 459.
Epps V, 'Self-Determination after Kosovo and East Timor' (1999–2000) 6 *ILSA Journal of International and Comparative Law* 445.
Epstein P, 'Behind Closed Doors: "Autonomous Colonization" in the Post United Nations Era – The Case for Western Sahara' (2009) 15 *Annual Survey of International and Comparative Law* 107.
Etzioni A, 'The Evils of Self-Determination' (1992–93) 89 *Foreign Policy* 21.
Falnes OJ, *Norway and the Nobel Peace Prize* (New York, AMS Press, 1938).
Fassbender B, 'The United Nations Charter as Constitution of the International Community' (1998) 36 *Columbia Journal of Transnational Law* 529.
Filmer R, *Patriarcha: Or the Natural Power of Kings* (London, Richard Chiswell, 1680).
Fine JVA, *The Early-Medieval Balkans: A Critical Survey from the Sixth to the Late Twelfth Century* (Ann Arbor, University of Michigan Press, 1991).
Fofana I, 'Afro-Asian Jurists and the Quest to Modernise the International Protection of Foreign-Owned Property, 1955–1975' (2020) 23 *Journal of the History of International Law/Revue d'histoire du droit international* 80.
Ford CA, 'Adjudicating Jus Cogens' (1994–95) 13 *Wisconsin Journal of International Law* 145.
Foster CE, 'Legal Consequence of the Construction of a Wall in the Occupied Palestinian Territory: The Advisory Opinion of the International Court of Justice, Human Security and Necessity' (2005) 2 *New Zealand Yearbook of International Law* 51.
French D, 'Introduction' in D French (ed), *Statehood and Self-Determination: Reconciling Tradition and Modernity in International Law* (Cambridge, Cambridge University Press, 2013).
Fuller L, *The Morality of Law* (New Haven, CT, Yale University Press, 1969).
Gewirth A, 'The Basis and Content of Human Rights' (1978–79) 13 *Georgia Law Review* 1143.
Gielis G and Soen V, 'The Inquisitorial Office in the Sixteenth-Century Habsburg Low Countries: A Dynamic Perspective' (2015) 66 *Journal of Ecclesiastical History* 47.
Gjerset K, *History of the Norwegian People*, vol 2 (New York, AMS Press, 1969).
Goldmann M, '„Ich bin Ihr Freund und Kapitän". Die deutsch-namibische Entschädigungsfrage im Spiegel intertemporaler und interkultureller Völkerrechtskonzepte' in P Dann, I Feichtner and J von Bernstorff (eds), *(Post-)Koloniale Rechtswissenschaft* (forthcoming).
Gordon E, 'Old Orthodoxies Amid New Experiences: The South West Africa (Namibia) Litigation and the Uncertain Jurisprudence of the International Court of Justice' (1971) 1 *Denver Journal of International Law and Policy* 65.
Gough JW, *The Social Contract: A Critical Study of its Development*, 2nd edn (Oxford, Clarendon Press, 1957).
Grimal H, *Decolonization: The British, French, Dutch and Belgian Empires 1919–1963*, tr S De Vos tr (Boulder, CO, Westview Press, 1978).
Hague E, 'National Tartan Day: Rewriting History in the United States' (2014) 38 *Scottish Affairs* 94.
Haines RM, *King Edward II: Edward of Caernarfon, His Life, His Reign, and Its Aftermath, 1284–1330* (Montreal, McGill-Queen's University Press, 2003).
Hanauer LS, 'The Irrelevance of Self-Determination Law to Ethno-national Conflict: A New Look at the Western Sahara Case' (1995) 9 *Emory International Law Review* 133.
Hanna RM, 'Right to Self-Determination in In Re Secession of Quebec' (1999) 23 *Maryland Journal of International Law and Trade* 213.
Hannum H, *Autonomy, Sovereignty and Self-Determination: The Accommodation of Conflicting Rights* (Philadelphia, University of Pennsylvania Press, 1990).
Hannum H, 'Rethinking Self-Determination' (1993) 34 *Virginia Journal of International Law* 1.
Hannum H, 'The Advisory Opinion on Kosovo: An Opportunity Lost, or a Poisoned Chalice Refused?' (2011) 24 *Leiden Journal of International Law* 155.
Harper D, '"Self-Determination" (n.)' (*Online Etymology Dictionary*, 2001–17).

Hartmann M, *Humanismus und Kirchenkritik: Matthias Flacius Illyricus als Erforscher des Mittelalters* (Stuttgart, Thorbecke, 2001).
Hegel GWF, *Grundlinien der Philosophie des Rechts*, 2 Auflage, ed G Lasson (Leipzig, Felix Meiner, 1921).
Held D, *Cosmopolitanism: Ideals and Realities* (Cambridge, Polity Press, 2010).
Herman LL, 'Western Sahara Advisory Opinion, ICJ Reports 1975, p 12 – An Analysis of the World Court Judgment in the Western Sahara Case' (1976–77) 41 *Saskatchewan Law Review* 133.
Hernández GI, *The International Court of Justice and the Judicial Function* (Oxford, Oxford University Press, 2014).
Hernández GI, *International Law* (Oxford, Oxford University Press, 2019).
Hernández GI and Sparks T, 'Categorising Self-Determination: Four Forms' (2020) 63 *German Yearbook of International Law* 223.
Higgins R, *The Development of International Law through the Political Organs of the United Nations* (Oxford, Oxford University Press, 1963).
Hill RMT, 'Belief and Practice as Illustrated by John XXII's Excommunication of Robert Bruce' (1972) 8 *Studies in Church History* 135.
Hilpold P, 'The International Court of Justice's Advisory Opinion on Kosovo: Perspectives of a Delicate Question' (2009) 14 *Australian Review of International and European Law* 259.
Hilpold P, '"Humanizing" the Law of Self-Determination – The Chagos Island Case' (2022) 91 *Nordic Journal of International Law* 189.
Hobsbawm EJ, *The Age of Revolution: Europe 1789–1848* (London, Weidenfeld and Nicolson, 1962).
Holland RF, *European Decolonization, 1918–1981: An Introductory Survey* (New York, St Martin's Press, 1985).
Holt MP, *The French Wars of Religion, 1562–1629* (Cambridge, Cambridge University Press, 1995).
Hoque A, 'Existence, Breach and Responses to the Breach of State Responsibility: A Critical Analysis' (2016) 53 *Journal of Law, Policy and Globalization* 136.
Hoveden R de, *The Annals of Roger de Hoveden: Comprising the History of England and of Other Countries of Europe from AD 732 to AD 1201*, vol I, tr HT Riley (London, HG Bohn, 1853).
Hoveden R de, *The Annals of Roger de Hoveden: Comprising the History of England and of Other Countries of Europe from AD 732 to AD 1201*, vol II, tr HT Riley (London, HG Bohn, 1853).
Howse R and Teitel R, 'Delphic Dictum: How Has the ICJ Contributed to the Global Rule of Law by its Ruling on Kosovo?' (2010) 11 *German Law Journal* 841.
Huberich CH, *The Political and Legislative History of Liberia*, vol 1 (New York, Central Book Co, 1947).
Iurlaro F, 'From Exemplary Individuals to Private Persons with Rights – International Law 1500–1647: Vitoria, Gentili, and Grotius' in T Sparks and A Peters (eds), *The Individual in International Law – History and Theory* (Forthcoming).
Jablonski JJ, Jr, 'The Dark Side of President Woodrow Wilson's Progressive Political Thought: Its Race-Historicism and Other Anti-democratic Aspects' (Unpublished Thesis, Claremont Graduate University, 2018).
Jacobs D, 'The Kosovo Advisory Opinion: A Voyage by the ICJ into the Twilight Zone of International Law' *The Hague Justice Portal* (12 October 2010).
Jacobs D, 'International Court of Justice, Accordance with International Law of the Unilateral Declaration of Independence in Respect of Kosovo, Advisory Opinion of 22 July 2010: Case Comment' (2011) 60 *ICLQ* 799.
Janis MW, 'The International Court of Justice: Advisory Opinion on the Western Sahara' (1976) 17 *Harvard Journal of International Law* 609.
Jansen JC and Osterhammel J, *Dekolonisation: Das Ende der Imperien* (München, CH Beck, 2013).
Jennings I, *The Approach to Self-Government* (Cambridge, Cambridge University Press, 1956).
Josephson H, 'Outlawing War: Internationalism and the Pact of Paris' (1979) 3 *Diplomatic History* 377.
Jovanović M, 'After the ICJ's Advisory Opinion on Kosovo: The Future of Self-Determination Conflicts' (2012) 3 *Annals of the Faculty of Law in Belgrade – International Edition* 292.

Jowitt J, 'Monkey See, Monkey Sue? Gewirth's Principle of Generic Consistency and Rights for Non-human Agents' (2016) 19 *Trinity College Law Review* 71.
Kammerhofer J, 'Uncertainty in the Formal Sources of International Law: Customary International Law and Some of its Problems' (2004) 15 *European Journal of International Law* 523.
Kant I, *Grundlegung zur Metaphysik der Sitten*, ed C Horn, C Mieth and N Scarano (Frankfurt am Main, Suhrkamp, 2007).
Kaplan LS, *Thomas Jefferson: Westward the Course of Empire* (Plymouth, Rowman & Littlefield, 1998).
Kavanagh R, 'Oil in Troubled Waters: The International Court of Justice and East Timor' (1996) 18 *Sydney Law Review* 87.
Kellas JG, *The Politics of Nationalism and Ethnicity*, 2nd edn (Basingstoke, Macmillan, 1998).
Kelsen H, *The Law of the United Nations: A Critical Analysis of its Fundamental Problems* (London, Stevens & Sons, 1951).
Kennedy JC, *A Concise History of the Netherlands* (Cambridge, Cambridge University Press, 2017).
Kesler CR, 'Woodrow Wilson and the Statesmanship of Progress' in BCS Watson (ed), *Progressive Challenges to the American Constitution* (Cambridge, Cambridge University Press, 2017).
Klabbers J, 'The Right to Be Taken Seriously: Self-Determination in International Law' (2006) 28 *Human Rights Quarterly* 186.
Knight DB, 'Territory and People or People and Territory? Thoughts on Postcolonial Self-Determination' (1985) 6 *International Political Science Review* 248.
Knox R and Tzouvala N, 'Looking Eastwards: The Bolshevik Theory of Imperialism and International Law' in K Greenman et al (eds), *Revolutions in International Law* (Cambridge, Cambridge University Press, 2021).
Köbler G, *Deutsches etymologisches Rechtswörterbuch* (Tübingen, Mohr, 1995).
Koenigsberger HG, *Monarchies, States Generals and Parliaments: The Netherlands in the Fifteenth and Sixteenth Centuries* (Cambridge, Cambridge University Press, 2001).
Kohen MG, 'Introduction' in MG Kohen (ed), *Secession: International Law Perspectives* (Cambridge, Cambridge University Press, 2006).
Kolb R, *The International Law of State Responsibility: An Introduction* (Cheltenham, Edward Elgar, 2017).
Korsgaard CM, *The Sources of Normativity*, ed O O'Neill (Cambridge, Cambridge University Press, 1996).
Korsgaard CM, *The Constitution of Agency: Essays on Practical Reason and Moral Psychology* (Oxford, Oxford University Press, 2008).
Koskenniemi M, 'The Pull of the Mainstream' (1990) 88 *Michigan Law Review* 1946.
Koskenniemi M, 'National Self Determination Today: Problems of Legal Theory and Practice' (1994) 43 *ICLQ* 241.
Krisch N, 'Crimea and the Limits of International Law' *EJIL:Talk!* (10 March 2014).
Kuźniak B and Kabat-Rudnicka D, 'Advisory Opinion or Judgment? The Case of the Chagos Archipelago' (2021) 13 *Przegląd Prawniczy Uniwersytetu im. Adama Mickiewicza* 45.
Lakoff G, *Women, Fire, and Dangerous Things: What Categories Reveal about the Mind* (Chicago, University of Chicago Press, 1987).
Langtoft P de, *The Chronicle of Pierre de Langtoft: In French Verse, from the Earliest Period to the Death of King Edward I*, vol 2, tr T Wright (London, Longmans, Green, Reader, and Dyer, 1866).
Larenz K, *Methodenlehre der Rechtswissenschaften*, 3rd edn, ed C-W Canaris (Berlin, Springer-Verlag, 1995).
Larsen K, *A History of Norway* (Princeton, NJ, Princeton University Press, 1948).
Law M, 'The Chagos Request: Does it Herald a Rejuvenation of the International Court of Justice's Advisory Function?' (2018) 9 *Queen Mary Law Journal* 25.
Lawson JP, *Historical Tales of the Wars of Scotland, and of the Border Raids, Forays, and Conflicts*, vol I (Edinburgh, A Fullarton, 1839).
Lenin VI, 'The Right of Nations to Self-Determination' in *VI Lenin: Collected Works*, vol 20, ed J Katzer, tr B Isaacs and J Fineberg (Moscow, Progress, 1964).

Lesaffer R, 'A Short Legal History of the Netherlands' in S Taekema (ed), *Understanding Dutch Law* (Den Haag, Boom Juridische Uitgevers, 2004).
Lesaffer R, 'Aggression before Versailles' (2018) 29 *European Journal of International Law* 773.
Levy GJ, 'Advisory Opinion on the Western Sahara' (1975–76) 2 *Brooklyn Journal of International Law* 289.
Libæk I, Sternersen Ø and Asle S, *The History of Norway after 1814*, tr J Irons (Oslo, Font Forlag, 2012).
Limm P, *The Dutch Revolt 1559–1648* (London, Routledge, 2014).
Lissitzyn OJ, 'International Law and the Advisory Opinion on Namibia' (1972) 11 *Columbia Journal of Transnational Law* 50.
Locke J, *Two Treatises of Government* (London, Awnsham Churchill, 1690).
Luard E, *A History of the United Nations: The Age of Decolonization, 1955–1965*, vol 2 (London, Macmillan, 1989).
Lucas S, 'Justifying America: The Declaration of Independence as a Rhetorical Document' in T Benson (ed), *American Rhetoric: Context and Criticism* (Carbondale, Southern Illinois University Press, 1989).
Lucas S, 'The Rhetorical Ancestry of the Declaration of Independence' (1998) 1 *Rhetoric & Public Affairs* 143.
Lumumba-Kasongo T, 'Why Katanga's Quest for Self-Determination and Secession Failed' in R Berekereab (ed), *Self-Determination and Secession in Africa: The Post-colonial State* (Abingdon, Routledge, 2015).
MacCormick N, *Legal Reasoning and Legal Theory* (Oxford, Clarendon Press, 1978).
MacDiarmid C, 'Masoud Barzani: Why it's Time for Kurdish Independence' *Foreign Policy* (15 June 2017).
Mackintosh J, *Historic Earls and Earldoms of Scotland* (Aberdeen, W Jolly, 1898).
Macklem P, 'Self-Determination in Three Movements' in FR Tesón (ed), *The Theory of Self-Determination* (Cambridge, Cambridge University Press, 2016).
MacMillan K, 'Secession Perspectives and the Independence of Quebec' (1999) 7 *Tulane Journal of International and Comparative Law* 333.
Maffei MC, 'The Case of East Timor before the International Court of Justice – Some Tentative Comments' (1993) 4 *European Journal of International Law* 223.
Makarova N, 'UN Court Ruling Doesn't Change Moscow's Stance on Kosovo' *RT* (5 August 2010).
Mälksoo L, 'The Soviet Approach to the Right of Peoples to Self-Determination: Russia's Farewell to the *Jus Publicum Europaeum*' (2017) 19 *Journal of the History of International Law/Revue d'histoire du droit international* 200.
Mann M, 'Little Ice Age' in T Munn, MC MacCracken and JS Perry (eds), *Encyclopedia of global environmental change*, vol 1 (Chichester, Wiley, 2002).
Maogoto JN, 'Somaliland: Scrambled by International Law?' in D French (ed), *Statehood and Self-Determination: Reconciling Tradition and Modernity in International Law* (Cambridge, Cambridge University Press, 2013).
Mar K del, 'The Myth of Remedial Secession' in D French (ed), *Statehood and Self-Determination: Reconciling Tradition and Modernity in International Law* (Cambridge, Cambridge University Press, 2013).
Marks TA, 'Spanish Sahara – Background to the Conflict' (1976) 75 *African Affairs* 3.
Marxsen C, 'The Crimea Crisis: An International Law Perspective' (2014) 74 *Zeitschrift für ausländisches öffentliches Recht und Völkerrecht* 367.
Mason RA, 'The Declaration of Arbroath in Print, 1680–1705' (2021) 72 *Innes Review* 158.
Matz N, 'Civilization and the Mandate System under the League of Nations as Origin of Trusteeship' (2005) 9 *Max Planck Yearbook of United Nations Law* 47.
Mayhew J, *A Discourse, Concerning Unlimited Submission and Non-Resistance to the Higher Powers: With Some Reflections on the Resistance Made to King Charles I, & on the Anniversary of His Death: In Which the Mysterious Doctrine of That Prince's Saintship & Martyrdom Is Unriddled: The Substance of Which Was Delivered in a Sermon Preached in the West Meeting-House in Boston the Lord's Day after the 30th of Jan., 1749–50* (Boston, D Fowle, 1750).

Mazower M, *Governing the World: The History of an Idea* (London, Penguin Books, 2013).
McCorquodale R, 'Self-Determination: A Human Rights Approach' (1994) 43 *ICLQ* 857.
McCorquodale R, 'Introduction' in R McCorquodale (ed), *Self-Determination in International Law* (Aldershot, Ashgate Dartmouth, 2000).
McGoldrick D, 'The Tale of Yugoslavia: Lessons for Accommodating National Identity in National and International Law' in S Tierney (ed), *Accommodating National Identity: New Approaches in International and Domestic Law* (The Hague, Martinus Nijhoff, 2000).
McLean I and McMillan A, *State of the Union: Unionism and the Alternatives in the United Kingdom since 1707* (Oxford, Oxford University Press, 2005).
Meester DH, 'The International Court of Justice's Kosovo Case: Assessing the Current State of International Legal Opinion on Remedial Secession' (2010) 48 *Canadian Yearbook of International Law* 215.
Mégret F, 'The Right to Self-Determination: Earned, not Inherent' in FR Tesón (ed), *The Theory of Self-Determination* (Cambridge, Cambridge University Press, 2016).
Meier V, *Yugoslavia: A History of its Demise*, tr S Ramet (London, Routledge, 1999).
Milanović M, 'Arguing the Kosovo Case' in M Milanović and M Wood (eds), *The Law and Politics of the Kosovo Advisory Opinion* (Oxford, Oxford University Press, 2015).
Milanović M, 'A Footnote on Secession' *EJIL:Talk!* (26 October 2017).
Milanović M and Wood M (eds), *The Law and Politics of the Kosovo Advisory Opinion* (Oxford, Oxford University Press, 2015).
Minas S, 'Why the ICJ's Chagos Archipelago Advisory Opinion Matters for Global Justice – and for "Global Britain"' (2019) 10 *Transnational Legal Theory* 123.
Moore M, 'Introduction: The Self-Determination Principle and the Ethics of Secession' in M Moore (ed), *National Self-Determination and Secession* (Oxford, Oxford University Press, 1998).
Morris CW, 'The Case for National Self-Determination' in FR Tesón (ed), *The Theory of Self-Determination* (Cambridge, Cambridge University Press, 2016).
Motha S, '"The Object Is to Frighten Him with Hope": Questioning the Tragic Emplotments of International Law and Decolonisation in the Chagos Archipelago' in S Chalmers and S Pahuja (eds), *Routledge Handbook of International Law and the Humanities* (London, Routledge, 2021).
Muharremi R, 'A Note on the ICJ Advisory Opinion on Kosovo' (2010) 11 *German Law Journal* 867.
Müller D, 'The Question Question' in M Milanović and M Wood (eds), *The Law and Politics of the Kosovo Advisory Opinion* (Oxford, Oxford University Press, 2015).
Musgrave TD, *Self-Determination and National Minorities* (Oxford, Clarendon Press, 1997).
Naldi G, 'Western Sahara: Suspended Statehood or Frustrated Self-Determination?' (2005) 13 *African Yearbook of International Law* 11.
Natarajan U, 'Creating and Recreating Iraq: Legacies of the Mandate System in Contemporary Understandings of Third World Sovereignty' (2011) 24 *Leiden Journal of International Law* 799.
Nierop H van, '*Alva's Throne* – Making Sense of the Revolt in the Netherlands' in G Darby (ed), *The Origins and Development of the Dutch Revolt* (London, Routledge, 2001).
Nollkaemper A, 'The Court and its Multiple Constituencies: Three Perspectives on the Kosovo Advisory Opinion' in M Milanović and M Wood (eds), *The Law and Politics of the Kosovo Advisory Opinion* (Oxford, Oxford University Press, 2015).
Norris O et al, '"Bellum Catilinae" by Sallust' (Utrecht University Library: Special Collections, July 2020).
Nozick R, *Anarchy, State and Utopia* (Oxford, Basil Blackwell, 1974).
Ntovas AXM, 'The Paradox of Kosovo's Parallel Legal Orders in the Reasoning of the Court's Advisory Opinion' in D French (ed), *Statehood and Self-Determination: Reconciling Tradition and Modernity in International Law* (Cambridge, Cambridge University Press, 2013).
Nzongola-Ntalaja G, *The Congo from Leopold to Kabila: A People's History* (New York, Zed Books, 2002).
O'Donoghue A, *Constitutionalism in Global Constitutionalisation* (Cambridge, Cambridge University Press, 2014).
Ohlin JD, 'The Right to Exist and the Right to Resist' in FR Tesón (ed), *The Theory of Self-Determination* (Cambridge, Cambridge University Press, 2016).

Oklopcic Z, 'The Referendum on Catalan Self-Determination (Part I): Endemic Rhetoric, Interpretive Hypocrisy and Legal Imagination' (*Völkerrechtsblog*, 22 September 2017).
Oklopcic Z, 'The Referendum on Catalan Self-Determination (Part II): Endemic Rhetoric, Interpretive Hypocrisy and Legal Imagination' (*Völkerrechtsblog*, 25 September 2017).
Orakhelashvili A, 'Legal Consequence of the Construction of a Wall in the Occupied Palestinian Territory: Opinion and Reaction' (2006) 11 *Journal of Conflict and Security Law* 119.
Orakhelashvili A, 'The International Court's Advisory Opinion on the UDI in Respect of Kosovo: Washing Away the "Foam on the Tide of Time"' (2011) 15 *Max Planck Yearbook of United Nations Law* 65.
Orford A, 'On International Legal Method' (2013) 1 *London Review of International Law* 166.
Osmond PJ, '"*Princeps Historiae Romanae*": Sallust in Renaissance Political Thought' (1995) 40 *Memoirs of the American Academy in Rome* 101.
Pahuja S, *Decolonising International Law: Development, Economic Growth and the Politics of Universality* (Cambridge, Cambridge University Press, 2011).
Parker S, *An Account of the Nature and Extent of the Divine Dominion and Goodnesse, Especially as They Refer to the Origenian Hypothesis Concerning the Pre-Existence of Souls, Together with a Special Account of the Vanity and Groundlessness of the Hypothesis Itself* (Oxford, R Davis, 1666).
Patten A, 'Self-Determination for National Minorities' in FR Tesón (ed), *The Theory of Self-Determination* (Cambridge, Cambridge University Press, 2016).
Pedersen S, *The Guardians: The League of Nations and the Crisis of Empire* (Oxford, Oxford University Press, 2015).
Pellet A, 'The Opinions of the Badinter Arbitration Committee: A Second Breath for the Self-Determination of Peoples' (1992) 3 *European Journal of International Law* 178.
Pellet A, 'Kosovo – The Questions not Asked: Self-Determination, Secession, and Recognition' in M Milanović and M Wood (eds), *The Law and Politics of the Kosovo Advisory Opinion* (Oxford, Oxford University Press, 2015).
Perritt HH, Jr, *The Road to Independence for Kosovo: A Chronicle of the Ahtisaari Plan* (Cambridge, Cambridge University Press, 2010).
Peters A, 'Does Kosovo Lie in the Lotus-Land of Freedom?' (2011) 24 *Leiden Journal of International Law* 95.
Peters A, 'The Principle of *Uti Possidetis Juris*: How Relevant Is it for Issues of Secession?' in C Walter, A von Ungern-Sternberg and K Abushov (eds), *Self-Determination and Secession in International Law* (Oxford, Oxford University Press, 2014).
Peters A, 'Has the Advisory Opinion's Finding that Kosovo's Declaration of Independence Was Not Contrary to International Law Set an Unfortunate Precedent?' in M Milanović and M Wood (eds), *The Law and Politics of the Kosovo Advisory Opinion* (Oxford, Oxford University Press, 2015).
Peters A, 'Populist International Law? The Suspended Independence and the Normative Value of the Referendum on Catalonia' *EJIL:Talk!* (12 October 2017).
Petrus Gedultius, *Concordantz und Zeiger über die gantze heilige biblische schrifft deß alten und Neuwen Testaments*, vol Erste Theil (Franckfurt am Mayn, Hieronymus Feyerabend/Georg Rab dÄ, 1571).
Philip JR, 'Sallust and the Declaration of Arbroath' (1947) 26 *Scottish Historical Review* 75.
Philpott D, 'Self-Determination in Practice' in M Moore (ed), *National Self-Determination and Secession* (Oxford, Oxford University Press, 1998).
Piirimäe P, 'The Westphalian Myth and the Idea of External Sovereignty' in H Kalmo and Q Skinner (eds), *Sovereignty in Fragments: The Past, Present and Future of a Contested Concept* (Cambridge, Cambridge University Press, 2010).
Pomerance M, 'The Badinter Commission: The Use and Misuse of the International Court of Justice's Jurisprudence' (1998–99) 20 *Michigan Journal of International Law* 31.
Potter PB, 'Origin of the System of Mandates under the League of Nations' (1922) 16 *American Political Science Review* 563.
Pratap D, *The Advisory Jurisdiction of the International Court of Justice* (Oxford, Clarendon Press, 1972).
Prestwich M, *Edward I* (New Haven, CT, Yale University Press, 1997).

Pribyl K, 'The Study of the Climate of Medieval England: A Review of Historical Climatology's Past Achievements and Future Potential' (2014) 69 *Weather* 116.

Puy H de, *Kossuth and His Generals* (Buffalo, NY, Phinney, 1852).

Quane H, 'The United Nations and the Evolving Right to Self-Determination' (1998) 47 *ICLQ* 537.

Radan P, 'Post-secession International Borders: A Critical Analysis of the Opinions of the Badinter Arbitration Commission' (2000) 24 *Melbourne University Law Review* 50.

Raič D, *Statehood and the Law of Self-Determination* (The Hague, Kluwer Law International, 2002).

Ramet SP, *Nihil Obstat: Religion, Politics, and Social Change in East-Central Europe and Russia* (Durham, NC, Duke University Press, 1998).

Rauschning D, 'Article 76' in B Simma et al (eds), *The Charter of the United Nations: A Commentary*, vol 2, 3rd edn (Oxford, Oxford University Press, 2012).

Raz J, 'The Rule of Law and its Virtue' in J Raz, *The Authority of Law: Essays on Law and Morality* (Oxford, Clarendon Press, 1979).

Raz J, 'Introduction' in J Raz (ed), *Authority* (New York, New York University Press, 1990).

Reid JP, *Constitutional History of the American Revolution: The Authority of Rights* (Madison, University of Wisconsin Press, 1986).

Reid RC, 'Edward de Balliol' (1956) 35 *Transactions of the Dumfriesshire and Galloway Natural History & Antiquarian Society* 38.

Riach A, 'Scotland Emergent IV: From Tales of Merlin and Arthur to the Agricola of Tacitus' *Glasgow University ePrints* (1 May 2018).

Riedel EH, 'Confrontation in Western Sahara in the Light of the Advisory Opinion of the International Court of Justice of 16 October 1975. A Critical Appraisal' (1976) 19 *German Yearbook of International Law* 405.

Rigo Sureda A, *The Evolution of the Right of Self-Determination: A Study of United Nations Practice* (Leiden, AW Sijthoff, 1973).

Rodríguez-Santiago E, 'The Evolution of Self-Determination of Peoples in International Law' in FR Tesón (ed), *The Theory of Self-Determination* (Cambridge, Cambridge University Press, 2016).

Ronen D, *The Quest for Self-Determination* (New Haven, CT, Yale University Press, 1979).

Ross A, *A Textbook of International Law: General Part* (London, Longmans, Green, 1947).

Rothermund D, *Decolonization: The Routledge Companion* (London, Routledge, 2006).

Rousseau J-J, *Du contrat social; ou principles du droit politique* (Amsterdam, Marc Michel Rey, 1762).

Rovine AW, 'The World Court Opinion on Namibia' (1972) 11 *Columbia Journal of Transnational Law* 203.

Rowen HH, 'The Dutch Revolt: What Kind of Revolution?' (1990) 43 *Renaissance Quarterly* 570.

Rydval M et al, 'Reconstructing 800 Years of Summer Temperatures in Scotland from Tree Rings' (2017) 49 *Climate Dynamics* 2951.

Samuel K, 'Can Religious Norms Influence Self-Determination Struggles, and with What Implications for International Law?' in D French (ed), *Statehood and Self-Determination: Reconciling Tradition and Modernity in International Law* (Cambridge, Cambridge University Press, 2013).

Scharf MP, 'Seizing the "Grotian Moment": Accelerated Formation of Customary Law in Times of Fundamental Change' (2010) 43 *Cornell International Law Journal* 439.

Scharf MP, 'Grotian Moments: The Concept' (2021) 42 *Grotiana* 193.

Scobbie I, 'Unchart(er)ed Waters?: Consequences of the Advisory Opinion on the Legal Consequences of the Construction of a Wall in the Occupied Palestinian Territory for the Responsibility of the UN for Palestine' (2005) 16 *European Journal of International Law* 941.

Scott RM, *Robert the Bruce: King of the Scots* (Barnes & Nobel, 1982).

Sebutinde J, 'Is the Right to Self-Determination Jus Cogens: Reflections on the Chagos Advisory Opinion' in D Tladi (ed), *Peremptory Norms of General International Law (*Jus Cogens*): Disquisitions and Disputations* (Leiden, Brill/Nijhoff 2021).

Sell L, *Slobodan Milosevic and the Destruction of Yugoslavia* (Durham, NC, Duke University Press, 2003).

Senese S, 'External and Internal Self-Determination' (1989) 16 *Social Justice* 19.

Shaw M, *International Law*, 8th edn (Cambridge, Cambridge University Press, 2017).
Shelton D, 'Righting Wrongs: Reparations in the Articles on State Responsibility' (2002) 96 *American Journal of International Law* 833.
Simma B, 'From Bilateralism to Community Interest in International Law' (1994) 250 *Recueil des Cours* 217.
Simma B and Alston P, 'The Sources of Human Rights Law: Custom, Jus Cogens, and General Principles' (1988–89) 12 *Australian Yearbook of International Law* 82.
Simon S, 'Western Sahara' in C Walter, A von Ungern-Sternberg and K Abushov (eds), *Self-Determination and Secession in International Law* (Oxford, Oxford University Press, 2014).
Simon TW, 'Remedial Secession: What the Law Should Have Done, from Katanga to Kosovo' (2011) 40 *Georgia Journal of International and Comparative Law* 105.
Simpson G, 'Judging the East Timor Dispute: Self-Determination at the International Court of Justice' (1993–94) 17 *Hastings International and Comparative Law Review* 323.
Smith FE, *International Law*, 4th edn (London, J M Dent, 1911).
Smith JJ, 'Western Sahara: The Failure and Promise of International Law' (2011) 69 *Advocate Vancouver* 179.
Smith, MA, Jr, 'Sovereignty over Unoccupied Territories – The Western Sahara Decision' (1977) 9 *Case Western Journal of International Law* 135.
Somos M, 'Boston in the State of Nature, 1761–1765' (2018) 3 *Jus Gentium* 63.
Somos M, *American States of Nature: The Origin of Independence, 1761–1775* (New York, Oxford University Press, 2019).
Somos M and Peters A, 'Introduction' in M Somos and A Peters (eds), *The State of Nature: Histories of an Idea* (Leiden, Brill, 2022).
Soroeta Liceras J, *International Law and the Western Sahara Conflict* (Wolf Legal Publishers, 2014).
Sparks T, 'Towards a Human-Centred International Law: Self-Determination and the Structure of the International Legal System' (Durham University, 2017).
Sparks T, 'Statehood in an Era of Sinking Islands' in T Jafry (ed), *Routledge Handbook of Climate Justice* (Abingdon, Routledge, 2019).
Sparks T, 'Grotian Moments in the Law of Self-Determination: Law, Rhetoric, and Reality' (2022) 43 *Grotiana* 159.
Sparks T, 'Reassessing State Consent to Jurisdiction: The Indispensable Third Party Principle before the ICJ' (2022) 91 *Nordic Journal of International Law* 216.
Sparks T and Somos M, 'Grotian Moments: An Introduction' (2021) 42 *Grotiana* 179.
Sterio M, 'The Case of Kosovo: Self-Determination, Secession, and Statehood under International Law' (2010) 104 *American Society of International Law Proceedings* 361.
Sterio M, 'A Grotian Moment: Changes in the Legal Theory of Statehood' (2010–11) 39 *Denver Journal of International Law and Policy* 209.
Sterio M, *The Right to Self-Determination under International Law: 'Selfistans', Secession, and the Rule of the Great Powers* (London, Routledge, 2013).
Sterio M, 'Do Kurds Have the Right to Self-Determination and/or Secession?' *Opinio Juris* (28 September 2017).
Sterio M, *Secession in International Law: A New Framework* (Cheltenham, Edward Elgar, 2018).
Stilz A, *Territorial Sovereignty: A Philosophical Exploration* (Oxford, Oxford University Press, 2019).
Strathopoulou K, 'Self-Determination, Peacemaking and Peace-building: Recent Trends in African Intrastate Peace Agreements' in D French (ed), *Statehood and Self-Determination: Reconciling Tradition and Modernity in International Law* (Cambridge, Cambridge University Press, 2013).
Summers J, 'The Internal and External Aspects of Self-Determination Reconsidered' in D French (ed), *Statehood and Self-Determination: Reconciling Tradition and Modernity in International Law* (Cambridge, Cambridge University Press, 2013).
Summers J, 'Kosovo' in C Walter, A von Ungern-Sternberg and K Abushov (eds), *Self-Determination and Secession in International Law* (Oxford, Oxford University Press, 2014).
Summers J, 'Decolonisation Revisited and the Obligation not to Divide a Non-Self-Governing Territory' (2018) 55 *Questions of International Law, Zoom Out* 147.

Summers J, '*Chagos*, Custom and the Interpretation of UN General Assembly Resolutions' in T Burri and J Trinidad (eds), *The International Court of Justice and Decolonisation* (Cambridge, Cambridge University Press, 2021).

Tams C, 'The Kosovo Opinion' *EJIL:Talk!* (6 August 2010).

Tanner R, 'Franco-Scottish Alliance' in R Crowcroft and J Cannon (eds), *The Oxford Companion to British History*, 2nd edn (Oxford, Oxford University Press, 2015).

Tesón FR, 'Introduction: The Conundrum of Self-Determination' in FR Tesón (ed), *The Theory of Self-Determination* (Cambridge, Cambridge University Press, 2016).

Thatcher OJ (ed), 'Act of Abjuration, 1581', *The Library of Original Sources*, vol V (Milwaukee, WI, University Research Extension Co, 1907).

The League of Nations, *The Mandates System: Origin – Principles – Application* (Series of League of Nations Publications, 1945).

Thirlway H, *The Law and Procedure of the International Court of Justice: Fifty Years of Jurisprudence*, vols I and II (Oxford, Oxford University Press, 2013).

Thirlway H, *The International Court of Justice* (Oxford, Oxford University Press, 2016).

Thornberry P, 'The Democratic or Internal Aspect of Self-Determination with Some Remarks on Federalism' in C Tomuschat (ed), *The Modern Law of Self-Determination* (Dordrecht, Martinus Nijhoff, 1993).

Tod MAL, 'The Narrative of the Scottish Nation and its Late-Medieval Readers: Non-textual Reader Scribal Activity in the MSS of Fordun, Bower and Their Derivatives' (PhD Thesis, University of Glasgow, 2005).

Tomuschat C, 'Foreword' in C Tomuschat (ed), *The United Nations at Age Fifty: A Legal Perspective* (The Hauge, Kluwer Law International, 1995).

Tomuschat C, 'Secession and Self-Determination' in MG Kohen (ed), *Secession: International Law Perspectives* (Cambridge, Cambridge University Press, 2006).

Trifunovska S, 'One Theme in Two Variations – Self-Determination for Minorities and Indigenous Groups' (1997) 5 *International Journal on Minority and Group Rights* 175.

Trinidad J, 'Self-Determination and Territorial Integrity in the Chagos Advisory Proceedings: Potential Broader Ramifications' (2018) 55 *Questions of International Law, Zoom Out* 61.

Trinidad J, *Self-Determination in Disputed Colonial Territories* (Cambridge, Cambridge University Press, 2018).

Tsagourias N, 'Non-State Actors in International Peace and Security: Non-State Actors and the Use of Force' in J d'Aspremont (ed), *Participants in the International Legal System: Multiple Perspectives on Non-State Actors in International Law* (London, Routledge, 2011).

Turack DC, 'Towards Freedom: Human Rights and Self-Determination in East Timor' (2000) 1 *Asia-Pacific Journal on Human Rights and Law* 55.

Twyman-Ghoshal A, 'State Co-offending: The Case of the Recolonization of the Chagos Archipelago and the Forced Eviction of the Chagossians' (2021) 29 *Critical Criminology* 311.

Tzouvala N, *Capitalism as Civilisation: A History of International Law* (Cambridge, Cambridge University Press, 2020).

Umozurike UO, *Self-Determination in International Law* (London, Archon Books, 1972).

Vashakmadze M and Lippold M, '"Nothing but a Road towards Secession"? The International Court of Justice's Advisory Opinion on Accordance with International Law of the Unilateral Declaration of Independence in Respect of Kosovo' (2010) 2 *Göttingen Journal of International Law* 619.

Verhoeven S, 'Advisory Opinion on the Legal Consequences of the Construction of a Wall in the Occupied Palestinian Territories' (2004) 6 *International Law Forum du droit international* 106.

Vermeer Z, 'Intervention with the Consent of a Deposed (but Legitimate) Government? Playing the Sierra Leone Card' *EJIL:Talk!* (6 March 2014).

Vidmar J, 'The Kosovo Opinion and General International Law: How Far-Reaching and Controversial Is the ICJ's Reasoning?' *The Hague Justice Portal* (11 October 2010).

Vidmar J, 'Unilateral Declarations of Independence in International Law' in D French (ed), *Statehood and Self-Determination: Reconciling Tradition and Modernity in International Law* (Cambridge, Cambridge University Press, 2013).

Vidmar J, 'Catalonia: The Way Forward Is Comparative Constitutional Rather than International Legal Argument' *EJIL:Talk!* (24 October 2017).

Vossen B van der, 'Self-Determination and Moral Variation' in FR Tesón (ed), *The Theory of Self-Determination* (Cambridge, Cambridge University Press, 2016).

Vyver JD van der, 'Self-Determination of the Peoples of Quebec under International Law' (2000) 10 *Transnational Law and Policy* 1.

Waldron J, 'Two Conceptions of Self-Determination' in S Besson and J Tasioulas (eds), *The Philosophy of International Law* (Oxford, Oxford University Press, 2010).

Wallace-Bruce NL, *Claims to Statehood in International Law* (New York, Carlton Press, 1994).

Walter C and von Ungern-Sternberg A, 'Introduction: Self-Determination and Secession in International Law – Perspectives and Trends with Particular Focus on the Commonwealth of Independent States' in C Walter, A von Ungern-Sternberg and K Abushov (eds), *Self-Determination and Secession in International Law* (Oxford, Oxford University Press, 2014).

Waters C, 'South Ossetia' in C Walter, A von Ungern-Sternberg and K Abushov (eds), *Self-Determination and Secession in International Law* (Oxford, Oxford University Press, 2014).

Webb P, 'The United Kingdom and the Chagos Archipelago Advisory Opinion: Engagement and Resistance' (2021) 21 *Melbourne Journal of International Law* 726.

Weber M, 'Wirtschaft und Gesellschaft' in K Borchardt, E Hanke and W Schluchter (eds), *Max Weber: Wirtschaft und Gesellschaft*, vol 23 (Tübingen, JCB Mohr (Paul Siebeck), 2013).

Webster B, 'Robert I (Robert the Bruce) (1274–1329)' in R Crowcroft and J Cannon (eds), *The Oxford Companion to British History*, 2nd edn (Oxford, Oxford University Press, 2015).

Weil P, 'Towards Relative Normativity in International Law?' (1983) 77 *American Journal of International Law* 413.

Weller M, 'Modesty Can Be a Virtue: Judicial Economy in the ICJ Kosovo Opinion?' (2011) 24 *Leiden Journal of International Law* 127.

Weller M, 'The Sounds of Silence: Making Sense of the Supposed Gaps in the Kosovo Opinion' in M Milanović and M Wood (eds), *The Law and Politics of the Kosovo Advisory Opinion* (Oxford, Oxford University Press, 2015).

Weller M, 'Secession and Self-Determination in Western Europe: The Case of Catalonia' *EJIL:Talk!* (18 October 2017).

Whelan A, 'Self-Determination and Decolonisation: Foundations for the Future' (1992) 3 *Irish Studies in International Affairs* 25.

Wilde R, 'International Court of Justice Advisory Opinion on the Consistency of Kosovo's Declaration of Independence with Principles of Self-Determination and International Administration' (2011) 105 *American Journal of International Law* 301.

Wilson W, *The Papers of Woodrow Wilson*, vol 19, ed AS Link (Princeton, NJ, Princeton University Press, 1975).

Wisehart D, 'The Crisis in Ukraine and the Prohibition of the Use of Force: A Legal Basis for Russia's Intervention?' *EJIL:Talk!* (4 March 2014).

Wolfrum R, 'Article 1' in B Simma et al (eds), *The Charter of the United Nations: A Commentary*, vol 1, 3rd edn (Oxford, Oxford University Press, 2012).

Woodward SL, *Balkan Tragedy: Chaos and Dissolution after the Cold War* (Washington, DC, The Brookings Institution, 1995).

Wooldridge F, 'The Advisory Opinion of the International Court of Justice in the Western Sahara Case' (1979) 8 *Anglo-American Law Review* 86.

Wright Q, *Mandates under the League of Nations* (Chicago, University of Chicago Press, 1930).

Wright Q, 'The United Nations, Self-Determination and the Namibia Opinions' (1972–73) 82 *Yale Law Journal* 533.

INDEX

Abi-Saab, Georges 118, 201
abuse of rights
American Declaration of Independence 26, 66–7, 69
colonial self-determination 17, 32, 37–8, 87
Crimea, Russian invasion and annexation of 2014 187–8, 191
French Declaration of the Rights of Man 86
Norway 1905 secession from Sweden 82, 84, 86
Plakkaat van Verlatinghe of 1581 55–6, 86
remedial self-determination 19, 69, 187–8, 229
academic opinion 9, 15, 178
Act of Abjuration *see* **Plakkaat van Verlatinghe (Act of Abjuration) of 1581**
Adams, John 67
African Charter on Human and Peoples' Rights (ACHPR) 150–1
African Commission on Human and Peoples' Rights (ACHPR) 188, 230 *see also* ***Katangese People's Congress v Zaire* (ACHPR)**
age of revolution (1789–1848) 4, 20, 26, 73–85, 86
Åland Islands dispute in 1920 40, 83–5
declarations of independence 73–5, 86
decolonisation 85, 86
legitimacy 82, 86, 87
long 19th century (1789–1920) 74, 86, 87, 127, 227, 229
Norway 23, 76–83
precedential reasoning 86
polity-based self-determination 20
remedial self-determination 74–5, 84–5, 87, 229
secessionary self-determination 23, 73–6, 77–8, 82–3
aggression 87
Ahtisaari, Martti 169
Åland Islands dispute (1920) 40, 83–5
Commission of Rapporteurs 83–5
Committee of Jurists 83–5
minority rights 85
remedial self-determination 84–5
secessionary self-determination 83–5, 144, 146, 183
sovereignty 83–5, 144, 151
territorial sovereignty, self-determination as subordinate to 85, 144, 151
Alba, 3rd Duke of (Fernando Álvarez de Toledo) 53–4, 56–7
Albania, secession of 167
Alexander III, King of Scotland 41
Alsop, Vincent 13
Alston, Philip 223
American Declaration of Independence 1776 4, 64–70, 227
abuses of rights 26, 66–7, 69
consent of the governed 66, 68, 71
Declaration of Arbroath of 6 April 1320 41, 60–3, 65, 229
French Declaration of the Rights of Man 70–1, 73
influence 70–1, 73–4
last resort, secession as remedy of 68–9
legitimacy 65, 67–9, 111–12
governments, of 67–8
states, of 67–8
origins 40–1
Plakkaat van Verlatinghe of 1581 50, 62–3, 65, 67, 229
polity-based self-determination 69–70, 87
popular sovereignty 65–6
precedential reasoning 63, 64–5
remedial self-determination 20, 26, 68–9, 74–5, 86, 179
secessionary self-determination 67–70
sources 61–3, 65
Stamp Act of 1765 66–7
state of nature 66–7
substance and form 74
syllogistic form 62, 67
totemic, as 40, 64
Wilson, Woodrow 93
Anghie, Anthony 89
Anjou, Duke of, Francis 51, 56–7

annexation
Crimea, Russian invasion and annexation of 2014 4, 18–19, 186–91, 192, 231
Wall advisory opinion 156–8
Aquinas, Thomas 66
Arafat, Yassa 155
arbitration *see* **Badinter Arbitration Commission**
ARSIWA (International Law Commission's (ILC) Articles on the Responsibility of States for International Wrongful Acts) 209–11, 216–17, 224–5
Armitage, David 61–2, 73–4, 145
Ascherson, Neil 62
Australia *see* ***East Timor*** **decision (ICJ)**

Badinter Arbitration Commission 129–32, 143–5, 230
declarations of independence from Yugoslavia 143–5
dissolution, Yugoslavia as in the process of 143–4
minorities, protection of 144–5
polity-based self-determination 145
referendums 144
secessionary self-determination 143–5, 146, 151, 183
Balé, Raymond 194–5
Balfour, Henry 92
Balliol, John, King of Scots 41–2
Barrow, Geoffrey Wallis Steuart 50
Barzani, Masoud 1–2, 6
Benedict XV, Pope 95
Berber independence war, Morocco (1921–1926) 90
Bernard of Kilwinning 47
Bianchi, Andrea 217
Bibliotheca Julia 58
Black Lives Matter (BLM) movement 88
Bolsheviks 30, 90, 91, 95
Brexit 11
Bruce, Robert 41
Bruce, Robert the *see also* **Robert I, King of Scots (Rob the Bruce)** 41, 43–50
Burke, Edmund 96

Callahan, Michael 99, 101
Canada *see* ***Quebec*** **decision (Canadian Supreme Court)**
Cassese, Antonio 71, 96, 108–9
Cataluña, unauthorised 2017 referendum in 2, 5–10
Constitution of Spain 7–8
European Commission 7–8
imprisonment of leaders 2, 10–11
international reaction 7–8
Kosovo advisory opinion 185–6, 193
police violence 2, 6–7, 10
secession 2, 5, 6, 23
support, lack of international 7
violence 2, 6–7, 10–11
categorisation as inherent element of law 35–6, 39
cessation of continuing acts, obligation of 209–11
Chagos Archipelago **advisory opinion (ICJ)** 4, 194–226
Charter of the UN 195, 197, 214, 218, 221
colonial self-determination 31–2, 194, 213–15, 218–19, 221–5, 231–2
consent to international adjudication 195, 196, 198–200, 202
continuing acts and obligation of cessation 209–11
cooperation, ICJ's duty of 200, 201–2, 211–12, 216–17
customary international law 212, 213, 218–19
Declaration on Friendly Relations 212, 218, 221
decolonisation 123, 195–226
discretion 196–203
East Timor decision 211–12
erga omnes norms 211–12, 215, 217
General Assembly 194–226
legal question, existence of a 197
requests for opinions 197–208
resolutions 194–9, 213–15, 219, 221, 232
international law 195–6, 200, 225–6
ius cogens 9, 211–12, 215–23, 232
jurisdiction 196–203
Kosovo advisory opinion 194, 196
Mauritius, separation from 4, 194–226, 231–2
opinio iuris 9, 214
polity-based self-determination 221–2, 225, 232
sovereignty 199, 210
spillover legitimacy 224–5, 232
substantive questions 203–12

territorial integrity 195, 210, 218
United Kingdom's administration of Chagos Islands 195–226
Charles I, King of England 66–7
Charter of the Economic Rights and Duties of States 118–19
Charter of the UN 8, 31, 88, 107–112
Article 1 8, 21–2, 107–11, 114–17, 120, 127, 221
Article 55 111, 149
binding obligations 108
Chagos Archipelago advisory opinion 195, 197, 214, 218, 221
colonial self-determination 31, 88, 104–12, 122–3, 221
Declaration of Friendly Relations 21, 124–5
develop self-government, obligation to 104–5
drafting 109–10
East Timor decision 9, 146–8, 149
ICCPR/ICESCR 119–20
importance 107
individual rights 108–9, 122
Kosovo advisory opinion 168–9, 174–5
legal norms 104, 221
legal rights 21–2, 108–10
legitimacy 111–12
maintenance of peace and security 108
non-interference/non-intervention, principle of 21, 110–11, 119, 127, 191
non-self-governing territories 104–5, 106, 146–8
political objectives 108
political self-determination 110, 111–12
polity-based self-determination 21–3, 87, 146, 228
purpose of UN, self-determination as a 107–11
self-defence, right to 191
Security Council 108, 111, 168–9
territorial integrity 174–5
Subcommittee I/1/A 109
trusteeship system 102–3, 111, 214
Wall advisory opinion 159
Western Sahara advisory opinion 141–2
Chimni, Bhupinder Singh 89–90
Christian Frederick, King of Denmark 79
Churchill, Winston 102
Cicero, Marcus Tullius 66
civil and political rights *see* **International Covenant on Civil and Political Rights (ICCPR)/International Covenant on Economic, Social and Cultural Rights (ICESCR)**
Clement V, Pope 44
Cobban, Alfred 13
colonial self-determination 3–5, 87–128, 130–1
1920–1970 87–128, 227
1960–1970 214–15
abusive colonial rule 17, 32, 37–8, 87
age of revolution 85, 86
borders, no modification of 121–2
Chagos Archipelago advisory opinion 31–2, 194–226
Charter of the UN 31, 88, 104–6, 107–12, 122–3, 221
colonial rule as wrong in itself 32, 87
customary international law 4, 33, 106, 117, 123, 127, 133
Declaration of Friendly Relations (UN) 88, 106, 124–7
decolonisation process 29–31, 87–128
definition 19, 228
East Timor decision 31, 146, 148–50, 159, 150, 222, 230
erga omnes norms 150, 228
First World War 29–31, 87–92, 127, 229
General Assembly (GA) 88, 106, 120–3, 127, 226, 229
historical roots 29
human rights 31, 88, 106, 112–20, 122
ICCPR/ICESCR 88, 106, 112–20, 127
illegitimacy of colonialism 30–1
imperialism and decolonisation 88–90
institutionalisation 88, 101–2, 127
internal/external dichotomy 16, 18, 227
international law 40, 89
interrelationship with other forms 35–8
ius cogens 4, 32, 33, 87–8, 107, 220–2, 226, 228, 232
Katangese People's Congress v Zaire 151–2
League of Nations 29–31, 88, 98–101, 105, 122–3, 127, 229
legal norm, as 4, 32, 37, 106–7, 111–12, 127, 134, 148, 226–31
Charter of the UN 221
crystallisation 31, 123, 205
East Timor decision 149
legitimacy 87

nationalism/anti-nationalism 97
Wall advisory opinion 158–9, 213–16
Western Sahara advisory opinion 141–2, 148
legal status 3–4, 37, 89, 220, 229
legitimacy 30–4, 39, 130
Lenin, role of 88, 90–2, 94–7
mandates system 30–1, 88, 98–101, 105, 122–3, 127, 229
Namibia advisory opinion 31, 136–7, 148, 159
nationalism, rejection of 91
opinio iuris 106
overlap with different forms 37–8
Plakkaat van Verlatinghe of 1581 58
political consensus and 30–2
political self-determination 87, 122
polity-based self-determination 32, 88, 127–8, 220, 225
Quebec decision 152–3
remedial self-determination 27, 32, 88
saltwater colonies 89, 91, 119, 228
secessionary self-determination 4, 87, 121–2, 220
Second World War 30–1, 87, 89
species of self-determination 37
spillover legitimacy 32, 34
state practice 106, 123, 213–14
trusteeship system (UN) 30–1, 101, 102–5, 122–3, 127, 229
UN 29–31, 101, 102–27, 229
Western Sahara advisory opinion 31, 141–2, 148, 150, 159
wider self-determination category 5
Wilson, Woodrow 30, 88, 90–7
Committee on Economic, Social and Cultural Rights (ICESCR) 116–17
Commonwealth countries, change in status from dominions to 90
Comyn family 45–6
Comyn, John (the Red Comyn) 43–6
conflicts and violence 6–11 *see also* **First World War**
Cataluña, unauthorised 2017 referendum in 2, 6–7, 10–11
Crimea, Russian invasion and annexation of 2014 187–91
Kosovo advisory opinion 166–8
Kurdish Autonomous Region of Iraq (KAR), referendum in 2, 6, 10, 185–6
Plakkaat van Verlatinghe of 1581 52–6
religious conflicts 52–6
secessionary self-determination 2–3
Second World War 30–1, 87–9, 103
self-determination problem 6–11
Syria, civil war in 10
Ukraine, Russian invasion of 2022
Yemen, civil law in 10
Congress of Berlin 165
consent to international adjudication 195, 196, 198–200, 202
continuing acts 209–11
cooperation, duty of 200, 201–2, 211–12, 216–17
Copiale prioratus Sancti Andreae 58
Crawford, James 182
Crimea, Russian invasion and annexation of 2014 186–91
abuses by Ukraine, allegations of 187–8, 191
constitutional law of Ukraine 190
Crimea's claim 189–91
Declaration of Friendly Relations 187–8
declarations of independence 190–1
effective control, threshold of 190
international law 163, 190–1
Kosovo advisory opinion 4, 18–19, 186, 187–91, 192, 231
opinio iuris 187–8
political self-determination 188–9
popular protest movement, triggered by 186–7
precedent 4, 18–19, 186, 187–91, 192
referendums 186–7, 190
remedial self-determination 187–8, 191
Russia's claim 187–9
secessionary self-determination 189–91, 231
Security Council (UN) 189–90
use of force, illegal 187–91
crimes against humanity 11, 167
Cristescu, Aureliu 115, 120
Croatia, declaration of independence of 143, 166–7
customary international law *see also* ***erga omnes*** **norms; legal norm of right to self-determination;** ***opinio iuris***
Chagos Archipelago advisory opinion 212, 213, 218–19
colonial self-determination 4, 33, 106, 117, 123, 127, 133, 212, 213
Declaration of Friendly Relations 124
Kosovo advisory opinion 179–80
Namibia advisory opinion 141

polity-based self-determination 4, 22, 33, 88, 131, 133
remedial self-determination 179–81
uti possidetis iuris principle 16, 122, 142–4
Western Sahara advisory opinion 141, 148

de Soulis, John 43
Declaration of Arbroath of 6 April 1320 4, 41–50, 71, 227
American Declaration of Independence 41, 60–3, 65, 229
Bannockburn, Battle of (1314) 46
Berwick massacre 43
circulation of copies 58–9
Comyn, John, murder of 44
divine right to kingship 47–8, 86
freedom 48, 50–1, 59, 61
French Declaration of the Rights of Man 229
influence 58
moral rights and legitimacy 50
national identity 57
nationhood, betrayal of 48–9
nationalism 50
Plakkaat van Verlatinghe of 1581 50–1, 58, 62–3
political propaganda, as 49
popular sovereignty 47–8
revolution, right of 48–9
Scotichronicon 58–9
Scottish War of Independence 41–6
sources 59–60
succession 41–6, 48
text 47–50
Declaration of Friendly Relations (UNGA) 88, 106, 124–7
Chagos Archipelago advisory opinion 212, 218, 221
Charter of the UN 22, 124–5
colonial self-determination 88, 106, 124–7
Crimea, Russian invasion and annexation of 2014 187–8
customary international law 124
human rights 125
Kosovo advisory opinion (ICJ) 124, 126
legal status of self-determination 124
Nicaragua case (ICJ) 124
non-intervention, principle of 116
opinio iuris 124
peoples, definition of 125
political self-determination 127, 188
polity-based self-determination 125
remedial self-determination 28, 125–6, 179–81
safeguard clause 125–6
secessionary self-determination 125–6, 179–80
territorial integrity 174, 188
text 124
Wall advisory opinion 157, 159
declarations of independence *see also* **American Declaration of Independence 1776**
age of revolution 73–5, 86
Badinter Commission 143–5
Crimea, Russian invasion and annexation of 2014 163, 190–1
Croatia 166–7
Flanders 27, 74
French Declaration of the Rights of Man 4
Hungary 27, 75
illegal acts, connection with 173, 176–9
India 90, 106
international law 163, 190–1
interpretation 176–9
Irish Republic 90
ius cogens 176–9
Kosovo advisory opinion 163–85, 231
legal norms 173, 179, 189
legitimacy 27
Liberia 27, 75
natural resources, sovereignty over 148
Norway 1814 secession 76
remedial self-determination 26–7
secessionary self-determination 25, 182–5
Slovenia 166–7
sovereignty, markers of 183
territorial integrity 173–4
UNGA Declaration on the Granting of Independence to Colonial Countries and People of 1960 31, 112, 120, 136, 204, 232
unilateral declarations 163–85
Venezuela 27, 75
Yugoslavia, dissolution of 143–4
decolonisation *see* **colonial self-determination**
democracy 68
Denmark's consensual union with Norway 76
divine right of kings 47–8, 55–6, 65, 70, 86
dominions to Commonwealth countries, change in status from 90
Dowthiltz, David 59

Dumas, Charles-Guillaume-Frédéric 61–2
Duursma, Jorri 10

***East Timor* decision (ICJ)** 129, 130, 145–50
  Chagos Archipelago advisory opinion 211–12
  Charter of the UN 9, 146–8, 149
  colonial self-determination 31, 146, 148–50, 159, 160, 222, 230
  economic co-operation 149
  erga omnes norms 146, 147, 159
  ICCPR/ICESCR 148, 149
  Indonesia's illegal annexation of East Timor, recognition by Australia of 145–50
  international law 145–7
  intervention, prohibition of 148
  legal status of self-determination 145
  natural resources, sovereignty over 147–8, 222
  political self-determination 148
  polity-based self-determination 22, 146, 148–9, 222
  remedial self-determination 146
  secessionary self-determination 146
  Wall advisory opinion 159, 160, 224–5
  Western Sahara advisory opinion 150
economic, social and cultural rights *see* **International Covenant on Civil and Political Rights (ICCPR)/ International Covenant on Economic, Social and Cultural Rights (ICESCR)**
Edward I, King of England 41–5, 47, 49
Edward II, King of England 46
Egypt in 1922, partial independence after civil resistance in 90
equality of states 16, 21, 110, 221
***erga omnes* norms**
  Chagos Archipelago advisory opinion 211–12, 215, 217
  colonial self-determination 150, 228
  East Timor decision 9, 146, 147, 159
  secessionary self-determination 228
  Wall advisory opinion 158–60, 215–16
ethnic cleansing 11, 167
ethnonationalism 94, 96–7
etymology of the term 12–14
European Union 7–8, 11, 143–4, 169
expropriation of property of non-nationals 118
external self-determination *see* **internal/ external dichotomy**

Field of Blackbirds 1389, battle on the 165–6
Finland *see* **Åland Islands dispute (1920)**
First World War
  Bolsheviks 90, 91
  colonial self-determination 14, 29–31, 87–92, 127, 229
  rhetoric 14, 90–2
  supplies, raw material and manpower of colonies 90–1
Flanders, declaration of independence of 27, 74
Floris V, Count of Holland 41
Floyd, George, death of 93
Fofana, Idriss 118
four forms of self-determination 19–39, 232
  see also **colonial self-determination; polity-based self-determination; remedial self-determination; secessionary self-determination**
France 88–9 *see also* **French Declaration of the Rights of Man and of the Citizen 1789**
Franklin, Benjamin 61
Franz Ferdinand, Archduke of Austro-Hungary 165
French Declaration of the Rights of Man and of the Citizen 1789 4, 40, 70–3, 227
  abuses of rights 86
  American Declaration of Independence 70–1, 73
  Declaration of Arbroath 229
  divine right of kings 70, 86
  Draft Constitution 71–2
  influence 73–4
  legitimacy 71, 73, 111–12
  non-intervention 21
  Plakkaat van Verlatinghe of 1581 229
  polity-based self-determination 20–1, 26, 70–1, 87
  popular sovereignty 13–14, 70
  precedential reasoning 63, 64
  remedial self-determination 26–7, 74–5
  self-government, right to 70
  text 71
  totemic, as 40, 64
  will of the people 26–7, 71
Fuller, Lon 36

Gandhi, Mohandas 90
genealogy of self-determination 3–5, 64

General Assembly (UN) *see also* **Declaration of Friendly Relations (UNGA)**
apartheid 135
Chagos Archipelago advisory opinion 194–226
colonial self-determination 31–2, 88, 106, 120–3, 127, 226, 229
Declaration on the Granting of Independence to Colonial Countries and People of 1960 31, 112, 120, 136, 204, 232
ICCPR/ICESCR 112–16, 118–19
Kosovo advisory opinion 163–5, 170–80, 192–3, 230
maintenance of peace and security 108
Namibia advisory opinion 135
Permanent Sovereignty over Natural Resources, declaration on 118–19
post-colonial self-determination, practice on 158–9
Resolution 1514 (XV) declaration on granting of independence to colonial countries and peoples 120–3, 127
resolutions
Namibia advisory opinion 135
Chagos Archipelago advisory opinion 194–9, 213–15, 219, 221, 232
colonial self-determination 31–2, 106, 120–3, 127, 226
Wall advisory opinion 155–6
Western Sahara advisory opinion 137–41
secessionary self-determination 121–2
Wall advisory opinion 155–6, 158–9
Western Sahara advisory opinion 137–41
genocide 11, 167
genus, self-determination as a 37
Grotius, Hugo 66

Haines, Roy Martin 46
Hanauer, Laurence 142
Hannum, Hurst 14
Hastings, John 41
Hegel, Georg Wilhelm Friedrich 13
Hernández, Gleider 37, 201
Herzog August Bibliothek, Wolfenbüttel 58
Hilpold, Peter 172, 225
Hobbes, Thomas 66, 93, 96
Hobsbawm, Eric 26, 64, 73–4, 229
Holbrooke, Richard 168–9
human rights *see also* **International Covenant on Civil and Political Rights (ICCPR)/International Covenant on Economic, Social and Cultural Rights (ICESCR)**
African Charter on Human and Peoples' Rights (ACHPR) 150–1
African Commission on Human and Peoples' Rights (ACoHPR) 188, 230
Charter of the UN 108–9, 122
colonial self-determination 31, 88, 106, 112–20, 122
Declaration of Friendly Relations 125
Quebec decision 154
regional human rights bodies 130
Universal Declaration of Human Rights 22, 116
Wall advisory opinion 157
Human Rights Committee (ICCPR) 116, 118
Hungary, declaration of independence of 27, 75

ICCPR *see* **International Covenant on Civil and Political Rights (ICCPR)/ International Covenant on Economic, Social and Cultural Rights (ICESCR)**
ICESCR *see* **International Covenant on Civil and Political Rights (ICCPR)/ International Covenant on Economic, Social and Cultural Rights (ICESCR)**
ICJ *see* **International Court of Justice (ICJ)**
identity
collective identity 12
identity-based self-determination 17, 19, 23–4, 130, 228
national identity 57, 165–6
self, identification of 5, 12, 34
separate character or identity of groups within states 23
several entities, groups with single identity split between 19
ILC Articles on the Responsibility of States for International Wrongful Acts (ARSIWA) 209–11, 216–17, 224–5
illegality
declarations of independence connected with illegal acts 173, 176–9
duty to end illegal situations 211–12

recognition of illegal situations 145–50, 158, 159–60, 212, 215–16
use of force 187–91
illiberal liberalism 94, 95–7
Illyricus, Matthias Flacius 58
imperialism and decolonisation 88–90, 99–100
independence, declarations of *see* **declarations of independence**
India, independence of 90, 106
Indonesia *see* ***East Timor*** **decision (ICJ)**
interference *see* **non-interference/ non-intervention, principle of**
institutionalisation 88, 101–2, 127
internal/external dichotomy 3, 5, 14–19, 39–40
categorisation as inherent element of law 36
colonial self-determination 16, 18, 227
definitions 15
external self-determination 17–19
internal self-determination 16–17
international law 11, 14–15, 227
non-interference/non-intervention, principle of 15, 16
political self-determination 16, 110
remedial self-determination 18
secession or autonomy claims of sub-state units (external element) 15, 17–18
unitary concept in international law, self-determination as a 5, 14–15
whole people within established borders (internal element) 15
International Court of Justice (ICJ) *see also* ***Kosovo*** **advisory opinion (ICJ)**
Chagos Archipelago advisory opinion (ICJ) 4, 9, 31–2, 129–30, 194–226, 231–2
customary international law 127
East Timor decision 9, 22, 31, 129–30, 145–50, 159–60, 222, 224–5, 230
individual rights 108–9
International Status of South-West Africa advisory opinion 132–3
maintenance of peace and security 108
mandates system 99
Namibia advisory opinion 31, 130, 132, 133–7, 141, 148, 159
Nicaragua decision 22
polity-based self-determination 21, 22
remedial self-determination 29
Wall advisory opinion 22, 130, 155–60, 212–16, 222, 224–5, 230
Western Sahara advisory opinion 31, 130, 137–42, 150
international courts and tribunals *see* **judicial treatment of self-determination (1945–2004)**
International Covenant on Civil and Political Rights (ICCPR)/International Covenant on Economic, Social and Cultural Rights (ICESCR) 8–9, 112–20
Badinter Commission 145
Chagos Archipelago advisory opinion 218, 221
Charter of the Economic Rights and Duties of States 118–19
Charter of the UN 119–20
colonial self-determination 88, 106, 112–20, 127
Committee on Economic, Social and Cultural Rights (ICESCR) 116–17
drafting 113–17
East Timor decision 148, 149
expropriation of property of non-nationals 118
General Assembly 112–16, 118–19
Human Rights Committee (ICCPR) 116, 118
interpretation and monitoring 116–17
legal right, self-determination as a 113
life, right to 119
minority rights 115
natural resources, sovereignty over 148
non-intervention/non-interference, principle of 116
non-self-governing territories 114–15, 117
peoples, definition of 120
Permanent Sovereignty over Natural Resources, GA declaration on 118–19
political self-determination 116–20, 145
polity-based self-determination 22, 116, 118–19
scope of self-determination 113–14
secessionary self-determination 120, 145
travaux préparatoires 106, 113–16
Wall advisory opinion 157
international humanitarian law (IHL) 157
international law 38, 130–2, 160
American Declaration of Independence 69
Badinter Commission 143

Chagos Archipelago advisory opinion 195–6, 200, 225–6
Charter of the UN 107
colonial self-determination 40, 89
Crimea, Russian invasion and annexation of 2014 163, 190–1
declarations of independence 190
East Timor decision 145–7
egregious violations of norms 176–9
internal/external dichotomy 11, 14–15, 227
Kosovo advisory opinion 163, 164, 172–9, 184–5, 231
legal norms 37, 69, 176–8, 220, 225
Namibia advisory opinion 136–7
polity-based self-determination 40, 220, 232
remedial self-determination 26, 33–4, 40, 191
secessionary self-determination 25, 33, 38, 40, 233
Ukraine, Russian invasion of 2022 163
unitary concept in international law, self-determination as a 5, 14–15
Wall advisory opinion 158

International Law Commission's (ILC) Articles on the Responsibility of States for International Wrongful Acts (ARSIWA) 209–11, 216–17, 224–5
***International Status of South-West Africa* advisory opinion (ICJ)** 132–3
intervention *see* **non-interference/ non-intervention, principle of**
Iraq *see* **Kurdish Autonomous Region of Iraq (KAR), independence referendum 2017 in**
Irish Republic in 1916 and 1919, independence declarations of 90
irredentism 38, 71, 144, 185, 228
Israel *see* ***Wall* advisory opinion (ICJ)**
ius cogens 160, 215–23 *see also* **legal norm of right to self-determination**
Chagos Archipelago advisory opinion 9, 211–12, 215–23, 232
colonial self-determination 4, 32, 33, 87–8, 107, 220–2, 226, 228, 232
declarations of independence 176–9
Kosovo advisory opinion 163, 176–9
polity-based self-determination 4, 22, 33, 88, 131, 220
serious breaches of peremptory norms 216–17

Jacobs, Dov 178
Janis, Mark 139
Jansen, Jan 89–90, 106
Jefferson, Thomas 61–2, 64–5
Jennings, Ivor 24
Johan, Karl 76–8
John XXII, Pope 46, 49–50
John of Fordun 58–9
Jovanović, Miodrag 175, 178
judicial treatment of self-determination (1945–2004) 9, 129–61, 229–32 *see also* ***Kosovo* advisory opinion (ICJ)**
Badinter Arbitration Commission 129–32, 143–5
Chagos Archipelago advisory opinion (ICJ) 4, 9, 31–2, 129–30, 194–226, 231–2
colonial self-determination 130–1, 133
customary international law 133
domestic courts 129
East Timor decision (ICJ) 9, 22, 31, 129–30, 145–50, 159–60, 222, 224–5, 230
erga omnes norms 160
international law 130–2, 160
International Status of South-West Africa advisory opinion (ICJ) 132–3
ius cogens 160
Katangese People's Congress v Zaire (African Commission on Human and People's Rights) 130, 150–2, 154, 180–1
legal status of self-determination 130–1
Namibia advisory opinion (ICJ) 31, 130, 132, 133–7, 141, 148, 159
over-inclusive, opinions as 222, 225
polity-based self-determination 130–1, 133
Quebec decision (Canadian Supreme Court) 130, 152–4, 180–1, 188, 230
regional human rights bodies 130
remedial self-determination 130–1
secessionary self-determination 130–1
Status of Eastern Carelia advisory request (PCIJ) 132
under-inclusive, opinions as 222, 225
Wall advisory opinion (ICJ) 22, 130, 155–60, 212–16, 222, 224–5, 230
Western Sahara advisory opinion (ICJ) 31, 130, 137–42, 150
Juncker, Jean-Claude 7–8
jurisdiction of ICJ 196–203

Kant, Immanuel 13, 63–4
***Katangese People's Congress v Zaire* (ACoHPR)** 130, 150–2
African Charter on Human and Peoples' Rights (ACHPR) 150–1
colonial self-determination 151–2
Democratic Republic of Congo (DRC), recognition of independence from 150–1
existence, inalienable right of peoples to their 151
inalienable right to self-determination 151
internally, self-determination as exercised 152
political status, inalienable right to 151
polity-based self-determination 152
remedial self-determination 152, 154, 180–1
secessionary self-determination 151
will of the people 152
KBR (formerly Koninklijke Bibliotheek) 58–9
Kellas, James 48
Kelsen, Hans 108–10
Kolb, Robert 209
***Kosovo* advisory opinion (ICJ)** 27, 129–30, 161, 162–93
academic opinion 178
Albania, secession of 167
background 164–70
Cataluña, unauthorised 2017 referendum in 185–6, 193
Chagos Archipelago advisory opinion 194, 196
Charter of the UN 168–9, 174–5
Crimea, Russian invasion and annexation of 2014 4, 18–19, 186, 187–91, 192, 231
Croatia, declaration of independence of 166–7
customary international law 179–80
Declaration of Friendly Relations 124, 126
declarations of independence, prohibition on 163–85, 231
after Kosovo 182–4
egregious violations of international law norms 176–9
illegal acts, connection with 173, 176–9
interpretation 176–9
ius cogens 176–9
territorial integrity 173–4
unilateral declaration of independence, legality of Kosovo's 163–85
decision of ICJ 173–85
ethnic conflict 166–8
expulsions 167
General Assembly
interpretation 164, 171–3
request to the ICJ 163–5, 170–80, 192–3, 230
resolutions 170
genocide, ethnic cleansing and crimes against humanity 11, 167
illegal acts, declarations of independence in connection with 173, 176–9
influence 162–3
international law 163, 164, 172–9, 184–5, 231
ius cogens 163, 176–9
Kosovo Diplomatic Observer Mission 168
Kosovo Liberation Army (KLA), Serbia's brutal response to 167–8
Kumanovo Accord 169
Kurdish Autonomous Region of Iraq (KAR), referendum in 185–6, 193
Lotus dogma 163, 184, 193, 230
national identity 165–6
NATO bombing campaign 169
opinio iuris 181, 187–8
political and cultural repression 167
prohibitive rules 171–3, 184–5
Rambouillet Conference 168–9
recognise Kosovo as independent, whether third states obliged to 171
remedial self-determination 163–4, 179–81, 184, 193, 194, 231
secessionary self-determination 25, 33, 163–85, 189, 194, 220, 231
Security Council (UN), resolutions of 168–70, 176
Serbia 165–85, 230–1
Constitution of the Kingdom of Serbs, Croats and Slovenes 1921 165
Field of Blackbirds 1389, battle on the 165–6
Gazimestan speech 165–6
independence declarations 166–7, 169
national identity 165–6
nationalism 165–6
Ottoman Empire 165
Slovenia, declaration of independence of 166–7
sovereignty 163, 169, 170, 183, 231
statehood, whether Kosovo had achieved 171, 173

territorial integrity 173–6, 185
Ukraine, Russian invasion of 2022
UN, Kosovo as under authority of 169, 183
unilateral declaration of independence, legality of Kosovo's 163–85
Kurdish Autonomous Region of Iraq (KAR), independence referendum 2017 in 1–2, 5–10
Constitution of Iraq 6
international reaction 6, 8
Kosovo advisory opinion 185–6, 193
legal right, existence of an international 6–9
legitimacy 7, 8
military force by Iraq, use of 2, 6, 10, 185–6
secession 1–2, 5, 6, 23, 185–6
sovereignty of Iraq 186

Lakoff, George 35
Lamberton, William, Bishop of St Andrews 43
Lamoral, Count of Egmont 52–3
Lazar Hrebeljanović, Prince of Serbia 165
League against Imperialism 89–90
League of Nations *see also* **Åland Islands dispute (1920); mandates system (League of Nations)**
colonial self-determination 29–31, 88, 98–101, 105, 122–3, 127, 129
Namibia advisory opinion 134–6
UN, replacement by 101
legal norm of self-determination 39, 219, 224, 232 *see also* **internal/external dichotomy; *ius cogens***
binary norms 34
categorisation 36
Charter of the UN 104, 221
colonial self-determination 4, 32, 37, 106–7, 111–12, 127, 134, 126–31
Charter of the UN 221
crystallisation 31, 123, 205
East Timor decision 149
legitimacy 87
Namibia advisory opinion 148
nationalism/anti-nationalism 97
Wall advisory opinion 158–9, 213–16
Western Sahara advisory opinion 141–2, 148
cooperation, duty to 212
crystallisation 31, 123, 188, 205
declarations of independence 173, 179, 189
international law 37, 69, 176–8, 220, 225
Kurdish Autonomous Region of Iraq (KAR), referendum in 5
legitimacy 87
nationalism/anti-nationalism 97
polity-based self-determination 4, 22, 33, 37, 88, 115, 119, 131, 228
remedial self-determination 4–5, 27, 37, 181, 191
secessionary self-determination 145
self-determination, meaning of 37, 39
territorial integrity 175–6
legitimacy 3, 5, 30–4
age of revolution 82, 86, 87
American Declaration of Independence 65, 67–9, 111–12
Charter of the UN 111–12
colonial self-determination 30–4, 39, 130
Declaration of Arbroath of 6 April 1320 50
declarations of independence 27
form of government 16
French Declaration of the Rights of Man 71, 73, 111–12
governments, of 67–8
identity-based self-determination 130
internal/external dichotomy 16–18
Kurdish Autonomous Region of Iraq (KAR), referendum in 7, 8
Norway 1905 secession from Sweden 82–3
polity-based self-determination 32–4, 39, 130
remedial self-determination 32–4, 39, 75, 130
secessionary self-determination 23, 32–4, 39
spillover legitimacy 18, 32, 34, 224–5, 230–2
states, of 67–8
Lenin, Vladimir Ilyich 29–30, 95, 98
colonial self-determination 88, 90–2, 94–6
First World War 90–2
mandates system 98
Marxism 86
nationalism 91, 97
Wilson, Woodrow 94–6
Liberia, declaration of independence of 27, 75
life, right to 119
Lippold, Matthias 183
Locke, John 48, 66
long 19th century (1789–1920) 74, 86, 87, 127, 227, 229
Lott, Trent 60–1

Low Countries *see* **Plakkaat van Verlatinghe (Act of Abjuration) of 1581**
Lucas, Stephen E 55, 62, 64–5, 67, 86
Lumumba, Patrice, murder of 150

McCorquodale, Robert 14–15
mandates system (League of Nations) 30–1, 88, 98–101
A, B and C mandates 98–9
civilisational logic 99–100
colonial self-determination 30–1, 88, 98–101, 105, 122–3, 127, 229
conditions for independence 101
defeated central powers, colonies of the 98
equivalency, declaration of 105
imperialism 99–100
Permanent Mandates Commission (PMC) 100–1
purpose 98–9
trusteeship system 30–1, 101, 102, 105, 132–3
tutelage, as a form of 99
Wilson, Woodrow 98
Margaret, Maid of Norway 41
Margaret of Palma 52–3
Mauritania 137–41
Mauritius *see* ***Chagos Archipelago*** **advisory opinion (ICJ)**
Mayhew, Jonathan 65, 66–7
meanings of self-determination 12–14, 63–4
etymology of the term 12–14
historical background 12–14
legal norms 37, 39
Selbstbestimmung, derivation from 12–13, 63–4
self, identification of 5, 12, 34
theological context 12–13, 63
Mégret, Frédéric 38
Michelson, Christian 80–1
Milanović, Marko 170
Milošević, Slobodan 165–9
minority rights 85, 95–6, 115, 144–5
Montesquieu, Charles de 66
moral-theoretical dimension of self-determination 12–13
Moray, Andrew 43
Morris, Christopher 18
Morocco
Berber independence war (1921–1926) 90
Ifni, status of 137–8
referendum on Western Sahara, opposition to 138
Western Sahara advisory opinion 137–41
Murad Hüdavendigâr (Murad I), Ottoman Sultan 165
Musgrave, Thomas 91
Mussolini, Benito 101

Namibia **advisory opinion (ICJ)** 130, 132, 133–7
apartheid 134–5
class C-mandate, SW Africa as 134–6
colonial self-determination 31, 136–7, 148, 159
customary international law 141
General Assembly resolutions 135
international law, development of 136–7
League of Nations, replacement of 134–6
sacred trust principle 136, 141
Security Council 133–7
South Africa in Namibia, conduct of 133–7
trusteeship 133–7
Western Sahara advisory opinion 141
Napoleon Bonaparte 76
Napoleonic wars 76–7, 81
national identity 57, 165–6
nationalism 14, 24, 39, 50, 91, 96–7, 165–6
NATO 11, 169
natural resources, sovereignty over 118–19, 147–8, 222
Nicaragua **case (ICJ)** 22, 124
non-interference/non-intervention, principle of
Charter of the UN 21, 110–11, 119, 127
East Timor decision 148
French Declaration of the Rights of Man 21
ICCPR/ICESCR 116
internal/external dichotomy 15, 16
polity-based self-determination 19, 21, 23, 87, 130–1, 148
self-defence, right to intervene in support of collective 191
Wall advisory opinion 160
non-self-governing territories/peoples
Charter of the UN 104–5, 106, 146–8
General Assembly Resolution 1514 (XV) 121–3
ICCPR/ICESCR 114–15, 117
internal/external dichotomy 16
principles of governance 104–5, 106
norms *see* ***erga omnes*** **norms; legal norm of right to self-determination**
Northern Ireland, re-starting Troubles in 11
Norway *see* **Norway 1814 secession; Norway 1905 secession from Sweden**

Norway 1814 secession 76–8
consensual union with Denmark 76
Convention of Moss 77–8
declaration of independence 76
Eidsvoll constitution 77–8
independent character of Norway 76–8
joint monarchy with Sweden 77–8
Napoleonic wars 76–7, 81
secessionary self-determination 23, 76–8, 82
Sweden under Treaty of Kiel, transfer of Norway to 76–8, 82
will of the people 77
Norway 1905 secession from Sweden 78–83
abdication of King 81
abuses of rights 82, 84, 86
consular service, veto by king on establishment of a Norwegian 80–1, 82
declaration on end of union 81
Eidsvoll Constitution
impeachment of ministers by government 79–80
Storthing alone, amendment by the 79–80, 82
veto of amendments by king 79–80
external competences of Norway and Sweden 80–1, 82
consular service, establishment of a Norwegian 80–1, 82
minister of foreign affairs as having to be Swedish, as 80
independent character of Norway, retention of 78, 80–2
joint monarchy 81
Karlstadt agreement of 1905 81
legitimacy 82–3
political and moral claim to secession 83
political structure of Norway/Sweden 79
secessionary self-determination 23, 76, 78–83
sovereignty, assertion of 78

opinio iuris
Chagos Archipelago advisory opinion 9, 214
colonial self-determination 106
Crimea, Russian invasion and annexation of 2014 187–8
Declaration of Friendly Relations 124
Kosovo advisory opinion 187–8
remedial self-determination 181
Quebec decision 154
Orakhelashvili, Alexander 178, 184–5
origins of self-determination (1320–1920) 40–86, 229
Oscar II, King of Norway 81
Osterhammel, Jürgen 89–90, 106
Otis Jr, James 66
Ottoman Empire 165–6

Pahuja, Sundhya 103, 105
Pakistan, independence of 90
Palestine *see* ***Wall* advisory opinion (ICJ)**
participation *see* **polity-based self-determination**
peace and security, maintenance of 108
Peace of Westphalia 57
Pedersen, Susan 100–1
peoples, definition of 24, 110, 120, 122, 125
Permanent Sovereignty over Natural Resources, General Assembly declaration on 118–19
Perrit Jr, Henry 169
Peters, Anne 192
Petrus Geduldius (Petrus the Patient) 12
Philip II, King of Spain 51–6, 62
Philip, JR 60
Plakkaat van Verlatinghe (Act of Abjuration) of 1581 4, 40, 50–7, 71, 227
abuses of rights 55–6, 86
American Declaration of Independence 50, 62–3, 65, 67, 229
background 51–5
civil war 51–3
colonialism, leading to 58
Declaration of Arbroath 50–1, 58, 62–3
divine right of kings 55–6, 65
Dutch East India Company, leading to 58
French Declaration of the Rights of Man and of the Citizen 1789 229
influence 57–8
limited government 55–6
national identity 57
nature, law of 51, 59
Pacification of Ghent 54
Peace of Westphalia 57
popular sovereignty 56, 65–6
religious conflict 52–6
remedial self-determination 56
Republic of the Seven Provinces 57, 58
sources 60
Spain, independence from 50–7, 62
syllogistic form 56–7, 62
text 51, 55–7
tyranny, resistance to 55–7

Union of Arras 54
Utrecht Union 54–5
Plato 66
political self-determination
Charter of the UN 110, 111–12
colonial self-determination 87, 122
Crimea, Russian invasion and annexation of 2014 188–9
Declaration of Friendly Relations 127, 188
East Timor decision 148
ICCPR/ICESCR 116–20, 145
internal/external dichotomy 16, 110
legal norm, as 110
Quebec decision 188
Wall advisory opinion 158, 160
Wilson, Woodrow 94, 95–7
polity-based self-determination 3–5, 20–3, 32–3, 130–1
age of revolution 20
aggression 87
American Declaration of Independence 20, 26, 69–70, 87
authority as distinct from power 20–1
Badinter Commission 145
Chagos Archipelago advisory opinion 221–2, 225, 232
Charter of the UN 21–3, 87, 146, 228
collective will of the people 20–1
colonial self-determination 32, 88, 127–8, 220, 225
customary international law 4, 22, 33, 88, 131, 133
Declaration of Friendly Relations 125
definition 19, 228
differentiating features 37
distinguishing features 34
East Timor decision 146, 148–9, 222
French Declaration of the Rights of Man 20–1, 26, 70–1, 87
historical roots 20–1, 25–6, 29
ICCPR/ICESCR 22, 116, 118–19
ICJ, practice of 21, 22
international law 40, 220, 232
interrelationship with other forms 35–8
ius cogens 4, 22, 33, 88, 131, 220
legal norm, as 4, 22, 33, 37, 88, 115, 119, 131, 228
legal status 3–4, 37, 130–1
legitimacy 32–4, 39, 130
non-interference/non-intervention, principle of 19, 21, 23, 87, 130–1, 148
outward-facing, as 21
overlap with different forms 37–8
remedial self-determination 25–9, 38
secessionary self-determination 23–4, 69, 225
Second World War 87–8
species of self-determination 37
sovereignty 22–3
spillover legitimacy 32, 34
United Nations 106–7
use of force, prohibition of 87
Wall advisory opinion 159, 160, 219, 222, 225, 230
wider self-determination category 5
popular sovereignty 13–14, 47–8, 56, 65–6, 70, 110
Portugal 145–50
practical implementation 2
precedential reasoning 4, 50, 86–7, 227
American Declaration of Independence 63, 64–5
Crimea, Russian invasion and annexation of 2014 4, 18–19, 186, 187–91, 192
French Declaration of the Rights of Man 63, 64
Wall advisory opinion 159
Princip, Gavrilo 165
Puigdemont, Carles 2
Putin, Vladimir 11

***Quebec* decision (Canadian Supreme Court)** 152–4
colonial self-determination 152–3
human rights 154
opinio iuris 154
political self-determination 188
remedial self-determination 153–4, 180–1
secessionary self-determination 23, 27, 130, 152–4, 180–1, 188
territorial integrity 154
threshold requirement 154
unilateral act, separation through a 152–4

racism
apartheid 134–5, 221
ethnonationalism 94, 96–7
racially designed communities 94
Wilson, Woodrow 88, 93–4
Raič, David 24, 72
recognise illegal situations, obligation of states not to 158, 159–60, 212, 215–16

referendums
Badinter Commission 144
Cataluña, unauthorised 2017 referendum in 2, 5–10, 23, 185–6, 193
Crimea, Russian invasion and annexation of 2014 186–7, 190
Kurdish Autonomous Region of Iraq (KAR), independence referendum 2017 in 1–2, 5–8, 10, 23, 185–6, 193
Norway 1905 secession from Sweden 81
Scotland, 2014 referendum on independence of 23
territorial delimitation 72
Ukraine, Russian invasion of 2022 192
Western Sahara advisory opinion 138, 141
regional autonomy 38
regional human rights bodies 130
remedial self-determination 3–5, 25–9, 32–3, 130–1, 232
abuse of rights 19, 69, 187–8, 229
age of revolution 74–5, 84–5, 87, 229
Åland Islands dispute 84–5
American Declaration of Independence 26, 68–9, 74–5, 86, 179
colonial self-determination 27, 32, 88
conflation of forms 29
Crimea, Russian invasion and annexation of 2014 187–8, 191
customary international law 181
Declaration on Friendly Relations 28, 125–6, 179–81
declarations of independence 26–7
definition 19, 228
differentiating features 37
distinguishing features 34
East Timor decision 146
external self-determination, as 5, 26, 29
French Declaration of the Rights of Man 26–7, 74–5
historical roots 25–6, 29
ICJ, case law of the 29
independence, claims to 26–7
internal/external dichotomy 18
international law 26, 33–4, 40, 191
interrelationship with other forms 35–8
Katangese People's Congress v Zaire 152, 154, 180–1
last resort, remedies of 19, 26, 33, 68–9, 152
legal norm, as 4–5, 27, 37, 181, 191
legal status 3–4, 33, 37
legitimacy 32–4, 39, 75, 87, 130
new state, right to a 33
overlap with different forms 37–8
philosophical foundations 26
Plakkaat van Verlatinghe of 1581 56
polity-based self-determination 25–9, 38
Quebec decision 153–4, 180–1
safeguard clause 125–6
secessionary self-determination 25–7, 29, 34, 69, 184, 227, 228
species of self-determination 37
spillover legitimacy 34
UN 106
wider self-determination category 5
Requesens y Zúñiga, Luis de 54
revolution/rebellion, right to 48–9, 56
right to self-determination *see* **legal norm of right to self-determination**
Rigo Sureda, Andrés 13, 72
Robert I, King of Scots (Rob the Bruce) 41, 43–50, 51
Rodríguez-Santiago, Elizabeth 40–1, 98, 100–1, 141
Roosevelt, Franklin Delano 102
Ross, Alf 22–3
Rothermund, Dietmar 102, 104–5
Rousseau, Jean-Jacques 48, 66
Roy, Guha 118
Russia *see also* **Crimea, Russian invasion and annexation of 2014; Ukraine, Russian invasion of 2022**
Bolsheviks 30, 90, 91, 95
Lenin 27, 29–30, 75, 86, 88, 90–2, 94–8
Soviet Union, dissolution of the 90

sacred trust principle 136, 141
safeguard clause 24, 125–6
Sallust 60
School of Salamanca 48
Scobbie, Iain 216–17
Scotichronicon 58–9
Scotland *see also* **Declaration of Arbroath of 6 April 1320**
referendum on independence 2014 23
secessionary self-determination 3–5, 23–5, 32–3, 130–1
academic writers 9
age of revolution 23, 73–6, 77–8, 82–3
Åland Islands dispute 83–5, 144, 146, 183
American Declaration of Independence 67–70
Badinter Commission 143–5, 146, 151, 183
Cataluña, unauthorised 2017 referendum in 2, 5, 6, 23

colonial self-determination 23, 25, 87, 121–2, 220, 225
conflicts and violence 2–3, 23
Crimea, Russian invasion and annexation of 2014 189–91, 231
customary international law 4
Declaration of Friendly Relations 125–6, 179–80
declarations of independence 25, 182–5
definition 19, 228
differentiating features 37
distinguishing features 34
East Timor decision 146
erga omnes norms 228
French Declaration of the Rights of Man 71–2
General Assembly (UN) 121–2
ICCPR/ICESCR 120, 145
identity-based claims 19, 23–4, 228
illiberal, as 24
internal/external dichotomy 15, 17–18
international law 25, 33, 38, 40, 233
interrelationship with other forms 35–8
irredentism 228
Katangese People's Congress v Zaire 151
Kosovo advisory opinion 25, 33, 163–85, 189, 194, 220, 231
Kurdish Autonomous Region of Iraq (KAR), referendum in 1–2, 5, 6, 23, 185–6
legal status 3–4, 37
legal norm, as 37, 145, 185, 188
legitimacy 18, 23, 32–4, 39
nationalism 24
Norway 1814 secession 23, 76–8, 82
Norway 1905 secession from Sweden 23, 76, 78–83
ought/is 24
overlap with different forms 37–8
people, definition of 24
political self-determination 180
polity-based self-determination 23–4, 69, 225
Quebec decision 23, 27, 130, 152–4, 180–1, 188
remedial self-determination 23, 25–7, 29, 34, 69, 184, 227, 228
safeguard clauses in proclamations of self-determination 24
Scotland, 2014 referendum on independence of 23
species of self-determination 37
separate character or identity of a group within a state 23
separatist movements 23
several entities, groups with single identity split between 19
spillover legitimacy 18, 34
State practice 25
territorial integrity 24, 173–6, 183
wider self-determination category 5
Wilson, Woodrow 95–6

Second World War 30–1, 87–9, 103

Security Council (UN)
Chapter VII, resolutions under 168–9
Charter of the UN 108, 111
Crimea, Russian invasion and annexation of 2014 189–90
declarations of independence 176
Kosovo advisory opinion 168–70, 176
maintenance of peace and security 108
Namibia advisory opinion 133–7
resolutions 155–6, 168–9, 176
Wall advisory opinion 155–6

Selbstbestimmung 12–13, 63–4

self-defence, right to intervene in support of collective 191

self-determination, meaning of *see* **meanings of self-determination**

self-determination problem 5, 6–19, 38

self, identification of 5, 12, 34

separatist movements 23

Serbia
Field of Blackbirds 1389, battle on the 165–6
Gazimestan speech 165–6
independence, declarations of 166–7, 169
Kosovo advisory opinion 165–85, 230–1
national identity 165–6
nationalism 165–6

Simma, Bruno 172, 184–5, 223, 230

Slovenia, declaration of independence of 143, 166–7

Smuts, Jan 98

social contract 93–4

Somos, Mark 66

South Africa *see* ***Namibia*** **advisory opinion (ICJ)**

Southern Rhodesia 176

sovereignty
Åland Islands dispute 83–5, 144, 151
Chagos Archipelago advisory opinion 199, 210
declarations of independence 183
Kosovo advisory opinion (ICJ) 163, 169, 170, 183, 231

Kurdish Autonomous Region of Iraq (KAR), referendum in 186
markers 183
Norway 1905 secession from Sweden 78
Permanent Sovereignty over Natural Resources, GA declaration on 118–19
polity-based self-determination 22–3
popular sovereignty 13–14, 47–8, 56, 65–6, 70, 110
territorial sovereignty 85, 140, 144, 151
Soviet Union, dissolution of the 90
Spain *see* **Cataluña, unauthorised 2017 referendum in; Plakkaat van Verlatinghe (Act of Abjuration) of 1581; *Western Sahara* advisory opinion (ICJ)**
species of self-determination 37
spillover legitimacy 18, 32, 34, 224–5, 230–2
state of nature 66–7
State practice 9, 25, 106, 123, 213–14, 224
State sovereignty *see* **sovereignty**
***Status of Eastern Carelia* advisory request (PCIJ)** 132
Statute of Westminster 1931 90
Sterio, Milena 14
sub-State units 15, 17–18, 125, 202–3
Sudan, conflict in 10
Summers, James 15
Sverdrup, Johan 80–1
Sweden *see also* **Åland Islands dispute (1920)**
Norway 1814 secession 76–8, 82
Norway 1905 secession from Sweden 78–83
syllogistic form 56–7, 62, 67
Syria, civil law in 10

Tams, Christian 164
taxonomy of self-determination 35–8, 130, 228
categorisation as inherent element of law 35–6, 39
genus, self-determination as a 37
species of self-determination 37
terra *nullius* 138–40
territorial integrity
Chagos Archipelago advisory opinion 195, 210, 218
Charter of the UN 174–5
Crimea, Russian invasion and annexation of 2014 188
Declaration of Friendly Relations 188
declarations of independence 173–4
Kosovo advisory opinion 173–6, 185
legal norms 175–6
negative treatment 175
obligation, not a right, as 174–5
Quebec decision 154
secessionary self-determination 24, 173–6, 185
Wall advisory opinion 222
territorial sovereignty 85, 140, 144, 151
Tesón, Fernando 6, 133
theological context 12–13, 63
Thirlway, Hugh 133
Tillerson, Rex 8
Tito (Josep Broz) 166
Tod, Murray 59
Tomuschat, Christian 107
Torra, Quim 7
trusteeship system (UN) 101, 102–5
Charter of the UN 102–3, 111, 214
colonial self-determination 30–1, 101, 102–5, 122–3, 127, 229
General Assembly Resolution 1514 (XV) 122–3
independence, move towards 102–3, 105–6
infrastructure and institutions, progressive development of 102
mandates system 30–1, 101, 102, 105, 132–3
Namibia advisory opinion 133–7
principles and objectives 102–6
Trusteeship Council 102–3
will of the people 102, 104
tyranny, resistance to 55–7
Tzouvala, Ntina 99–100, 103–4

Ukraine *see* **Crimea, Russian invasion and annexation of 2014; Ukraine, Russian invasion of 2022**
Ukraine, Russian invasion of 2022 191–2
Donetsk and Luhansk, recognition of independence of 191–2
international law 163
intervene in support of collective self-defence, right to 191
justification 191
Kherson and Zaporizhia 192
Kosovo advisory opinion 192, 193
nationhood, suppression of 11
NATO membership 11
referendum 192
Russian decline post-Cold war 11
Umozurike, Umozurike Oji 14

United Kingdom's administration of Chagos Islands 195–226
United Nations (UN) *see also* **Charter of the UN; General Assembly (UN); Security Council (UN); trusteeship system (UN)**
colonial self-determination 29–31, 102–27
core purposes 2–3
ius cogens 107
Kosovo as under authority of UN 169, 183
Kurdish Autonomous Region of Iraq (KAR), referendum in 8
law of the UN 105–27
League of Nations 101
legal status of self-determination 131
polity-based self-determination 106–7
remedial self-determination 106
United Provinces *see* **Plakkaat van Verlatinghe (Act of Abjuration) of 1581**
United States *see* **American Declaration of Independence 1776**
Universal Declaration of Human Rights (UDHR) 22, 116
use of force, illegal 87, 187–91
***uti possidetis iuris* principle** 16, 122, 142–4

Van Alstyne, Richard 94–6
Vashakmadze, Mindia 183
Vattel, Emer de 61, 66
Venezuela, declaration of independence of 27, 75
violence and disorder *see* **conflicts and violence**
vocabulary 35
von Braunschweig-Lüneburg, Duke Heinrich Julius 58

Wagner, Marcus 58
Waldron, Jeremy 17–18, 69
***Wall* advisory opinion (ICJ)** 22, 130, 155–60
annexation, wall as amounting to *de facto* 156–8
Charter of the UN 159
colonial self-determination 158–9, 213–16, 222
Declaration on Friendly Relations 157, 159
East Timor decision (ICJ) 159, 160, 224–5
erga omnes norms 158–60, 215–16
General Assembly 155–6, 158–9
human rights 157
international humanitarian law, violation of 157
ius cogens 222
legal right, self-determination as a 157
non-interference/non-intervention, principle of 160
occupied territory, Palestine as an 159, 222
political self-determination 158, 160
polity-based self-determination 22, 159, 160, 219, 222, 225, 230
positive obligations to promote self-determination 158
post-colonial self-determination, practice on 158–9
precedents 159
recognise illegal situations, obligation of states not to 158, 159–60, 212, 215–16
Security Council resolutions 155–6
territorial integrity 222
Wallace, William 43
war *see* **conflicts and violence; First World War**
***Western Sahara* advisory opinion (ICJ)** 130, 137–42
Charter of the UN 141–2
colonial self-determination 31, 141–2, 148, 150, 159
customary international law 141, 148
decolonisation of Spanish holdings in North Africa, GA calls for 137–8
East Timor decision (ICJ) 150
General Assembly resolution 137–41
historical title 140–1
Ifni, status of 137–8
legal status of self-determination 142
Mauritania 137–41
Morocco 137–41
Ifni, status of 137–8
referendum on Western Sahara, opposition to 138
Nambia decision 141
referendum on Western Sahara 138, 141
sacred trust, objective of the 141
Spain, control of Western Sahara by 137–42
terra nullius, whether territory was 138–40
territorial sovereignty 140
uti possidetis iuris principle 142
Whelan, Anthony 15
Wilde, Ralph 182
will of the people
collective will of the people 20–1
form of government, legitimacy of 16

French Declaration of the Rights of Man 26–7, 71
Katangese People's Congress v Zaire 152
Norway 1814 secession 77
trusteeship system 102, 104
Wilson, Woodrow 96
William V, Prince of Orange 62
William of Nassau, Prince of Orange (William the Silent) 52–4
William of Ockham 66
Wilson, Woodrow 14, 92–8
colonial self-determination 30, 88, 90–7
ethnonationalism 94, 96–7
First World War 90–2
Fourteen Points 95–6
illiberal liberalism 94, 95–7
Lenin 94–6
national minorities, rights of 95–6
nationalism 97
political philosophy 92–5
racially designed community 94
racism 88, 93–4
social contract 93–4
states, basis for authority of 93–4
Wishart, Robert, Bishop of Glasgow 44
Wolfrum, Rüdiger 108
Wright, Quincey 99

Yanukovych, Viktor 186
Yemen, civil law in 10
Yugoslavia, dissolution of 143–4 *see also* ***Kosovo*** **advisory opinion (ICJ)**

Zaire *see* ***Katangese People's Congress v Zaire*** **(ACHPR)**
Zeid Ra'ad Al Hussein 7

www.ingramcontent.com/pod-product-compliance
Ingram Content Group UK Ltd.
Pitfield, Milton Keynes, MK11 3LW, UK
UKHW020250290926
15470UKWH00002B/846

9 781509 945061